Fort St. Joseph Revealed

UNIVERSITY PRESS OF FLORIDA

Florida A&M University, Tallahassee
Florida Atlantic University, Boca Raton
Florida Gulf Coast University, Ft. Myers
Florida International University, Miami
Florida State University, Tallahassee
New College of Florida, Sarasota
University of Central Florida, Orlando
University of Florida, Gainesville
University of North Florida, Jacksonville
University of South Florida, Tampa
University of West Florida, Pensacola

Fort St. Joseph Revealed

The Historical Archaeology of a Fur Trading Post

EDITED BY MICHAEL S. NASSANEY

UNIVERSITY PRESS OF FLORIDA

Gainesville Tallahassee Tampa Boca Raton

Pensacola Orlando Miami Jacksonville Ft. Myers Sarasota

First cloth printing, 2019
First paperback printing, 2021

26 25 24 23 22 21   6 5 4 3 2 1

Library of Congress Cataloging-in-Publication Data
Names: Nassaney, Michael S., editor.
Title: Fort St. Joseph revealed : the historical archaeology of a fur trading
    post / edited by Michael S. Nassaney.
Description: Gainesville : University Press of Florida, 2019. | Includes
    bibliographical references and index.
Identifiers: LCCN 2018054096 | ISBN 9780813056425 (cloth : alk. paper) |
    ISBN 9780813068497 (pbk.)
Subjects: LCSH: Fur trade—Michigan—Fort Saint Joseph—History. | Fur trade—
    Michigan—Niles—History. | Excavations (Archaeology)—Michigan—Fort Saint Joseph.
    | Excavations (Archaeology)—Michigan—Niles. | Fort Saint Joseph (Mich.)—History. |
    Niles (Mich.)—History.
Classification: LCC F1059.5.F666 F67 2019 | DDC 971.3—dc23
LC record available at https://lccn.loc.gov/2018054096

The University Press of Florida is the scholarly publishing agency for the State University
System of Florida, comprising Florida A&M University, Florida Atlantic University,
Florida Gulf Coast University, Florida International University, Florida State University,
New College of Florida, University of Central Florida, University of Florida, University of
North Florida, University of South Florida, and University of West Florida.

University Press of Florida
2046 NE Waldo Road
Suite 2100
Gainesville, FL 32609
http://upress.ufl.edu

Contents

Figures

Tables

Preface

If I had not answered that random phone call from Hal Springer, then president of Support the Fort, Inc. (STF), in 1997, I probably would not be writing these words of gratitude. I have jokingly quipped on numerous occasions that when I casually agreed to help STF find Niles's long-lost fort, Hal neglected to tell me that others had been searching for it for nearly a century! Buoyed by enthusiasm, our timely survey led us to a collector and a collection of colonial artifacts from the banks of the St. Joseph River, where Joseph Peyser predicted they would be found, and the rest is history, as they say. My colleague, Bill Cremin, envisioned that Fort St. Joseph could occupy me for the rest of my career; his prophecy was correct. Since 1998, the people of Niles have welcomed me and my team of archaeologists and interdisciplinary researchers as we have drained, dug, and deciphered the remnants of the Four Flags Fort. While we have published extensively on our findings, after nearly twenty years of investigations it seemed time to publish a synthetic overview of much of what we have learned about the history and archaeology of this place. It is a moving target, to be sure, and it has taken scores of eager volunteers, interested citizens, student archaeologists, and dedicated staff associated with the Fort St. Joseph Archaeological Project—a proverbial village—to get us where we are today. The project began as a partnership that has mobilized the energy of countless individuals in sustaining our collaborative efforts.

As I sit back and reflect on the past two decades of mud, sweat, and tears and the production of this volume, I'm faced with both a pleasurable and daunting task in attempting to call out all the groups, associations, colleagues, and friends who have helped in countless ways to reveal Fort St. Joseph. First and foremost are the principal partners, Western Michigan University and the city of Niles, who have the vision to commit time and resources to investigating and interpreting the remains of the fort in order to educate students and the public. WMU administrators assist by stepping in and stepping back as needed to support our efforts to operate the longest-running archaeological field school in the country. The city of Niles has always provided logistical assistance and made Niles a home away from home for me and my crews. Thanks to the Niles City Council, former mayor Mike McCauslin, current mayor Nick Shelton, Juan Ganum, Sanya Vitale, Ric Huff, Carol Bainbridge, Christina Arseneau, and Mollie Watson for their hospitality and good humor. Always in the background (when they weren't leading the charge) are the stalwart and indefatigable members of Support the Fort, Inc., whose mission to teach the world about Fort St. Joseph informs our vision. Although their numbers are dwindling, they were a formidable force in the past and always reminded anyone who would listen that the Niles fort was and is a special place deserving of further study. We could not ask for better partners than Mary Ellen Drolet and her family, Barb Cook, the late Grif Cook, Janine Frizzo, Larry Horrigan, and the late Joseph L. Peyser. They overlap with a talented group of performative historiographers led initially by LisaMarie Malischke and later by Bob Myers. Since 2006, our reenactors have brought the archaeology alive with their demonstrations and first-person interpretations at our annual open house and other events.

The project has benefited greatly from various grants and financial gifts made available by generous donors and individuals including the Michigan Humanities Council; the Joseph L. Peyser Endowment for the Study of New France; the WMU Cultural Events Committee; the Conference on Michigan Archaeology; the Office of the State Archaeologist; Support the Fort; the French-Canadian Heritage Society of Michigan; the General Society of Colonial Wars; the Society of Colonial Wars in the State of Michigan; the Leighton-Oare Foundation, Inc.; the Quebec Government Office in Chicago; the late Nancy Butler; Sharon Carlson; Tom Dietz; Mary Ellen Drolet; Gordon Marshall; Nancy McCarty; members of the Peyser family (Jann, Randy, and the late Julia Peyser); and Larry Sehy. I am especially grateful to the Society of Colonial Wars in the State of Michigan for funding to subsidize the publication of this book.

Much of the work in the archives, on the ground, and in the lab has been conducted by a swarm of students enrolled in the WMU archaeological field schools since 2002 and in our archaeology summer camp program. They have all labored alongside and under the supervision of numerous staff, teaching assistants, professional associates, and seasoned volunteers who deserve recognition, most notably Andy Beaupré, Tim Bober, José António Brandão, Amanda Brooks, John Cardinal, Jim Clark, Erin Claussen, the late Bill Cremin, Meghan Cook, Erica D'Elia, Kelly Hagenmaier, Erika (Loveland) Hartley, Neil Hassinger, Joe Hearns, Ian Kerr, Dan Lynch, LisaMarie Malischke, Terry Martin, Cynthia Nostrant, the late Jan Personette, Emily Powell, Bill Sauck, the late Larry Simpson, and Gary Thompson. Many colleagues visited the site over the years and contributed ideas that have influenced my thinking, including Dean Anderson, Sonya Atalay, Sean Dunham, Kent Lightfoot, Karen Marrero, Doug Scott, Heather Walder, Jason Wesaw, Sophie White, Mike Zimmerman, and members of the Fort St. Joseph Archaeology Advisory Committee. Living in Niles makes it possible for us to fully engage in community archaeology; housing has been provided by the Butler family, the Niles school system, and the Layman family.

I have tried to pay my intellectual debt to the many French colonial archaeologists and Fort St. Joseph aficionados who came before me by citing their work. In addition, thanks to those who provided permission to reproduce artwork, photographs, and previously published text and to all the authors who worked with me, cheerfully met my stringent demands, and delivered insightful essays that reflect their current understandings of the fort. Also, thanks to Meredith Babb and her able staff at the University Press of Florida for their role in making our ideas tangible in the form of this handsome volume in such a timely manner. Finally, this volume is dedicated to my wife, Nadine, and my sons, Andrew and Alexander, for their generosity and love. Family and friends have nurtured me on this journey, always sincerely inquiring about my latest discoveries. Sharing my stories has revealed to me the broad interest in the archaeological past.

1

Revealing the History and Archaeology of Fort St. Joseph

For nearly two decades, historical archaeologists have been revealing the con-
tours of everyday life at Fort St. Joseph, one of the most important French colonial outposts in the western Great Lakes region, also known as the *pays d'en
haut* (the Upper Country) in New France. After the French founded a mission
along the St. Joseph River in the mid-1680s, they recognized the significance
of this location for their imperial ambitions and soon established a permanent
settlement amid their Miami and Potawatomi allies (Idle 2003; Peyser 1992).
By the 1720s, the post supported a commandant and several officers, eight
to ten enlisted men, a priest, an interpreter, a blacksmith, about fifteen fur
traders, and their French, French Canadian, and Native American wives and
children (Brandão and Nassaney 2006). For decades, the site was the hub of
a large multiethnic community that featured intermarriage between French
and French Canadian men and Native American women and intense cultural
interaction between Europeans and Native Americans. The fort was a strategic
stronghold for the French and English for nearly a century before it was abandoned in 1781 (Idle 2003; Peyser 1992).

Despite the importance of Fort St. Joseph in the political and commercial
aspirations of the French empire, it was underreported and seldom referenced
from the time of its abandonment through much of the nineteenth century.
Yet it was never forgotten. The site was commemorated with the dedication of
a stone marker in 1913 in the general location where artifacts were being recovered by a few local collectors (Beeson 1900; Coolidge 1915; Nassaney 2008a)

(Figure 1.1). By the mid-twentieth century, however, the site proved difficult to locate on the ground due to limited and forgotten documentation and landscape modifications associated with industrial developments. Its precise location was lost to living memory until 1998, when Support the Fort, Inc., a local group of history enthusiasts, invited Western Michigan University (WMU) archaeologists to search for material evidence of the long-lost fort (Nassaney 1999). Using background research provided by Joseph L. Peyser (1992) and other local historians (e.g., Beeson 1900), we excavated shovel test pits and backhoe trenches in high-probability areas and encountered a low density of Late Woodland (ca. AD 600–1600) and colonial-era objects (20BE10) on a terrace where previous investigators had searched (Figure 1.2). The paucity of remains led us to rule out this area as the location of the fort.

As luck would have it, a local collector approached us as we were completing our survey and shared the contents of a proverbial shoebox filled with artifacts, including gunflints, flintlock hardware, faience, and French clasp knife blades,

Figure 1.1. This 65-ton commemorative boulder was dedicated near the site of Fort St. Joseph in 1913 amid considerable pomp that included a mile-long parade, songs by a girl choir, and speeches from local dignitaries. Courtesy of the Fort St. Joseph Archaeological Project.

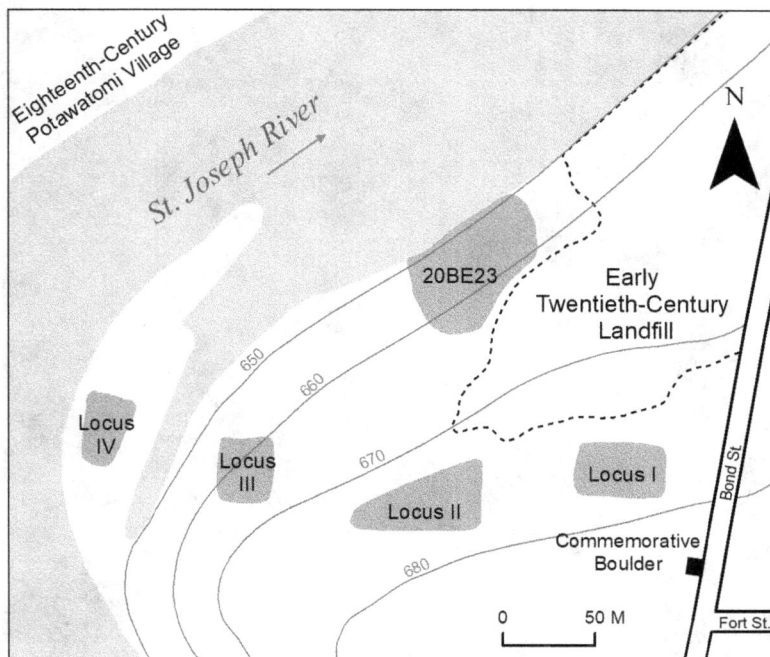

Figure 1.2. Map showing the locations of Fort St. Joseph (20BE23), the Lyne site (20BE10; Loci I–IV), and an eighteenth-century Potawatomi village. Drawn by Jason Glatz.

along with other related materials that he had recovered with the aid of a metal detector. He subsequently led us to the floodplain along the St. Joseph River (Figure 1.2), where our testing revealed dense deposits of eighteenth-century French and English artifacts (20BE23), which we surmised might represent the remains of the old fort (Nassaney et al. 2003). Unfortunately, the artifacts lay beneath the water table, owing to the rise in river elevation due to the construction and enlargement of an industrial dam immediately downstream in the late nineteenth and early twentieth centuries. We were unable to evaluate the integrity of these finds in our initial survey because the high water table prohibited us from recognizing features and undisturbed artifact deposits that would have enabled us to establish the site's integrity. In 2002, we installed a dewatering system to lower the groundwater table, performed a geophysical survey, and conducted more intensive investigations to examine magnetic and other geophysical anomalies in a site evaluation (Nassaney et al. 2002–2004).

Figure 1.3. This stone fireplace, designated Feature 2, provides clear evidence for the presence of undisturbed eighteenth-century archaeological deposits at Fort St. Joseph. Courtesy of the Fort St. Joseph Archaeological Project.

Subsurface testing revealed undisturbed archaeological deposits in the form of fireplaces (Figure 1.3), pits, and trash middens—definitive material evidence that Fort St. Joseph had been found (Nassaney and Cremin 2002b). Select materials recovered from the floodplain (20BE23) and the terrace (20BE10) are the subject of this book (Figure 1.2).

Different soil types and the depositional context of archaeological materials resulted in different excavation strategies and data recovery procedures in each of these areas. The initial survey grid was used to record provenience on the terrace. A separate grid was established in the floodplain (Figure 1.4). The terrace exhibits a dark-brown, sandy loam plow zone underlaid by a yellow-brown B horizon. The soil profile in the floodplain begins with a circa 20-centimeter stratum of highly organic alluvium that is underlaid by a nineteenth-century plow zone that contains numerous eighteenth-century artifacts. Undisturbed deposits appear at about 45 cm below the ground surface. Excavations followed

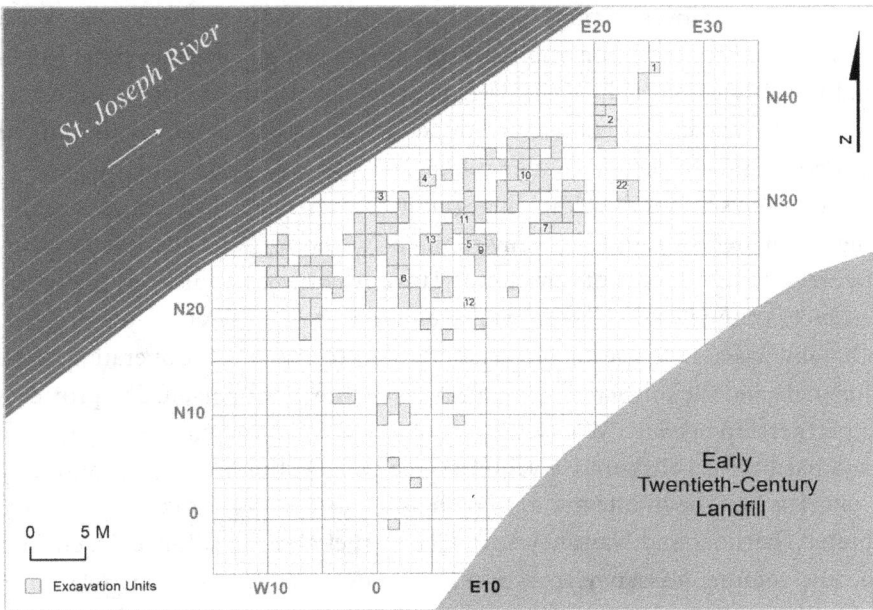

Figure 1.4. Excavation units dug in the floodplain (2002–2018) have revealed dense deposits of archaeological materials associated with Fort St. Joseph (20BE23). Numbers correspond with the locations of select features. Drawn by Jason Glatz.

five-centimeter levels within stratigraphic units in one- by one-meter and one-by two-meter units. Features are defined as soil anomalies, artifact concentrations, and architectural remains immediately beneath the plow zone in both areas. We initially used dry screening procedures with mostly quarter-inch mesh in both areas until we adopted water screening and eighth-inch mesh in the floodplain to improve recovery of small finds in the silty clay sediments that predominate there. We take flotation samples from feature and nonfeature contexts for comparative purposes. Although all of these samples have been processed, few have been sorted and analyzed (Cremin and Nassaney 2003; Hughes-Skallos and Allen 2012; Martinez 2009). Artifacts and other materials discussed in this volume derive from systematic excavations and are supplemented with collections curated in local repositories antiquarians made in the late nineteenth and early twentieth centuries (Stone 1974a). Because this is not a technical report, we have not presented data on all the artifact classes we recovered in our investigations. For example, glass beads (Malischke 2009) and containers, ceramics, iron and blacksmithing products, and gun parts (Jones n.d.) await detailed analyses that were not completed at the time of this publication. These and other data classes will provide important new insights into our understanding of daily life at this colonial outpost.

Fourteen seasons of fieldwork beginning in 2002 have focused on examining the materiality and built environment of the fort and the relationships between the fort residents and local Native American populations under the auspices of the Fort St. Joseph Archaeological Project (hereafter the project). Our aim has been to use historical archaeology to examine the operation of the fur trade and the impact of colonialism in southwest Michigan. The project is a partnership between WMU, the city of Niles, and other community groups and has been a collaborative venture since its inception in 1998. Community concerns have been integral to how the site has been investigated and interpreted (Berliner and Nassaney 2015; Claussen et al. 2013; D'Elia et al. chapter 9, this volume; Nassaney 2011, 2018a). The outcome has been an awarding-winning public archaeology program in which archaeologists, students, community groups, and individuals engage in an ongoing dialog to ensure public participation, outreach, and education as we reveal the past.

Frontier Forts Yesterday and Today

Europeans constructed defensive facilities in tandem with their earliest settlements in order to serve as the vanguard for population expansion (Babits and Gandulla 2013). Most Americans know about nineteenth-century frontier forts as arenas where Manifest Destiny was enacted in the process of dislocating Native American peoples in order to appropriate their land (Starbuck 2011). Forts (perhaps more accurately blockhouses) fueled the mythology of the Wild West expressed in literature, tourist sites, Hollywood movies, and other iconic imagery (Maher 2016; Starbuck 2011). Indeed, forts continue to capture the imagination of scholars and the general public alike and experience more than their share of visitation among heritage sites for a variety of reasons. Because fortifications were places where identities were negotiated, contested, transformed, and enacted, they are ideologically charged loci that are important for examining the lived experience of colonial interaction and exchange and deconstructing the perceived wisdom that they symbolize (Tveskov and Rose 2019).

Indeed, how we remember and commemorate forts serves to legitimize contemporary social relations by erasing some historical narratives while elevating others (Maher 2016; see Trouillot 1995). The inherent ambiguity of the evidence available to us regarding colonialist relations leaves ample room for political relations to influence our understandings. Suffice it to say that our interpretations are sensitive barometers of broader sociopolitical factors and are constantly shifting (Nassaney, chapter 10, this volume).

Contemporary imaginings of the nature and outcomes of cultural interactions on the so-called frontier are products of intellectual inquiry that developed in response to the acculturation paradigm of the mid-twentieth century that viewed European goods as technologically superior and Native American adoptions as a means of emulating the dominant culture (Nassaney 2015). Post-acculturation approaches to cultural encounters emphasized the entangled nature of interaction and highlighted cultural mixing (i.e., hybridization, creolization, and *métissage*), challenging the essentialized identities associated with earlier understandings (e.g., Beaudoin 2013; Dawdy 2000; Jordan 2009; Panich 2013; Turgeon et al. 1996). Yet it appears that as Native American peoples were accorded greater agency in political charades on the colonial stage, various groups drew from a reservoir of behavioral and material practices to ensure their survival under colonialism. Cultural borrowing was not emulation but an expedient strategy that furthered each groups' interests (e.g., Nassaney 2019; Nassaney, chapter 10, this volume). This reading shifts attention toward understandings grounded in more pragmatic solutions that agents employed to expand cultural practices and secure political autonomy under new social conditions that accompanied colonialism (Witgen 2012). This more nuanced perspective frames much of the archaeological and historical data that the contributors to this volume reveal about Fort St. Joseph.

Reconstructing Eighteenth-Century Materiality and Frontier Life

Documentary sources provide an understanding of the cultural contexts of exchange and interaction that occurred on the frontier of New France. While these sources are important for framing the broad outlines of colonialism and the fur trade, they remain of limited value in revealing the mundane activities that people conducted on a daily basis and the ways that colonial agents imbued their material world with meaning. In contrast, the material goods that were made, used, deposited, and discarded at Fort St. Joseph provide insight into the lived experience and identities of the site occupants along the lines of gender, status, race, and ethnicity as they negotiated the new conditions associated with colonialism and frontier life.

Archaeologists have long recognized that the spatial, temporal, and formal dimensions of the material world can illuminate aspects of daily life that are not recorded in written documents (Deetz 1977). For example, while trade lists and account books enumerate the goods that were produced and exchanged for use on the frontier, archaeological evidence points to the myriad ways users reimagined and modified materials in ways that their makers did not anticipate (Bradley 1987a). Moreover, archaeological materials are particularly valuable when written documents are silent. Few people at Fort St. Joseph could read and write; those who could write were seldom interested in expressing ideas about mundane activities and events, leaving serious gaps in our understanding of subsistence practices, architectural forms, adornment styles, settlement locations, and other aspects of lived experience and material life that are critical to fully understanding fur trade society.

Scope of This Book

This book juxtaposes archaeological and documentary sources to reveal the history and culture of a colonial outpost that participated in the fur trade. It synthesizes observations derived from documents, cultural features, plant and animal remains, and various types of artifacts to examine fur trade society from the perspective of a single place in the western Great Lakes region. The authors also highlight the importance of Fort St. Joseph in both the past and in the present. Many of the interpretations offered in this collection derive from discussions nurtured in collaborations between archaeologists and community groups (Nassaney 2018b). Input from the public, descendants, Native American participants, students, and other stakeholders have shaped the discourse and the ways we conducted this archaeology, including the questions we asked, the data we collected, the analyses we conducted, and the ways we have disseminated our results (see D'Elia et al. chapter 9, this volume; cf. Low 2018).

Fort St. Joseph was known through documents long before systematic archaeological investigations began. Both the French and the English used written records to communicate information to further their imperial goals. In chapter 2, José António Brandão and I rely on predominantly extant records (e.g., letters, correspondences, church records, government documents, maps, and other written sources) to trace the development of Fort St. Joseph and discuss its roles in shaping the history and culture of the Native American and European groups who lived in and near the fort.

Documentary sources indicate that colonial powers encouraged their subjects to become self-sufficient to lessen the economic burden on the empire. The lack of local sources of raw materials (e.g., lead, iron ore) and the absence of infrastructure for producing finished goods (e.g., cloth, glass, ceramics) required most colonists to be dependent on imported commodities from the homeland. However, it was more difficult to transport food over long distances, especially perishable goods such as meat and dairy products. The alternative was to derive these products locally or do without. The French quickly adopted and adapted to Native American cuisine, as indicated by the well-preserved assemblage of faunal remains derived from our excavations at the fort. In chapter 3, Terrance Martin, Joseph Hearns, and Rory Becker examine the use of animals for fur, food, and raw material at Fort St. Joseph. Animal remains provide data on the types of species exploited, how they were butchered, and their spatial patterns to determine their contribution to the diet and the fur trade economy. The authors demonstrate that the Fort St. Joseph faunal assemblage and activities represented at the site illustrate the complexity and idiosyncrasies of daily interactions that occurred among local Native Americans, French creole habitants, commercial agents, and military personnel. The abundant and well-preserved faunal assemblage demonstrates that the fort's inhabitants acquired and processed hides and consumed meat (Nassaney and Martin 2017). Whereas both subsistence and fur trade activities occurred at the site, analyses of the faunal remains provide detailed information on the wild animals that were procured, the local habitats from which these animals were acquired, and unique examples of traumatic injuries, bone tools, ornaments, and gaming pieces. The spatial distribution of the various specimens suggests refuse disposal patterns and distinctive activity areas where animals were processed for their hides, meat, and bone marrow.

Much of the discard occurred in domestic contexts among the habitation structures revealed through archaeology. In the absence of any detailed maps, drawings, or descriptions of the physical appearance of the site, archaeology has helped us identify several buildings at the fort. In chapter 4, Erika Hartley and I discuss the architectural evidence associated with the remains of a series of fireplaces that mark the locations of several residential structures. Structural features and artifacts associated with these fireplaces include foundation walls, postholes, hand-wrought nails, architectural hardware (e.g., hinges, pintles, keyhole escutcheons), window glass, daub, and structural stone. These remains provide important information about the construction methods, materials, size, and layout of the buildings present at the fort and insights about the buildings' functions and the identities of their occupants. They also demonstrate that the French used local resources when available to recreate traditional architectural styles, suggesting the conservative nature of architecture in New France (Mann 2008).

Ethnic identity is distinctly expressed through architecture at Fort St. Joseph, along with items associated with dress and adornment that were clearly visible markers on the body and hence inextricably linked with personal identity. Textiles were arguably one of the most popular commodities in New France (Anderson 1994). They were essential for keeping warm and served as a medium of stylistic expression. They were also important in the exchange network that connected France with its North American frontier territories. Because cloth and clothing seldom preserve in the ground, archaeologists must seek out alternate media that complement historical records to monitor the direction, volume, and nature of imported textiles that entered the fur trade. In chapter 5, Cathrine Davis analyzes a sizable collection of lead seals from Fort St. Joseph to learn more about the types of cloth that fort residents used and their implications for trade, transport, and identity formation. These small metal tags and their imprinted designs and lettering enable researchers to relate sites and their occupants to the distribution of textiles in the Atlantic World. Davis details the lead seals and textile consumption at Fort St. Joseph and compares the seals to similar artifacts from other French colonial sites in the region to identify varying patterns of consumer choice on the frontiers of New France.

Cloth can be modified to express new forms of social identity by fashioning it into distinctive cuts of clothing and adorning it with beads, buttons, brooches, and bangles. Beads are among the most ubiquitous type of material culture recovered from fur trade sites throughout North America (Nassaney 2015, 103–104). Produced almost exclusively in the Old World (Italy, France, Holland) for domestic and external markets, glass beads come in a wide array of colors, shapes, and sizes, all of which could be put to distinctive uses based on personal and cultural preferences. Numerous bead types that were used in a variety of ways have been recovered from Fort St. Joseph, including specimens of glass, shell, ivory, and stone (Malischke 2009). Preliminary analysis indicates that glass beads intended for trade reflect local Potawatomi and Miami ideas regarding color symbolism. Those found within French households provide evidence for a multiethnic community of French, *métis*, and Native American visitors; Native American servants; and enslaved Native Americans who occupied and frequented the site, although further study is needed to confirm this inference. Ivory beads from rosaries express the deep faith of the fort's inhabitants, as suggested by other religious items from the site (see Brandão and Nassaney 2008). Wearing glass and shell beads and displaying them on garments and in wampum belts were visual signs of the malleable and fluid identities of people in the fort community.

Once objects were imported into North America, their makers could not predict how they would be used. For example, Natives in the upper Midwest and Plains regions often melted and fused blue glass beads to create pendants in the eighteenth century (Billeck 2016). Similarly, brass kettles served as a raw material for producing various new objects such as arrow points, awls, and scrapers, to name just a few examples (Bradley 1987a). The crafting of novel artifact forms was a process that came to distinguish the occupants of Fort St. Joseph from their ancestors and cousins in Paris, La Rochelle, Quebec, and Montreal.

The study of craft production in the context of interactions between Native Americans and Europeans during the eighteenth century in the western Great Lakes region has emerged as a topic of scholarly interest (Morand 1994). Among the objects that were produced at Fort St. Joseph, the tinkling cone—a small, decorative ornament made of imported copper base metal—had its precedent in Native American forms and local raw materials such as bone. In our analysis of tinkling cone production and labor organization, Brock Giordano and I (chapter 6) demonstrate how European raw materials were being transformed into new shapes with varying functions. We focus on the technological histories of tinkling cones, an approach that enables us to establish that tinkling cone production was conducted in independent workshops as an opportunistic activity to fit the demands of life at the colonial outpost of Fort St. Joseph.

Artifacts (e.g., lead seals), features (e.g., fireplaces), and ecofacts (e.g., animal bones) undoubtedly provide significant insight into fur trade society. Of course, Europeans are only one component of the fur trade—their Native American partners were the primary producers of the furs that were processed and the consumers of significant quantities of imported European goods. Although Native American peoples are represented in the material remains associated with several habitation structures, more information can be obtained regarding their role in the fur trade by examining Native American sites beyond the fort to ascertain their activities and associated settlement patterns. Historical and archaeological records document the locations of some Native American settlements in the region, though few of these have been investigated systematically (e.g., Bettarell and Smith 1973; Jelinek 1958; Nassaney et al. 2000).

During the initial survey to locate the fort, we recovered a low density of what appeared to be Native American–style artifacts, including flakes, low-fired earthenware, and three stone smoking pipes on the terrace above the floodplain, suggesting an occupation that might overlap temporally with the fort (Figure 1.2). Subsequent investigations of the Lyne site (20BE10)—the designation given to the archaeological remains in this area—have revealed more artifacts, including European imports that can be securely dated to the eighteenth century, such as gunflints, flintlock hardware (i.e., a trigger and a sideplate), lead shot and musket balls, a pewter brooch, numerous copper alloy scraps, hand-blown glass container fragments, and a piece of trade silver that was perforated for ornamental use (Nassaney 2015, 175–176). Although much of the material is confined to the plow zone, several truncated features have been identified, including a series of smudge pits filled with carbonized corncobs and other burned organic matter. A radiocarbon date and associated artifacts suggest that these features are contemporaneous with the fort and can shed light on the intensified hide-processing activities that accompanied the fur trade. Eric Teixeira Mendes and I (chapter 7) examine the occupational history and cultural formation processes that produced these deposits. Their morphology and contents assist us in placing these features into a cultural context and demonstrate the types of activities that a multiethnic population engaged in cross-cultural exchange conducted on the margins of a commercial fur-trading post in the western Great Lakes region.

Participants in and the impact of the fur trade—clearly a global process—extended well beyond the Fort St. Joseph vicinity. Researchers have noted that Native American groups adapted to the commercial, political, and social opportunities European settlements provided (Lightfoot 2005). Native Americans astutely incorporated sites such as Fort St. Joseph as another node in their seasonal round and aggregated nearby to take advantage of the materials and services Europeans offered. In our study of the changing cultural landscape of the lower St. Joseph River valley, Mark Hoock, Allison M. Hoock, and I examine the spatial distribution of Native American and Euro-American sites in southwest Michigan and northwest Indiana in the periods immediately prior to, during, and after the abandonment of Fort St. Joseph (chapter 8). We use geographic information system (GIS) analysis to monitor changing settlement patterns. The distribution of settlements indicates that Native American peoples were actively making locational decisions related to resource availability and alliance formation in the context of local and regional political-economic relations before and after they were attracted to the fort.

The history of Fort St. Joseph is marked by a close alliance between Native American peoples and their French allies. Exchanging goods, services, and marriage partners were among the strategies that both groups used to meet their daily needs and ensure their survival (Nassaney 2019). The French were dependent on Native American peoples for resources, information, and technological goods such as canoes and moccasins, much as the Native Americans depended on the French for cloth, iron implements, and other imports. Similarly, archaeologists and the local community have entered into a long-term collaborative agreement to facilitate and enhance site investigations. In chapter 9, Erica A. D'Elia, Kelley Berliner, Sue Reichert, and I discuss how the Fort St. Joseph Archaeological Project aims to be a collaborative, community-based research program that provides various community groups opportunities to offer input, build capacity, and learn more about archaeology. Our discussion demonstrates that collaboration requires a delicate balance between maintaining professional standards of data recovery and curation while at the same time ensuring inclusivity.

In the concluding chapter, I reflect on how the public and scholarly audiences have conceptualized Fort St. Joseph and how its shifting narratives have been constructed to meet social and political needs. The site was initially venerated as a place that exhibited evidence for the dominance of colonizer over colonized, civilized over savage, and Christian over heathen (Coolidge 1915). By the end of the twentieth century, researchers had begun to emphasize the reciprocal exchanges between the French and their Native American allies, effectively blurring the boundaries between cultures. More recent interpretations highlight the ways that both the French and Native Americans sought to conserve their cultural values, even as they adopted each other's material accoutrements.

The study of Fort St. Joseph affords us the opportunity to look at the past while simultaneously seeing ourselves in the present as we chart a course for the future. Indeed, our vision of the history and the archaeology of this eighteenth-century French colonial outpost continues to shift as new observers unearth and scrutinize further evidence under changing social and political conditions. I invite you to explore what this current group of researchers has revealed about Fort St. Joseph and consider how these narratives may change tomorrow and well into the future.

2

The Historical and Cultural Context of Fort St. Joseph

JOSÉ ANTÓNIO BRANDÃO AND
MICHAEL S. NASSANEY

Fort St. Joseph was located in the St. Joseph River valley in the area that is now the city of Niles in southwest Michigan. This region played a strategic role in French aspirations for the *pays d'en haut* (Upper Country) and consequently has attracted considerable historical interest (e.g., Ballard 1973; Beeson 1900; Coolidge 1915; Cunningham 1961; Idle 2003; Peyser 1978, 1992). Historians have used oral traditions and documentary sources such as letters, official correspondences, maps, and a marriage and baptismal register to provide data on local Native American groups and the importance of Fort St. Joseph in the history of New France (e.g., see Brandão and Nassaney 2006; Clifton 1977; Peyser 1978, 1992). In this chapter we use documentary, material, and oral evidence to establish the antiquity and movement of Native American peoples in the area prior to the establishment of Fort St. Joseph. We then turn to written records that provide information about the fort's religious, military, and commercial significance. Although these documents are limited, they provide some understanding of the cultural and historical context of Fort St. Joseph.

Indigenous History

Although Native American peoples occupied southwest Michigan for millennia before European contact, the names of these groups and the relationships between them and subsequent populations remain poorly understood. The fluid nature of Native American social organization and patterns of movement and migration make it difficult to define sociopolitical entities or bounded ethnic units (Witgen 2012). Various sources of historical data suggest that the Potawatomis had moved into western Lower Michigan after they separated from their Ojibwe and Ottawa kin at the Straits of Mackinac sometime before the seventeenth century (Figure 2.1; Clifton 1977, 1986; Nassaney et al. 2012, 58). Once they were established in their new homeland, they adopted a mixed economic strategy that included maize agriculture.

Sometime in the early seventeenth century, the Potawatomis abandoned this area and moved to northeastern Wisconsin. Rock Island appears to have been one of several refugee centers brought about by the domino effect of Iroquoian incursions or their perceived threats from New York State (Mason 1986). It was in multiethnic communities such as the village on Rock Island that the underlying premise of alliance—mediation as a source of influence—emerged, perhaps accompanied by the spread of the calumet, a smoking-pipe

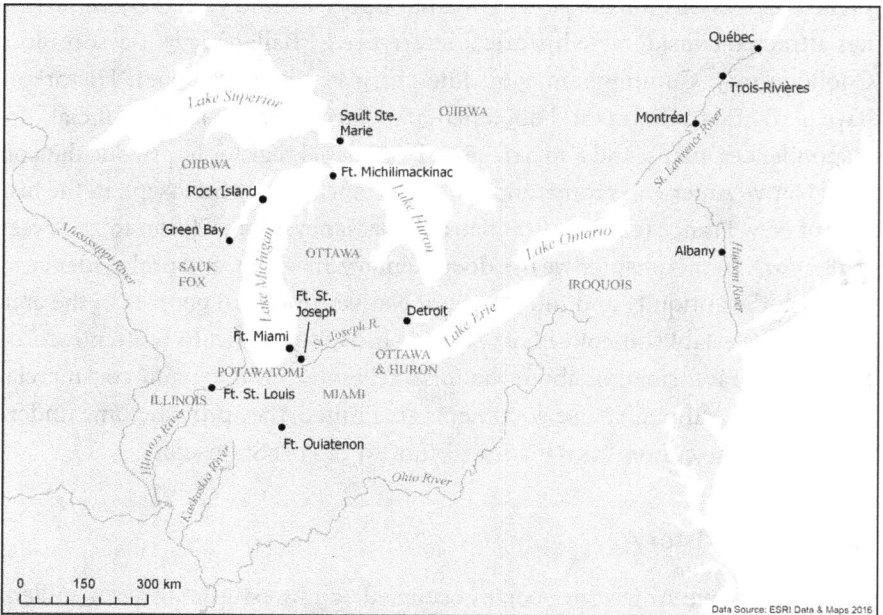

Figure 2.1. Select places and peoples in the *pays d'en haut* and adjacent regions, ca. 1730. Drawn by Jason Glatz.

ritual used in intercultural negotiations. The Potawatomis perfected this essentially Algonquian practice and showed the French how their "role as mediators has made them the most influential group at Green Bay" (White 2011, 35). This environment offered the Potawatomis social and strategic advantages by providing temporary security from Iroquois raids, direct access to French trade goods, and a political climate that presented opportunities for expansion and cultural growth (Clifton 1978, 726).

The Miamis moved into southwest Michigan from La Salle's Fort St. Louis on the Illinois River in the 1680s, possibly accompanied by the Jesuit missionary Father Claude Allouez (Myers and Peyser 1991, 12). In 1695, the vanguard of a Potawatomi expansion from their refuge in northeastern Wisconsin numbering 200 strong relocated to the "River of the Miamis," as it was then known to the French, and soon became the dominant force in the valley (Nassaney et al. 2012, 60). An incomplete 1736 census listed 100 Potawatomis, ten Miamis, and eight Illinois Kaskaskias for the area (Idle 2003, 92). While these Algonquian groups spoke mutually intelligible languages,

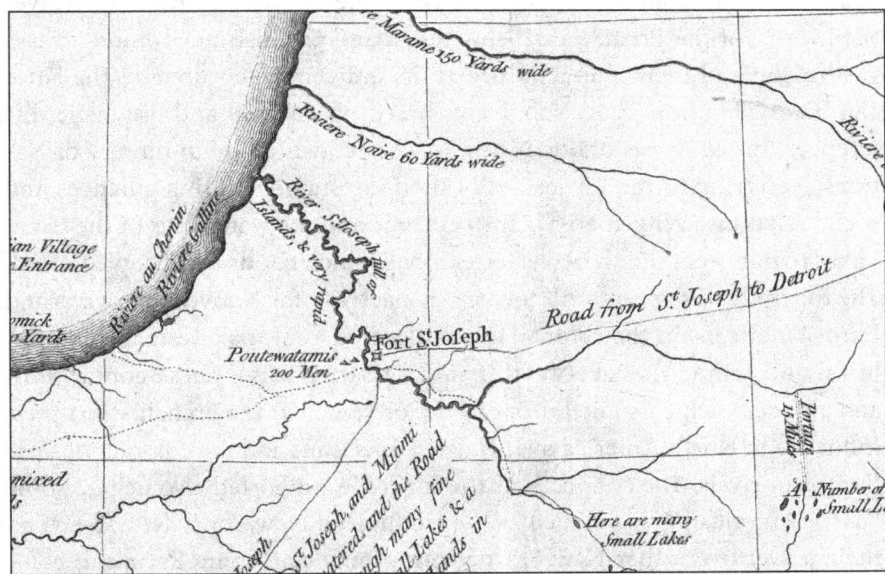

Figure 2.2. Hutchins's 1778 map of the St. Joseph River valley based on his 1762 visit. Courtesy of the David Rumsey Map Collection, www.davidrumsey.com.

their relationships, the locations of their villages, and the nature and degree of their interactions are poorly understood. The English surveyor Thomas Hutchins [1762] documented the presence of 200 Potawatomi men immediately across the river from Fort St. Joseph (Figure 2.2). Their proximity to the fort suggests amicable relations with the French. For most of the eighteenth century the Potawatomis occupied the entire lower valley, from the river's mouth to just above South Bend, Indiana. Although their population would gradually decline, there were still 790 Potawatomis in six semi-permanent villages along the river in 1819. Their numbers were surpassed only by Euro-Americans a decade later, when government treaties made land available to white settlers (see Hoock et al., chapter 8, this volume). Further information about Native American languages, architecture, material culture, subsistence, conversion, and village organization during the early nineteenth century and into the removal period can be found in Clifton (1978, 1986), Schurr (2006, 2010), Secunda (2006), Sleeper-Smith (2001), and Tanner (1987).

Means and Motivations of French Settlement in North America

The history of northeast North America—from Hudson Bay to the Chesapeake Bay and from the Atlantic Coast to the Mississippi River—involves the history of the French, English, Dutch, and Swedish newcomers to this vast region and their interactions with its indigenous occupants. The latter can be divided into many subgroups based on cultural and linguistic differences. In the words of one historian, they constituted "an infinity of Nations," referring to the intricacies of their constantly shifting alliances and social relations (Witgen 2012). The fur trade and the waterways of the Great Lakes region were the shared arteries along which goods and people flowed. The fur trade was an important economic activity for Native Americans and Euro-Americans in the colonial era and served a means of establishing political and military ties between them (Nassaney 2015). These connections and alliances helped some European nations, such as the French, exert their influence in North America over Native Americans and the colonies of their European rivals. The connections the fur trade supported also helped some Native American groups, such as the Iroquois of New York State, to extend their power over other Native American groups and some European colonies. What is now Michigan, in general, occupied an important place in the French fur trade empire.

The fur trade in northeast North America was a consequence of Christopher Columbus's failure to find a water route west to Asia. The possibility of finding either the passage Columbus had sought or places with vast riches attracted the efforts of French, English, and Dutch rulers. Unable to explore the lands Spain claimed, which clearly blocked the way to the Far East, the other nations searched for a northern passage. The French, however, did not entirely concede the southern regions of North America to the Spanish and continued to explore and colonize in the Gulf of Mexico and the Caribbean (Pritchard 2004). John Cabot (Giovanni Caboto) sailed for England and in 1497–1498 explored the New England coast. In 1534, French explorer Jacques Cartier traveled up the St. Lawrence River into the interior of the North American continent. In 1603, Samuel de Champlain, also sailing for France, returned to the area to continue Cartier's explorations, but he too could not find the passage. In 1608, Englishman Henry Hudson, sailing on behalf of the English Muscovy Company, tried an Arctic route but also failed to find the elusive route west (Bentley and Ziegler 2003, 607–635; Eccles 1978).

While a western passage to Asia eluded European explorers, they did find exploitable natural resources, among other opportunities. The ocean was filled with fish, the furs local inhabitants traded proved to be sought after in Europe, there was a vast amount of land, and they could harvest souls by converting the people they met to Christianity. There seemed to be some value, if not actual mineral riches, in northern America, and European nations strove to claim some part of it for themselves. The French, English, and Dutch promoted (with varying degrees of enthusiasm and via different mechanisms) the establishment of colonies in North America to stake their claims to areas they had explored and the resources they had found (although the settlements were not always located where the explorers had first gone). Champlain founded the village of Quebec by a cliff overlooking the St. Lawrence River in 1608, and James Smith established a settlement at Jamestown in Virginia in 1607. In 1609, Henry Hudson, trying a more southern route and now sailing for the Dutch, traveled up the Hudson River, where, in 1614, the Dutch built a fort that eventually became Albany, New York. In 1620, a group of English Pilgrims founded a settlement at Plymouth.

Even though the French did not find the fabled route westward to Asia, they never really stopped trying. Of the fifty-three major voyages of exploration the French launched up to 1751, twenty-six were attempts to find a water passage westward. By the mid-eighteenth century, they were looking for an overland route to the Pacific. Of those exploratory voyages, thirty-nine, or 73 percent, took place before 1701 (Ruggles and Heidenreich 1987, Plate 36). Equally important was the search for furs and the economic and political connections that they provided. Of the fifty-three voyages of exploration, thirty were also undertaken to find more fur-bearing lands and to develop trade and political relations with the Native Americans who trapped the furs (Ruggles and Heidenreich 1987, Plate 36). This combined passion for exploration and for expanding the fur trade (for both the wealth and political power that could result from claiming the land and its resources) had led the French as far west as the Rocky Mountains by the 1750s (Eccles 1997, 149–202). Not surprisingly, it was a group of French traders, led by Alexander Mackenzie, a Scottish fur trader working for the North West Company of Montreal, who were the first Europeans to reach the Pacific over land in July 1793, a decade before Lewis and Clark made their famed expedition.

A number of factors made this exploration and expansion of trade possible. French explorers had support from the French Crown, relied on knowledge of the interior gained from Native Americans, were remarkably tough explorers, and were motivated by a desire for wealth and a desire, fueled by national pride, to discover new lands in advance of other Europeans (Heidenreich 1997, 68–71). But most important, the French had settled along the main artery into the interior. Quebec (and later Montreal) were located on the St. Lawrence— the central river system that drained the Great Lakes and was fed by tributaries from the north, west, and south. The French recognized their strategic placement and sought to maintain their geographic advantage. They worked hard to explore westward and made alliances with Native American groups in the hopes of gaining exclusive trading rights with them. They worked to ensure peaceful relations between Native American groups because warfare hindered trapping and trading activities. Sometimes they sought to destroy those who opposed their plans, as they did with the Fox/Mesquakies in the early eighteenth century (Eccles 1978; Edmunds and Peyser 1993; Havard 2003; Heidenreich 1997; White 1991). To facilitate this policy, they built a vast network of some 106 forts and trading posts and missions (Havard 2000; Zitomersky 1994). Fort St. Joseph was among them.

By the late 1690s, however, the fur trade had become a problem for the French. The lure of adventure and wealth, aided by lack of government control, was leading men to trade rather than farm and according to Crown officials was undermining the colony's development (Eccles 1978, 110–111). No more than 800 men were ever engaged as legal or illegal traders, but that was a large proportion of the male population. Louise Dechêne (1974, 220–221) puts the number of *coureurs du bois* (literally "runners of the woods" or unsanctioned traders) at the turn of the seventeenth century at around 668 men, or 12 percent of the male population of New France at that time. Some communities, such as those of Montreal and Three Rivers, provided a disproportionately larger number of men for the trade. The proportion of *voyageurs* also varied over time. From 1690 to 1709, about 17.5 percent of the male population undertook at least one trade voyage (Beauchamp et al. 1978, 120–133). Worse than the attraction of the trade that undermined labor to conduct other economic pursuits, the demand for beaver pelts decreased in the late seventeenth century and the fur trade was no longer as profitable. In 1696, King Louis XIV of France ordered the posts in the interior closed and traders were prohibited from obtaining furs. Officials in Montreal suggested that the forts at St. Joseph and Michilimackinac be kept open for economic and military reasons, but by 1698 all the western posts were closed and trading was prohibited (Allaire 1980; Eccles 1978, 125–128; Peyser 1992, 61–62; Peyser and Brandão 2008, 112–120; Zoltvany 1974, 37–8). Western trade was not reopened and posts were not officially regarrisoned until 1715.

Despite the initial closure of posts, the fur trade continued to expand in volume and western exploration resumed. After 1715, the fur trade provided a steady flow of wealth and became even more vital for other reasons. While the fur trade had been very profitable, the French had competed with the English in seaboard colonies and with the Dutch in New Netherland for control of the land and for the allegiance of the Native American peoples who traded with them. As the vast extent of North America became known, mostly through French efforts, the French and English raced to claim lands for expansion and to prevent their European rivals from growing more powerful. By 1700, both countries envisioned growing settlements in North America that would produce goods not found in Europe and that could serve as markets for European goods. The French were less enthusiastic about this than the English were, but they were not prepared to let the English take over North America (Pritchard 2004). For the French, who by 1700 numbered only 10,000 people and by 1760 only 70,000, this meant reliance on Native American peoples. The French needed the military support of Native Americans to fend off the English and the Indians wanted manufactured goods and weapons for a variety of reasons. To stop trading was to lose the connection to the Indians and the support they provided (Eccles 2003; Zoltvany 1974). In the end, the fur trade became more important to maintain even as it began to cost money to operate (Eccles 1987). Indeed, the French Crown subsidized the costs of some goods and maintained posts in some areas for military security rather than for economic reasons.

Few places were as important for the French as the *pays d'en haut*—the western Great Lakes (Huron, Michigan, and Superior) region and the areas to the immediate north, south and west. This region was important because of its large Native American population and extensive riverine system that supported beaver populations and served as the transportation network for westward expansion. It was vital then, that the French control the region and be on good terms with its peoples. A quick glance at any map will reveal the centrality of what came to be Michigan in this system (Figure 2.1).

To maintain good relations through trade and diplomacy with the nations in the *pays d'en haut*, the French built a number of posts including one at Michilimackinac, one on the St. Joseph River (Niles, Michigan), and one at Detroit. Some posts, often where trade profits were surpassed by their strategic importance, were run as a Crown monopoly. Others, such as Michilimackinac, Detroit, and the post at the St. Joseph River, were garrisoned by French troops and run by French commanders who contracted with merchants to actually manage the business end of matters (Allaire 1987). Throughout the country, the trade was carried out by *congé*, a fur trade license. A licensing system had been developed in 1681 to try to control the number of men who could go into the interior. Limiting the number of traders was intended to control the volume of trade and who would have contact with Native Americans. The latter was an important consideration, since bad traders could cause diplomatic problems. The *congé* specified where the holder could trade, the type of merchandise he could send, and the number of canoes and men he was permitted to send in any one trading season. The holder would then make contracts with the men who took the goods upriver, or *engagés* (Eccles 1978, 113; Peyser and Brandão 2008, 59–62). Wages, length of service, how much (if any) personal trade items the canoe men could take, and even where a man was placed in the canoe were all considerations that figured into the contract (Allaire 1980). *Congé* holders were either merchants in Montreal or Quebec or contracted with merchants to bring in trade items from France. *Congés* were also given to widows and orphans, who then sold or leased them to merchants (Havard 2003, 293–294, 339–340). The license holders then had to sell the furs to either a Crown monopoly or a group of private citizens who had been granted the monopoly (depending on the period in question) to buy and ship all the fur to France.

At the height of the fur trade in 1755, eighteen licenses were assigned to Michilimackinac, which was established on the south side of the Straits by 1715. Detroit, which was established in 1701, had thirteen licenses in 1755, and the post on the St. Joseph River, which began operations in 1691, had four. All in all, these three forts shipped 1,950 packs of furs and hides, or about 195,000 pounds of furs and hides (over 97 tons) (Heidenreich and Françoise Noël 1987, Plate 40). This volume of trade represents 29.3 percent of all furs and hides traded in Canada, Louisiana, and the Hudson's Bay District and about 38 percent of all furs from Canada. This breaks down as follows: Detroit, 900 packs (13.5 percent of total); Michilimackinac, 650 packs (9.8 percent of total); and St. Joseph, 400 packs (6 percent of total) (Heidenreich and Françoise Noël 1987: Plate 40). These forts, in the same order, ranked first, second, and fourth among all French forts in terms of volume of furs shipped through their gates. The volume of trade varied from year to year, of course but the general importance of these places in the French trade and in military and diplomatic relations did not.

The Historical Context of French Activities in the St. Joseph River Valley

The French recognized the importance of the St. Joseph River valley, and as early as 1679, La Salle built what has come to be called Fort Miami at the mouth of the river. Little more than a seasonal staging area, the post did not last long. By 1686, the Society of Jesus, usually called the Jesuits, who had been doing missionary work in the region before La Salle, had been granted a tract of land for a house and chapel along the river and by 1691 the French had built a trading post near the present-day southern boundary of Niles, Michigan (Peyser 1992, 43–46). The fort, mission, and river were all named after St. Joseph, the patron saint of New France. This post "among the Miamis," later to become Fort St. Joseph, was one of the most important frontier outposts in the North American interior. It was situated near a strategic portage that linked the River of the Miamis (now the St. Joseph River) and the Great Lakes basin to the Mississippi drainage (Idle 2003, 11; Nassaney et al. 2003). It became the keystone of French control of the southern Lake Michigan region and served as a hub of commercial, military, and religious activity for local Native American populations and European colonial powers for nearly a century (Brandão and Nassaney 2006).

Despite the fact that it was first established as a mission, Fort St. Joseph served primarily as a commercial and military center. Its military significance was demonstrated when the Iroquois sought to destroy the post soon after it was constructed because of the threat it posed to their ambitions (Brandão 1997, Appendix D, Spring 1695). This mission-garrison-trading post complex initially consisted of a palisade, a commandant's house, and a few other structures (Faribault-Beauregard 1982, 1:175). Governor-General Frontenac of New France established it in an attempt to solidify French relations with the local Miami Indians and other Native American groups to the west and north of the area. Frontenac also hoped that a permanent French presence supported by the military would stimulate the fur trade in the region and check the expansion and power of the Iroquois Confederacy and their English allies (Brandão 1997; Eccles 1978, 1972; Myers and Peyser 1991). Once the French established Fort St. Joseph, the area again became home to various Native American groups with populations numbering in the hundreds by the early eighteenth century. By the early 1720s, the fort was supporting several officers, including a commandant, eight to ten enlisted men, a priest, an interpreter, a blacksmith, and about fifteen fur traders and their French, French Canadian, and Native American wives and children (Idle 2003; Peyser 1978, 44). For decades, the site was the locus of a multiethnic population that included French or French Canadian and Native American couples and intense cultural interaction. Jesuit priests baptized Native American women and their mixed-heritage offspring and Native American women served as godmothers, testifying to the sincerity of their beliefs and their full integration into the life of the community (Nassaney et al. 2012, 69).

Fort St. Joseph figured prominently in interactions between Native American peoples and French and English colonial powers throughout the eighteenth century. It served as a central staging point and supply base for the French military during its savage and destructive wars against the Fox Indians (Mesquakies) in Illinois in the 1720s and 1730s and later against the Chickasaws in Mississippi (1736–1740). These wars were vital to French expansion to the west and south of the Great Lakes.

Documentary sources contain information about the types of imported goods that the French supplied to the Native Americans, from which we can infer related activities. Joseph Peyser (1978) translated a number of French-language manuscripts from the 1730s and 1740s pertaining to Fort St. Joseph that describe goods and services merchants provided to Native Americans and others conducting official business for the Crown (Peyser 1978, 86). Among these are vouchers that list goods and services associated with the capture and processing of fur-bearing animals. For example, Fort St. Joseph merchants Louis Hamelin and Louis Gastineau (Gatineau?) supplied Antoine De Hestre and Joseph Lepage with a total of 875 deerskins. We do not know if these were produced at Fort St. Joseph or elsewhere and we do not know what their intended use was, but they point to the volume of goods involved in the fur trade. The Crown also paid various blacksmiths at the fort to repair and maintain Native American guns (Peyser 1978, 99). Musket balls, buckshot, lead, gunpowder, vermilion, and tallow are some of the other manufactured or processed goods the French traded with Native Americans at Fort St. Joseph.

Dunning Idle (2003, 82–84) compiled information on the number of canoes sent to the St. Joseph River and the permits that were issued in the period 1721–1745. While they do not specify the types of goods traded, the data indicate that the French were importing significant quantities of goods for distribution to Native American allies. Less is known about the types of furs that were collected and shipped back to Montreal from the fort. An undated report claimed that the fort could "furnish four hundred parcels of racoon, bear, wildcat, dwarf deer, [and] elk" (Peyser 1978, 30a). In 1757, the French explorer Bougainville estimated that Fort St. Joseph could produce the same number of "packages of pelts of cats, bears, lynx, otters, deer, and stags" (Idle 2003, 121). Curiously, no mention is made of beaver.

The English surveyor Thomas Hutchins remarked on the fort's population of fur traders and their economic activities during his visit in 1762:

> It is inhabited by about a dozen French families who chiefly support themselves by the trade they carry on with the Indians and notwithstanding the country is very rich about them, they raise nothing more than some Indian corn and make a little hay to support their horses and mules and a few milch cows, which seems to be all the stock they have. (Cunningham 1961, 72–73)

A year earlier, Lieutenant Dietrich Brehm, a British cartographer, had also provided a brief description of the fort:

> Fort St Joseph is made of Oak Stokados, about 7 years ago rebuilt, in a pretty good order, but no Plattforms in the Bastions or any part of it. there is no House for a officer, who has taken a Privat House, in which the Priest used to live; four Familys live hier, have a little Land improved. and rise some wheat, but are obliged to sent to Detroit to be grainded.
> (Quoted in Widder 2013, 251)

Commanders at the fort and Native Americans from the region were key players in events related to the Seven Years' War, the first major war for empire in North America. As a result of this war, France lost Canada to the English (Idle 2003, 151–52; Myers and Peyser 1991; Peyser 1992). Once the English gained control, relationships changed. Lord Jeffrey Amherst, governor-general of British North America after the French defeat, discouraged the practice of providing Native Americans with what he considered to be lavish gifts, including gunpowder and alcohol in fur trade negotiations, as the French had done. He reasoned that such gifts made Native Americans less industrious about acquiring furs. Native American discontent with English practices and attitudes instigated Pontiac's Rebellion in the spring of 1763, in which supporters of the Ottawa leader attacked Fort St. Joseph to remove the English from the area and encourage the return of the French (Widder 2013, 157–159). This forced the English to establish a policy to limit colonial expansion into the interior via the Proclamation of 1763. After 1763, French fur traders were allowed to remain at the fort and continued to trade for furs. Following a daylong raid and occupancy by the Spanish in 1781, the site was abandoned and the area came under American control. Independent and company traders such as William Burnett and Joseph Bertrand continued trading for fur in the St. Joseph River valley into the nineteenth century (Cunningham 1967; Johnson 1919, 108–109). After the US government acquired the area through treaties, it had the land surveyed (1827) and began selling it to pioneers, who soon modified it for cultivation, slowly eradicating the habitats of fur-bearing animals and effectively ending the fur trade.

The Cartographic Record and Other Documentary Sources

Fort St. Joseph was clearly a well-known outpost located along major land and water routes. However, visitors to the fort and others who sought to place the post on maps left vague, imprecise, and at times conflicting information about its location. In 1721, the French missionary Pierre-François-Xavier Charlevoix visited the fort. He wrote that the post was twenty leagues from the mouth of the river on the same bank as that of the Potawatomi village, but he failed to specify which bank of the river that was (Charlevoix 1761, 94, 99). On September 23, 1754, Father Jacques-François Forget Duverger traveled overland from Detroit to Fort St. Joseph on his way to take up his mission at Cahokia (Illinois). He placed the post on the right side of the St. Joseph River, twenty leagues from Lake Michigan and about fifteen to sixteen leagues from the river's headwaters.[1] The French commander Louis-Antoine de Bougainville, writing three years later, in 1757, also placed the fort on the right bank of the St. Joseph River twenty leagues from Lake Michigan (Bougainville in Margry 1867, 53). An anonymous observer who wrote around 1763 and who may not have visited the fort personally, claimed that the fort was 25 leagues from the mouth of the river on the same side as the Potawatomi village but also did not specify which bank that was.[2]

French maps of the period are not much more help. Even though the post was marked on many early French maps, the maps are not detailed enough to locate the fort on the ground. Worse, early map makers who never visited the site relied on the written descriptions of those who had placed the fort on different maps on each side of the river. The most reliable map of the fort's location comes from an English cartographer. Thomas Hutchins, who was sent as an envoy on behalf of English officials to quiet Native American fears after the capitulation of New France, visited the fort in August 1762. His journal does not indicate the location of the fort, but a map attributed to him locates the fort on the east side of the river across from the Potawatomi village. According to the scale of the map, the fort was about thirty miles from the mouth of the St. Joseph River.[3] Hutchins repeated that location in a 1778 map (Figure 2.2). In the early 1990s, Joseph L. Peyser sorted through much of this contradictory material and concluded that the fort was on the east bank, the right side as one travels toward the mouth of the St. Joseph River, at or very near a commemorative boulder placed at that point in 1913 (Figure 1.1; Peyser 1992, 71–78). The contradictory information about the location of Potawatomi and Miami villages remains unresolved and may reflect the Native American practice of periodic village relocation.

As early as 1900, Lewis H. Beeson, a local historian who lived near the fort, claimed that he had found the actual site of the fort and left a detailed legal description of an area that had yielded copious amounts of French and English artifacts (Beeson 1900). There is also an anonymous map from that period (ca. 1900), probably produced by Beeson, that places the fort on the eastern side of the river in Niles, Michigan (Peyser 1992: Figure 6). Collectors working in the Niles area had turned up many French-period artifacts but failed to pinpoint the location of the fort until 1998, when Western Michigan University initiated the Fort St. Joseph Archaeological Project. A reconnaissance survey conducted in the area Beeson described and Peyser confirmed revealed a deposit of eighteenth-century colonial artifacts and animal remains in the floodplain northwest of the boulder (Nassaney 1999). Subsequent work established the integrity of the deposits, and excavations have continued at the site almost every year since then (Nassaney et al. 2002–2004).

In addition to maps, Fort St. Joseph is known through a variety of French-language (and some English-language) documents that provide limited insights about what the fort looked like, who lived there, and the relationships between French and Native American peoples in and around the fort. Despite the shortcomings of these sources, historians have discussed the fort in works dealing with the fur trade, religious life, and the military and imperial history of New France (Idle 2003; Malchelosse 1957, 1958, 1979; Myers and Peyser 1991; Paré 1930–1931; Peyser 1992).

The quality of numerous popular works on the fort ranges from the derivative to the deeply flawed. Among the former is Ballard (1973) and Cunningham (1961). Among the latter is Webster and Krause (1990), who revive the false notions, which Malchelosse conclusively put to rest in 1957, that Fort St. Joseph was the same as La Salle's earlier, temporary fortification and that both forts and the mission were located near the mouth of the river.

Historians have written less about daily life, relations among the French, and the process of cultural exchange between French and Native Americans and identity formation at the post. These topics have been the focus of subsequent archaeological research. We know only a little more about the built environment, material culture, and demographic profile of this important frontier community. The emphasis of previous work, understandably enough, has been upon trying to ascertain where the fort was located, who served there, and what the fort's role was in the imperial and commercial affairs in the Great Lakes region and of New France in general.

By using that pioneering scholarship and some of the primary sources related to the fort's history, we can construct a broad picture of the fort's fur trade society and its material conditions. According to one observer, Fort St.

Joseph was built more to facilitate trade than defense: "within a few yards of navigable water, commanded by two high banks one on each side of the River" (Hutchins 1762). It had entrances on the north and south sides of the palisade line. Shortly after 1691, it enclosed a small commander's house, a building that could garrison twenty men, and some buildings used to store trading goods and furs.[4] The palisade was not especially secure, and in 1695 the Iroquois Indians were able to put their guns through its gaps to shoot into the fort (Relation de 1694–95 in Margry 1876–1886, 5:71). That the Iroquois could get that close to the fort suggests that it had no platforms or bastions from which to fire upon the attackers, as Brehm's remarks confirmed in 1761 (see Widder 2013).

Records from 1701 suggest that no major additions had been made to the fort (Margry 1701, 5:281, 283), and the palisade was reported to still be less than ideal in 1721 (although apparently it was repaired a few years prior to 1761). According to the Jesuit Pierre-François-Xavier Charlevoix, who visited the fort in 1721, the commander's house, "which is but a sorry one, is called the fort from its being surrounded by an indifferent pallisado" (Charlevoix 1761, 2:93). Austerity and disrepair were common conditions of smaller forts, where, according to Bougainville, "the house where the commanding officer resides, being surrounded by stakes [stuck in the ground], is honoured by the name of fort" (quoted in Margry 1867, 58). Still, a visitor in 1753 indicated that a palisade was intact and noted one door in the wall.[5] A 1763 description of the fort commented on its palisade of "rounded stakes" stuck in the ground.[6]

In 1753, the post contained "fifteen huts which the owners call houses."[7] That number of houses, even though Brehm noted only four families, seems to have remained fairly constant over the next few decades (see Widder 2013). A census of the French-speaking inhabitants who were deported from the post to Fort Michilmackinac in 1780 lists the names of fourteen household heads, "each in their own house" (Malchelosse 1958, 169). There is no written information about how the houses were built (see Hartley and Nassaney, chapter 4, this volume). In 1750, a ten- by eight-foot jail made of cut stone and provided with "iron work" for security was ordered to be constructed (Peyser 1978, document 140). By the 1740s, a Native American leader asked the French to build him a house with two doors; the structure required 400 linear feet of squared timber (Peyser 1978, document 123 [2]). French sources refer to a chapel (1721) and a church (1741 and 1752), but it is not clear if they were located in the fort or in the nearby Indian village. The references relate to Indian converts (Idle 2003, 64; Paré and Quaife 1926, 219, 222–223).

The question of the "ethnic" or "cultural" identity of the fort's inhabitants is vexing (see Nassaney 2008b). Even with a detailed genealogical analysis of each person, one could not say with certainty how residents viewed themselves, how others viewed them, and which view was "real" or counted for official purposes or for purposes of social interaction (see Sommerville 2014, 22–31.) Moreover, documentary sources and material remains can be interpreted as evidence of cultural change, continuity, and ethnogenesis, as Nassaney and Brandão (2009) and Nassaney (2019; Nassaney chapter 10, this volume) argue. Written records can provide only crude generalizations based on names, on how those who maintained records chose to identify individuals, and on the occasional scrap of information in a document that may clarify whether a person was "French" or "Indian" or "*métis*." The criteria later scholars chose to use to identify a Euro-American inhabitant of the fort as "French" rather than "French Canadian" is also subject to debate. Indeed, such distinctions by modern writers may have little or no bearing on the historical agents' sense of self or their place in society at the time. For the purposes of this chapter, "French" or "Miami" or other labels related to nationality or group means more or less the static and crude categories that can be inferred from the limited sources and the categories those sources assigned to people.

Demography, the Built Environment, and Cultural Interactions at Fort St. Joseph

How many people lived at the fort and what the composition of that population was are also difficult to ascertain. The garrison at the fort was, at most, twenty men strong. In the early 1720s, a list of military personnel noted ten soldiers and eight officers at the post, although this seems to be somewhat out of proportion (Peyser 1978, document 44). The names of the officers may include those who led the companies from which the men were drawn rather than who was present at the fort. Some forty years later, the fighting strength of the fort, including the soldiers and inhabitants, was estimated to be eighteen to twenty men.[8] The French Canadian historian Gérard Malchelosse, without citing a source, claimed that by 1730 thirty families were living around the fort and that by 1750 forty families were there (Malchelosse 1958, 150). That would have meant as many as 100 men, including traders, soldiers, and *engagés* at the height of the summer before the traders returned to their various points of origin. In claiming such a large number of families, Malchelosse may have been counting French and Native American households that were formed, sometimes for periods of a lifetime, each summer as traders returned to the area. However, a study of licenses to trade in the area reveals that in peacetime, only about four to ten *engagés* were sent to the fort each year in the 1720s. On average, only about eight men were sent to the fort each year in the 1740s (Idle 2003, 83, 118). The few eyewitnesses who comment directly on population size indicate quite clearly that approximately a dozen French families living in about fifteen houses made the fort their home throughout the year.[9] Those numbers seemed to hold well into the period of English occupation of the fort, when forty-five people were evacuated from fourteen households (Malchelosse 1958, 161, 169).

The Native Americans who lived in and near the fort came from a variety of nations, including the Algonquian-speaking Illinois, Miami, Ottawa, and Potawatomi groups, but their exact number is unknown. Writing in 1710, Antoine Raudot estimated that some 800 Miami warriors were spread across six bands located at St. Joseph and elsewhere (Raudot 1904, 135). A roughly equal distribution of warriors would lead to about 100 or so warriors at Fort St. Joseph. Multiplied by the accepted factor of five (one warrior and four other family members) produces a total of about 500 Miamis. Reports from a decade later reveal that the Miamis and Potawatomis each still had villages nearby and regularly visited each other to play lacrosse and games of chance, but these reports offer no population data or hints about the nature of their relationships (Charlevoix 1761, 94, 102). In 1757, Bougainville estimated 400 Potawatomi and some Miami warriors (or 2,000 people) in the area (Bougainville in Margry 1867, 53). In 1762, a visitor estimated 200 (1,000 people), while one year later the number of warriors was said to have been 250 Potawatomis (or 1,250 people).[10]

The occupational roles of some of the residents can be determined from written sources and by inference. Lists of commanders and soldiers reveal a military presence at the fort and an interpreter to assist in dealings with Native Americans (Peyser 1978, document 44). Marriage and baptismal records identify French and Native American women and enslaved Indians in the community (Faribault-Beauregard 1982, 179–189). Payment records indicate that a gunsmith/blacksmith, Antoine Dehaître (also known as Dehestre, Dehastre, de Hestre, etc.) lived at the fort from at least 1731 to 1749 (Faribault-Beauregard 1982, 181; Peyser 1978, documents 99[2], 121, 123[2], 130). Around 1739, Dehaître listed Michel Durivage Baillonjeu as his partner in the blacksmithing trade

(Peyser 1978, document 99). The same records reveal that several traders had shops in the fort, that a master carpenter lived at Fort St. Joseph in 1745, and that priests were also often present there (Faribault-Beauregard 1982, 182–3, 188). Trade licenses indicate that *engagés* were frequent visitors, bringing supplies to the king's men and goods for the local inhabitants (Malchelosse 1958, 148).

Some of the fort's residents may have practiced horticulture or maintained small garden plots near their homes, but French observers who commented on the matter in 1711, 1721, and 1763 noted only Native American farming practices.[11] Father Charlevoix (1761, 2:100) mentioned that cleared fields surrounded the post, but he did not describe the extent and nature of any crops. Brehm observed in 1761 that the residents raised some wheat (which had to be ground in Detroit), whereas Hutchins (1762) only noted Indian corn and hay. The French did not adopt extensive farming practices in the *pays d'en haut*, in contrast to their agricultural practices in settlements in the Illinois Country and the mid–Mississippi River Valley. French officials routinely chided residents of Fort Michilimackinac for not farming and for relying on Native Americans to supply them with food in exchange for manufactured goods and castigated those at Fort Ouiatenon for failing to exploit the land for anything but small garden plots (de Lotbinière 1976, 9).

The post was by no means self-sufficient, although surpluses were sometimes available. In 1740, Nicolas-Antoine Coulon de Villiers, the post commander, authorized the purchase of meat and grain to sustain two families living there (Peyser 1978, document 104), and in 1754, seven men from the area went to Detroit to purchase wheat to get them through the winter (*RAPQ* 1928, 404). In contrast, the historical records often refer to purchases of meat for the soldiers and Indian allies who came to the post, suggesting that livestock was raised at Fort St. Joseph. In the 1740s and early 1750s, Marie Réaume and Antoine Dehaître, among other habitants at the post, sold pigs, cows, and oxen to the fort's commander (Peyser 1978, documents 121[3], 123, 151). In 1762, Hutchins noted horses, mules, and cows at the fort. And while it seems reasonable to suggest that some, if not all, of the livestock was raised at the post, faunal analysis reveals that wild game, deer in particular, dominated the diets of the fort's residents (see Martin et al., chapter 3, this volume; Nassaney and Martin 2017).

The French did what they could to maintain good relations with the Indians in the area. In times of war, as one would expect, the Indians received gifts of supplies and services at the king's expense (Peyser 1978, documents 93, 121,

121[3]). But the French also seemed to provide Indians with the sort of help that suggests genuine concern for neighbors. For example, families of warriors were given food and clothing assistance while the men were fighting (Peyser 1978, document 101). In 1739, two blankets were given to cover the body of Chief Arikikon, an Odawa chief who had died (Peyser 1978, document 88). In 1747, post commander Piquotée de Belestre arranged for Antoine Dehaître to build a coffin for the son of the local headman, Pinchicaché, and a house for the grief-stricken father (Peyser 1978, document 123[2]). A few years later, Belestre was instructed to intervene in the family affairs of Canasa, a local Native American, to ensure peace between him and his brother (Peyser 1978, document 138). While such gestures likely earned goodwill and support, they nonetheless can also be said to show compassion.

Good relations with the Indians should come as little surprise. While some Indians came and went in time of war and trade, others stayed to make lives with the fort's French inhabitants. The admittedly incomplete marriage and baptismal records reveal one such French-Indian marriage in the period up to 1763. Jean-Baptiste Baron, a voyager from Boucherville, Quebec, married Marie-Catherine 8ekioukoue,[12] an Illinois woman. They had at least three children together in the period 1729 to 1733 (Faribault-Beauregard 1982, 179). These are the ones recorded as having been baptized. Marie-Catherine later served as godmother to the child of Gabriel Bolon and Susanne Ménard, both of whom are indicated as being French in marriage records (Faribault-Beauregard 1982, 121, 180). Marie-Catherine's role in the latter event suggests the degree to which Indians were, or at least could be, accepted in the life of the community.

Marie-Catherine's marriage in the church and her role as godmother also reveal that Native Americans in the area converted to Catholicism. Pierre Mekabikanga, a Miami, married twice in the Catholic Church; the first time to another Miami and, after that wife died, to Marianne Pi8assik8, an Ottawa woman (Faribault-Beauregard 1982, 179). Eight Native American adults were baptized, as were about twenty-five infants. About eleven of these infants died shortly after (Faribault-Beauregard 1982, 186–189). These conversions reflect a clear willingness on the part of Native Americans to link their fortunes and cultures to that of the French and reflect the continued practice of a Catholic faith among the denizens of the community (see also Brandão and Nassaney 2008).

Life on the frontier, despite popular images of isolation, also seems to have involved a fair amount of movement among and interactions with communities at a substantial distance from Fort St. Joseph, both for traders and others, as documented in the biographical information presented here from Faribault-Beauregard (1982). The names of fort residents appear in archives associated with other French colonial sites (e.g., Detroit, Michilimackinac) suggesting the extent of their geographic mobility, perhaps influenced by opportunities that resettlement provided. The entries in a baptismal register for Jean-Baptiste Baron, a voyageur from Boucherville, Quebec, and Marie-Catherine Sagatchioua or Ouekeoukoue, an Illinois woman who was baptized in 1727, both of whom have been already mentioned above, are telling. While the records do not reveal when Jean-Baptiste Baron and Marie-Catherine Ouekeoukoue were married, they do indicate that they were married according to the rites of the Roman Catholic Church. Jean-Baptiste and Marie-Catherine had three children: Joseph Baron (1729) (whose godmother was Marie Josephe Rheaume), Susanne Baron (1730) (whose godmother was Susanne Ménard, and after whom she was named), and Marguerite Baron (1733). Marguerite was baptized summarily, which suggests that she may have been at risk of dying. Her godmother was Anne Charlotte Chevalier.

Pursuing in more detail some of the individuals mentioned in the baptism records offers more insight about the life of denizens at Fort St. Joseph and other distant trading posts. Marie Josephe Rheaume, godmother to Joseph Baron in 1729, was a *métis* woman, the daughter of Jean-Baptiste Réaume, an interpreter at the post in Green Bay, Wisconsin, and Simphorose Owaouagoukoue, a Native American woman. Marie was married to Jean-Baptiste Jourdain at Michilimackinac in 1746. At least five of her children were baptized at the fort from 1747 to 1759, but three of them had been born in Green Bay. One daughter, Josette Jourdain, was married at Michilimackinac in 1764 at the age of 17. She was among those who had been born at Green Bay; she was baptized at Michilimackinac in 1747. Marie Josephe lost one child at birth.

Susanne Ménard, godmother to Susanne Baron, was the wife of Gabriel Bolon, a soldier in the garrison of Fort St. Joseph. Susanne and Gabriel were married at Michilimackinac in 1726. Susanne Ménard had at least six children between 1726 and 1740 at Fort St. Joseph. She and Gabriel Bolon returned the honor Jean-Baptiste Baron and his wife had bestowed on them by having Marie-Catherine Ouekeoukoue Baron as the godmother to Marie Louise Bolon in 1728. Susanne and Gabriel baptized four more children at Fort Michilimackinac. Indeed, they seem to have been a rather mobile couple. One of the children baptized at Michilimackinac was, in fact, born at a winter hunting camp at Kalamazoo in 1745. His name was Joseph. Marie Louise, their daughter baptized at Fort St. Joseph with Marie-Catherine Ouekeoukoue Baron as the godmother, was married at Michilimackinac in 1747 at the age of 19.

The above, admittedly dry, set of facts reveals information about social relations, including the sharing and retention of cultural practices in the course of intimate interactions. Marie-Catherine Ouekeoukoue Baron's role as the godmother to Marie Louise Bolon in 1728 is an indication of the sincerity of her conversion and how readily she was accepted into Catholic kin networks. Moreover, the godparents of Susanne Ménard's other children were her sister and the post commander—the latter representing the highest echelon of fort society. The fact that a *métis* couple practiced elements of an enduring cultural tradition in the form of baptisms with godparents at a great distance from the seats of civil and ecclesiastical authority may also speak to the endurance of French Catholicism.

These records also point to the mobility of people across a vast geographic span: from Fort St. Joseph to Michilimackinac to Green Bay and the St. Lawrence towns of Montreal and Quebec. Equally evident are the rigors of living in a harsh environment where death at birth was not uncommon. The pursuit of a living and food did not keep even pregnant women from traveling in the harsh conditions of a Michigan winter. Women married young, did not remain widows for very long, and continued to bear children so long as they were fertile. All of this suggests ways that people established social networks across wide spatial areas: French and Indians trying to build networks of support through marriage and fictive kin relationships; French and Indians trying to overcome the isolation by forging links across communities; and French and Indians interacting, in multiple ways, with their new neighbors in order to better survive in a rapidly changing world. From this set of records, we learn that the French, even those of mixed ancestry, tried to maintain elements of what they considered central to their culture, in particular religious practices (cf. White 1991; see Nassaney, chapter 10, this volume).

Concluding Thoughts

Documentary sources provide a cultural context for the colonial motivations and efforts of the French in the heartland of the continent and hint at how

Native American groups responded to the new challenges and opportunities afforded by the international fur trade. Of course, these records were not written with the questions that contemporary researchers have in mind. As a result, new questions are constantly being generated, some of which may be answered by new archival research and others potentially through archaeological investigations. The archaeological record is particularly telling with regard to the materiality of eighteenth-century lives, including the appearance of the fort, the activities conducted there, the ways that fort residents reimagined and reused objects, and the identities of the participants. Ongoing archaeological excavations are revealing the size, construction methods, styles, and functions of structures at Fort St. Joseph (see Hartley and Nassaney, chapter 4, this volume). Recovery of faunal and floral remains and small finds are indicative of daily activities and the extent to which the French and Native Americans adopted each other's practices (see Martin et al., chapter 3, this volume; Davis, chapter 5, this volume; Giordano and Nassaney, chapter 6, this volume). Settlement distributions demonstrate the impact Fort St. Joseph had on the cultural landscape of the lower St. Joseph River valley (Hoock et al., chapter 8, this volume). The detritus of eighteenth-century life and its distribution can illuminate what life was like for those who sought to live in a distant outpost of empire, had to serve the ambitions of their king, needed to provide for themselves and their families while adjusting to new ways and peoples, and at the same time sought to preserve what they knew and valued of their own culture.

Archaeological investigations in conjunction with new readings of the extant archival record will give scholars the ability to place Fort St. Joseph more fully in the scholarship on the networks of French posts in the distant interior and allow comparisons of the fort and its culture to that of other posts and to the better-studied French settlements in the St. Lawrence River valley and beyond (Armour 2000; Gauthier-Larouche 1974; Greer 1997; Lessard and Marquis 1972; Moogk 2000; Séguin 1967; Walthall 1991; Walthall and Emerson 1992). In the end, investigation of Fort St. Joseph can reveal insightful understandings of what worked and what failed and offer lessons about cultural interactions, collaboration, and conflict—aspects of human social relations that become ever more important in our increasingly globalized contemporary world.

Acknowledgments

Portions of this chapter have appeared previously in Brandão (2008) and Brandão and Nassaney (2006). They are reproduced here with permission of the Michigan State University Press and the French Colonial Historical Society. Other sections are rewritten from Nassaney et al. (2012) and Nassaney (2015). This work is a synthesis that has grown out of fifteen years of collaborative research between the two of us. In the course of this work we have relied on the scholarship and intellectual generosity of many people. Our intellectual debts are made clear in the sources we cite, but we want to offer special thanks to Christina Arseneau, Carol Bainbridge, the late William M. Cremin, Lisa-Marie Malischke, Terrance Martin, Robert Myers, the late Joseph L. Peyser, William Sauck, and the members of the Support the Fort organization, whose enthusiasm for the history of the area and whose knowledge and historical reenacting have helped us better "see" the world we uncovered in the field and archives. We remain responsible for the contents of this chapter. We hope it reveals to the people of Niles the depth and richness of the history and archaeology of Fort St. Joseph and the ways the study of this place can enhance our understandings of ourselves. We dedicate this chapter to the memories of Drs. William M. Cremin and Joseph L. Peyser. Bill recognized the scope of the effort that would be required to recover and interpret the archaeological remains of one of the most important French colonial sites in Michigan and Joe laid the groundwork that enabled us to approach the site with confidence about its location and a deeper understanding of the place of Fort St. Joseph in the French empire.

Notes

1. Forget Duverger was actually more precise; he located the door of the fort at "46 degrees, 16 minutes"; "Relation D'un voyage Intéressant au Canada, [26 juin, 1753–22 novembre, 1754]," in "Variétés Philosophiques et Litteraires," Miscellanea, Tome VII, ms 213, ff. 79r–79v, Bibliothèque Universitaire de Rennes. The document is unsigned, but internal evidence and information from other sources leave little doubt that Forget Duverger was the author. See "Mémoire sur les postes du Canada . . . Par le Chevalier de Raymond," in *RAPQ* 1927–1928, 323–429. Forget Duverger accompanied Chevalier de Raymond as far as Detroit and he notes Forget Duverger's departure for St. Joseph on September 3, 1754 (ibid., 401). In his account, Forget Duverger wrote that he left Detroit on Tuesday, September 3 to "go to the St. Joseph river" (Relation D'un voyage Intéressant au Canada," f. 78v.). All translations from French, unless otherwise noted, are by Brandão.

2. The document in question is printed in two parts. See "Memoire sur la partie occidentale du Canada, depuis Michillimakinac, jusqu'au fleuve du Mississipi," in *Bulletin des Recherches Historiques* 26, no. 1 (Janvier 1920): 25–32 and 26, no. 2 (Fevrier 1920): 56–64. The dating of the document is discussed in an unnumbered note on page 25 of the January issue and the locational data is found at page 56 of the February number. The league as a unit of distance varied from place to place in France; today, estimates are that a league was roughly equal to three statute miles ("League," *Oxford English Dictionary*; "lieue," *Le Nouveau Petit Robert*.)

3. The map, which is misleadingly titled, is discussed in William A. Jenks, "The 'Hutchins' Map of Michigan," *Michigan History Magazine* 10, no. 34 (January 1926): 358–373. An abbreviated version of this article is reproduced as "Supplementary Note: The 'Hutchins' Map of Michigan," in Louis Karpinsky, *Bibliography of the Printed Maps of Michigan, 1804–1880* (Lansing: Michigan Historical Commission, 1931), 71–79. The map's actual title is "A Tour from Fort Cumberland North Westward round the part of the Lake Erie, Huron and Michigan, including part of the Rivers St. Joseph, the Wabash, and Miamis, with a Sketch of the Road from thence by the Lower Shawanoe Town to Fort Pitt [1]762." Hutchins's name is nowhere on the map, but the route laid out on the map and the locations there fit those that Hutchins describes in his journal. (On the journal see, Jenks, "The 'Hutchins' Map of Michigan," 365–373). The map also includes a wealth of detail about the locations listed and the number of Indian warriors each village could furnish. This too fits with the information Hutchins was asked to gather on this trip. Both Jenks articles have a section titled "Remarks on the Face of the Map." In reality, there is a great deal more information on the map than Jenks reproduced. He did not even reproduce all the information on the map relevant to Michigan.

4. Malchelosse (1958, 144). He offers no authority for this assessment of the fort's built environment. The only reference in the paragraph in which this detail is found is to a letter dated October 25, 1693, from Governor Frontenac to the minister of the marine in France. A copy of that letter (*RAPQ* 1928, 68–74), makes no mention of the fort's contents. Marthe Faribault-Beauregard adds another house to this total, also without citing authority but probably following Malchelosse, whose work is listed in the bibliography; see *La population des forts français d'Amérique (xviiie siècle)* (Montreal: Éditions Bergeron, 1982), 1:175.

5. Forget Duverger, "Rélation D'un voyage Intéressant au Canada," f. 79v.

6. "Memoire sur la partie occidentale du Canada, depuis Michillimakinac jusqu'au fleuve du Mississipi," *Bulletin des Recherches Historiques* 26, no. 2 (1920): 56.

7. Forget Duverger, "Rélation D'un voyage Intéressant au Canada," f. 79v.

8. "Memoire sur la partie occidentale du Canada," 56.

9. Forget Duverger, "Rélation D'un voyage Intéressant au Canada," f. 79v. See also Hutchins [1762].

10. "Memoire sur la partie occidentale du Canada," 56; [Hutchins], "A Tour from Fort Cumberland," [1762].

11. Father Marest to Father Germon, November 9, 1712, in *The Jesuit Relations and Allied Documents, 1610–1791*, edited by R. G. Thwaites (Cleveland: Burrows Bros., 1896–1901), 66:281; Charlevoix (1762, 2:99); "Memoire sur la partie occidentale du Canada," 56.

12. Seventeenth- and eighteenth-century French writers used a symbol, written like the

number "8," to represent a sound in Algonquian and Iroquoian languages that most closely resembled the *ou* sound in French. The 8 and the *ou* were often used interchangeably, but the 8 at the start of word more often emulates the "w" sound of the French word for 8, *huit* (phonetically, wheet/wheat). In time, the 8 was dropped for a regularized use of *ou* (e.g., Louis 8akouts became Louis Ouakouts.)

3

The Use of Animals for Fur, Food, and Raw Material at Fort St. Joseph

TERRANCE J. MARTIN, JOSEPH HEARNS, AND RORY J. BECKER

The faunal assemblage and activities represented at Fort St. Joseph illustrate the complexity and idiosyncrasies of daily interactions that occurred among local Native Americans, French creole habitants, commercial agents, and military personnel who occupied this eighteenth-century settlement. Abundant well-preserved animal remains indicate that the fort's inhabitants acquired and processed hides and consumed meat (Nassaney and Martin 2017). Analyses of the faunal remains provide detailed information on the wild animals that were procured, the local habitats from which these animals were acquired, and unique examples of traumatic injuries. Inspection of faunal specimens also revealed modifications of certain elements to create bone tools, ornaments, and gaming pieces. Our attention to the spatial distribution of animal remains was an attempt to identify refuse disposal patterns and distinctive activity areas where animals were processed for their hides, meat, and bone marrow.

Methods

The junior authors initially identified samples of animal remains from the Fort St. Joseph site using reference animal skeletons as part of their masters' theses at Western Michigan University (Becker 2004; Hearns 2015). The senior author selected additional samples as materials for zooarchaeology workshops that Western Michigan University archaeological field school students and participants in various archaeology summer camps that were attended by middle school students, high school students, teachers, and lifelong learners examined (see D'Elia et al., chapter 9, this volume). Whereas Becker and Hearns placed a priority on features for their respective analyses (a total of more than 7,600 specimens from fourteen features), samples for zooarchaeology workshops over several years were based on size and the condition of the remains so that attempted identifications would result in positive experiences instead of creating frustration with samples that consisted of small unidentifiable long-bone shaft fragments. The senior author also selected additional samples in order to complete units, levels, or features that workshop students examined. Samples from locations outside features consist of more than 24,700 animal remains that were obtained from areas of alluvium, plow zone, occupation zone, stratigraphic transition zones, and wall profiles within numerous excavation units across the site (Table 3.1; see Figure 1.4). Recovery techniques for the samples reported in this chapter include wet screening sediments through quarter-inch and eighth-inch mesh screens. Although animal remains were sporadically encountered during excavations at the Lyne site on the terrace (Figure 1.2), our discussion in this chapter is restricted to the floodplain. Ultimately, all of the animal remains were examined and previous identifications were verified at the Illinois State Museum's Research and Collections Center in Springfield, Illinois, where an extensive collection of modern vertebrate skeletons and freshwater mussel shells are available for reference. Information for each identified specimen and each lot of unidentified specimens was entered on tags that were printed on acid-free, archive-quality paper. Specimens and accompanying tags were placed within 2 mil or 4 mil polyethylene zipper bags. Included on the specimen tags is information on archaeological provenience, animal taxon, anatomical element, side, portion of element, condition of epiphyseal closure (if present), specimen completeness, weight of the specimen in grams, natural modifications (e.g., gnaw marks made by carnivores and/or rodents), and cultural modifications (e.g., burning and cut marks). Standard lengths were estimated for each identified fish bone by referring to bones from modern fish of known size in the reference collection. For all animal classes, single specimen counts were tallied in the case of refitted broken specimens and rejoined epiphyses and shafts. All information was then entered into computer files in order to facilitate the analysis.

Table 3.1. Faunal samples by feature and strata at the Fort St. Joseph site

Feature/Strata	NISP[a]	NISP Weight (g)	Biomass (kg)[b]	Number of Taxa
Feature 1	24	85.7	1.579	4
Feature 2	724	769.7	12.230	15
Feature 3	102	64.1	1.162	4
Feature 4	29	61.3	1.164	6
Feature 5	1,839	3,843.1	51.879	16
Feature 6	557	787.2	11.910	14
Feature 7	1,885	2,668.4	36.021	19
Feature 9	5	55.8	1.037	3
Feature 10	661	709.7	11.000	9
Feature 11	1,263	3,176.1	42.666	13
Feature 12	177	851.5	11.864	9
Feature 13	99	341.8	5.268	10
Feature 19	224	167.0	3.008	6
Feature 22	81	382.3	6.063	6
Feature totals	7,670	13,963.7	196.851	
Alluvium to top of plow zone	1,180	1,770.0	25.551	14
Plow zone	15,739	21,735.2	241.777	38
Plow zone to occupation zone transition	1,829	3,202.4	42.731	21
Occupation zone	5,744	10,101.5	122.246	34
Occupation zone to B-horizon transition	98	92.5	1.798	8
Wall profiles	185	361.7	5.905	8
Grand totals	32,445	51,227.0	636.859	56

[a] Number of identified specimens.
[b] Biomass in kilograms was calculated from the sum of the biomass calculated from NISP weights for individual features and strata using allometric formulae presented by Reitz and Scarry (1985, 67).

Summary calculations are presented in tables and include the number of identified specimens (NISP), minimum number of individuals (MNI) per taxon, total weight of specimens per taxon (in grams), and biomass (in kilograms) for each taxon. Scientific and common names for animals follow the Integrated Taxonomic Information System website.[1] Estimates of MNI were calculated from individual features (using the maximum distinction approach [Grayson 1973]), which assumes that specimens from one individual did not occur in multiple features or other contexts, and from the site at large (using the minimum distinction approach [Grayson 1973]), which assumes that specimens from one individual could occur in multiple contemporaneous features or other contexts. MNI counts for a given taxon are based on most numerous skeletal elements, element portion, symmetry of skeletal elements, and biological age or body size indicated by particular elements. Spatial impacts on MNI estimates are more likely to be significant for animals of small and medium body size than for large animals (e.g., cattle, wapiti, swine, white-tailed deer, and black bear) for which body portions may have been shared or dispersed over larger areas. MNI estimates for animal taxa for which dozens or more specimens were recovered will tend to be imprecise, since specimens from the same individual may occur in multiple strata and/or excavation units. The dense occupation debris at the site and nearly a century of continuous occupation also make ordinal estimates of MNI for the most abundant taxa tenuous and likely conservative. Reitz and Wing (1999, 194–199) summarize the many factors that affect MNI estimates.

Biomass estimates were derived from allometric scaling (Reitz et al. 1987; Reitz and Scarry 1985; Reitz and Wing 1999, 225–228). Reitz and Scarry (1985, 18) describe this method: "the weight of the archaeological bone is used in an allometric formula [see Reitz and Scarry 1985, 67] to predict the quantity of biomass for the skeletal mass recovered rather than the total original weight of the individual animal represented by the recovered bone." This approach avoids the problem of basing meat estimates on MNI and determining whether the meat from entire animals was consumed at the site where the archaeological sample was acquired. For the Fort St. Joseph site, biomass values were calculated for each taxa separately by individual feature and stratigraphic division and then summed. Weights of antler fragments were excluded from biomass calculations for white-tailed deer, wapiti, and unidentified cervids. Despite the problems inherent in the various techniques used to estimate biomass and usable or edible meat, the interpretive value of such measures is the relative importance of the various taxa rather than the absolute quantities.

Composition of the Fort St. Joseph Faunal Assemblage

Excavations have demonstrated that the majority of items recovered from typical excavation units at Fort St. Joseph are animal remains. The proveniences that were selected for faunal analysis varied in the density and amount of animal remains each contained and represent a variety of areas and functions. Of the fourteen features that were included, those with the largest samples include a large pit (Feature 7), a possible house floor (Feature 5), and a bone midden (Feature 11). There is a tendency for particular proveniences with the largest samples to contain the greatest number of taxa, a quantitative principle that was demonstrated long ago (Grayson 1984; Styles 1981). Whereas the combined unit samples from the plow zone yielded thirty-eight taxa, the second-largest stratigraphic sample, the undisturbed occupation zone exclusive of features, provided thirty-four taxa. Although the overall analyzed faunal assemblage contains a grand total of fifty-six taxa—twenty varieties of mammal, eighteen birds, nine fish, five reptiles, three species of bivalves, and one amphibian (Table 3.2), nearly 73 percent of all identified specimens (i.e., specimens identified more specifically than the level of class) consist of white-tailed deer. Despite the presence and influences of Europeans, domestic animals constitute a small part of the analyzed sample.

Table 3.2. Species composition of animal remains from the Fort St. Joseph site

Animal taxa	NISP[a]	MNI[b]	NISP Weight (g)	Biomass (kg)[c]
Class: Mammals	29,450	110–166	49,901.7	620.305
Eastern cottontail, *Sylvilagus floridanus*	3	1–3	1.4	0.040
Gray squirrel, *Sciurus carolinensis*	1	1	0.3	0.009
Fox squirrel, *Sciurus niger*	4	1–3	1.0	0.028
Tree squirrel, *Sciurus* sp.	2	—	0.7	0.019
Beaver, *Castor canadensis*	254	8–24	687.8	11.450
Muskrat, *Ondatra zibethicus*	3	1–3	1.6	0.045
Porcupine, *Erethizon dorsatum*	82	5–17	136.6	2.571

Animal taxa	NISP[a]	MNI[b]	NISP Weight (g)	Biomass (kg)[c]
Medium-sized rodent	1	—	0.1	0.003
Gray wolf, *Canis lupus*	1	1	5.6	0.124
Dog/coyote, *Canis* sp.	8	1	25.1	0.531
Gray fox, *Urocyon cinereoargenteus*	1	1	0.8	0.022
Black bear, *Ursus americanus*	132	4	1,062.7	16.719
Raccoon, *Procyon lotor*	310	17–39	456.0	7.797
Marten, *Martes americana*	1	1	0.5	0.014
Striped skunk, *Mephitis* cf. *M. mephitis*[d]	1	1	0.2	0.006
Bobcat, *Lynx rufus*	6	1	12.8	0.279
Medium-sized carnivore	2	—	0.7	0.020
Small/medium-sized carnivore	1	—	0.5	0.014
Horse, *Equus caballus*	3	1	39.5	0.770
Swine, *Sus scrofa*	92	5	533.1	8.996
Wapiti, *Cervus elaphus*	18	2	199.1	3.672
Wapiti, *Cervus* cf. *C. elaphus*	1	—	22.3	0.430
White-tailed deer, *Odocoileus virginianus*	4,031	56	25,684.2	301.832[e]
Wapiti/white-tailed deer, family Cervidae	2	—	15.5	—
Cf. Bison, *Bison* cf. *B. bison*	1	1	6.6	0.144
Cattle, *Bos taurus*	14	1	333.3	5.838
Cattle, *Bos* cf. *B. taurus*	3	—	73.3	1.343
Large bovid, family Bovidae (cattle/bison)	9	—	131.6	2.375
Large artiodactyl (cattle/wapiti)	2	—	38.9	0.752
Unidentified very large mammal	14	—	98.7	1.818
Unidentified large mammal	8,510	—	14,290.6	169.413
Unidentified medium-sized/large mammal	14,139	—	4,736.0	63.176
Unidentified medium-sized mammal	348	—	181.9	3.345
Unidentified small/medium-sized mammal	28	—	2.8	0.072
Unidentified small mammal	25	—	2.0	0.054
Unidentified mammal	1,397	—	1,117.9	16.584
Class: Birds	1,193	77–88	1,010.1	15.335
Pied-billed grebe, *Podilymbus podiceps*	2	2	0.3	0.007
Trumpeter swan, *Cygnus buccinator*	25	4	114.9	1.797
Canada goose, *Branta canadensis*	76	7	153.3	2.244
Mallard/black duck, *Anas platyrhynchos/ rubripes*	4	4	2.4	0.052
Bay duck sp., *Aythya* sp.	1	1	0.3	0.007

continued

Table 3.2.—*continued*

Animal taxa	NISP[a]	MNI[b]	NISP Weight (g)	Biomass (kg)[c]
Common merganser, *Mergus merganser*	2	1	2.4	0.045
Hooded merganser, *Lophodytes* cf. *L. cucullatus*	1	1	0.5	0.011
Unidentified large duck, subfamily Anatinae	51	5	32.6	0.555
Unidentified medium-sized duck, subfamily Anatinae	27	4	16.2	0.288
Unidentified small duck, subfamily Anatinae	11	1	3.0	0.061
Unidentified duck, subfamily Anatinae	7	5	3.2	0.067
Soaring hawk, cf. *Buteo* sp.	1	1	0.1	0.003
Domestic chicken, *Gallus gallus*	13	4–8	5.5	0.112
Ruffed grouse, *Bonasa umbellus*	3	1–3	1.5	0.032
Greater prairie-chicken/sharp-tailed grouse, *Tympanuchus cupido/phasianellus*	1	1	0.4	0.009
Unidentified gallinaceous bird, subfamily Phasianinae	2	—	0.3	0.007
Wild turkey, *Meleagris gallopavo*	146	17–26	326.9	4.635
Sandhill crane, *Grus canadensis*	3	1	5.0	0.094
Small shorebird, order Charadriiformes	1	1	<0.1	—
Passenger pigeon, *Ectopistes migratorius*	64	11–17	9.1	0.193
Barred owl, *Strix varia*	1	1	1.4	0.028
American crow, *Corvus brachyrhynchos*	1	1	0.1	0.003
Common grackle, *Quiscalus* cf. *Q. quiscula*	1	1	0.1	0.003
Medium-sized passerine, order Passeriformes	3	1	<0.1	—
Small passerine, order Passeriformes	1	1	<0.1	—
Unidentified large bird	430	—	256.0	3.742
Unidentified medium-sized/large bird	76	—	22.0	0.408
Unidentified medium-sized bird	138	—	30.4	0.535
Unidentified small/medium-sized bird	8	—	0.7	0.016
Unidentified small bird	8	—	0.3	0.008
Unidentified bird	85	—	21.2	0.373
Class: Reptiles	80	8–16	48.6	0.931
Spiny softshell turtle, *Apalone spinifera*	4	1–4	3.2	0.079
Blanding's turtle, *Emydoidea blandingii*	3	1–2	5.8	0.128
Eastern box turtle, *Terrapene carolina*	5	1–5	3.7	0.113
Painted turtle, *Chrysemys picta*	41	4–6	22.6	0.297
Common map turtle, *Graptemys* cf. *G. geographica*	1	1	0.5	0.020

Animal taxa	NISP[a]	MNI[b]	NISP Weight (g)	Biomass (kg)[c]
Semiaquatic pond turtle spp., family Emydidae	22	—	11.5	0.237
Unidentified turtle	4	—	1.3	0.057
Class: Amphibians	2	2	0.1	—
Frog sp., *Rana* sp.	1	1	<0.1	—
Frog/toad sp., order Anura	1	1	0.1	—
Class: Fishes	32	11–19	11.4	0.288
Lake sturgeon, *Acipenser fulvescens*	15	3–11	9.8	0.242
Gar sp., *Lepisosteus* sp.	1	1	<0.1	—
Bowfin, *Amia calva*	1	1	0.1	0.005
Northern pike, *Esox lucius*	1	1	0.4	0.015
Carp, *Cyprinus carpio*	1	1	0.4	—
Sucker sp., family Catostomidae	2	1	<0.1	—
Brown bullhead, *Ameiurus nebulosus*	1	1	0.1	0.002
Black bass, *Micropterus* sp.	1	1	0.2	0.007
Walleye/sauger, *Sander* sp.	1	1	0.1	0.004
Unidentified fish	8	—	0.3	0.013
Unidentified Vertebrata	1,634	—	156.0	—
Bivalves	54	15	99.1	—
Spike, *Elliptio dilatata*	6	6	32.0	—
Mucket, *Ortmanniana ligamentina*	1	1	3.0	—
Plain pocketbook, *Lampsilis cardium*	2	2	35.1	—
Unidentified freshwater mussel	45	6	29.0	—
Grand totals	32,445	223–306	51,227.0	636.859
Totals identified below the level of class	5,552	217–300	30,281.2	377.302
Percentage identified below the level of class	17.1		59.1	59.2

[a] Number of identified specimens.
[b] Minimum number of individuals (ranges reflect minimum distinction and maximum distinction estimates).
[c] Biomass in kg was calculated from the sum of the biomass calculated from NISP weights for individual features and strata using allometric formulae presented in Reitz and Scarry (1985, 67). No estimates are presented for vertebrate taxa that are not considered to have been human food items (including intrusive specimens) or for invertebrates.
[d] Following Lucas (1986).
[e] Weight of antler fragments is not included in total specimen weights that were used for the calculation of biomass for white-tailed deer and wapiti. Both unidentified Cervidae (wapiti/white-tailed deer) specimens are antler fragments.

Mammals

Specimens from mammals are the most numerous of any class of animals at the site, representing 90.8 percent of the total assemblage and 90.1 percent of specimens identified more precisely than class (Table 3.2). Not surprisingly, mammals also constitute more than 97 percent of the estimated biomass. Percentage by number of individuals for mammals is more difficult to calculate but ranges from 44 to 49 percent.

Rodents and Lagomorphs

Beaver is the most abundant species in this group in terms of number of specimens, number of individuals, and biomass. These data attest to its importance for the local fur trade in the eighteenth century. A total of 254 specimens from this large rodent were present in ten of the fourteen features and all six stratigraphic categories. A minimum of eight individuals are represented if all beaver specimens are viewed as one sample; however, at least twenty-four individuals can be calculated if all features and strata are considered separately and then summed. The distal shaft of an ulna from N23W2 exhibits remodeling after an injury to the front leg. Knife cut marks were noted on a proximal ulna, a proximal femur shaft, an ilium, and an ischium. The importance of beaver for the French fur trade in the Great Lakes region in the seventeenth and eighteenth centuries is well known (Innis 1962; Johnson 1919; Nassaney 2015). Although beaver is mentioned in various historical accounts of the St. Joseph River valley (Baker 1899; Cunningham 1967; Johnson 1919), local populations of the semiaquatic rodent were soon depleted as a result of intense trapping (Baker 1983, 253). Curiously, a roster of mammal pelts for Fort St. Joseph in 1757 does not include beaver (Idle 2003, 121).

Muskrat is another aquatic rodent that was important commercially for its pelt, but it is surprisingly underrepresented in the Fort St. Joseph collection. Only three specimens have been identified, including one from Feature 7. Muskrat pelts are more prevalent in lists of fur-bearing species in the nineteenth century, after beaver was depleted (Baker 1983, 332; Johnson 1919, 97–98). The Fort St. Joseph faunal collection also contains only seven bones from tree squirrels. Gray squirrel was associated with the occupation zone in N27E8. Four fox squirrel specimens (distinguished from gray squirrel by their larger size) were recovered, including two teeth from Feature 7. Eastern cottontail is also rare, but the sample includes a specimen from Feature 7.

The most unexpected species in this group is porcupine. A total of eighty-two specimens (eighteen cranial bones, thirty-six teeth, and twenty-eight postcranial bones) were associated with eight features (thirty-two specimens, including thirteen from Feature 5, six from Feature 11, and five from Feature 7) and the alluvium (two specimens), the plow zone (thirty-seven specimens), and the occupation zone outside of features (eleven specimens). A minimum of five individuals is indicated for the total assemblage, but consideration of separate contexts leads to an estimate of at least seventeen individuals. Baker (1983, 373) states that porcupines were formerly present in southern Michigan but vanished after Euro-American settlement of the area. Population densities increased during winter, when multiple individuals congregated at denning sites (Dodge 1982, 359). Although porcupines are not a fur bearer, Great Lakes Indians used their quills to decorate clothing and containers (Densmore [1929] 1979, 172–173; Rogers 1978, 766) and local Indians consumed their meat (Baker 1983, 378; Cook [1889] 1974, 65). Neither Peyser (1978) nor Idle (2003) mentioned porcupine at Fort St. Joseph, but it was identified at the precontact Upper Mississippian Moccasin Bluff site (AD 1100–1600), located about twelve miles downstream from Fort St. Joseph, where it was the fifth most abundant mammal in terms of number of specimens and ranked fourth in MNI among all animal classes (Bettarel and Smith 1973, 132–133). An unidentified medium-sized rodent incisor fragment from plow zone contexts is comparable to that of a tree squirrel or muskrat.

Carnivores

Raccoon was the most abundant carnivore at the site; the sample includes ninety-five specimens from eight features. Estimates of MNI for raccoon vary from seventeen for the site at large to thirty-nine if individual features and strata are given primary consideration. Feature 5 alone contributed at least seven individuals, Feature 11 contributed four individuals, and Feature 7 contributed three individuals. All skeletal portions are present, including sixty isolated teeth. A distal fibula from Feature 5 was remodeled after a traumatic injury. Knife cuts were seen on a proximal ulna, a radius midshaft, and a proximal femur. Raccoon pelts had been a substantial part of the fur trade since the eighteenth century but along with muskrat became more popular in the nineteenth century after the decline of beavers (Johnson 1919). Baker (1983, 450–451) also notes that the meat of raccoons has long been a delicacy among rural residents.

Black bear ranks second in this group; the sample includes 132 specimens that occurred in eight features and all six of the strata. Nearly 42 percent of the bear specimens are from the feet (i.e., carpals, tarsals, metapodials, and phalanges). Twenty-one percent are rib fragments. The remaining 37 percent consists of cranial fragments (two mandibles and nine isolated teeth), proximal forequarters (i.e., scapula, humerus, radius, and ulna), vertebrae, and proximal hindquarters (i.e., femur, tibia, fibula, and patella). Given the dispersed site contexts for bear specimens, a conservative MNI estimate of four is based on the whole collection of bear specimens. At least three adult and one subadult individuals are represented, but several individuals are probably represented among this dispersed collection. A dorsal rib fragment from N23W2 and a fused distal tibia and fibula from N19W7 both reveal remodeling after severe injuries. Knife cuts were noted on the midshaft of a rib and on a right distal tibia. Historical accounts mention the local presence of black bears and humans' encounters with them (Baker 1899, 7; Cook [1889] 1974, 63, 66). A robust commerce involving New France, the Illinois Country, and Lower Louisiana entailed black bear commodities such as hams, oil, and skins (Morgan 2010, 106–108; Surrey [1916] 2006). In the western Great Lakes region, the Ojibwe stored bear oil and used it as a food additive (Henry 1985, 95); bear oil was added to soups that were consumed by *voyageurs* (Lavender 1964, 28). In the Illinois Country, bear oil (*huile d'ours*) was substituted for olive oil (Brown 2002, 8) and was also used to maintain guns and other metal items (Morgan 2010, 106–107). Although often mentioned, the specific commercial uses of bear oil at sites such as Michilimackinac and Detroit are not as well documented and there is no mention of bear oil in the Fort St. Joseph manuscripts Peyser translated (1978).

Three varieties of mammals of the family Canidae were identified. A large proximal tibia shaft (right side) from the plow zone of N25W2 is identical in size and morphology to tibiae of reference skeletons of gray wolves in the Illinois State Museum zoology collection. The gray wolf was present throughout Michigan when Euro-American settlement began and wolves were reported from the Detroit vicinity and in Berrien County in the early eighteenth century (Baker 1983, 403). Wolves were a serious threat in southwestern Michigan until well into the nineteenth century (Cook [1889] 1974), and wolf pelts were among those listed in a 1796 ledger for the St. Joseph River valley (Johnson 1919, 97–98). Although some Indians and Euro-Americans used wolf fur for shoes, caps, robes, and garment trimming (Paradiso and Nowak 1982, 470), its low value may help explain the rarity of wolf specimens at Fort St. Joseph.

An additional eight canid specimens are comparable in size to coyote (*Canis latrans*) and moderate-sized domestic dogs, except for a proximal radius shaft from a large individual (smaller than a wolf) that was found in N23W1. The remaining dog and/or coyote specimens were associated with Feature 5, the plow zone (an ulna from N21W7 and a third metacarpal from N19W7), the occupation zone (a proximal tibia shaft from N39E20 and a lumbar vertebra fragment from N25W2), and the plow zone to occupation zone transition (two caudal vertebrae from N23W2). No dog burials were encountered, and although the isolated dog bones shared the same contexts as the other animal remains, none exhibited cut marks.

The third canid identified at the site is a gray fox, which is represented by the posterior portion of a parietal from the plow zone of N24E2. The gray fox prefers wooded habitats, in contrast to the red fox (*Vulpes vulpes*), which tends to occur in more open areas (Baker 1983, 426).

The only felid remains at the site are from bobcat. Feature 12 yielded a claw (third phalanx), and five other bones, either from the same or a second individual, were recovered from N23W2. Conceivably from the same individual, these specimens consisted of a cranial fragment along with a calcaneus and three metatarsals from a right foot. Bobcats were formerly present in southwestern Michigan and their pelts were part of the fur trade (Baker 1899, 7; Baker 1983, 554, 558–559). No remains of domestic cat (*Felis catus*) or cougar (i.e., mountain lion or puma, *Puma concolor*) were encountered, although cougars were known to occur in the vicinity (Baker 1983, 539; Cook [1889] 1974, 22).

Two species of mustelids are present. The right distal humerus of a marten was recovered from the occupation zone in N23W2 and an isolated left lower canine tooth from the plow zone of N27E8 was tentatively identified as striped skunk. Both species were formerly present in the area (Baker 1899, 7; Baker 1983, 457, 518) and were included in the French colonial fur trade, and American Indians ate their meat and used their skins (including skulls and foot bones) as parts of personal or medicine bundles (Parmalee and Klippel 1983, 278). Three isolated canine teeth could not be identified with confidence and may be from small canids, mustelids, or possibly raccoons.

Ungulates

At least five species of hoofed mammals were identified. By far the most frequently encountered animal at the site is white-tailed deer. Deer constitute 80.8 percent of the identified mammal specimens and 72.6 percent of identified specimens from all classes, 82.5 percent of the biomass from identified mammals, 80 percent of the biomass from all identified taxa, 45–49 percent of the mammal MNI, and 20–24 percent of all MNI. Deer are ubiquitous in that they were present in all analyzed features and all strata. Early historical accounts (e.g., Baker 1899, 6–7; Cook [1889] 1974) and local archaeological investigations (Bettarel and Smith 1973; Garland et al. 2001; Martin 2003) attest to the abundance of white-tailed deer in southwestern Michigan. For the French in the St. Joseph valley, deer were as important for their hides as for their meat. Peyser (1978, document 123) noted expenses for making moccasins from deer hides. Moccasins that non–Native Americans made were also an important part of locally manufactured wardrobes in eighteenth-century Detroit (Cangany 2014, 85–105).

A conservative assessment of the sexual composition of deer in the Fort St. Joseph assemblage is possible on the basis of nineteen pelvis fragments, eleven of which were from bucks, and eight were from does. Although specimens from fawns (deer one year or less in age) were occasionally recovered, they are rare. These include four mandibles, five isolated deciduous teeth and one unerupted tooth, two distal scapulae (plus one from a fetal deer), one radius shaft, and a first rib. Epiphyseal fusion occurs just prior to or during the deer's first autumn in the proximal radius and the distal humerus; it occurs by the deer's first year of life in the phalanges (Purdue 1983). The Fort St. Joseph analyzed faunal collection includes only four distal humeri with open epiphyses and no proximal radii or phalanges with unfused epiphyses. Although the bones and teeth of fawns are more fragile than those of mature deer, the excellent preservation of animal remains at the fort indicates that hunters targeted mature deer for their meat and hides. Assuming that local deer herds were healthy and were heavily hunted by indigenous peoples and Euro-Americans, the age composition would be dominated by younger individuals if deer were being taken at random (see Hesselton and Hesselton 1982, 891).

Calculation of deer MNI is problematic given the overall abundance of deer specimens and their presence in all features and strata. This estimate of fifty-six individuals is likely to be highly conservative and includes at least fifty-one adults, four fawns, and one fetal deer.

Three deer bones exhibit pathologies. All are bones from front legs that were remodeled after traumatic injuries: a left proximal radius from N27E8 (plow zone), a left ulna midshaft from N33E15 (plow zone to occupation zone transition), and a nearly whole right radius and ulna from N23W1 (Figure 3.1). Speci-

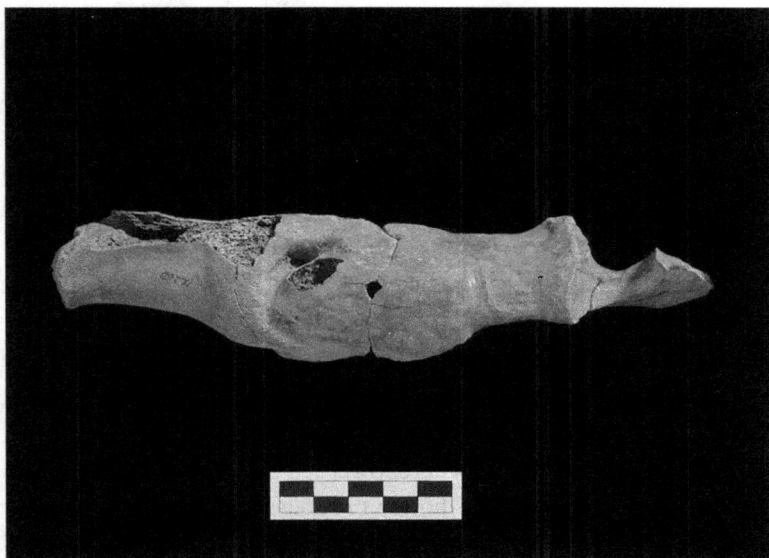

Figure 3.1. White-tailed deer radius and ulna remodeled after traumatic injury. Photo by Doug Carr, Illinois State Museum.

mens such as these show the resiliency of individual deer to survive injuries that initially might be considered to be fatal (Martin and Lawler 2014).

Knife cuts were observed on eighty-two deer bones (sixteen humeri, twelve femurs, twelve tibiae, nine ribs, eight scapulae, six radii, six pelves, two crania, two ulnae, two thoracic vertebrae, two lumbar vertebrae, two calcanei, one astragalus, one cuboid, and one sternum). These cut marks indicate dismemberment (cutting ligaments or muscle mass at proximal or distal ends) and filleting of muscle from bone (usually along the long-bone shafts and vertebral dorsal spines). Only one bone was sawed—a pelvis that was separated at the pubis bone. Nearly all deer bones occurred as fragments; some were chopped (as if with hatchets) and many specimens had green-fracture breaks. Several specimens were used as raw material for artifacts. These are described below in the section on bone, antler, and shell artifacts.

All parts of the deer body are represented at the site. Table 3.3 presents quantities for the various skeletal portions. Becker's original database for the 2002 samples is inaccessible; this prevented the reconstitution of skeletal portion tabulation by feature. However, this affects only the 2002 sample (Becker

2004, 81), resulting in a discrepancy of 87 (2.1 percent) between the total number of deer specimens in Tables 3.2 and 3.3. Hearn's study (2015) used some of the data from the same features Becker originally analyzed so that some counts are apparently redundant. Despite this, the proportions shown in Table 3.3 are nearly identical. The significant finding, however, is the underrepresentation of bones from the lower legs and feet; they account for only 6 percent. This contrasts with early historic Native American habitation sites such as the Zimmerman site in the upper Illinois River valley (Martin 2015), where distal leg and foot bones contribute nearly 33 percent of 311 deer specimens; the Iliniwek Village site at the mouth of the Des Moines River (Martin et al. 2003), where these bones constitute 26 percent of 245 deer specimens; and the precontact Upper Mississippian Wymer West Knoll site (AD 1100–1400) in the lower St. Joseph valley (Garland et al. 2001), where lower leg and foot bones make up 43.5 percent of 115 deer specimens. Although breakage of deer long bones may have occurred as part of the process for acquiring marrow for food, some ethnographic and ethnoarchaeological accounts suggest that Native American hunters preferred fat from the extremities (i.e., metacarpals and metatarsals) over fat from the axial bones and shoulder blades for food and for technological uses (Binford 1978; also see Logan 1998, 359). Although brains of deer and wapiti were commonly employed in the hide tanning process, a variety of fatty substances such as bone grease (Grinnell 1972, 216, cited in Vehik 1977, 171) and bone marrow (Teit 1900, 184–185) were also used. Innis (1962, 14) also stated that the inner side of beaver pelts were "scraped and rubbed with the marrow of certain animals." Perhaps lower legs of deer were systematically collected from the Fort St. Joseph site and transported to nearby locations such as the

Table 3.3. White-tailed deer skeletal portions (NISP) from the Fort St. Joseph site

Anatomical Part/Skeletal Portion	Fort St. Joseph Site[a]		Fort St. Joseph Site, 2002[b]	
	NISP	%	NISP	%
Crania	188	3.1	9	3.3
Antler	6	0.2	1	0.4
Mandible	48	1.3	1	0.4
Hyoid	7	0.2	1	0.4
Isolated teeth	328	8.7	32	11.8

Anatomical Part/Skeletal Portion	Fort St. Joseph Site[a]		Fort St. Joseph Site, 2002[b]	
	NISP	%	NISP	%
Cervical vertebrae	92	2.4	—	—
Thoracic vertebrae	106	2.8	—	—
Lumbar vertebrae	234	6.2	—	—
Vertebrae, cervical-lumbar	—	—	34	12.5
Sacrum	28	0.7	—	—
Costal cartilage	4	0.1	1	0.4
Sternum	7	0.2	—	—
Rib	740	19.6	49	18.1
Innominate bone (pelvis)	148	3.9	5	1.8
Subtotal: Axial/Cranial	1,936	50.3	133	49.1
Scapula	154	4.1	13	4.8
Humerus	297	7.9	20	7.4
Radius	251	6.6	10	3.7
Ulna	142	3.8	12	4.4
Femur	359	9.5	30	11.1
Patella	49	1.3	1	0.4
Tibia	422	11.2	38	14.0
Subtotal: Proximal Appendicular	1,674	43.5	124	45.8
Carpals	45	1.2	3	1.1
Metacarpal	14	0.4	—	—
Astragalus	22	0.6	1	0.4
Calcaneus	36	1.0	1	0.4
Tarsals	41	1.1	1	0.4
Metatarsal	27	0.7	4	1.5
Metapodial fragments	16	0.4	1	0.4
Phalanx 1	20	0.5	—	—
Phalanx 2	9	0.2	—	—
Phalanx 3	6	0.2	—	—
Phalanx 1–3	—	—	3	1.1
Sesamoid	1	0.03	—	—
Subtotal: Distal Appendicular	237	6.2	14	5.2
Grand Totals	3,847	100.0	271	100.1

[a] Grand totals excluding 2002 specimens identified in Becker (2004, 81).
[b] Based on quantities recovered in 2002 and presented in Becker (2004, 81).

Lyne site, where hide processing occurred (see Mendes and Nassaney, chapter 7, this volume; and Nassaney and Martin 2017).

Wapiti (elk) is another cervid species that was identified in three features (Features 2, 5, and 7) and five strata. A total of eighteen specimens plus a rib that was tentatively attributed to wapiti represents a minimum of two individuals based on the presence of two left patellae. Other bones include fragments of a mandible, a scapula, a carpal, thoracic vertebrae, pelves, a distal femur, and distal tibiae. Filleting cut marks were noted on a thoracic vertebra dorsal spine. Prior to the mid-nineteenth century, wapiti inhabited woodlands and open grasslands throughout most of the Lower Peninsula of Michigan and the St. Joseph River valley (Baker 1899, 7; Baker 1983, 568–569; Bettarel and Smith 1973, 135–136; Johnson 1919, 97–98; Peyser 1978, document 30). Surely the large meat package of wapiti would have been appreciated by local hunters as they procured food for the local settlement (Baker 1983, 569, 574).

Three antler fragments could not be distinguished with certainty between white-tailed deer and wapiti. A specimen from Feature 11 had been carved, but its intended function is unknown. A small piece from the occupation zone in N19W7 was sawed and may have been modified to be used as a tool handle. A third fragment is from Feature 13, but it has no obvious signs of modification.

Just less than 100 bones and teeth from swine were recovered; it is the most abundant domesticated mammal at the site. Swine specimens were identified in seven features and four strata. The two features having the most swine remains are Feature 5 (twenty-two specimens) and Feature 11 (thirteen specimens). Features 1, 2, 7, 10, and 22 also contained swine (ranging from one to three specimens). When all swine elements are viewed as one sample, there is a minimum of only five adult individuals and at least two juveniles. Half of the recovered swine specimens are represented by isolated teeth (29 percent) and bones from the lower legs and feet (21 percent). A left fibula is unique in that it has a remodeled shaft indicative of a healed traumatic injury. Only two bones exhibit cut marks: a left distal humerus shaft and a right pelvis. Biomass from swine contributed only 2.5 percent of all biomass from identified mammals at Fort St. Joseph.

Fourteen large bovid specimens are diagnostic of domestic cattle. Seven came from four features (Features 5, 7, 11, and 22). The specimens consist of a lower incisor, a cranial fragment (palatine), fragments of left and right scapulae, right and left proximal radii, two cervical vertebrae, a thoracic vertebra, pelvis, a distal metatarsal shaft, a first phalanx, and a third phalanx. A proximal radius and the metatarsal had been chopped with an ax or cleaver; the first phalanx had a cut mark made with a knife. Although as a collection these represent an MNI of one, contextual consideration of dates of feature would probably increase this estimate to multiple individuals. Three additional bones were tentatively identified as cattle: a thoracic vertebra fragment, a femur midshaft, and a first phalanx. Cattle were transported to Michigan as early as 1704, when Cadillac brought oxen to Detroit from the St. Lawrence Valley (Ekberg 1998, 205). Hutchins ([1778] 1904), quoted in Cunningham 1961, 72–73) mentions that he observed "a few milch cows" at Fort St. Joseph during his 1762 visit. In the Illinois Country cattle were used as draft animals and a source of dairy products and meat (Ekberg 1998, 206).

Baker (1899, 6, 7, 39) alludes to place names associated with bison in three locations: south of Niles ("Parc aux vaches"), at the portage between the St. Joseph and Kankakee Rivers, and a prairie southwest of the portage landing ("La Prairie de Tete la Boeuf"). Except for the much longer and more robust thoracic vertebra dorsal spines, frontal bone cranial morphology, and orientation of the horn cores, osteological differences between cattle and bison are subtle (see Balkwill and Cumba 1992; Olsen 1959, [1960] 1974). A fragment of a left distal tibia from the occupation zone in N25E4 is the only large bovid bone from Fort St. Joseph that is comparable to bison. It is likely that the meat of bison was transported with a minimum of bones when the kill site was any significant distance from the fort due to the great weight of bison and the difficulty of hauling such a large animal over land or by river. Thus, bison may have been acquired opportunistically and consumed at the fort without much of a trace.

Nine specimens are attributed to either cattle or bison; these consist of one incisor and two molar fragments, fragments of a lumbar vertebra (from Feature 5) and a thoracic vertebra, two ribs, a distal femur fragment, and a radius shaft. Seven bones were recovered from plow zone contexts. Two additional bones could not be distinguished between large bovid and wapiti: a fragment of a distal tibia epiphysis from Feature 5 and a rib dorsal articular process from an area of the occupation zone that is not a feature.

The role and importance of horses at Fort St. Joseph is unclear. Three horse specimens were identified. The only feature context was Feature 5, which yielded a left metatarsal. The other specimens came from the plow zone and include a right ulnar carpal from N24E2 and left upper third incisor tooth from N30E2. None had cut marks or were burned. Unlike cattle and swine, horses were likely acquired from the Spaniards in the Southwest by way of Indian traders (Ekberg 1998, 205). Although gristmills in the Illinois Country were powered only by horses (Ekberg 1998, 266), oxen were preferred over horses as draft animals (Ekberg 1998, 21, 177, 179). The English surveyor Thomas Hutchins observed horses and mules at St. Joseph during his 1762 visit (Cunningham 1961, 72–73). Even though French colonials used rivers to travel, the presence of horse remains at Fort St. Joseph may indicate that the St. Joseph Trail was important for trade and communication between the lower St. Joseph River drainage and Detroit (Lewis 2002, 26–27). Alternatively, horse specimens from plow zone contexts may postdate the French occupation.

Birds

Avian remains constitute the second most abundant class in terms of NISP, MNI, and biomass. Although bird remains contribute only 8.1 percent of all identified taxa, the eighteen varieties represent a rather diverse array of habitat preferences. Because many avian species are migratory, some species would have been available only during certain seasons. Whereas birds would have been hunted to provide food, some species may have been more significant to Native American inhabitants for their plumage or for their symbolic or ceremonial usages.

Waterfowl

The most abundant single group of birds is waterfowl, which compose 45.6 percent of all identified bird bones, 38 to 43 percent of the estimated MNI for birds, and 51.2 percent of the biomass from identified birds. Only Features 1, 9, 19, and 22 lacked waterfowl remains. Canada goose was the single most numerous waterfowl species; seventy-six bones were recovered from at least seven individuals in four features (2, 5, 6, and 7) and five strata. The only knife cut mark is on the anterior articular portion of a right scapula. Although widely regarded as a migratory species, Canada geese nested widely in the Midwest as late as the early nineteenth century, especially in favorable locations such as the Kankakee Marsh and would have been available year round (Barrows 1912, 118; Brewer 1991, 41).

Trumpeter swan bones were recovered from six features (a total of seven bones from Features 2, 6, 10, 11, 12, and 13) and from nonfeature contexts in the occupation zone and the plow zone. The total was twenty-five bones representing at least four individuals. A left proximal humerus exhibits a knife cut mark. In addition to wings, the presence of sternum fragments, sacrum, vertebrae, and leg bones indicate that whole swan carcasses were brought to the site. Although early historical records do not substantiate the early presence of trumpeter swan as a breeding bird in Michigan, Brewer (1991, 36) suggests that records for nesting swans in Illinois and the Kankakee Marsh in northwestern Indiana provide supportive evidence. He is also of the opinion that the commercial harvest of their skins by nineteenth-century fur trade companies led to the extirpation of trumpeter swans in Michigan.

Just over half of the waterfowl bones are from ducks, which represent 66.7 percent of the waterfowl MNI and 21.2 percent of the biomass from this group. Duck bones were identified in ten features (they were absent only from Features 1, 9, 19, and 22) and five strata. Whereas most of the specimens were identified to subfamily and distinguished as large (e.g., mallard), medium-sized, or small duck (e.g., teals [*Anas discors, A. crecca*] or bufflehead [*Bucephala albeola*]), eight bones were identified more precisely. Four bones (specimens from Features 4, 6, and 11) were assigned to mallard or black duck. A sternum from Feature 13 was identified as one of the bay ducks (*Aythya* sp.). A coracoid and carpometacarpal were identified as common merganser, and a femur was from a hooded merganser.

Miscellaneous Swimming and Wading Birds

Two right pied-billed grebe humeri representing two individuals and an unidentified small shorebird coracoid were recovered from plow zone contexts. Pied-billed grebes are most common in southwestern Michigan, where the secretive, diving bird inhabits lakes, ponds, and marshes from late February through October (Brewer et al. 1991, 100). All three sandhill crane specimens (an anterior scapula from Feature 12, a coracoid, and a cervical vertebra) were associated with the undisturbed occupation zone. Sandhill cranes inhabit southern Michigan from early March through late October, and although they nest mostly in the southern three tiers of counties in the central part of the state, the large birds may have been more widespread prior to the drainage of many of the region's wetlands for modern agriculture. They also sought bulbs, seeds, insects, frogs, snakes, and mice in upland fields and open forests (Barrows 1912, 150; Brewer et al. 1991, 202). Sandhill cranes have been identified at French colonial contexts in the Illinois Country (Jelks et al. 1989, 82; Martin 1988, 229; Martin 2010, 199; Martin and Masulis 1988).

Galliformes

By far, the most significant bird at Fort St. Joseph is the wild turkey, which represents 32.6 percent of the identified bird bones, 19 to 34 percent of the estimated MNI for birds, and 45.2 percent of the biomass from identified birds. Wild turkey bones were identified in eleven features (they are absent only from Features 1, 3, and 9) and all five strata. Wild turkeys were abundant in southern Michigan until the late nineteenth century; they resided there year round amid mast-producing stands of mature oak, beech, and hickory (Barrows 1912, 236; Brewer et al. 1991, 188).

Only three ruffed grouse bones were identified, representing from one to three individuals. All were associated with the undisturbed occupation zone that includes Feature 9. Present year round, ruffed grouse require stands of aspen for food and for nesting sites. Populations likely remained small until Europeans began clearing virgin pine and hardwood forests for homesteads and cultivation (Brewer et al. 1991, 184). A greater prairie-chicken was identified from the anterior part of a coracoid in the occupation zone of N27E8. Prairies and oak openings in southwestern Michigan were favorable habitats for prairie-chickens (Brewer et al. 1991, 51), and flocks apparently remained throughout the year (Barrows 1912, 233).

Remains of domestic chickens are limited to thirteen bones that were recovered from Features 2, 6, and 10 and from nonfeature contexts in the occupation and plow zones. Two unidentified gallinaceous bird bones that are probably chicken were also found in Feature 2. At least four individuals are indicated by age and size differences among the various bones, but the minimum may be as many as eight individuals when considering features and spatial distribution. The absence of eggshell fragments from small-mesh water-screen recovery samples and the relatively low number of chicken bones suggest that domestic birds were not numerous at Fort St. Joseph.

Miscellaneous Birds

The passenger pigeon ranks fourth in number of identified specimens. Just more than half of the sixty-four bones recovered were associated with the occupation zone, including twenty specimens that were recovered from eight features. The remaining thirty specimens were recovered from plow zone or transitional plow zone strata. Our MNI estimates range from eleven to seventeen but are probably conservative. Prior to the extinction of the species in the early twentieth century, flocks of the migratory passenger pigeons inhabited all parts of Michigan from April through autumn. Although small colonies and isolated pairs nested wherever oak and beech mast was available, the large, dense concentrations of nesting birds described in the latter part of the nineteenth century in northern parts of the state may have occurred after the clearing of forests in southern Michigan (Barrows 1912, 238; Brewer 1991, 35).

Remains of two raptors were found in the occupation zone. A whole right femur from a barred owl was recovered from the occupation zone in N25E4. This owl is present year round and prefers mature deciduous and coniferous forests, including heavily wooded swamps and river bottoms (Brewer et al. 1991, 242). A distal part of a foot phalanx that is most comparable to an unidentified species of hawk was recovered from Feature 10.

A total of six bones from the order of perching birds (Passeriformes) were recovered. A wing bone (the second digit of the first phalanx) from an American crow and a coracoid that is comparable to a common grackle were both recovered from plow zone contexts. Unidentified medium-sized passerine bones consist of a distal tibiotarsus from Feature 19, a right proximal ulna from the plow zone to occupation zone transition in the same unit (N19W7), and a left whole ulna from the plow zone to occupation zone transition in N23W2. A proximal tarsometatarsus from an unidentified small perching bird was recovered from the occupation zone in N21W7.

Reptiles and Amphibians

A total of eighty turtle specimens were identified. Eleven occurred in five features, nine in the occupation zone outside of features, and sixty in the plow zone. Five species of turtles are represented with a minimum of from eight to eleven individuals. Although painted turtles (four to six individuals) are most numerous, contributing 95 percent of the bones from carapaces and plastrons, none of the specimens were recovered from features or the occupation zone. The painted turtle is the most abundant turtle in the area and prefers quiet, permanent water with soft substrates and abundant vegetation (Harding [1997] 2006, 213). Single bones from the carapace of the eastern box turtle were identified in Feature 11 and the occupation zone of N39E20, and two other carapace bones and an epiplastron were recovered from plow zone contexts. Unlike the other turtles encountered in the Fort St. Joseph faunal assemblage, the eastern box turtle is terrestrial and occurs mainly in deciduous or mixed woodlands where they have access to water (Harding [1997] 2006, 197). Two Blanding's turtle bones were identified in Feature 7 along with a carapace fragment from the plow zone of N27E8. This turtle usually inhabits weedy ponds and backwaters (Harding [1997] 2006, 203). A hypoplastron fragment from the occupation zone in N27E4 was tentatively identified as common map turtle, an aquatic species that prefers larger rivers and lakes (Harding [1997] 2006, 208). The spiny softshell is another aquatic turtle from the site and is rarely found away from water (Harding [1997] 2006, 223). The species was identified from single bones from four different units, only one of which occurred in the occupation zone. Aside from a mandible from a large individual, all other specimens are from the carapace or plastron, which are distinguished by external surfaces that resemble "the dimpling on a golf ball" (Sobolik and Steele 1996, 27). Except for one proximal femur shaft fragment, the remaining twenty-five turtle remains consist of small fragments of carapace and plastron from unidentified turtles, twenty-two of which are from the pond turtle family (Emydidae). Unidentified turtle specimens were found in Features 2, 4, 5, and 7.

Two amphibian remains were also recovered. A frog humerus was identified from Feature 12 and a bone from Feature 7 could not be distinguished as either frog or toad. Because most bones of anurans are small and fragile, the recovery of only two bones does not attest to whether the site's inhabitants consumed frogs and toads or if the bones are intrusive.

Fishes

The most underrepresented vertebrate class at the site is fish. Nine fish taxa were identified. However, nearly 63 percent of the identified fish specimens are from lake sturgeons. Unidentified sucker (including a rib from Feature 19) is the only other fish taxon that is represented by more than one bone. Unlike most other freshwater fish, lake sturgeons have cartilaginous endoskeletons that do not survive at archaeological sites. Remains consist of bony cranial plates, a pair of prominent pectoral spines, and five rows of bony scutes along the sides of the body (Auer 2013, 11–12). Sturgeon remains were recovered from nine units (six specimens from the occupation zone, including Feature 7, and nine from the plow zone or plow zone to occupation zone transition).

These consist of eleven dermal bone fragments from crania, three scutes, and one right pectoral spine. The pectoral spine is from a sturgeon that was approximately 152 cm (5 feet) in total length, one dermal scute is comparable to a larger individual, and most of the other specimens appear to be from fish of similar large sizes. Wesley and Duffy (1999, 55) note that the "abundance of lake sturgeon made the area around Niles famous in the mid-to late-1800s" and that large fish were speared from a series of large rocks in the river and from temporary weirs. Lake sturgeon remains were also plentiful at the Moccasin Bluff and Wymer West sites downstream from Fort St. Joseph. Local indigenous residents would surely have relied on this important annual resource, as sturgeons returned to the St. Joseph River (and all of the other major rivers in western Michigan) each spring for spawning runs (Auer 2013, 15; Bettarel and Smith 1973, 136–137; Cleland 1966, 79, 212–217; Garland et al. 2001). American Indians in the region also retain traditions in which lake sturgeons have significant spiritual importance (Martin 2008b; Mitchell 2013). Thus, their paucity at Fort St. Joseph is perplexing.

All other fish at Fort St. Joseph were identified from single specimens. A northern pike vertebra from the occupation zone in N25E4 is from an individual that was 72–80 cm in standard length. A brown bullhead dentary fragment was identified in Feature 6 from an individual in the size class of 16–24 cm. A vertebra from the occupation zone of N30W23 is most comparable to a walleye or sauger of 30–35 cm in standard length. Another vertebra from that same unit was tentatively identified as a black bass of 24–32 cm in standard length. The plow zone strata yielded bowfin (a vertebra from an individual of 48–56 cm in total length), a gar scale, and common carp (a spine from an individual 32–40 cm long). Because the common carp was introduced in the 1870s (Smith 2010, 35), its presence in the plow zone does not imply an association with the eighteenth-century occupation.

The relatively small proportion of fish in the Fort St. Joseph faunal assemblage is difficult to explain. Wesley and Duffy (1999, 54) state that "97 species of fish were native to the St. Joseph river basin," and faunal collections from late prehistoric sites elsewhere in the river valley attest to the capture of numerous fish by indigenous populations. Although fish may have been processed at some area of the site that has not been investigated, such spatial segregation of animal remains has not been encountered at other French colonial sites such as Fort Michilimackinac, Fort Ouiatenon, or Fort de Chartres.

Bivalves

A total of fifty-four freshwater mussel shells were encountered in the assemblage. This count includes whole bivalve shells and small fragments. Although mussel shells were found in five features, twenty-three shells were recovered from plow zone contexts. Only three species were identified. All are common in a variety of medium and large river habitats, especially in sand and gravel substrates where there are moderate to strong currents (Cummings and Mayer 1992). Wesley and Duffy (1999, 61, 205) report that twenty-three native freshwater mussel species (including the species identified at Fort St. Joseph) have been recorded for the St. Joseph River and that commercial harvesting was a major activity for the shell button industry. The intended use of mussels and mussel shells at Fort St. Joseph is unknown, but to date, no modified freshwater shell artifacts have been found from the Western Michigan University excavations at the site. Although not especially abundant, mussels more commonly recovered at Moccasin Bluff (Bettarel and Smith 1973, 138–139) and Wymer West (Garland et al. 2001), where they presumably provided minor dietary supplements.

Bone, Antler, and Shell Artifacts

Excavations yielded several specimens of bone, antler, and shell that had been made into artifacts. Utilitarian artifacts include a projectile point (Figure 3.2a), an awl or perforating tool (Figure 3.2b), and a decorated scale for a knife handle (Figure 3.3). At least three antler fragments were carved, possibly to function as tool handles. Recreational specimens include round disks made from mammal bone or antler that were used as dice in games of chance (see Clifton 1978, 733–734; Figure 3.4), two cup-and-pin gaming pieces made from deer phalanges (Figure 3.5), and a specimen with a serrated edge that may have been a rasp (Figure 3.6). The posterior portion of a black bear mandible fragment from N25E2 was ground and may have functioned as a gaming piece. Personal artifacts include a bone comb (Figure 3.7) and adornment pieces such as two thin, delicately cut and carved mammal bone specimens from Feature 11 (Figure 3.8). A small tubular white shell bead found in N27E8 is similar to other purple and pink shell beads, or wampum, that were made from marine shells from the East Coast. Similar to the case at Fort Ouiatenon, many of the bone and shell artifacts from Fort St. Joseph reflect close contact and daily interactions with local Native American groups in the eighteenth century (see Martin 1991b).

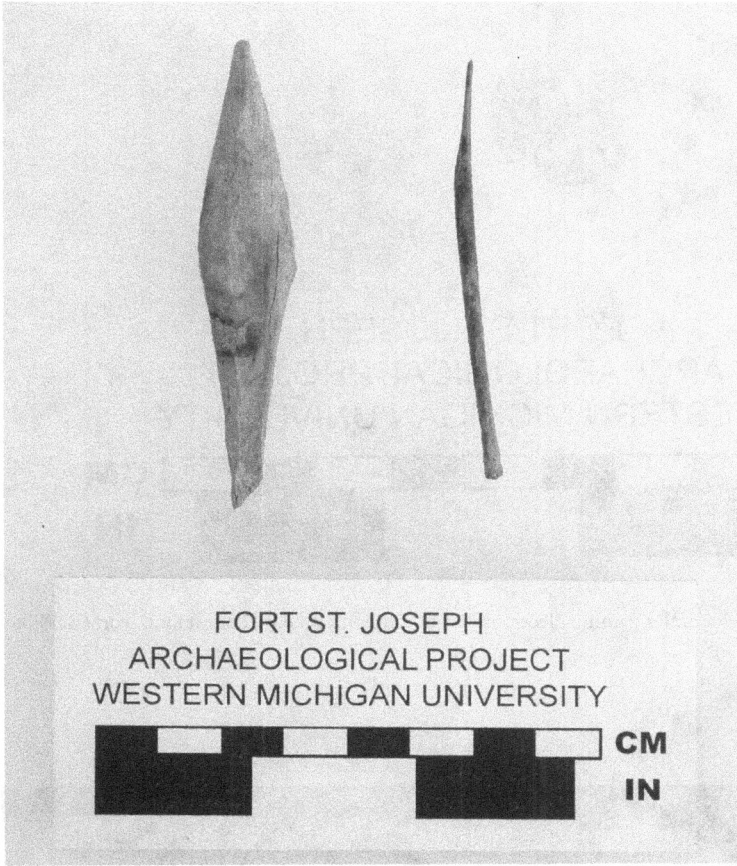

Figure 3.2. Bone artifacts: *left*, projectile point; *right*, awl or perforating tool. Photo by John Lacko.

Figure 3.3. Bone knife handle. Photo by Brock Giordano.

FORT ST. JOSEPH
ARCHAEOLOGICAL PROJECT
WESTERN MICHIGAN UNIVERSITY

Figure 3.4. Bone or antler gaming pieces similar to examples used by Potawatomi women. Photo by John Lacko.

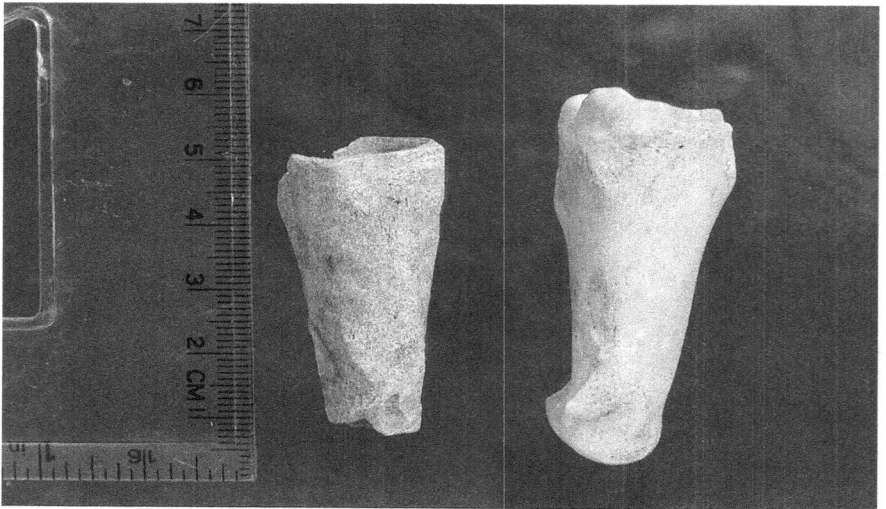

Figure 3.5. White-tailed deer phalanx and cup-and-pin gaming piece. Photo by Rory Becker.

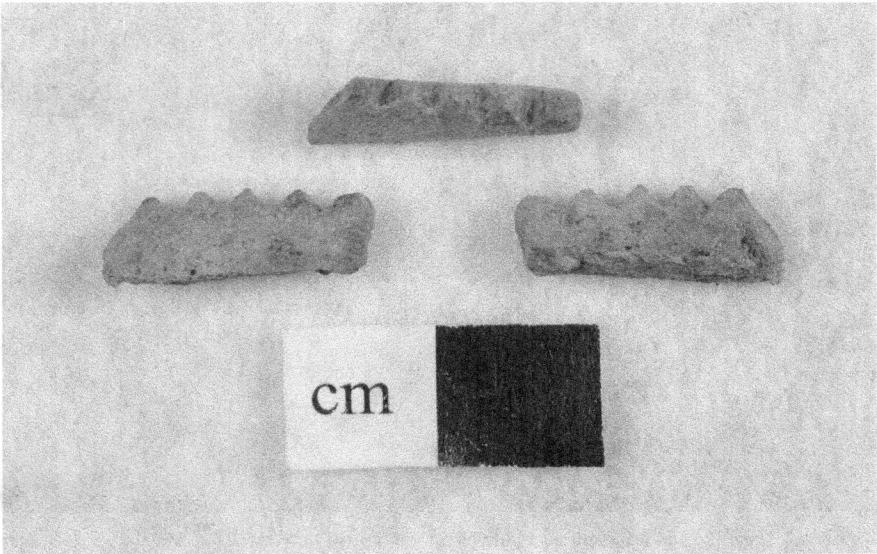

Figure 3.6. Bone or antler rasp. Photo by Genevieve Perry.

Figure 3.7. Bone comb. Photo by John Lacko.

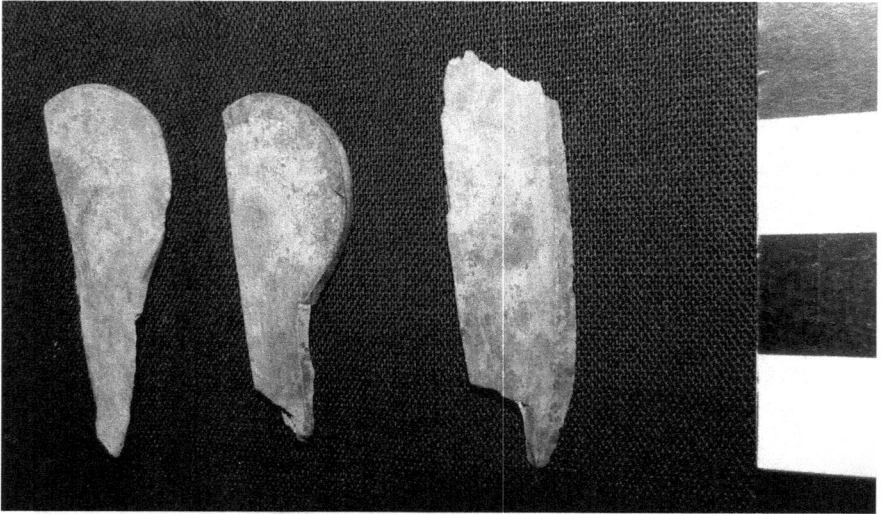

Figure 3.8. Fragments of adornments made of carved bone. Photo by Claire Martin, Illinois State Museum.

Spatial Analysis of Faunal Remains at Fort St. Joseph

A basic principle for archaeological research contends that the materials recovered are present as a consequence of culturally meaningful decisions the human populations that occupied these sites made. Animal remains are no exception. The species present in an archaeological assemblage and the patterns related to the processing and consumption of these animals and the disposal of their remains provide evidence for specific activities that occurred at a site (Hockett 1998; Lapham 2005). The spatial distribution of animal remains can reveal important information about the use of space and refuse disposal patterns (Bamforth et al. 2005; Sakaguchi 2007). Consideration of Fort St. Joseph's animal remains addressed spatial relationships and attempted to infer activities related to subsistence, hide processing, discard patterns, and taphonomy at the site.

A sample of 15,271 animal remains from eight excavation units across the site was analyzed to gain insights into spatial relationships (Hearns 2015). The units were selected to sample all areas of the site and the features that were discovered within those units. These features include (from units west to east) a metal cache in N19W7 and N21W7 (Feature 19); small, filled pits or postholes in N23W2 (no feature numbers assigned); an extensive bone midden in N27E8 (Feature 11); a large pit in N28E15 (Feature 7); a fireplace in N31E14 (Feature 10); and a small concentration of stones in N42E25 (Feature 1). The objective was to use the distribution of animal remains across the Fort St. Joseph site to understand more about the creation of the site and where distinct activities may have occurred (Lapham 2005). Variables examined included taxonomic richness; specimen sizes and completeness; frequency of burned specimens; occurrence of bone modifications such as rodent gnawing, carnivore damage, chopped bones, and knife cuts; and the distribution of skeletal portions of large mammals. The analysis used Surfer 11, a contour-mapping program used in spatial studies (e.g., Bamforth et al. 2005; Enloe et al. 1994). Within each excavation unit, the identified remains were grouped by strata and the data were analyzed separately for each attribute in order to perceive patterns in vertical relationship.

For the various attributes we considered, contour maps showing taxonomic richness are most informative. The plow zone context contained the highest diversity of taxa, especially in the central and western portions of the site, as shown by the lighter shading in Figure 3.9. The darker shades show areas having smaller numbers of discrete taxa. Moreover, the tight contour lines indicate numbers of taxa east of unit N27E8 and reflect the abrupt transition from high to low diversity. The nonfeature occupation zone shows a similar distribution pattern (Figure 3.10), with some key differences. The greatest diversity occurs near N27E8, where there is less diversity in the more western units and low taxonomic diversity in the eastern units.

Taxonomic diversity by feature follows a similar pattern (Figure 3.11). The area of high diversity is attributable to the fact that Feature 11 is an extensive bone midden and to the possibility that N23W2 includes pit features. The structural remnant (Feature 1) and the fireplace (Feature 10) show the least diversity, but the metal cache (Feature 19) in the westernmost units also has low taxonomic diversity.

White-tailed deer, raccoon, beaver, and black bear occur in most stratigraphic zones in all units, which is understandable given the overall abundance of remains from these species at the site. Greater taxonomic richness consists of small quantities of specimens that rarely represent more than a single individual. Mammals recovered from areas that have the most diversity are smaller-bodied animals, such as bobcat and marten, whose furs were also valuable (Jordan 2008). Birds—mainly waterfowl and wild turkey—do not occur in the same proportions as mammals. Fish, reptiles, and bivalves are also

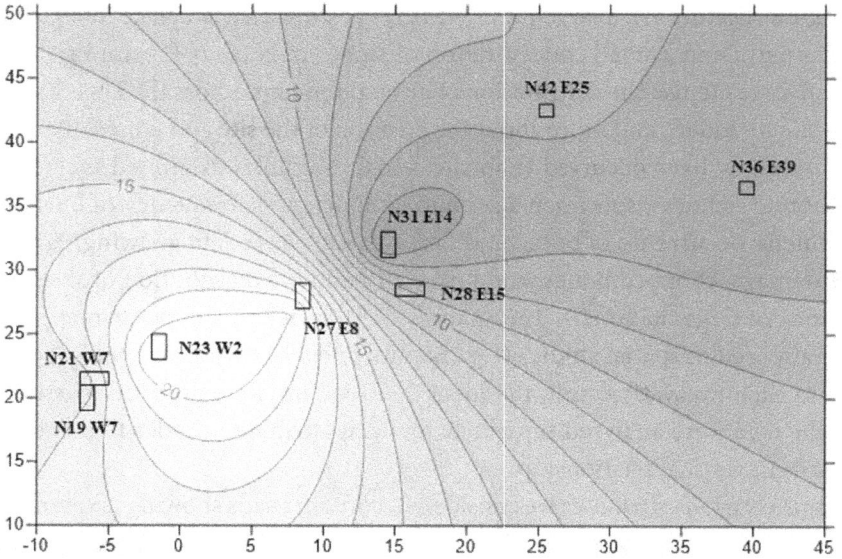

Figure 3.9. Distribution of animal remains from the plow zone by taxonomic richness. Lighter shading indicates greater taxonomic richness. Contour image by Joseph Hearns.

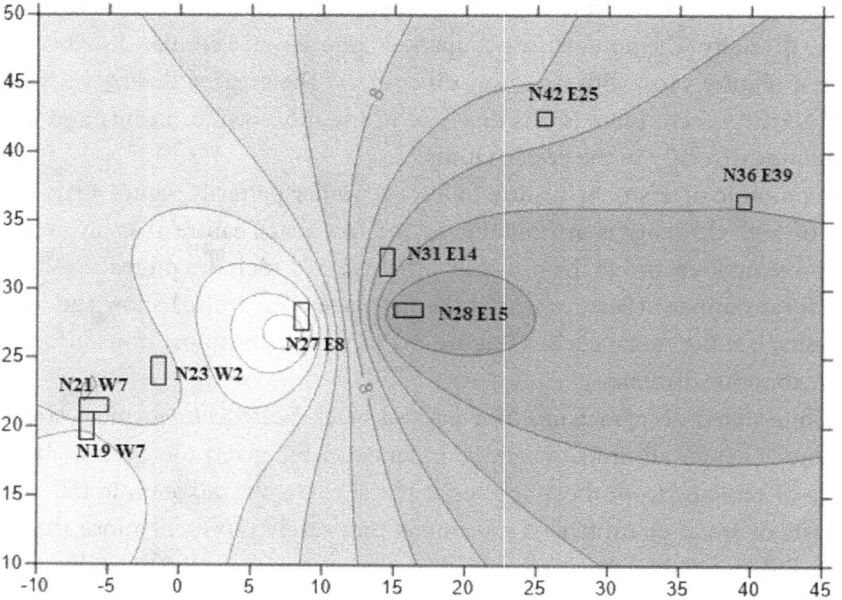

Figure 3.10. Distribution of animal remains from the occupation zone, excluding features, by taxonomic richness. Lighter shading indicates greater taxonomic richness. Contour image by Joseph Hearns.

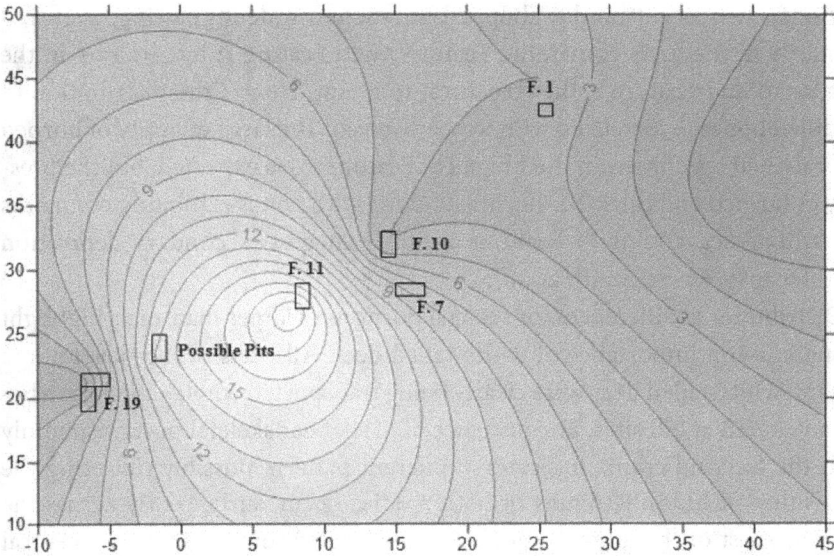

Figure 3.11. Distribution of animal remains from feature contexts by taxonomic richness. Lighter shading indicates greater taxonomic richness. Contour image by Joseph Hearns.

present in surprisingly small quantities. In this regard, Fort St. Joseph's faunal profile is an anomaly in comparison to other French fur trade posts in the western Great Lakes region and the Illinois Country (Becker 2004).

Consideration of the other faunal attributes adds subtle insights into the distribution of animal remains. Highly fragmented bones account for only 17 percent of the specimens identified below the level of class (e.g., "mammal," "bird," "reptile"). This pattern is consistent for all contexts at the site, regardless of sample size in each unit. Disturbance within the plow zone does not seem to have contributed significantly to additional fragmentation. The small variation in sizes of specimen mirrors the patterning noted above: slightly greater average size in N27E8, the unit containing the bone midden, and slightly smaller average size in and around the units containing the Feature 1 structural remnants.

Faunal remains that were subjected to incineration were more prevalent in the plow zone of western units and in the units containing a fireplace (Feature 10), a pit feature (Feature 7), and the bone midden (Feature 11). Other modifications, such as cut marks, chopped bones, and rodent gnawing, occurred primarily in the units containing Feature 7 and Feature 11 but are rare in the Feature 10 and Feature 1, the structural remnant. Hence, the distribution of modified bones is correlated with waste disposal. The large quantity of burned and calcined specimens in the fireplace (Feature 10) is expected, but the presence of burned and calcined specimens along with bones exhibiting cut marks and animal scavenging in Features 7 and 11 suggests secondary deposition (Schiffer 1987, 64–71; Smith 2006).

Distributional differences for skeletal portions of larger mammals highlight the paramount importance of white-tailed deer. All parts of the skeleton are present; white-tailed deer were clearly being transported whole rather than being butchered at kill sites. The presence of black bear skeletal portions mainly from the feet and crania indicates a different pattern, possibly reflecting the acquisition of hides. Remains of both species occur fairly evenly across the site, but most of the larger animal remains were recovered from the central units and the plow zone of the western units. Proportional representation of the various deer skeletal portions was found to be rather homogeneous across the site, whether viewing the plow zone (52 percent of the deer specimens), the nonfeature occupation zone (17 percent of the deer specimens), or the seven features (32 percent of the deer specimens). No area suggests distinctive deer-processing activities such as hide or meat preparation.

Not surprising for a site that was continuously occupied for many decades, maintenance activities seem to have affected the spatial distribution of animal remains. Structural features that were associated with human habitation have less faunal refuse. Fireplaces (e.g., Feature 10) were probably cleaned out periodically, leaving behind only smaller faunal specimens. In contrast, sheet middens and refuse pits outside dwellings, such as those exposed in the central units, received larger butchered bones and refuse from swept areas (Smith 2006).

Changes in how spaces were used also affected distribution patterns. The plow zone of the western units appears to be similar to occupation zones with secondary discard. Units N19W7, N21W7, and N23W2 seem to indicate areas inside structures that include hearths or fireplaces. Animal remains decrease in quantity significantly below the plow zone. Schiffer (1987, 61–62) notes that abandoned structures, pits, and areas of previous secondary refuse disposal are often attractive areas for the discard of high densities of refuse. The area of the structure tentatively identified in the western area might have been abandoned during the site's occupation and then repurposed for refuse disposal, as indicated by the accumulation of material in the plow zone and its similarity to other areas of repeated discard at the site.

Finally, although discard patterns and use of space may have changed over time, the species procurement and processing activities seem to have strong continuity. There was a special emphasis on locally obtained animals and an underrepresentation of domesticated animals compared to other French fur trade posts. The Gete Odena site on Grand Island provides an interesting comparison. Much like the sample analyzed for Fort St. Joseph, the Gete Odena sample contained a disproportionate emphasis on fur trade species such as beaver, muskrat, river otter, black bear, and white-tailed deer, along with fewer-than-expected quantities of birds and fish (Skibo et al. 2004). Furthermore, a series of smudge pits similar to those at Gete Odena were encountered on the terrace of the Lyne site (see Mendes and Nassaney, chapter 7, this volume), in addition to a single smudge pit at the site of the fort (Cremin and Nassaney 2003). Thus, areas of Fort St. Joseph and the Lyne site reflect activities related to procuring and processing animals for their meat *and* hides, especially white-tailed deer.

A Regional Perspective on Fort St. Joseph

Long-term archaeological and historical studies have been pursued at two French colonial fur trade sites in the Upper Country of New France (*pays d'en haut*). Specifically zooarchaeological analyses have been conducted at Fort Michilimackinac at the Straits of Mackinac in northern Michigan (Carlson 2012; Cleland 1970; Scott 1985, 1991) and at Fort Ouiatenon in the Upper Wabash River valley of Indiana (Martin 1986, 1991b). Faunal assemblages from both sites reveal the importance of wild animals over domesticated species. This has been attributed to geographic isolation, the importance of fur trade activities, and daily interactions with local indigenous populations. However, studies of additional sites in the French colony of Louisiana have also shown a preference for wild animal resources in the Illinois Country (Martin 1991a, 2008a) and in Old Mobile (Clute and Waselkov 2002) and New Orleans (Dawdy 2008, 84; Scott and Dawdy 2011). In contrast to the English colonists' practice of free-range animal husbandry along the East Coast (Anderson 2004), French colonists actively embraced conditions in New France, a place that many perceived as wild, or "*sauvage*," in order to integrate these resources and experiences into their colonial landscapes and persona (Parsons 2017). Similarly, according to Shannon Lee Dawdy,

> French colonial Louisiana's palate was an adventurous one but, at the same time, one that sought to domesticate native foods into familiar recipes. The raw ingredients may have been conceived as wild, native, and local, but the preparation and presentation methods were imagined to be French, "civilized," and imported. [In contrast, the English] tended to limit their tastes to those foods having close equivalences in English cooking (e.g., deer, rabbit, and buffalo, but not swan or unfamiliar fish species). (Dawdy 2010, 407–408)

Consistent with Tordoff's (1983) hierarchical model for French fur trade sites in the Midwest, local wild game species are prevalent in faunal assemblages at local distribution centers (e.g., Fort St. Joseph, Fort Ouiatenon, and the early Fort Michilimackinac), whereas sites that functioned as regional distribution centers (e.g., the later Fort Michilimackinac and Fort de Chartres in Upper Louisiana) exhibit greater consumption of domesticated animals such as swine, cattle, and domestic chickens. Proportions of white-tailed deer in the faunal assemblages at Fort St. Joseph and Fort Ouiatenon are much higher. This may be because people at these outposts had little desire to acquire domestic animals. Most of the *habitants* at Fort St. Joseph were creole; that is, people who were not born in France but in the St. Lawrence River valley of Quebec. When they arrived in the western Great Lakes, southwestern Michigan, and the St. Joseph River valley they still needed to adjust to the new natural and social environments. Many other permanent residents or frequent visitors were *métis*. Interactions with local indigenous groups may have also contributed to the greater reliance on local wild animal populations.

The distinctive nature of the Fort St. Joseph animal exploitation pattern can best be understood by comparing its archaeological faunal assemblage to those that were recovered at Fort Michilimackinac and Fort Ouiatenon. Figure 3.12 presents a comparison of the three trading-post sites using estimated biomass because that measure has meaning with regard to human subsistence practices. Furthermore, bone weight allometry (see methods section) was used to calculate biomass for all three sites (Carlson 2012; Martin 1986; Scott 1985).

The biomass calculated for domesticated mammals in the Fort Ouiatenon assemblage (35 percent) may be somewhat inflated. In addition to swine, sev-

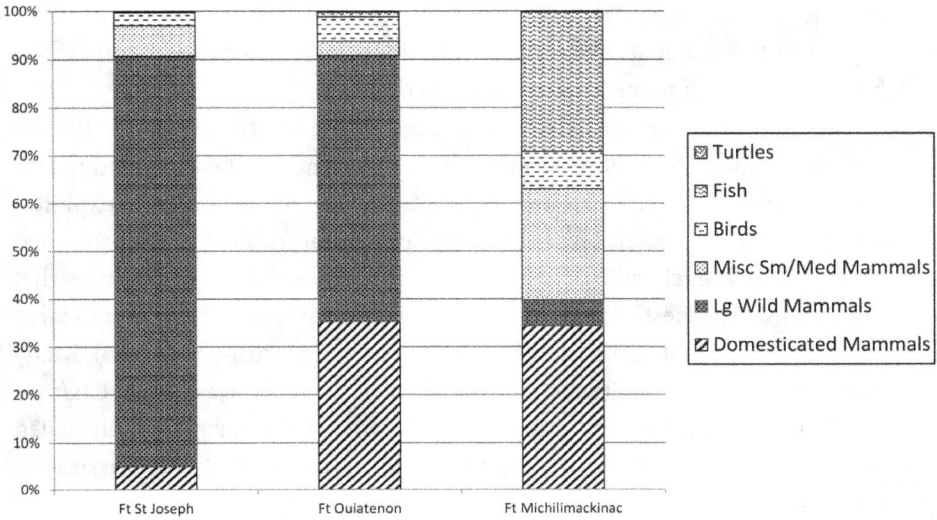

Figure 3.12. Comparison of animal groups by biomass at Forts St. Joseph, Ouiatenon, and Michilimackinac. Graph by Terrance Martin.

eral horse bones are included, and just over 7 percent of the biomass calculated for cattle are from diagnostic cattle bones. Even though the rest of the fragmented large bovid specimens were attributed to cattle, some of these could possibly be from bison. Although only one bison bone was identified, written accounts indicate that bison were occasionally encountered on the Wea Plains across the river. Thus, although selected cuts of bison meat were probably consumed, most of the large bones were probably left at kill sites. Fish remains were more abundant and diverse than at Fort St. Joseph, but as a class, fish appear to have been a minor supplement to the overall diet.

Fort Michilimackinac is located in a very different environmental setting than Fort Ouiatenon, namely in the transition between deciduous and coniferous woodlands and on the shore of Lakes Michigan and Huron. During the French occupation, dietary contributions from wild animals reflect a scarcity of large mammals such as white-tailed deer and wapiti; an abundance of medium-sized mammals such as beaver, porcupine, river otter, mustelids, and squirrels; and a reliance on deepwater fish such as lake trout (*Salvelinus namaycush*), lake whitefish (*Coregonus clupeaformis*), and lake sturgeon. The percentage by biomass of domesticated animals, which are represented by swine and cattle, was comparable to that at Fort Ouiatenon. Interestingly, even during the British occupation, biomass from domesticated mammals still ranged from only 10 to 34 percent (Scott 2001, 64).

The importance of agriculture and the production of wheat in the Illinois Country along with a more formal military presence at the third and fourth sites of Fort de Chartres resulted in yet another variation in animal exploitation patterns. Livestock (swine and cattle) produced locally were supplied to the larger French military garrison. This is reflected by the findings that biomass from domesticated mammals ranged from 65 to 70 percent and large wild mammals contributed only 22 to 25 percent (Martin 2008a, 196). Many creole residents of the French communities of Cahokia, Kaskaskia, Chartres, and Prairie du Rocher still procured wild game in the form of white-tailed deer, bison, and black bear along with wild birds, turtles, and Mississippi River fish.

Conclusions

The diversity of animals represented by the faunal remains that were recovered from the site of Fort St. Joseph suggests that the fort's fur trade inhabitants exploited species in addition to those that were valued for their hides and their meat. Written accounts often mention only beaver as the local target fur trade species (Peyser and Myers [1991] 1997, 5, 7). Hutchins also referred to the presence of horses, mules, and "milch cows" at the settlement (Cunningham 1961, 72–73). Although archaeological data attest to the paramount importance of white-tailed deer for food and for furs, many other varieties of wild mammals and birds were hunted and trapped. The recovery of healed bones from white-tailed deer, black bear, beaver, and raccoon demonstrates the resiliency of some of these wild animals. Given the rich aquatic resources in the St. Joseph River, we should also not be surprised that turtles, fish, and freshwater mussels were also procured. Perhaps most unexpected is the discovery that domesticated species such as cattle, swine, and chickens contributed so little to the residents' diet. The current result of the ongoing faunal analysis is reinforcing the impression that lifeways at the site were those of residents who consisted largely of creoles, *métis*, and local Indians along with French and Indian traders who visited the site. Moreover, they were not using dietary practices to express their French identity, unless this occurred through preparation and presentation methods, as Dawdy (2010, 407) argued was the case for New

Orleans. The occurrence of utilitarian, decorative, and recreational artifacts that were made from bones, antlers, and shells also reflects interactions with Native Americans.

The identification of migratory waterfowl and other avian species together with aquatic turtles, lake sturgeon, and juvenile deer indicates that the site was occupied year round. Despite these findings, the underrepresentation of fish is puzzling. Not only is the site located in immediate proximity to the St. Joseph River, the interactions of local *habitants* with local indigenous people would have resulted in a mutual awareness of the seemingly unlimited bounty of the potamodromous lake sturgeons, white suckers, and varieties of redhorse that ascended the river from Lake Michigan each spring to spawn.

Analysis of deer skeletal portions at the site indicates that all deer body parts are represented. However, when proportions of specimens by skeletal portion are compared to Native American habitation sites, we observed that bones from the lower legs and feet are underrepresented. This same bias also was found for deer remains at the Fort Ouiatenon site. Since metapodials are known to provide high-quality marrow that Native Americans sought as a dietary staple, this pattern would seem to be significant. Elsewhere, Nassaney and Martin (2017) have suggested that bone marrow may have been used as a supplement to deer brains for tanning hides.

Although structural remnants, fireplaces, refuse pits, a smudge pit, and a bone midden have been discovered, apparent continuous occupation of the site along with sweeping and secondary refuse discard complicate our ability to perceive discrete activities involving animal remains. Intrasite differences in distributions by taxonomic richness, specimen size, burning, and culturally and naturally modified specimens have been observed, but the homogeneous dispersal of deer skeletal portions across the site has prevented us from recognizing significant spatial differences that would enable us to identify special processing areas for hides or for food. Such challenges await future excavations and investigations that will employ larger data sets and more innovative approaches, techniques, and ideas to reveal heretofore undetected patterns in the use of animals by the Fort St. Joseph occupants.

Acknowledgments

We acknowledge Christina Arseneau and Carol Bainbridge, current and former directors, respectively, of the Niles History Center, for permitting access to the faunal collections from the Fort St. Joseph site. We are also grateful to the Illinois State Museum for access to the zoology reference collection and laboratory facilities at the Research and Collections Center in Springfield, Illinois. Thesis committee members for Rory Becker were Michael Nassaney, William Cremin, Michael Chiarappa, and Terrance Martin. Michael Nassaney, LouAnn Wurst, and Terrance Martin were committee members for Joseph Hearns. Becker and Hearns thank these individuals for their patience, encouragement, and guidance in various stages of data analyses and writing. Martin is obliged to WMU archaeological field school students and individuals who participated in the summer camp training program in previous years of the Fort St. Joseph Archaeological Project for their participation in zooarchaeology workshops, which provided significant additional data for inclusion in this chapter.

Note

1. Information retrieved May 17, 2016, from the Integrated Taxonomic Information System online database, http://www.itis.gov.

4

Architectural Remains at Fort St. Joseph

ERIKA K. HARTLEY AND MICHAEL S. NASSANEY

Throughout New France, Native Americans and Europeans frequently interacted as they exchanged goods and forged alliances. This intense entanglement among close allies influenced how these fur trade participants expressed their cultural identities. Historical archaeologists can examine the materiality of their lives to explore this dynamic process. Identity formation can take a variety of forms, from the foods people ate and the clothes they wore to the dwellings they built and inhabited (e.g., Becker 2004; Davis, chapter 5, this volume; Mann 2008; Martin et al., chapter 3, this volume; Nassaney 2008b). Architectural remains are particularly informative because inhabitants construct their buildings in accordance with their needs and cultural values (Bourdieu 1970; Loveland 2017; Loveland and Nassaney 2017). Archaeological and documentary records indicate that a wide range of raw materials were used to create building forms in New France (Loveland and Nassaney 2017). Available technology, cultural practices, and the desired architectural outcomes dictated the use of straw, sticks, clay, wood, stone, glass, iron, and various combinations of these materials (Loveland and Nassaney 2017; Thurman 1984). Evidence of structural remains provide important clues about the ways people constructed their buildings, the types of raw materials they used, and how they occupied these spaces. Because building forms were influenced by intended function, their remains provide information about the identities of their makers and users. The cultural interactions that took place in the St. Joseph River valley after the French settled there in the late seventeenth century provide a laboratory for investigating the extent to which the French were able to impose Old World architectural styles on the edge of empire.

This chapter reveals the architectural remains recovered at Fort St. Joseph. Prior to systematic investigations, little information existed about the built environment at the fort (see Brandão and Nassaney, chapter 2, this volume). Unlike the documentation we have for other colonial settlements, no detailed maps, drawings, or descriptions have come to light to illuminate the physical appearance of the fort. Here, we trace the origins of French colonial architectural styles and how they were adapted in the New World. We then use archaeological and documentary sources to ascertain the types of buildings that may have existed at Fort St. Joseph, what their functions likely were, and what they may have looked like. This information will help us interpret the function, techniques, and materials used to construct buildings as revealed through the architectural remains and associated structural materials found at Fort St. Joseph. This examination of eighteenth-century buildings in New France provides a better appreciation and understanding of colonial architecture and the conservative nature of French building practices.

Domestic Architectural Styles in New France

Houses and building techniques can serve as material expressions of ethnic identity (Bourdieu 1970; Mann 2008). French colonial building styles in North America derive from the half-timbered vertical log structures of northwest France that date back to the French Renaissance (Brazier 2013; Eccles 1964; Edwards 1986; Ekberg 1985; Peterson 1965; Sheldon et al. 2008; Thurman 1984). Modifications were made in the St. Lawrence Valley, the Great Lakes region, and the Mississippi Valley to adapt architecture to resource availability, group size, and (perhaps most important) environmental conditions. For example, Charles Peterson (1965) provided valuable information on French houses by studying extant structures in St. Louis and examining their derivation from and similarities to buildings in France and other French colonies. Buildings in the central Mississippi River Valley combined the floor plan of the French Canadian house (*maison canadienne*) with porches (galleries) from the Caribbean to create a new architectural form distinctive to this region (Ekberg 1985; Peterson 1965; Thurman 1984).

Archaeological studies, historical documents, and standing structures can inform us about French colonial building styles. Most buildings were constructed using one of four methods: 1) *poteaux en terre* (posts in the ground); 2) *poteaux sur sole* (posts on a sill); 3) *pièce-sur-pièce* (squared timbers); or 4) stone masonry (Brazier 2013; Ekberg 1985; Heldman 1991; Kornwolf 2002; Moogk 2002; Peterson 1965; Sheldon et al. 2008; Thurman 1984). These construction methods were used for buildings that served various functions, including as powder magazines, guardhouses, prisons, warehouses, churches, barracks, commandants' quarters, kitchens, simple dwellings, henhouses, and smithies (Loveland and Nassaney 2017).

Many buildings, particularly in frontier settings, were simple *poteaux en terre* structures (Figure 4.1) that were built by setting upright posts in a trench and filling the interstices with *bousillage* (clay and mud mixed with straw, grass, or Spanish moss), then covered with whitewash (a mixture of lime and water to protect the walls from the elements) (Brazier 2013; Ekberg 1985; Gums 2002; Mann 2008; Moogk 2002; Peterson 1965; Sheldon et al. 2008; Thurman 1984). This type of building was relatively quick and easy to construct, albeit short lived since wooden posts inserted directly in the ground were susceptible to moisture rot and insect damage. Sometimes the wall posts would be pegged and nailed into a horizontal wooden sill, which sat either on the ground or on a stone foundation using a technique known as *poteaux sur sole* (Figure 4.2). This method of construction resulted in a more durable structure but required more time and skill. In both techniques, a mortise and tenon system of timber framing was used. A plate, or the upper large hewn timber, was used to frame the top of the structure to match the wall trench or sill at the bottom (Thurman 1984). To support the plate, upright posts were needed at each corner and beneath the splicings (Thurman 1984). These construction techniques remained common well into the eighteenth century, even though structures that were more weatherproof were preferred in colder climates (Brazier 2013; Heldman 1991; Kornwolf 2002). *Pièce-sur-pièce* involved squared horizontal timbers, as found in the reconstructed church of Ste. Anne at Fort Michilimackinac. This technique combined with masonry construction was typically used for special-purpose and more permanent buildings found in settlements such as the Fortress of Louisbourg, Fort Niagara, Montreal, and Quebec (Brazier 2013).

Stone fireplaces and hearths with wattled-and-daub chimneys were often placed at the ends or corners of habitation rooms (Brazier 2013; Moogk 2002). Fireplaces were used for cooking and to warm the home (Moogk 2002). They

Figure 4.1. *Poteaux en terre* method of French colonial building construction. Adapted from Thurman (1984, Figure 1). Redrawn by Michael S. Nassaney.

Figure 4.2. *Poteaux sur sole* method of French colonial building construction. Adapted from Thurman (1984, Figure 1). Redrawn by Michael S. Nassaney.

also were a source of light in dwellings, allowing for domestic activities such as sewing and craft production to occur when natural light was insufficient. Windows made of glass or oiled paper were placed on adjacent sides for cross-ventilation (Moogk 2002). A steep hipped roof of long wooden rafters was covered with boards, wooden shingles, or pieces of bark to shed rain and snow and divert water from building foundations (Crompton 2012; Edwards 1986; Gums 2002; Kalm 1937; Kornwolf 2002; Moogk 2002). Attics or lofts may have been built in French-style homes for sleeping areas and for storing dry foods and goods used in the fur trade (Farah 2011; Moogk 2002). Structures had earthen or wooden floors; the latter were typically raised off the ground to keep the wood from rotting (Gums 2002; Kalm 1937; Kornwolf 2002; Moogk 2002). Joists or stones held up the floorboards, which were secured in place by nails or the tongue and groove method (Thurman 1984).

These four building techniques could be adapted to structures of various size. In the seventeenth century, the average size of a dwelling ranged from 3 to 4 *toise* (5.85–8.5 m) long by 2.4 to 3.5 *toise* (4.68–6.8 m) wide, employing a length-to-width ratio of 5:4 (a *toise* is a French unit of measurement equal to 6 feet, 4.75 inches) (Moogk 2002, 132). At Fort Michilimackinac, high-status artifacts indicate that individuals of better means most likely occupied slightly larger buildings even though the dwellings were constructed in similar *pote-aux en terre* styles (Heldman 1991). Building size also depended on function; most residences typically featured one room containing a fireplace with an occasional additional room that served as a storage or sleeping area (Brazier 2013). Some inhabitants lived in row houses, like those found at Fort Michilimackinac (Heldman 1991). These were long one-story buildings with three to six interconnected rooms and attics for storage (Heldman 1991). Interior walls were typically mere partitions that were narrow compared to the exterior walls. Outbuildings such as barns and sheds were constructed using these techniques in the Illinois Country and the Upper Country (Gums et al. 1991; Moogk 2002).

The French used both local and imported raw materials to construct their structures. Early explorers and settlers could make do with local raw materials of wood, stone, and clay for construction (Sheldon et al. 2008). They also sought "to acquire, produce, and maintain products of Old World technology" (Nassaney 2018b, 60). Through an extensive trade network the French built in North America, construction materials not locally available such as window glass and wrought iron were imported (Jones and Sullivan 1989; Roache-Fedchenko 2013). Glass would have been carefully transported as small panes cut in diamond, triangular, and other shapes to prevent breakage en route from large production areas in Europe. These would be taken by canoe to forts and settlements across New France (Brown 1971a; Jones and Sullivan 1989; Moogk 2002). Blacksmiths at the fort and abroad made various types of iron hardware, such as nails, pintles, locks, keys, and hinges for the *habitants* to use in their buildings (Roache-Fedchenko 2013). An increase in population and skilled labor and the need for permanent architecture in New France contributed to the diversity and complexity of French colonial styles (Loveland and Nassaney 2017).

The construction styles in New France varied from urban to frontier settings and over the duration of the French regime, depending on the availability of raw materials and the needs and desires of the builders (see Harris 1987, 138–141). Of course, many of these buildings have long disappeared. Fortunately, these structures often left archaeological signatures in the form of fireplaces, postholes, and foundation walls associated with architectural debris, allowing archaeologists to discern the techniques, size, and materials once used to shelter the inhabitants of New France.

The Built Environment of Fort St. Joseph

Fort St. Joseph was a relatively small but intensely occupied mission, garrison, and commercial center for much of the eighteenth century (Brandão and Nassaney 2006). Despite its importance to French imperial ambitions, documentary records provide little information about the built environment of the fort. Virtually no detailed maps, drawings, or building descriptions are known to exist (Brandão and Nassaney 2006). Thus, the appearances, construction techniques, and sizes of the buildings can be revealed only through archaeological investigations.

By the early eighteenth century, the post supported a commandant, ten to fifteen soldiers and officers, a blacksmith, an interpreter, an occasional priest, and up to fifteen additional households occupied by fur traders, their wives, and children (Brandão and Nassaney 2006, chapter 2, this volume; Idle 2003, 149–154; Nassaney 2008b; Peyser 1992). All of these occupants and their specialized activities required structures for security and protection from the elements and from potential enemies. Fort St. Joseph never became a strong military post even though it played an important role during the Fox and Chickasaw Wars (Brandão and Nassaney 2006; Peyser 1992). One account suggests that Fort St. Joseph was defended by a wooden palisade with an entrance gate on the north and south sides, enclosing homes for the commandant and his soldiers and the storage buildings needed for the fur trade (Benston 2010; Brandão and Nassaney 2006, 65). The palisade is thought to have been somewhat flimsy because "in 1695 the Iroquois Indians were able to put their guns through its gaps and shoot into the fort" (Brandão and Nassaney 2006, 65). Since the attackers were able to get that close to the palisade, there were probably no platforms in the bastions for defensive fire (Brandão and Nassaney 2006, chapter 2, this volume). Archaeological evidence of military fortifications or a powder magazine has not yet been found.

Frequent interactions between Native Americans and Europeans occurred at the fort throughout the eighteenth century. French survival on the edge of empire depended upon close cooperation with Potawatomi and Miami allies. Fort St. Joseph played a major role in the fur trade, as indicated by the fort's high ranking (fourth) in volume of furs traded among all of the posts in New France in the mid-eighteenth century (Brandão and Nassaney, chapter 2, this volume). European manufactured goods were exchanged for furs trapped and processed and for food the Native Americans had procured (Brandão and Nassaney 2006; Juen and Nassaney 2012; Nassaney 2008b, 2015, 164–196). While a storehouse has not yet been archaeologically discovered at Fort St. Joseph, it is likely that some buildings at the fort were used to store trading goods and furs (Brandão and Nassaney 2006).

A payment voucher indicates that Commandant François-Marie Picoté de Belestre ordered the construction of a jail in 1750 (Brandão and Nassaney 2006; Peyser 1978, document 140). The Crown paid the fort's blacksmith, Antoine Deshêtres, to provide the necessary ironwork and a lock for a ten-by-eight-foot square cut-stone building (Peyser 1978, document 140). Material evidence of this structure at the site is needed to determine if the construction of the jail was ever completed.

In 1753, documentary evidence reported that the fort "contained 'fifteen huts which the owners call houses'" (Brandão and Nassaney 2006, 65). This report was consistent with a 1780 census of the French *habitants* who were deported from the fort. The census specifies that fourteen households, totaling about forty-five settlers, were evacuated (Brandão and Nassaney 2006). Furthermore, the historical record reveals some information on the occupations and identities of a few of Fort St. Joseph's inhabitants, which included religious and military personnel, an interpreter, a blacksmith/gunsmith, *voyageurs*, and French and Native American women (Brandão and Nassaney 2006; Nassaney 2008b).

The material remains found associated with individual habitations allow inferences about the identities of the occupants. Personal adornment objects (e.g., buttons, buckles, tinkling cones, finger rings, religious items, jewelry, and wampum) suggest that French traders, Native Americans, and *métis* peoples lived in the area that has been the focus of excavation since 1998 (Kerr 2012). Animal remains (Martin et al., chapter 3, this volume) indicate the importance of white-tailed deer at the site in both hide production and consumption practices. While glass and ceramic items, such as faience and creamware, have not yet been studied extensively at Fort St. Joseph, the large quantities recovered from across the site provide evidence for domestic spaces and activities occurring at the fort. Thus, studies of the contents of the buildings and associated midden deposits suggest a well-integrated, multiethnic population that shared material culture and borrowed cultural practices from each other (Becker 2004; Hearns 2015; Kerr 2012; Nassaney 2008b). Yet some cultural practices may have been more resistant to syncretism than others.

Architectural Remains

Archaeological investigations of Fort St. Joseph have revealed evidence of structural remains from which we can ascertain building size, function, and methods of construction at the site (see Loveland 2017; Loveland and Nassaney 2017; Nassaney 2015, 178–180). Information collected thus far and the associated artifacts suggest the presence of several structures, probably for habitation, along the St. Joseph River (Figure 4.3) (Brandão and Nassaney 2006; Loveland 2017; Nassaney 2008, 2015; Nassaney and Brandão 2009). To date, excavations have located a series of six fireplace features, four of which have been interpreted as components of residential structures based on previous examination of the personal adornment items found in their vicinity (Kerr 2012). Kerr examined personal adornment items associated with the fireplaces (designated Feature 2, Feature 6, Feature 10, and Feature 14) and with Feature 5, which was previously thought to be a fireplace. Kerr did not examine the Feature 20 fireplace found in Structure 4 and the newly uncovered Feature 27 fireplace that are discussed below. His study adds to the significance of

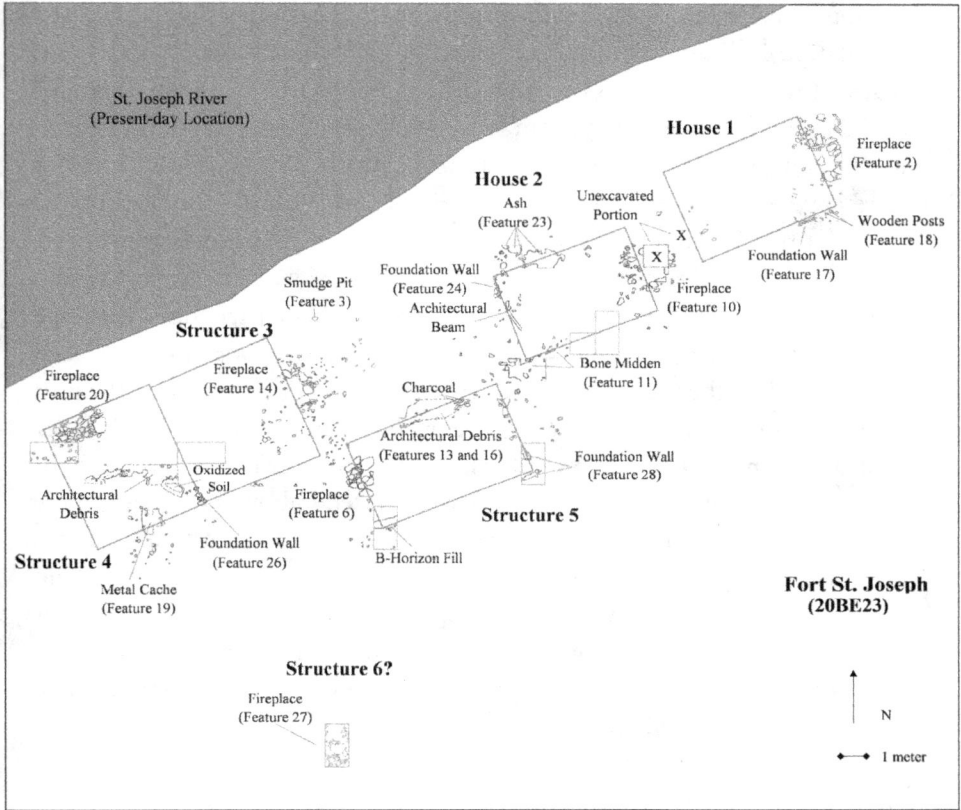

Figure 4.3. Building locations identified at Fort St. Joseph through archaeological excavations. Map by Erika Loveland.

this architectural analysis and the need for an interpretation of the buildings' function and the identity of their occupants. While the personal adornment objects suggest that French traders, Native Americans, and *métis* occupied these houses, this chapter discusses another line of evidence—architectural remains—to discern the ethnic identities of the fort's occupants.

House 1

House 1 has a fireplace (Feature 2) along the east wall and a stone foundation (Feature 17) and two upright posts (Feature 18) that define the south wall and southeast corner of the house. The fireplace consists of large stones (10–50 cm long) that open to the southwest inside the structure (Figure 1.3). The foundation is at least 90 cm long, consisting of smaller stones (10–15 cm) that rest on top of one another in a linear pattern that is oriented parallel to the river. A larger stone (38 cm long) was placed underneath, perhaps to fill in a low area or to provide additional structural support. These stones were covered in mortar and intentionally placed in this construction. The extent of this foundation is unknown, as it has not yet been fully exposed. The two upright wooden posts appear to be in line with the stone foundation and were placed along the southeastern wall of the structure. The large post (15 cm in diameter) may be a load-bearing corner post, as it is placed 2.30 m south of the fireplace. A soil core was used to determine that the post extends to a depth of just over 60 cm below the foundation wall. The smaller post (10 cm in diameter) is located just southwest of the larger post, perhaps to provide additional support. It appears to extend about 34 cm below the foundation wall. Archaeological evidence of the north and west walls has not been uncovered yet. However, based on the proximity of the fireplace and foundation posts, it appears that the fireplace was located close to the center of the east wall rather than the northeast corner of the house. From this, the width of House 1 has been approximated to be about 5 m (ca. 2.5 *toise*), while the length remains unknown.

House 2

Southwest of House 1, another stone fireplace (Feature 10) is associated with a stone foundation wall (Feature 24) and a hewn board. Together, these features make up House 2 and bear formal similarity to House 1. The fireplace includes large stones (15–50 cm long) located along the east wall and opens to the southwest of the structure. The partially exposed foundation wall is at least one meter long, consisting of smaller stones (10–20 cm long) that rest on top of one another in a linear arrangement along the west wall. A hewn board was found aligned with the wall immediately to the south (Figure 4.4). Its location suggests it may be a sill, perhaps for a door since it is directly across from the fireplace. An ash pit (Feature 23) found where the north wall is thought to have been located may suggest the presence of a window where the home's residents could dispose of ash buildup from the fireplace. Excavations have also revealed a large bone midden (Feature 11) south of the structure, possibly representing accumulated debris immediately adjacent

FORT ST JOSEPH SITE
20BE23
N29E8

66 CMBD
WOOD
PLAN VIEW
AUGUST 8 2013

Figure 4.4. A hewn pine board unearthed during excavation, possibly a plate or a sill. Photo by Katelyn Hillmeyer.

to the outside wall (Figure 1.4). While there is no conclusive evidence (e.g., wall foundations, wooden posts, postholes) for the locations of the north and south walls, the presence of the ash pit and bone midden suggest that the walls would have been located within this perimeter. House 2 is estimated to be approximately 4 by 7 m (ca. 2 by 3.5 *toise*) in size. These dimensions are comparable to other French houses and individual rooms in row houses and barracks found throughout seventeenth- and eighteenth-century New France (see Loveland 2017, 40).

Structures 3 and 4

Located to the southwest of House 1 and House 2 lie the proposed Structures 3 and 4. These two structures are similar in some respects to the previously described structures. Structure 3 is composed of a fireplace (Feature 14) along the east wall made of large stones (10–50 cm), opening to the southwest. While this fireplace is slightly smaller than those in House 1 and House 2, its style, the presence of oxidized soil, and the structural stones employed in its construction are very similar. The proposed Structure 4 consists of a substantial concentration of large structural stones (10–70 cm) associated with heavily mottled oxidized soil, specifically near the south edge of the feature. This concentration, designated as Feature 20, has not been fully exposed, but it is at least 2.30 by 1.40 m in size. Feature 20 has been interpreted as a fireplace, although its appearance is much different from the others found at the site. The other fireplaces have a clear outline and opening, whereas this feature appears to be rectangular. Perhaps this is a result of the lower portion of the fireplace caving in on itself or it may have had a different function (forge?) from the other fireplaces at the site. Feature 20 is also located along the north wall of the proposed Structure 4, which differs from the other three fireplaces described previously. The significance of these differences remains unknown.

In addition to the fireplace features associated with Structures 3 and 4, there is a stone foundation wall (Feature 26) that could be associated with either or both structures. This wall consists of five structural stones covered in mortar (15–40 cm) and a few smaller stones (10 cm) placed around them. The foundation wall is at least 95 cm long and may continue farther north. At present, we cannot determine the relationship between this foundation wall and the two adjacent structures, though there are several hypotheses. One is that this foundation wall is located between the two structures and could be associated with the west wall of Structure 3 or the east wall of Structure 4. A second hypothesis is that the buildings may have been constructed at different times during the fort's occupation and the *habitants* may have wanted to reuse the architectural remains of one building to construct the other. A third hypothesis is that it is possible that these two buildings are connected and the foundation is the base of a partition wall between the two rooms. The latter hypothesis is most likely and can be supported by the types of features found in and around the proposed layout of these structures, which ultimately suggest the presence of blacksmithing activities.

Payment records from 1739 to 1752 reveal that someone who could forge metal and repair guns lived at the fort and baptismal records further indicate that a blacksmith, Antoine Deshêtres, resided there as early as 1731 (Brandão and Nassaney 2006). Two archaeological features (Features 4 and 19) are indicative of metal working at the site (Figure 1.4). Feature 4, located about 7 meters northeast of the Structure 3 fireplace, is a large cache of more than 100 gun parts, including 22 gun cocks, 29 breech plugs, 22 frizzens, 2 lock mechanisms, related flintlock hardware, and other metal artifacts (see Jones n.d.). Feature 19 is another large metal cache located just 5 meters south of the heated stone concentration feature in Structure 4. This cache contained two ax heads, some lead sprue, an iron chisel, a gun cock, a brass butt plate, a lead whizzer, a gun lock, iron screws, hand-wrought nails and nail fragments, lead shot, and unidentifiable iron and copper alloy fragments.

In addition, a smudge pit (Feature 3) is located just 3 meters north of the Structure 3 fireplace. This circular pit is 20 cm in diameter and 9 cm deep, having been truncated by plowing (Nassaney 2008b). Native Americans commonly used smudge pits to tan hides; thus, this feature could represent hide processing activities (Binford 1967; Mendes and Nassaney, chapter 7, this volume). At Fort Ouiatenon, excavations have revealed a smithy represented by a packed earthen floor associated with three pits, iron tools, bone, and other artifacts (Tordoff 1980, 22). One pit contained a large amount of clay, ash, and iron oxide staining, while the remaining two contained charred corncobs, which may have been used for tanning hides (Tordoff 1980). Gun parts, iron tools, and unidentifiable iron fragments were found in all three pits, suggesting that they were used for refuse related to forging activities (Tordoff 1980). The association of these features and artifacts at Fort Ouiatenon suggest that blacksmiths may have conducted a range of activities besides metalworking that involved fire.

Limited evidence suggests that Structures 3 and 4 and their associated features may represent the blacksmith's house and his workshop. Workshops on the frontier are thought to average no larger than 7.7 by 7.5 m (Roache-Fedchenko 2013, 70), which is consistent with the proposed size of Structure 4 (5 by 7 m). Feature 20 compares favorably in size to French forges identified at Fort Michilimackinac (see Roache-Fedchenko 2013, 100–111). It is also not uncommon for the blacksmith's living quarters to be attached to their workshop (Roache-Fedchenko 2013, 80–81). For example, at Fort Pentagouet in Maine, the smithy consisted of three rooms: a workshop, a storage space, and living quarters (Faulkner 1986). While Kerr's (2012) analysis did not include Feature 20, which is located in Structure 4, he did interpret the area associated with Feature 14, located in Structure 3, as a domestic space. Future analysis of the slag and various iron material found in Structure 4 is needed in addition to an intrasite comparison of these materials among the buildings identified at the site. If Structure 4 is the blacksmith's workshop, it would arguably contain a greater quantity of iron and slag than the other buildings at the fort.

Structure 5

The proposed Structure 5 consists of a fireplace (Feature 6) and the remains of two walls. This fireplace feature has not yet been fully excavated; however, the size of the structural stones (10–70 cm) resemble those found in the other fireplace features. It appears that the fireplace may open to the east due to the location of the oxidized soil found in association. This orientation correlates with the heavy amounts of architectural debris found to the northeast of the fireplace, designated as Features 13 and 16, and the remains of two wall trenches that form a corner (Feature 28).

Feature 28 has been interpreted as the southeast corner of Structure 5. This feature consists of two linear light-gray clay soil zones tentatively identified as wall trenches that form a 90-degree angle but do not intersect; these are associated with large quantities of charcoal. At least one possible posthole was found in association with these soils along with a B-horizon fill zone located along the outside of the east wall, perhaps backfill from the excavation of the trench. The fill zone is very similar to the B-horizon sediments found in another unit located 5 meters to the southeast that appears to align with the Feature 28 south wall foundation. Further investigation of this feature is needed to determine the construction techniques and materials used in this building.

Possible Structure

Large stones and oxidized soil have been uncovered and designated as Feature 27, a potentially new fireplace feature, in an excavation unit dug over a series of years by participants in the project's archaeology summer camp (see D'Elia et al., chapter 9, this volume). Feature 27 consists of stones ranging in size (15–40 cm) along with oxidized soil, ash, and charcoal. The orientation of this feature is unclear, although it bears some similarities to the other five fireplaces identified at the site. More archaeological work is needed around this fireplace feature to establish the orientation of the fireplace and the size, construction techniques, and function of an associated structure.

Summary

The clustering of these buildings near the St. Joseph River and their contents and construction techniques suggest that they may represent some of the "huts" that sheltered fur traders as observed by the English prior to deporting the inhabitants. They were all built using a combination of the *poteaux en terre* and *poteaux sur sole* construction techniques, as revealed by the three stone foundations and two posts uncovered thus far at the site. The size, orientation, and other formal similarities between House 1 and House 2 suggest that these structures conform to a regular template derived from French Canadian building traditions (Table 4.1). While slightly smaller in size, the appearance of the Structure 3 fireplace also compares favorably to the fireplaces in House 1 and House 2, suggesting that it was constructed using the same design principles.

The similarities in design, layout, size, and features present in House 1, House 2, and Structure 3 suggest that these buildings may have served similar functions. Given the personal adornment objects associated with these three buildings and Structure 5, we propose that these structures had domestic functions, serving as habitations for the fort's French traders, Native Americans, and *métis* occupants (see Kerr 2012). Future excavation will be oriented toward uncovering additional architectural remains of Structures 3, 4, and 5 and the potential Structure 6 and to search for evidence of some of the other "fifteen huts" and other buildings that have not yet been discovered on the site.

Construction Materials Employed at Fort St. Joseph

At Fort St. Joseph, the French used both locally available raw materials and imported manufactured materials to construct their buildings using traditional Old World techniques (Loveland 2017; Loveland and Nassaney 2017). These materials underscore the permanence of the buildings in contrast with their more ephemeral Native American counterparts (Loveland and Nassaney 2017, 10, 30–32). The archaeological record documents the use of wood, stone, clay, glass, and iron hardware in the construction of buildings at the fort (Loveland 2017; Loveland and Nassaney 2017). Wood was sourced from the immediate area to construct walls, sills, and roofs. The wooden sill in House 2 has been identified as white pine (*Pinus strobus*) (Katie Egan-Bruhy, personal communication 2016), which would have been easy to cut but not as durable as local hardwoods. Wood charcoal of ash, beech, black elm, walnut/butternut, hickory, maple, oak, and white pine have also been found in situ at the site (DesJardins 2003).[1] Both unmodified and modified pieces of wood were used to construct the forts' buildings. The wood identified as a sill was intention-

Table 4.1. Architectural and morphological attributes of structures identified at Fort St. Joseph

Structure and Fireplace Feature	Location of Fireplace Feature	Orientation of Fireplace Feature	Size of Fireplace Feature	Fireplace Stone Sizes	Associated Foundation Wall/s	Associated Posthole/s and Hewn Boards
House 1 (Feature 2)	Along the east wall	Opens to the southwest	2.25 × 1.30 m	10–50 cm	Feature 17: At least 90 cm long, 10–15 cm stones resting on and around one larger stone (38 cm long)	Feature 18, Posthole 1: 15 cm in diameter; 60 cm deep Feature 18, Posthole 2: 10 cm in diameter; 34 cm deep
House 2 (Feature 10)	Along the east wall	Opens to the southwest	2.50 × 1.40 m	15–50 cm	Feature 24: At least 1 m long, 10–20 cm stones	Hewn Board: 1.4 m long by 12 cm thick
Structure 3 (Feature 14)	Along the east wall	Opens to the southwest	1.90 × 1.10 m	10–50 cm	Feature 26: At least 95 cm long, 15–40 cm stones with four 10 cm stones placed around them	Undetermined
Structure 4 (Feature 20)	Along the north wall	Oxidized soil is located to the south of the stones	At least 2.30 × 1.40 m	10–70 cm	Feature 26: At least 95 cm long, 15–40 cm stones with four 10 cm stones placed around them	Undetermined
Structure 5 (Feature 6)	Along the west wall	Oxidized soil is located to the east of the stones	At least 1.80 × 1.40 m	10–70 cm	Feature 28: Two linear light gray clay soil zones with heavy amounts of charcoal	Undetermined
Structure 6 (Feature 27)	Undetermined	Oxidized soil is located to the north of the stones	At least 1.70 × 1.15 m	15–35 cm	Undetermined	Undetermined

ally hewn, perhaps with an ax. Concave log impressions found on pieces of baked clay suggest that some wooden posts were unmodified and retained their convex shape.

The stones used in the foundations and fireplaces were most likely found in or along the banks of the St. Joseph River. The similarities in the size of stones used to construct wall foundations and fireplaces demonstrates that the stones were carefully selected for specific purposes. Large stones were used as a base for the fireplaces, whereas smaller stones were selected for the foundations. The inhabitants of the fort used mortar (a mixture of sand, lime, and water) to further secure the stones in place; it was found on many of the structural stones unearthed at Fort St. Joseph.

Clay mixed with water, soil, and straw or grass to produce *bousillage* served as a binding agent to fill the interstices of upright posts and to form chimneys. At Fort St. Joseph, there are close to 10,000 pieces of baked clay, or daub, varying in weight and size found through excavation. Some "fist-sized pieces" present in the collection "exhibit log and straw impressions, and white-washed surfaces suggesting that they represent chinking (*bousillage*)" used in the construction of *poteaux en terre* and *poteaux sur sole* structures (Nassaney 2008b, 303). The log impressions found in the *bousillage* suggest that some logs used in the construction of these buildings were unmodified; that is, they were not hewn. This interpretation is supported by the circular-shaped wooden posts (Feature 18) in House 1.

Some materials such as glass and iron were produced in Europe and transported along extensive trade networks that the French grafted onto preexisting Native American exchange systems (Loveland 2017; Loveland and Nassaney 2017). Just under 2,000 fragments of window glass have been found in excavations at Fort St. Joseph. They range in thickness from 0.30 to 3.40 mm (average 1.20 mm; standard deviation ± 0.37 mm) and provide evidence for the use of glass windows across the site (Loveland 2017, 50). The ubiquity of fragments of window glass at Fort St. Joseph indicates that the *habitants* had ready access to this fragile commodity.

French-style buildings required various types of iron hardware such as hand-wrought nails, pintles, locks, and hinges that blacksmiths across New France produced. Whether the raw iron ore or the finished iron hardware was transported to Fort St. Joseph is not clear, as the available documents do not discuss the manufacturing or trading of these types of materials at the site and archaeological evidence of smelting has not been recovered (Peyser 1978). At Fort Michilimackinac, a larger trading post complex, most metal arrived in the form of finished goods (Roache-Fedchenko 2013). As Roache-Fedchenko notes, "Fort Michilimackinac was receiving iron goods from France from 1715 until shortly after 1736. After this period, iron may have been imported to the fort from either France or the St. Maurice Forges at Montreal"; these practices continued until the British occupation in 1761 (Roache-Fedchenko 2013, 62). Thus, it seems likely that some finished products were sent to Fort St. Joseph (Loveland 2017). This is not to say, however, that there were not occasional shipments of iron bars to the site for the blacksmith to use to forge and repair items for the fort's residents and Native American neighbors. These may be represented by the large, undiagnostic pieces of scrap iron that have been recovered archaeologically.

Approximately 2,000 hand-wrought nails and nail fragments have been found at the site before 2018. Of these, Loveland (2017, 53) examined 672 complete hand-wrought nails and identified 455 nails from the nail typology Stone created (1974b). Nail types recognized at the site include rose head with a pointed shank, rose head with a flattened shank, L-head with a pointed shank, L-head with a flattened shank, offset head, T-head, large nail head with a small shank, and square head (Loveland 2017, 53–54). It was not surprising that the most common type found at Fort St. Joseph was the rose head with a pointed shank end (n = 237), since this type of nail was commonly used for general construction purposes (Stone 1974b, 231). The presence of L-head and T-head nails at the site was unexpected because these types of nails are thought to have been used for more specialized purposes such as nailing finer trim boards, stairways, and flooring (LeFever 2008; Mullaley 2011). The presence of these types of nails at Fort St. Joseph indicates that the structures were not "huts" and had wooden flooring, lofts, and perhaps even two stories (Loveland 2017). The large quantity of nails and nail fragments unearthed at the site further suggests that the inhabitants were constructing permanent residential structures and using nails to firmly secure upright posts to the buildings' frames.

Architectural hardware such as hinges, pintles, hook-and-eye latches, latch bar catches, keys, keyhole escutcheons, and locks have also been found archaeologically. Several pieces of hardware have been found relating to locks and those involved in securing windows, doors, and gates. Items relating to locks include two keys, two lock fragments, and one keyhole escutcheon (Loveland 2017, 56–57). The two keys recovered were from the same one- by two-meter excavation unit near the proposed Structure 3. Based on their small size and the absence of notches on their blades, both keys may have been used in padlocks. One of the lock pieces has not been identified by type due to its fragmentary state; however, the top of the keyhole is present. The other fragment is part of a lock spring used in rim door locks. The keyhole escutcheon is a complete oval-shaped plate tapering to a point at the proximal and distal ends with the keyhole located in the center.

Hardware related to securing windows, doors, and gates include three staples, one hook and two eye latches, three iron hinge strap elements from self-contained hinges, one complete strap hinge and five fragments, and two complete pintles and three pintle fragments (Loveland 2017, 57–58; Loveland and Nassaney 2017). The staples uncovered may have been used as keepers for door-latch bolts, although they may have also been repurposed for a variety of functions (Stone 1974b, 235). The hook-and-eye latches were used to secure doors, shutters, or gates. The fragments of self-contained iron strap hinges may have been used for attaching shutters to window frames or gates to a post, as self-contained hinges were used for these purposes. The pintles would have been secured by driving or embedding the shank into the wood frame. None of the pintles require nails or screws to attach them to a frame. Based on their large size, the strap hinge and hinge fragments were probably used on doors. The complete strap hinge recovered from the site has a spear-shaped finial with nails in each of its four nail holes (Figure 4.5). The nails are bent, which may suggest that they were clinched against the back of a door that was about four cm thick.

Figure 4.5. Iron strap hinge with a spear-shaped finial attached to four hand-wrought nails that were bent to secure the hinge in place. Recovered from Fort St. Joseph. Photo by John Lacko.

Most of the iron hardware artifacts were found near or in the proposed layouts for each of the buildings (Loveland 2017, 56, 58). This somewhat uniform distribution suggests that residents of all structures identified to date chose to use elements of French-styled iron hardware. Documentary evidence compiled on the fort does not mention if these hardware items were manufactured locally or imported (Peyser 1978). However, their presence indicates that the items were manufactured or, more likely, transported to the fort at the request of the buildings' inhabitants, demonstrating the people living at the fort were actively selecting the French-style architectural hardware found in the archaeological record.

Concluding Thoughts

The architectural evidence recovered thus far derives from domestic buildings rather than barns, jails, powder magazines, and/or storehouses. The Fort St. Joseph inhabitants constructed these dwellings in accordance with their needs and cultural values. They viewed their homes as shelters and as places to sleep, conduct domestic activities, and store goods. Large quantities of calcined bone and adornment items found in association with the fireplaces of House 1, House 2, Structure 3, and Structure 5 indicate that these buildings served as habitations where people slept, cooked, and conducted other daily activities (Hearns 2015; Kerr 2012; Martin et al., chapter 3, this volume). Examination of the architectural features and artifacts found at Fort St. Joseph reveals that European-style building techniques and materials were used to construct these houses for occupants identifying as French or *métis* and their families. Architectural features (e.g., foundation walls and wooden posts) identified at the site demonstrate the use of *poteaux en terre* and *poteaux sur sole* construction methods. The types of structural materials (wood, stone, *bousillage*, glass) and architectural hardware (locks, nails, pintles, hinges, latch hooks) associated with these buildings provide evidence that European materials and construction styles were preferred by their inhabitants.

These material remains contrast markedly with the more ephemeral structures that Native Americans constructed and used in the region and reflect different cultural attitudes toward building permanency, settlement patterns, and land use practices in New France (Loveland 2017; Loveland and Nassaney 2017). While some cultural aspects (adornment and foodways) of the fort's residents may provide evidence for ethnogenesis among Native Americans and French occupants (Becker 2004; Hearns 2015; Kerr 2012), we suggest that the architectural remains at this site indicate that the occupants were retaining characteristics of their French identity through construction techniques (see Nassaney 2019). Despite the close social, political, and economic relationships between Native Americans and the European inhabitants at Fort St. Joseph, the architecture there retained a conservative aspect of French culture.

The continued use of Old World–style construction methods and materials at the fort may be explained by their practicality and functionality in meeting the needs of their inhabitants. The utility of these more permanent architectural forms is supported by a Native American's request for assistance in building a French-style structure somewhere in the vicinity of the fort (Peyser 1978, document 123, page 2, voucher 11). This request suggests that Native American peoples in this area did not know how to construct this type of building and/ or perhaps did not have an interest in learning. It also indicates that Native American peoples recognized some symbolic or utilitarian benefits of these European-style structures. The permanence, functionality, and warmth these *poteaux en terre* and *poteaux sur sole* buildings provided appealed to those who lived permanently in this region, perhaps as mobility decreased when Native Americans settled near the fort (see Hoock et al., chapter 8, this volume).

The research presented here suggests that not all aspects of identity and culture are transformed in the context of colonialism and intense cultural interaction. Some aspects, in this case architecture, remain relatively unchanged, perhaps to provide a sense of identity and ethnic pride (Mann 2008). The examination of material culture at sites throughout New France provides historical archaeologists with an opportunity to uncover the various expressions of Native American and European cultural identity. The record demonstrates that while groups may share some cultural practices in contexts of intense social and political interaction, they may retain some material expressions as they successfully coexist with each other.

Acknowledgments

This chapter stemmed from the research we performed while co-authoring the third installment in the Fort St. Joseph Archaeological Project's booklet series entitled "Sheltering New France" and further developed from Hartley's (formerly Loveland) MA thesis, "Archaeological Evidence of Architectural Remains at Fort St. Joseph (20BE23), Niles, MI." We would like to extend our sincere gratitude to the many individuals who assisted in those endeavors by providing feedback and support, including Elizabeth Scott and Doug Wilson. We would also like to thank everyone associated with the Fort St. Joseph Archaeological Project. We appreciate the professional and academic opportunities the project has provided us.

Note

1. Arthur DesJardins, "Summary Comments on Examination of 2003 Fort St. Joseph Wood Charcoal," letter report dated December 19, 2003, on file at Department of Anthropology, Western Michigan University, Kalamazoo.

5

Lead Seals from Colonial Fort St. Joseph

CATHRINE DAVIS

The fur trade was a vast social, political, and economic network that linked Old World centers of production with settlements on the periphery (Nassaney 2015). Considerable research has focused on the operation of this system, including what goods were exchanged (e.g., Allaire 1999; Dechêne 1988; Gladysz 2011; Lohse 1988; Quimby 1966), how they moved in space (e.g., Ray and Freeman 1979; Anderson 1994), how they were used (e.g., Malischke 2009; Morand 1994; White 1998; White 2012), and the types of relationships the fur trade engendered (e.g., Havard 2003; Sleeper-Smith 2001; Trigger 1986; White 2011). Documentary sources such as trade lists provide data about the goods that were produced for exchange. However, they are not always clear about the destination of the goods and the ways they were used by local consumers. Material evidence recovered from archaeological contexts provides complementary data to inform us about this aspect of the exchange.

Durable items such as ceramics, glass, gunflints, and metal tools dominate archaeological assemblages and in the past have led archaeologists to overestimate their importance in the trade. However, historical accounts and trade lists reveal that cloth was the most important trade good category by both volume and value; it accounted for 60 percent of the items by volume sent from Montreal into the *pays d'en haut* (Anderson 1994, 109–111; Dechêne 1988, 151–153, 505; White 2011, 138). Even though cloth preserves poorly, its presence is implicated by various related objects such as buttons, straight pins, needles, scissors, and lead seals. It remains for the archaeologist to interpret these remains in order to gain a better understanding of cloth and its role in New France.

Lead seals are commonly found at colonial sites in North America, albeit in smaller numbers than hand-wrought nails, glass, ceramics, and other objects used in everyday life. Still, these small finds hold important keys to unlocking a wealth of information about trade networks, consumer choice, and social identity at the places where they were ultimately deposited (see Loren and Beaudry 2006). In this chapter, I focus on the interpretive potential of the lead seals associated with Fort St. Joseph. The lead seals antiquarians collected from the vicinity of the fort that are curated in local museums complement an assemblage from known provenience recovered through recent excavations conducted under the auspices of the Fort St. Joseph Archaeological Project (Davis 2014). Many of these seals are documentary artifacts par excellence—they exhibit iconography that encodes information about varieties and quality of cloth and how it was produced and imported. I begin with a brief introduction to lead seals, then I examine the use of cloth at Fort St. Joseph and other French colonial sites and discuss how lead seals reveal connections to European merchants. A comparison of Fort St. Joseph with the nearby site of Fort Michilimackinac provides some perspective on patterns of consumption and the role cloth played at Fort St. Joseph at the height of its commercial importance.

Lead Seals: Reweaving the Past

Although lead seals are still in use as anti-pilfering devices on various cargos on trains, ships, and trucks, they are unfamiliar to most people today. Despite their small size (1–3 cm in diameter) and seeming insignificance, lead seals were relatively common in the colonial period and would have been generally recognizable. Lead seals of the seventeenth and eighteenth centuries were a new iteration of an even older tradition in the western world. As early as the Roman period (around the 1st century BCE), seals served to mark official documents and goods circulating in shipments throughout the Mediterranean world (Egan et al. 1995, 8–9; Sabatier 1912, 2–3; Still 1995, 1:26–27). They peaked in popularity in the seventeenth and eighteenth centuries, beginning as document markers and expanding to serve as customs markers and later as trademarks for textile manufacturers (Still 1995, 28–30).

Seventeenth- and eighteenth-century lead seals are found archaeologically in France, England, Spain, the Netherlands, Germany, Russia, and other European countries and former European colonies (Egan 1995, 18; Sabatier 1912, 444–486). Seals recovered from North American sites have received particular attention in the past half-century due to their connection with colonial economic activity, especially the fur trade. Their appearance in the archaeological literature is widespread because they appear at a variety of English, French, Dutch, and Spanish colonial sites (e.g., Bense 2003; Baart 2005; Stone 1974b; for lists of other sites where lead seals have been found, see Adams 1989, 38; Kent 2001, 943–944).

Although the most intensive studies of lead seals have been conducted by Europeans (e.g., Egan et al. 1995; Sabatier 1912), many North Americans have included them in site reports and typological analyses (Hulse 1977; Noble 1983; Stone 1974b). They have also been the focus of specialized studies (Adams 1989; Baart 2005). Diane Adams's MA thesis (1987) is perhaps the most notable study devoted to lead seals on French North American sites. She examined lead seals from Fort Michilimackinac and related them to various cloth types. Her study helped clarify the use of lead seals; she argued that not all lead seals are "bale seals" used to package or mark bundles of trade goods. Furthermore, many seals hold significant clues about the nature of colonial cloth at trade-related sites. Since Fort St. Joseph was once a major hub in the fur trade of the western Great Lakes region, the analysis of lead seals from the site contributes to our understanding of cloth circulation in the Atlantic world.

Fort St. Joseph and Beyond: Commerce, Cloth, and Culture in the Atlantic World

Fort St. Joseph was ideally situated to act as a commercial hub in the western Great Lakes region. In a world where the main transportation corridors were waterways, it was at the juncture of several strategic routes. The St. Joseph River connected to Lake Michigan in the west and other tributaries to the east and crossed preexisting Native American trails, including the Great Sauk Trail (modern-day Old Route 12, which runs from Detroit to Chicago). The fort was also located near the portage to the Kankakee River, which eventually joins the Mississippi (Nassaney et al. 2003, 107; Nassaney 2015, 167). This placed the fort at the intersection of trade routes leading from the St. Lawrence River Valley, the nucleus of French colonization in North America, to as far away as Louisiana. Trading posts such as Fort St. Joseph were thus part of a grand trade network that not only spanned North America but also connected the interior of the continent to Europe and the larger Atlantic world (Figure 5.1).

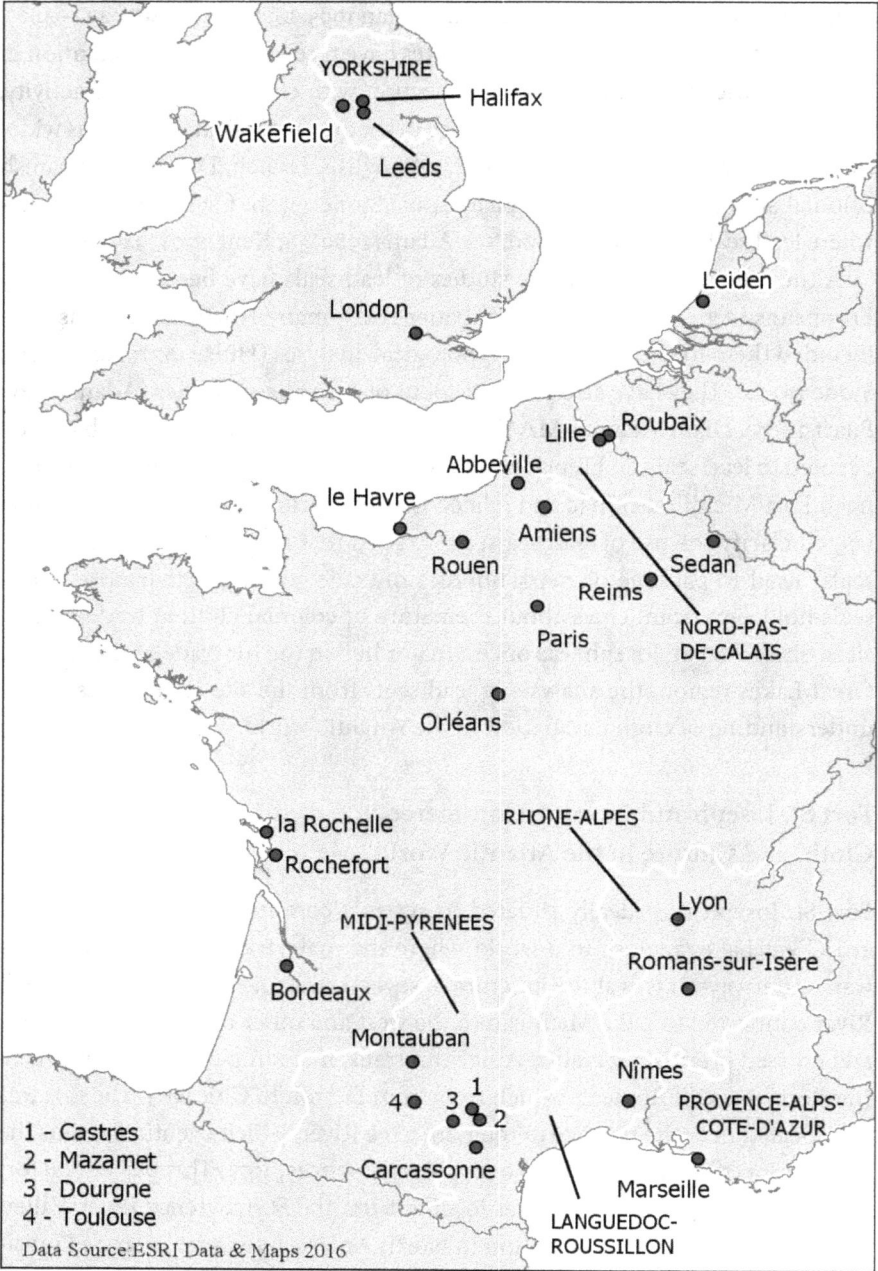

YORKSHIRE

Halifax

Wakefield

Leeds

Leiden

London

Lille

Roubaix

Abbeville

le Havre

Amiens

Sedan

Rouen

Reims

NORD-PAS-DE-CALAIS

Paris

Orléans

RHONE-ALPES

la Rochelle

Rochefort

Lyon

MIDI-PYRENEES

Romans-sur-Isère

Bordeaux

Montauban

Nîmes

4 3 1
   2

PROVENCE-ALPS-COTE-D'AZUR

1 - Castres
2 - Mazamet
3 - Dourgne
4 - Toulouse

Carcassonne

Marseille

LANGUEDOC-ROUSSILLON

Data Source:ESRI Data & Maps 2016

Figure 5.1. Cloth production centers in England and France that linked Europe to overseas colonies in the Atlantic World. Map by Jason Glatz.

The fur trade was far more than a commercial and economic system. Far from the metropolitan areas of Québec and Montreal, economic interaction led to complex exchanges of material culture, ideas, and spouses between Native Americans and the French. The fur trade was the "middle ground," a point of convergence whereby strangers and elements of their material culture were integrated into existing social, cultural, and economic networks (White 2011). Europeans and European goods were evaluated and assigned positions in the Native American worldview through the processes of intermarriage, gift giving, alliances, wars, and other interactions (Nassaney 2015, 11; White 1998; Witgen 2012). Native American settlements thus became the western reach of European trade networks. Their dominance of the territory figured into European political decisions and elements of their culture and society were exported, examined, and imitated by European writers, ballerinas, and artists (Cangany 2012; Delâge 1992, 38–39).

This cautious integration was born out of practicality, expediency, or convenience rather than a desire to imitate the other for altruistic or ideological reasons (Nassaney 2015, 33–34, 101; Nassaney 2019; Nassaney, chapter 10, this volume). When practical or timesaving European objects were available for a reasonable price, Native Americans adopted them. If they were too expensive, of low quality, or not easily accessible, Native Americans simply reverted to or continued to use traditional objects or technologies (White 1998, 123). Likewise, the French adopted Native American clothing elements such as moccasins or *mitasses* (woolen or hide thigh-high leggings) because they were practical for navigating rugged and wooded North American landscapes, the same reason that birch bark canoes became the preferred mode of transportation for delivering cloth to consumers.

The practical use and reuse of objects is reflected in the artifacts recovered from Fort St. Joseph and other sites in New France (see Giordano and Nassaney, chapter 6, this volume; Morand 1994). At Fort St. Joseph and elsewhere, worn copper kettles were cut apart and shaped into tinkling cones and other useful objects (Bradley 1987a; Nassaney 2015, 188), musket barrels were flattened into hide scrapers (Nassaney and Martin 2017, Figure 4.4), and silver trade objects were cut into smaller ornaments (Nassaney 2015, 176). Cloth was not exempt from this material manifestation of cultural convergence: many accounts note that Native American groups present in the *pays d'en haut* and the Northeast were avid consumers of European textiles and used them to create clothing that was consistent with the style of their traditional garments (Bougainville 2003, 93; Duplessis 2015, 105; Pouchot 2003, 263–268).

Native Americans used European cloth as much for its aesthetic appeal as for its versatility and practicality (DuPlessis 2015, 48–49; Havard 2003, 570–571; Nassaney 2015, 99–100; White 1998, 123). Compared to the skins and plaited plant fibers that were still largely in use at the time of first contact (DuPlessis 2015, 47–48), European textiles were faster to dry and easier to sew (Anderson 1994, 111; DuPlessis 2015, 99). Once the amount of time required to sew clothing for other members of the tribe was reduced, women could reallocate their labor to preparing pelts and skins and doing other tasks (Anderson 1994, 111).

Even in areas of greater French influence farther south in Upper and Lower Louisiana, where many Native Americans were dressing in more "Frenchified" styles, including *mantelets* (jackets) and petticoats, many traditional elements of Native American apparel were translated into the medium of European cloth and incorporated into everyday dress (White 2012, 62–63,70–71, 74). As Diana DiPaolo Loren (2009, 115–116) has noted, Natchez and Tunica sites show evidence that these groups incorporated recycled trim from European manufactured garments into indigenous-style clothing. In addition, burial sites from these tribes have yielded evidence for the adoption of European-style frock coats, a practice also observed in Michigan (Brown 1971b, 132; Loren 2009, 117; Loren 2010, 85; Mainfort 1985, 562–565). This suggests that across regions, tribes were using European cloth and clothing styles in traditional ways, adopting cloth for its practicality and workability, imbuing it with new meanings and values, and using it to facilitate social interactions with Europeans (Anderson 1994, 111; Loren 2009, 115; 120; Loren 2010, 85).

Europeans also altered their appearance to express attachment to social groups. They relied on dress styles adapted to the physical and social geography of North America. *Voyageurs*, militia, and even *canadien* officers used breechcloths (*brayets*) and leggings (*mitasses*) to integrate themselves into the Native American world or elicit the support of indigenous allies.

In addition to using European cloth in Native American styles, colonists used cloth in familiar ways. Since only 5 percent of the cloth that left Montreal in the period 1650 to 1720 was produced in New France, French Canadians relied on imported European cloth (Dechêne 1988, 151–152). At Fort St. Joseph, European colonists likely purchased cloth to create traditional European styles, which they then used as a marker of social status. However, it is equally likely that sumptuary laws were less rigidly followed in New France and that class divisions in dress were less apparent than in France. Departures from the prescribed dress codes and consumption patterns in colonial contexts are expressed archaeologically (e.g., lead seals) and have been noted by modern scholars and contemporary eyewitnesses alike (Loren 2001; Séguin 1967, 114–116). This relaxation of rules can be attributed to the difficulty of effectively regulating an expanding colonial territory in a world before communication was expedient (Hodson and Rushforth 2010, 103–105). The spatially expansive Atlantic territories that France possessed were not conducive to control via a highly centralized and localized source of power. Indeed, "the most important limitation on absolutism was not theoretical but practical" (Beik 2000, 4). In a colonial world where governments struggled to enforce regulations, the rules of fashion may have been regularly bent by individuals of various social classes and economic positions for a wide variety of reasons that have largely been lost to time.

Generally, the patterns of consumption of imported cloth among the denizens of New France in the St. Lawrence Valley varied between the urban and the rural; the elite, the middling class, and the working class; and among men, women, and children (DuPlessis 2009, 234, 238; DuPlessis 2015, 219–220). Residents of urban areas consumed more silks, cottons, and finer woolens and linens, while those in more rural, agricultural areas opted for less expensive goods, including basic-quality woolens, linens, and occasionally *toile du pays* and *étoffe du pays* (domestically produced rough linen and woolens of low quality) (DuPlessis 2015, 218–220). Colonists in the western Great Lakes region may also have followed these trends. Lower- and middle-class inhabitants of Fort St. Joseph who came from rural communities in the St. Lawrence River Valley would likely have continued to use the basic woolen and linen clothing and dress styles that were convenient, comfortable, and practical for working. Upper-class individuals may have used more expensive fabrics reserved for elites to distinguish themselves from working-class colonists in accordance with European custom (Loren 2010, 27–28, 48). The fact that various groups may have been present in the population at Fort St. Joseph make it a challenge to isolate who was using what cloths to dress in which fashions, and although trade lists can provide information about what is being transported to Fort St. Joseph and other posts in the region, they generally do not specify what goods were destined for which consumers. Future household archaeology at the Fort St. Joseph site and the associations of lead seals with various structures there could elucidate ties between identified cloth and specific consumers, as could continued research at other French and Native American sites.

Extant Trade Lists

Despite the importance of cloth in the fur trade, the only known trade lists from Fort St. Joseph that mention textiles date to 1694, 1739, and 1740 (Idle 2001, 16; Peyser 1978, documents 86, 88, 89, 101, 104, 123). The 1694 trade list shows the importance of cloth even in the early days of the post; it includes three lace-trimmed jackets, three pairs of breeches, and two sails among other nontextile goods bound for the Miamis (Idle 2001, 16). Another shipment to the Miamis from the same year lists six pairs of stockings, nine chemises, and a *capot* (Idle 2001, 16). Among the goods enumerated in 1739 are 2 cloth blankets, 2 ½ ells of *toile de Lyon*, along with 5 ells and 2 ½ ells of two other simply listed "cloths" (Peyser 1978, document 86).

The 1739 record notes that two blankets were being sent to the fort for use in the burial of an Ottawa chief (Peyser 1978, document 88). The use of new blankets in Native American burials is also possibly shown in the discovery of a lead seal in a mortuary context at a Tunica cemetery in Louisiana dating to the French regime. However, Brain notes that it was "not definitely associated with the burial," since it appeared to have been deposited with the soil used to fill the grave (Brain 1988, 172–173, 410). Because the seal was "unmarked" and was interpreted as a bale seal, its function as a possible textile marker does not appear to have been considered (Brain 1988, 410). Its position at the foot of an individual burial is thought provoking nonetheless, since any given textile seal would have been attached to the extremity of a new blanket or piece of cloth (Waselkov 1991, 346). Other sources attest to the use of European textiles in Native American mortuary contexts and lend support to the hypothesis that this seal may have marked a new blanket included in the burial Brain mentioned (Nassaney 2015, 100–101).

Lists from 1739 and 1740 show the presence of both pre-made clothing items and blankets, including leggings, chemises, women's chemises, a breechcloth, a blue blanket, and a four-point blanket (Peyser 1978, documents 89, 101, 104, 123). These lists distinguish women's chemises from those for men, which suggests that these shirts may have been intended for use by women dressing in a European style at the fort, since period accounts mention that Native American men and women wore chemises of the same cut and style (Bougainville 2003, 93; Pouchot 2003, 264–265). The blankets may have been for Native American use as part of everyday dress either as material for *machicotés* (wrap skirts) or as blanket wraps, although the largest point blankets mentioned as apparel by Pierre Pouchot had only three points (2003, 276). Because of the intensity of cross-cultural influence on the colonial frontier, these trade lists do not allow us to attribute particular cloth types to specific consumers, but they provide other valuable insights into the quantity and origins of textiles destined for the site. When these data are considered in conjunction with material evidence, a picture emerges of the role of cloth in everyday life.

Textiles and the Economy in Eighteenth-Century France and New France

Mercantilism, Cloth, and the French Economy

Cloth played an important role in the French colonial experience and the relationship between France and her colonies. The purpose of a colony was to enrich the mother country not only by providing natural resources but also by consuming finished goods. New France fulfilled this latter role almost too well. Since the time of Jean-Baptiste Colbert and Jean Talon in the third quarter of the seventeenth century, there had been efforts to establish and maintain manufactories in the colony, including the iron works at Forges de Saint-Maurice and experiments in textile production elsewhere (Jean and Proulx 1995, 93–95; Kent 2001, 663). These attempts were designed to encourage some degree of self-sufficiency and decrease the burden of supplying a colony in constant need. Colbert even mentioned in a letter to Talon that "one of the greatest needs of Canada is to establish there manufactures, and to attract there the artisans for the things of everyday use; up till now it has been necessary to take to that country the cloth to clothe the inhabitants and even the shoes for them to wear" (Cole 1964b, 78). However, many manufacturing initiatives ultimately failed.

French cloth producers met the needs of the entire nation, its colonies, and foreign consumers. In the seventeenth and eighteenth centuries, mercantilism was the predominant economic system in France and in the rest of Europe. Mercantilism, which was both economically and politically aggressive, emphasized the accumulation of capital, especially in the form of precious metals such as gold and silver (Cole 1964a, 3). The collection of specie, sometimes referred to as bullionism (Cole 1964a, 337), was essential to the mercantilist mindset because precious metals were thought to exist in only a finite amount (Minard 1998, 15). By accumulating wealth, a nation could undertake internal improvements and innovations and would be able consequently to fortify its military strength (Cole 1964a, 3). Rivals that possessed lesser wealth would be unable to compete with nations of greater economic and military power.

Since mercantilism put such a heavy emphasis on material wealth, it follows that dominance in international trade would be the main goal of any given European country. Here, we see the true value of textiles. Textiles had been among the most demanded, common, and costly commodities on the European market for centuries (De Vries 1976, 98; Lemire 2009, 211–212). A country that could produce higher-quality textiles than its rivals had a competitive advantage (Cole 1964a, 9). Domestic manufacturing theoretically kept the circulation of gold and silver currency within a country: creating and selling high-quality goods to locals would prevent them from purchasing lower-quality foreign products and would stimulate the local economy (Cole 1964a, 9, 117).

Mercantilist inspections and quality standards were in place for many different products throughout Europe, and many countries installed inspection systems for textiles on a local level, as evidenced by the existence of cloth halls such as the Lakenhal in Leiden or the Piece Hall in Halifax (Yorkshire).[1] However, the obsession with state control and regulation of the textile industry was greatest in France, where that industry had been steadily growing since the fifteenth century (Cole 1964a, 3). The financial ministers of Louis XIV worked to create and perfect a more intense variant of mercantilism, culminating in a system known as Colbertism (after the financial minister Colbert) (Minard 1998, 15). This system was put in place both to protect consumers from faulty products and to attempt to establish a nearly self-sufficient France. As Colbert thought, "it is always very advantageous for the state to make within the kingdom the goods that come from outside" (Cole 1964a, 348).

Textile Production, Inspection, and Sealing

Cloth production in early modern France was a combination of a cottage and a guild industry, nearly unchanged from the medieval period. Textile merchants had little control over the supply of finished cloth. A merchant might invest in the raw material to produce a piece, but spinners, weavers, dyers, and fullers worked on their own time and controlled the knowledge needed to produce the fabric the merchant had commissioned (Conseil d'État de la France 1754, 5–6; De Vries 1976, 105–106). Cloth makers probably stitched their marks or names into the selvedges (finished ends, also known as lists) of the pieces they created (Sabatier 1912, 212). In some cases, cloth was produced in hospitals run by religious orders, just as monks produced beer as a way of earning money to support their abbeys. Often these hospitals functioned in a way that was similar to English poorhouses; it was believed that the poor could benefit both themselves and the state economy by working to produce various commodities (Cole 1964a, 264, 275). Since textiles were supposed to conform to various government standards, state officials sometimes seized incorrectly manufactured or low-quality cloth and fined the associated cloth merchants, producers, and even cloth inspectors (Conseil d'État de la France 1743, 1–4). Several levels of inspection were instituted to ensure quality control.

Once a piece was completed, the inspections began. The first stop for newly produced textiles was the *bureau de visite*.[2] These offices existed in most cloth-producing towns in France and were put in place by the cloth makers of a community (usually together as a guild) in order to protect themselves against charges that the textiles they produced were of poor quality. *Guardes jurés*, locally elected "sworn guards," inspected and marked pieces with lead seals. Once a piece had passed this inspection, the producer would pay a fee of one sol per piece and it would be sealed with the mark (lead seal) of the office, indicating that the piece had met the standards in place.[3] The work of the *guardes jurés* was in turn inspected by government-appointed regional inspectors, the *commis aux manufactures*. These inspectors were there to enforce government regulations during and after production and to prevent corruption in the trade (Minard 1998, 20–21, 23).

Next would be the *bureau de contrôle*, which inspected textiles bound for sale or consumption outside the town of production. The merchants of a region and their *guardes jurés* ran the *bureaux de contrôle*, much in the same way that the makers ran the *bureaux de visite*. The *bureaux de contrôle* were often located at fairs, markets, or cloth halls in a town (Minard 1998, 21). A 1730 act listed Abbeville, Amiens, Carcassonne, du Mans, Montauban, Nîmes, Paris, Reims, Romans, Rouen, and Sedan (see Figure 5.1) as towns that had a *bureau de contrôle* (Conseil d'État de la France 1730, 5). The act also indicated that cloth distributed in or outside France and originating from towns that did not have a *bureau de contrôle* or *de visite* had to be brought to one of those towns to be

> seen, visited (inspected), and marked with the leads (seals) of Controlle of the aforementioned offices, if they are found to be made, dyed, and prepared in conformity with the Standards: His Majesty wishes, that the aforementioned cloths be then packaged in these same Offices, & the bales corded and sealed with the same seal; so that the aforementioned bales will be exempt from inspections of the Bureaux de Controlle along their route, & will be able to go freely to their destination without being subjected to inspections other than those of the seal of Controlle. (Conseil d'État de France 1730, 5)[4]

In this act, the *Bureaux de Marchands Drapiers & Merciers* (Office of Cloth Merchants and Haberdashers) were the officials acting as the *bureaux de contrôle*.

Cloth entering a town for sale from elsewhere in France or from outside the country was often inspected by yet another office, the *bureau foraine* (MacDonald 2012, 8; Sabatier 1912, 326). Cloth entering and exiting the country would also be put through customs (*douanes*) inspections before reaching the *bureau foraine* of a given town. The word *forain* today often describes activities related to fairs (or markets), but at the time it would have been used to mean "foreign" (Académie Française 1694, 473). When the words *forain(e)* or *étrangèr(e)* were used, they often applied to goods coming from elsewhere in France at a time when the country was divided between an area known as the Cinq Grosses Fermes (a union of thirteen northern provinces formed in 1664) and the *provinces reputées étrangères* (areas of France proper that were not included in the Cinq Grosses Fermes) (Cole 1964a, 416–417; Minard 1998, 17).

At each of these inspection offices and customs offices, a piece of cloth and the seals previously attached to it would be verified and a new seal would be attached to signify that the piece had passed inspection at that office. Thus, it was common for a piece to have multiple seals attached to its selvedge, depending on the rigor and frequency of the inspections. Textiles bound for the colonies or other European nations would travel through the markets of France and through the gauntlet of bureaucratic inspection and customs offices until they were finally purchased by a merchant or trading company for sale abroad. This would begin the next step in the long voyage of textiles bound for New France.

Native American Preferences and the Influence
of Indigenous Consumers on Cloth

The production and inspection of cloth in Europe, particularly in France, was
greatly influenced by Native American demand. Many period accounts mention Native American preferences in some detail and testify to their shrewdness and selectivity. In his *Mémoire sur l'État de la Nouvelle-France* (1757),
Louis-Antoine de Bougainville noted:

> The Compagnie des Indes gives Native Americans blankets for [the men
> and] their wives, and *machicotés* in red and blue woolens with black
> bands; [the compagnie] is obligated to [obtain] these from English man-
> ufactures; [it] wanted to take those from Carcassonne, but the natives did
> not want them. It is not because the woolens [from Carcassonne] are not
> better and are not also as beautifully colored, but we can still not make
> bands in a nice black there; in general our merchandise is worth more for
> the quality than those of the English, but the natives prefer theirs; they
> better capture their tastes. (Bougainville 2003, 89)[5]

Bougainville also mentions the woolen manufactures of Carcassonne earlier
in his description, stating that the producers there should "work to make red
and blue woolens to attract that branch of commerce that we carry out in Canada, supplying blankets to the natives" (2003, 83).[6] Throughout much of the
eighteenth century, producers in Carcassonne attempted to produce imitation
écarlatines to compete with the popular English variety (Havard 2003, 569).
Meanwhile, as Bougainville mentions, the Compagnie des Indes defied French
policies of economic protectionism by importing the English variety to fulfill
Native American demands (Innis 2001, 86). Other archival sources attest to the
constant temptation English textiles, particularly woolens, posed both to Native
Americans and French colonists, but this attraction appears to have been fueled
by the lower prices offered at Albany as much as by differences in quality.[7]

While the availability of certain colors strongly influenced trade decisions,
quality and price were also of great concern to Native Americans. A close study
of Native American relations with the Hudson's Bay Company reveals that at
times, indigenous consumers would seek French traders and textiles because
the quality and the price was better; sometimes they even brought examples
they had purchased of these superior goods to British posts so they could show
traders what they desired (Ray and Freeman 1979, 226–227). If they were not

impressed with the quality of goods traders offered, they would often refuse to trade for them (Ray and Freeman 1979, 226), especially if they knew better-quality goods or prices were available elsewhere. Bégon (the intendant of New France from 1712 to 1726) mentions an extreme example of informed consumerism (quoted in Havard 2003, 569):

> It is important that these pieces of [British] *écarlatine*, in equal regards to the color as to the quality, should be so well imitated so that one cannot tell the difference because the natives are so refined that they know the quality of cloth as well as the most experienced *négociants* [merchants], [taking] enough care to burn the hair [nap] of a sample in order to see the weave.[8]

In a world where trade helped maintain alliances between empires, one can argue that cloth was literally the fabric of diplomacy and that its production was of key importance in maintaining colonial possessions and relations in North America.

Lead Seals Recovered from Fort St. Joseph

To explore the ways that cloth was implicated in the Atlantic trade at Fort St. Joseph, I conducted an analysis of sixty-six lead seals and seal fragments from the site in the collections of two separate institutions in the Michiana region (Davis 2014).[9] Forty-three of these seals and fragments are housed and curated at the Fort St. Joseph Museum in Niles, Michigan. Of these, seventeen were recovered in the archaeological excavations conducted under the auspices of the Fort St. Joseph Archaeological Project. The others were recovered from the site and its environs by local collectors beginning in the early twentieth century and were later donated to the museum (Hulse 1977, 15–16). Although Hulse (1977, 55) mentions and describes thirty-one seals in his inventory of artifacts from Fort St. Joseph, only twenty-six were accessible for study, largely because they were included in temporary exhibitions elsewhere or were on loan (Davis 2014, 21). The History Museum (formerly the Center for History) in South Bend, Indiana, houses the other twenty-three seals included in my study. These seals were acquired in the 1990s from a collector along with many other eighteenth-century artifacts from the fort site (Davis 2014, 21). In the discussion that follows, the seals from the Fort St. Joseph Museum will be identified using the letters I assigned them in my previous work (Davis 2014) or by accession number when possible; these numbers begin with "FSJ." Those from The History Museum (THM) will be identified by letters assigned within the group catalog number (94.3.317).

Classifying Lead Seals

Although today's plastic and paper price tags are easily removed, lead seals were not so easily attached and detached. There are a few attachment styles with varying usage among different cultures and geographical locations. These various attachment styles fall under three main types (Stone 1974b, 281; see also Sabatier 1912, 7–13).

Series A seals, or "*sceaux à plateau*" (Sabatier 1912, 8–9), consist of two flat plates of the same size, one with a projection (knob) and the other with a hole (loop), connected by a thin strip of lead (a flange) (Figure 5.2). To attach these

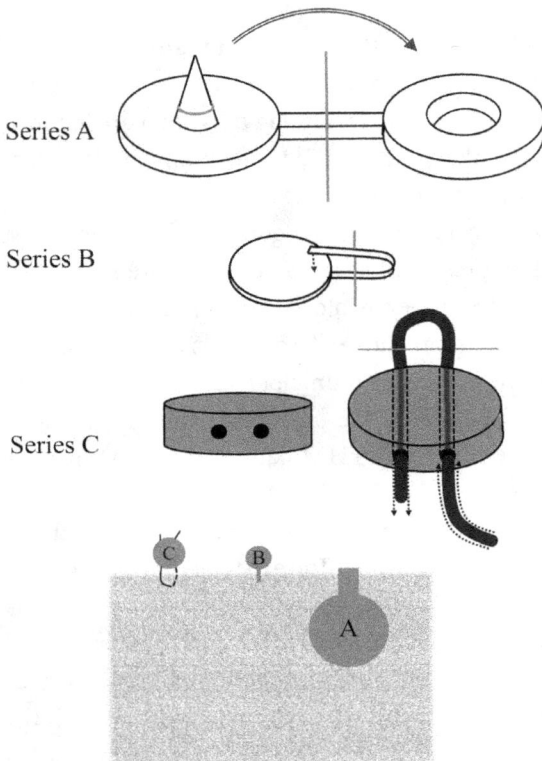

Figure 5.2. Attachment styles for lead seals. Drawing by Cathrine Davis.

seals to cloth, the knob would be forced through the fabric, possibly damaging the area of attachment, and the plate with the loop would be bent to align with it before the two plates were hammered together (Sabatier 1912, 7–8).

The other two types of seals are less common. The rarest are series B seals, which have only one plate and are closed by pressing the end of a long flange back onto the plate. These are often identified as bag seals (Figure 5.2). Series C seals, or "*sceaux à tunnel*" (Sabatier 1912, 7), consist of a single, thick disk of lead with one or more tunnels running through it. A wire or thread is passed through the tunnels and through the textile and the disk is pressed or hammered closed, collapsing the tunnels and securing the thread inside the seal (Figure 5.2). Every seal has an obverse (front) side and a reverse (back) side. In my work, I assume that the obverse side of a seal is the side that shows the flattened plug within the looped plate and that the reverse side is completely flat, consisting of the backside of the plate with the knob.

French Seals at Fort St. Joseph

Of the sixty-six seals that I examined, twenty-five (37 percent) are of French origin, two (3 percent) are British, and thirty-nine (60 percent) are of unknown origin. The dominance of French seals at the site among those that are identifiable is likely a result of the closed colonial trade and protectionist policies that France maintained with its North American colonies (DuPlessis 2015, 57), and the presence of predominantly French residents and goods at the site for most of the occupation. Prominently represented in the assemblage are seals from southern France, especially those from the town of Mazamet (Table 5.1). Seals from Mazamet generally exhibit the impression of a *coq gaulois* (Gallic rooster) on the obverse side, a symbol present in the municipal coat of arms. Two of these seals appear to have originated from the *bureau de contrôle* of Mazamet. Two seals from The History Museum (THM 94.3.317 K, THM 94.3.317 A) are marked "DE / [C]ONTROLL / DE / [M]AZAMET / 174[8]" (Figure 5.3).[10] These indicate that cloth was produced in or around Mazamet and was approved for sale by the local *bureau de contrôle*. The existence of this seal suggests that Mazamet was an important enough producer of cloth that it had its own *bureau de contrôle* in 1748, eliminating the need for cloth to be transported to nearby Carcassonne, Montauban, or Nîmes for inspection. The reverse face of seal THM 94.3.317 K suggests that this seal was used in inspection with the phrase "PVLCH au MAZAMET." The word "pulch," which is probably rooted

Table 5.1. Frequency of French lead seals from Fort St. Joseph and Fort Michilimackinac by place of origin (region, production center, or trading company)

	Fort St. Joseph[a]		Fort Michilimackinac[b]	
	N	%	N	%
Languedoc Region	9	36	39	35
Carcassonne	2	8	1	1
Mazamet	4	16	12	11
Montauban	3	12	6	5
Nîmes	0	0	20	18
Nord Pas-de-Calais Region	2	8	1	1
Lille	2	8	0	0
Roubaix	0	0	1	1
Rhône-Alpes Region	0	0	2	2
Lyon	0	0	2	2
Compagnie des Indes	3	12	26	23
French seals of unknown origin	11	44	46	41
Total French seals	25	100	113	100

[a] Updated from Davis (2014, 66).
[b] Adams (1989).

in the Latin adjective "*pulcher*," or "excellent, fine," suggests that it was meant to convey information about the quality of the cloth.[11]

The main product of Mazamet was *mazamet*, which may have either been a type of *molleton* or a *cordelat* that was named after the town (Peuchet 1799, 646). *Molletons* are very heavy, thick woolens with a short nap (a layer of fuzz worked up by brushing the woven fabric) over a distinctive diagonal twill weave (Kent 2001, 663; Savary des Bruslons 1732b, 757; Tichenor 2002, 31). *Cordelats* are similar but are described as lesser-quality woolens (Savary des Bruslons 1732a, 1505). In 1742, 889 yards of *molleton* were shipped to Fort St.

Figure 5.3. Lead seals from Mazamet: *top*, 94.3.317 A; *bottom*, 94.3.317 K. Drawing by Cathrine Davis. Courtesy of The History Museum, South Bend, Indiana.

Joseph (Kent 2001, 663). It is possible that some of these *molletons* were of the *mazamet* variety. This 1742 mention also supports the lead seal evidence because both attest to the presence of a large amount of woolen cloth at Fort St. Joseph from Mazamet and elsewhere. The other two seals from Mazamet are marked for the *bureau de visite* and the *bureau foraine* in Mazamet, respectively (FSJ seals G and F) (not shown). The mark of the *bureau de visite* of Mazamet would have probably been applied to cloth produced in Mazamet, while the mark of the *bureau foraine/ bureau de visite foraine* would have been attached to goods coming from places outside Mazamet, possibly from other French provinces or from other towns and cities in Languedoc such as Castres, Dourgne, or Montauban (Cazals 1992, 166–167). These towns all produced significant amounts of woolens. While *mazamet* had a reputation for being of a high quality (Cazals 1992, 165), woolens of lesser quality from Languedoc are represented in sources that document imports to Fort St. Joseph in 1742, notably *dourgne* (282 yards [Kent 2001, 664]) and *cadis* (an unknown quantity [Kent 2001, 665]). *Mazamet* had a variety of uses, including as material for *capotes* (Kent 2001, 569–570), for the *veste* (waistcoat) of French marine uniforms that were sometimes produced locally in the Illinois country (Gallup and Shaffer 1992, 61, 74), and as a high-quality woolen that was likely exchanged with Native Americans.

Two other seals from Fort St. Joseph are from a *bureau foraine* but come from the town of Lille in northern France. One is Seal A in the Fort St. Joseph Museum and the other was recovered in excavation (MacDonald 2012, 8; Sabatier 1908, 10; Sabatier 1912, 254, plates 11 and 12, no. 183). Lille was one of the main arteries through which foreign textiles came into France, particularly from neighboring Spanish Flanders and the Netherlands, which imported Italian and Spanish goods (Cole 1964a, 369–370; MacDonald 2012, 8). Lille was also a major exporter of French textiles produced in the surrounding region and from more distant production centers such as Paris and Rouen (Cole 1964a, 369–370). Germany and Belgium, especially the towns of Strasbourg and Tournai (in modern Belgium), received a significant quantity of textiles from Lille (Cole 1964a, 369–370). Since Lille was a hub for international trade, the *bureau foraine* in that town would have marked many different types of textiles of various origins, making it difficult to link these seals to any specific cloth. These seals all have a double knob attachment style: they have two plugs and two holes but only one plate (Series A Type II), a characteristic that Sabatier attributes both to foreign seals and to those from northern France (1908, 11, 1912, 9).

Fort St. Joseph has yielded several seals associated with the Compagnie des Indes (CDI), the French Company of the Indies. Two designs the CDI used that are found at Fort St. Joseph feature the company's arms on the reverse (Figure 5.4). It should be noted that although several iterations of the Compagnie des Indes Occidentales were in existence throughout history, the version on these seals is the company that John Law established in 1717 (Sabatier 1908, 387; Vidal and Havard 2008, 130).

Though both versions of the CDI seal feature this crest on the reverse side, the obverse sides are quite different. One (THM seal 94.3.317 M; FSJ seal Y) shows a wreath of laurels encircling the company's initials with a symbol that resembles two C's back to back under the initials. This design is surrounded by a very prominent beaded *grenètis*.[12] The other design (THM seal 94.3.317 W) includes a tear-shaped crest with a striped field and three fleurs-de-lys inside an elaborate crowned frame. The center crest is surrounded by a corded *gre-*

Figure 5.4. Lead seals of the Compagnie des Indes: *top*, THM 94.3.317 W; *bottom*, THM 94.3.317 M. Drawing by Cathrine Davis. Courtesy of The History Museum, South Bend, Indiana.

nètis and fragments of the company motto, "*florebo quocumque ferar*," which is best translated from Latin as "I flower wherever planted" (Figure 5.4). It is important to note that on the reverse side of these seals, the company coat of arms is flanked by two Native American figures. Sabatier hypothesizes that this latter seal type might date from after 1749, as indicated by the font style and an *arrêt* (court order) that mandated a design change in 1748–1749 (Sabatier 1908, 403–406). The other seals of the company must postdate 1717 and predate 1769, the end of the company's charter (Sabatier 1908, 391). As previously discussed, the CDI was the only organization the French government allowed to import British *écarlatines*, which were reserved exclusively for use in the fur trade (Dechêne 1988, 153). However, the CDI may also have supplied posts with various patterned and plain cottons or muslins, though *indiennes* (printed cottons) remained restricted until after 1759 (Sabatier 1908, 390). These materials would have been likely used by French inhabitants of the fort or by their partners in trade as material for chemises, *machicotés*, and European-style elements of dress for men and women (DuPlessis 2009, 233–235; DuPlessis 2015, 115, 120–122). These series C seals would probably have been used in conjunction with stamped parchment tags, as mandated in company documents (Sabatier 1908, 390–396).

It is worth noting that the seal of the city of Nîmes is often misidentified as a seal of the CDI (Hume 1969, 269–270; Kent 2001, 941). This is best shown in examples from Fort Michilimackinac (Adams 1989, 42; Stone 1974, 292). The seal of Nîmes includes a crocodile chained to a palm tree, surrounded by the letters "COL NEM." Though at first one of these appears to be an abbreviation for the Compagnie des Indes (if mistakenly read as "CDI ND"), it is actually part of the crocodile and palm motif that the Romans who first colonized the Nîmes area used (Maucomble 1767, 90; Ménard 1856, 9; Sabatier 1912, 254–255). The abbreviation COL NEM is short for the Roman name for Nîmes, Colonia Nemausensis (Adams 1989, 42).

Carcassonne, like Mazamet and Montauban, is also situated in the belt of woolen-producing centers in southern France. The seals from Fort St. Joseph that come from Carcassonne (FSJ seals H and I) show fragments of the phrase "FABRIQUE DE CARCASSONNE" and "DRAP." The use of the word "*drap*" identifies this seal as a mark used on bolts of broadcloth manufactured in Carcassonne. Bougainville's writings seem to support the idea that these seals could have marked imitation British-style *écarlatines* created in Carcassonne for the North American market. However, since Bougainville wrote about the importation of British *écarlatines* in 1757, it seems unlikely that fort residents would have imported these woolens from Carcassonne. The manufacturers there would have had only one year to improve their textiles and successfully export them to Michigan before French supply lines were severed when the British captured Fort Frontenac in 1758. Thus, these earlier French woolens may have been less prized by Native Americans at the fort (Anderson 2001, 262).

At least one seal from Fort St. Joseph is traceable to a French merchant family. Seal THM 94.3.317 Q reads "MARI[E]TTE NÉG[OCIAN]T[S] MO[NTAUBAN]" (Figure 5.5). Other seals of the Mariette family, a prominent dynasty of merchants in the city of Montauban, also appear at Fort Ticonderoga (formerly Fort Carillon) and Fort Ouiatenon (Calver and Bolton 1950, 272–273; Noble 1983, 271). Because several generations of the Mariette family were involved in the Canada trade (Bosher 1987, 42, 100, 128, 181), some change in design occurred over time. On the seal from Fort Ticonderoga (Calver

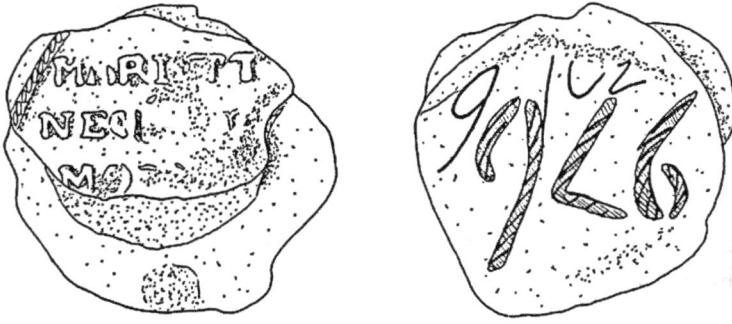

Figure 5.5. Lead seal (THM 94.3.317 Q) related to the Mariette family found at Fort St. Joseph. Drawing by Cathrine Davis. Courtesy of The History Museum, South Bend, Indiana.

and Bolton 1950, 272–273), a fragment of the name "Dumas" is evidence of a partnership between the Dumas and Mariette families, both of Montauban (Bosher 1987, 42; Jean and Proulx 1995, 146). Any seals related to the Mariette family must predate April 1760, when the family declared bankruptcy after the French lost Québec to the British (Bosher 1987, 198). The relation between different impressions on lead seals from Fort Ticonderoga also enables us to identify at least one product the Mariette family shipped to New France. The mark of the Mariette family is found on the opposite side of the seal from the mark of the Hôpital Saint-Joseph de la Grave, a hospital in Toulouse (a major town near Montauban).[13] This hospital mark is found on the obverse of a seal marked "MANUFACTURE DE COUVERTURES DE TOULOUSE" (Calver and Bolton 1950, 272–273). Several other seals from the site reinforce these relationships. In the late seventeenth and early eighteenth centuries, the manufacturing that was done in hospitals was also subject to the control of mercantilist policies. Since the poor who were housed in hospitals (many of which resembled poorhouses) were thought to be best served if they were taught a skill and given work, the manufactured goods and cloths they produced would provide benefits to both the workers and the state (Cole 1964a, 264, 347). We know that cloth was manufactured in the hospital system of Toulouse at about the time of Colbert (Cole 1964a, 275).

The evidence suggests that the Hôpital Saint-Joseph de la Grave in Toulouse employed the poor to produce blankets that the Mariette family purchased (possibly in partnership with the Dumas family) and shipped to New France, where other yet-undiscovered connections made these goods available to consumers. It appears that most of the connections of the Mariette family were in Québec City (Bosher 1987, 100, 137; Jean and Proulx 1995, 146), which suggests that some of these goods must have arrived by way of Canada and not from Louisiana and up the Mississippi River system. Since Montauban is situated in a major wool-producing area, it is likely that this seal and others from Montauban marked either blankets or woolens. The seals that have been identified as French but whose origins in France are unknown are classified based on the presence of the fleur-de-lys, the coat of arms of France, French words or word fragments (often evidenced by vowel combinations), or part of a motif previously seen on other identified French seals.

British Seals

Though only two of the seals from Fort St. Joseph are of British origin, they are quite informative. The first seal (seal U) from the Fort St. Joseph Museum resembles a specimen from a Revolutionary War site (Calver and Bolton 1950, 165–166). It is identified as belonging to James Eyre, a successful woolen merchant from Leeds in Yorkshire (Calver and Bolton 1950, 166). In the eighteenth and nineteenth centuries, Leeds was the center of the Yorkshire wool-producing region (Atkinson 1956, x, xi). Although the main textile produced in the region was kersey, a course, lightweight woolen often used in military uniforms (Kent 2001, 665), Leeds was also a renowned manufacturer of broadcloths (*draps*), a heavier and higher-quality woolen (Atkinson 1956, 70). Kersey was imported to Fort St. Joseph in 1742, but because British cloth was then illegal in the French colonies, it may or may not have come from Yorkshire (Kent 2001, 665). Other woolens manufactured in Yorkshire included bays (baize), which was woven using a weft thread of woolen yarn and a warp thread of worsted yarn (Atkinson 1956, 69). A collection of Yorkshire woolen swatches displays a variety of colors of broadcloth and bays (Atkinson 1956, frontispiece).

The second British seal allegedly found at Fort St. Joseph is from Halifax, another major wool-producing town in Yorkshire. This seal (FSJ seal P) once marked the products of Buck and Kershaw, woolen merchants of Halifax. The earliest mention of this company is an 1814 notice in the *London Gazette* announcing the dissolution of a partnership between William Kershaw (of Buck and Kershaw) and a certain Edward Swain (Neuman 1814, 939). The Buck and Kershaw duo appears to have been alive and well in an 1818–1820 commercial directory.[14] The Halifax store of Buck and Kershaw was located on Union Street, not far from Piece Hall, where cloth would be inspected, measured, and sealed. William Kershaw and Sons, merchants located at Warley-House in Halifax, are also listed in this commercial directory.[15] A later commercial directory for 1834 notes that Buck and Kershaw were still located on Union Street in that year.[16] Although records for the company are elusive, they would have probably also sold a range of locally produced woolens. The existence of this seal at the site could indicate commercial activity that possibly continued into the late eighteenth or early nineteenth century, provided the specimen is actually associated with Fort St. Joseph and does not derive from some other location where the fur trade persisted long after the abandonment of the fort (see Hoock et al., chapter 8, this volume).[17]

Comparisons with Lead Seals from Other Sites in the Region

Many of the seals discussed above also appear at sites throughout the western Great Lakes region, including Forts Michilimackinac and Ouiatenon (Adams 1989; Noble 1983; Stone 1974b). The most obvious similarity between Fort St. Joseph and other sites in the region is the preponderance of French seals, despite the fact that the British occupied the fort during and after the French and Indian War (i.e., 1761–1781). Table 5.1 compares the French seals from Fort St. Joseph with those from Fort Michilimackinac (Davis 2014). Of the French lead seals identified in this table, those from the southern region of Languedoc outnumber the seals from other regions. Some similarities between woolen consumption at Fort St. Joseph and Fort Michilimackinac are represented by the seals present at both sites, particularly seals from the town of Mazamet. This indicates that cloth from in and around Mazamet was preferred throughout the region, or at least that it was readily available. Seals from Mazamet are the most common at both Fort St. Joseph and Fort Michilimackinac, accounting for 16 percent and 11 percent of identified French seals at each site, respectively. Based on the seal from Mazamet marked "PV-LCH" (Seal 94.3.317 K from The History Museum) and on descriptions of Native American shrewdness with regard to quality, it is probable that this seal and others represent the finer version of *molleton* woolens from Mazamet and not the lower-quality *cordelats*.

Interestingly, these are the only real similarities of the lead seals from Michilimackinac and Fort St. Joseph. A significant number of seals from Michilimackinac originated in Nîmes, an important producer of silks (Table 5.1). In fact, Adams identified the seals in her study as Nîmes silk seals for cloth or stockings because of their tiny size (< 1 centimeter) and distinctive design (Adams 1989, 42; Sabatier 1908, 129; Sabatier 1912, 331–332, 361). The presence of silk at Michilimackinac may indicate that part of the French population of the fort dressed in clothes more suited to metropolitan settlers or the upper class, such as officers and their families who were part of the French Canadian nobility (Cassel 1987, 79). However, we cannot rule out the possibility that Native Americans were using silk. After all, Pouchot observed silk ribbons being used to decorate *machicotés, mitasses,* and blankets in his encounters with Native Americans of various ethnicities in the eastern Great Lakes region, so silk could have been used in a similar fashion farther west at Fort St. Joseph (Pouchot 2003, 265–268). The current absence of Nîmes silk seals at Fort St. Joseph may attest to a slight difference in taste or availability between the two sites. Of course, this difference may be the result of preservation bias at the site, an indication about the occupants of the excavated portions of the site, or a difference created by the amount of archaeology conducted at Fort St. Joseph and Michilimackinac. The apparent scarcity of silk at Fort St. Joseph should not necessarily be interpreted as an indicator of a comparatively low population of upper-class French residents at the site in relation to Fort Michilimackinac, since almost the same number of commandants, officers, and their families were present at both Fort St. Joseph and Fort Michilimackinac throughout their existence (Idle 2003, 151; Stone 1974b, 8).

There are also numerous seals of the CDI at Michilimackinac. If these seals can be linked definitively to woolens, that would align Michilimackinac more favorably with Fort St. Joseph, a site where woolens dominated. It is also important to consider the origins of lead seals found at Fort St. Joseph and Michilimackinac, the types of cloth associated with each, and some of the different cloths the CDI imported (Table 5.2). Since these company seals are difficult to attribute to a specific cloth type out of the many the company imported, their connection to woolens cannot be assumed, despite historical evidence that often points to the company as the importer of *écarlatines.* Likewise, although seals marked "*écarlatine*" are not found at Fort St. Joseph, as they are at Michilimackinac (Stone 1974b, 288, figs. B and E; Adams 1989, 24), this popular trade woolen may still have been imported and marked with seals of the CDI or Carcassonne.

Table 5.2. Cloth types associated with identified seals and their occurrence at Forts St. Joseph and Michilimackinac

Origin	Major Cloth Types Associated with Location or Entity	Seal(s) Present at Fort St. Joseph	Seal(s) Present at Michilimackinac (Adams 1989)
Carcassonne	*Écarlatines* (heavy woolen)	Yes	Yes
Lille	Camlet (cotton), *polimiez, persianes* (light woolens), lace, linens	Yes	No
Lyon	Bombazine (cotton; Kent 2001, 672), fustian (cotton; Kent 2001, 672), *coutil* (denim, cotton; Kent 2001, 673), taffeta (silk/satin; Kent 2001, 647)	No, but "Lyon cloth" recorded in documents (Peyser 1978)	Yes
Mazamet	*Mazamet* (woolen), other woolens	Yes	Yes
Montauban	Woolens, cloths from nearby towns	Yes	Yes
Nîmes	Silks (Sabatier 1912, 332), serge (woolen; Kent 2001, 663), *perpetuana* (woolen; Kent 2001, 667)	No	Yes
Roubaix	Woolens	No	Yes
Compagnie des Indes	*Écarlatines,* muslins (cotton), bleached cotton cloths, striped and plaid cotton cloths (late eighteenth century)	Yes	Yes
Halifax	Kersey (light worsted woolen), bays (worsted/woolen combination cloth), broadcloths (woolen), stuffs	Yes	No
Leeds	Kersey (light worsted woolen), broadcloths (woolen)	Yes	No
Wakefield	Woolens (Adams 1989, 41)	No	Yes
London	Unknown, cloths from elsewhere in England for export, packer's seals	No	Yes

Source: Unless otherwise specified, the data on this table is updated from Davis (2014, 66).

The seal of the Bureau Foraine de Lille (n = 2) from Fort St. Joseph has also been found at the Ghost Horse site farther south in the Illinois country, although with different markings on the reverse side (Mazrim 2011, 210–211). None of these seals have been found at Michilimackinac, which has yielded at least two seals from Lyon, a prominent center of cloth production in France that is not represented in the assemblage from Fort St. Joseph.

Although both sites have produced British seals that have been tied to specific merchants, there is no overlap in the merchants represented at the two sites (Adams 1989, 38–44). Whether these patterns will persist and whether they represent distinct differences in supply or preferences at the two sites remains to be answered in future investigations as more lead seals are discovered and identified.

Conclusions

Lead seals are important sources of information about the distribution and consumption of textiles and have implications for sartorial styles at Fort St. Joseph and other sites in New France. First, most of the identified seals present in the Fort St. Joseph collections derive from textiles that were produced in France. This, in conjunction with previous understandings of French economic protectionism and the dates of French and British occupation of the fort, indicates that the occupants of the fort may have obtained the majority of their cloth from French producers for over half a century. If contraband British cloths were being used or trafficked at the site during the eighteenth century, they do not appear to have been marked by lead seals. The only identified British seals from the site are associated with later periods of occupation.

Second, many of the textiles that were traded at the fort were from Languedoc in southern France (Figure 5.1), a major woolen-producing area involved in the Canada trade. The fortunes of southern France and Languedoc were tied to trade with Canada and consumer choices there led to profits and losses for French merchants and changes in production due to supply and demand. The residents of Fort St. Joseph might have had some influence on the changes made to the textile industry during the eighteenth century due to their demands for certain textiles for trade and personal consumption. The seals also suggest that New France acquired some cloth from northern France near Lille. Original import lists to Québec and Louisbourg indicate that the two main outlets for goods bound for Canada in the first part of the eighteenth century were La Rochelle and Rochefort, but other ports may have also shipped to Canada or transferred goods to these main export sites in France.[18]

The intimate economic connection between France and New France that the colonial demand for French textile goods created led to changes in France following the loss of Canada. Although the economic havoc created by the fallout of the Canadian credit system and unpaid merchant debt can be seen in one way or another throughout the parts of the kingdom most implicated in the Canada trade, many of the impacts have yet to be fully explored. Many small French towns and villages have forgotten transatlantic histories veiled by years of economic downturn, archival lacunae, and social change. A prime example of these economic impacts that may attract work in the future as a case study is the bankruptcy of the Mariette family and much of the mercantile town of Montauban in 1760 as a result of the loss of Canadian markets (Bosher 1987, 198).

Interestingly, later trade at the site is represented in the collections by the two late eighteenth- and early nineteenth-century British seals, which may provide additional information about trade at the site after the 1750s. Knowing that these seals were attached to woolens suggests that type of textile was still popular in the region during and after the eighteenth century, although the sources and likely the quality of the woolens were different. When compared with seals from other French sites in North America, it appears that Fort St. Joseph had access to similar goods as posts in the *pays des Illinois* and in the St. Lawrence and Champlain Valleys. The seal of the CDI is also omnipresent at nearly every site examined in the western Great Lakes region and at sites in the eastern United States, Canada, and Louisiana. The wide distribution of goods associated with the CDI shows the extent of its economic influence in New France.

Many seals have escaped archaeological detection because they were reused as a convenient source of lead on the frontier. This explains their scarcity at some sites and poses a problem in the analysis of sites where seals do exist. Even at sites with large numbers of seals, such as Michilimackinac, there is evidence of reuse (Adams 1989, 37; Morand 1994, 40–44); seals were made into projectile points and simple toys such as whizzers, whereas unknown and uncounted seals may have been melted down or reworked beyond recognition into fishing weights, musket balls, lead shot, or gunflint patches.

Although this issue complicates the study of seals, extant specimens are nonetheless useful in the study of the normally perishable goods they are associated with. Robert DuPlessis has underlined some of the major problems historians face who rely on archival sources to learn more about textiles in the colonial Atlantic world (DuPlessis 2015, 8–14). He notes that the many archival sources available for the study of textiles, such as probate inventories, descriptions in journals, account books, and other written and pictorial sources, were produced by European colonists and thus contain information viewed and amended through the lens of a European worldview (DuPlessis 2015, 12–14). Because of this bias and the fact that many documents, especially inventories, are concerned with the activity of European individuals whose estates required documentation to facilitate division or inheritance, we are left with a significant gap in our understanding of textile use by culturally (e.g., Native Americans and African Americans) and economically (e.g., indentured servants, enslaved people) marginalized groups and individuals (DuPlessis 2015, 8–9). Thus, lead seals present at sites associated with underdocumented groups have a high potential to contribute new information about textile consumption patterns. In the case of Fort St. Joseph, a site with limited documentation, seals open a window into the textiles present at the site and reveal how French *voyageurs* and soldiers, their Native American trading partners, and later British and American occupants may have used them.

This study shows that despite their distance from the more urban and populated centers of New France, the people in and around Fort St. Joseph relied on the fur trade system to bring imported cloth from France to meet their demands for clothing materials. The presence of a large percentage of French lead seals seems to indicate that at Fort St. Joseph, contraband British cloth was uncommon. It may have been difficult to import illegal British goods. Since trade lists and seal evidence indicate that trade woolens and broadcloths represent most of the cloth imported to the site, it might be suggested that Native Americans in the region were using the cloth for *machicotés* and blankets. Documentary and archaeological evidence also seems to suggest that local indigenous groups used some of these valuable woolens to clothe both the living and the dead. French Canadian inhabitants of the site would have likely brought elements of their existing wardrobes (which generally consisted of lighter woolens and linens) with them to the site from their former residences in the St. Lawrence Valley, where there were skilled tailors who were able to produce European-style clothing (Gousse 2013). However, some imported cloth might have been used to sew simple clothing items that required only basic skills, which would explain the straight pins and sewing implements found at the site (Juen and Nassaney 2012). Soldiers garrisoned at Fort St. Joseph may have used the same varieties of woolens as uniform material when necessary.

The terrain of the *pays d'en haut* may have encouraged soldiers, *voyageurs*, and colonists to fashion Native American–style garments such as *mitasses* for use in daily life. This might explain the importation of pre-made *mitasses* to the site and would further implicate colonists in the consumption of the woolens that were once marked by these lead seals. As revealed through comparison with seals found at Michilimackinac, it appears that life at Fort St. Joseph lacked many of the niceties, such as silk and cotton, that were available at Michilimackinac. The reasons for this are yet to be explored, but this difference could perhaps be explained by the latter fort's proximity to Georgian Bay and the main trade route between Montreal and the Great Lakes.

The seals from Fort St. Joseph reveal the trade networks, textile consumption, and economic forces that linked the fur trade at a post in the interior of New France to a greater Atlantic world in the seventeenth and eighteenth centuries (see also Adams 1989; Baart 2005). Yet there are still aspects of lead seals that merit further attention and research. Notably, the numbers etched onto the backs of seals, if identified, might be directly linked to merchant records or ship manifests. If these codes can be deciphered, more information will become available about various types of textiles, their owners, and their route of transmission from France to North America. Also, the analysis of unintentional fabric imprints on the interior of lead seal plates might indicate the variety of textile they marked. Although this study has focused on the information available using the intentional markings and designs impressed into the lead, imprint analysis may also assist in understanding historic cloth—especially considering the difficulty of deciphering the period terminology for various fabrics, which were often named based on their place of origin and were rarely described in detail ("Lyon cloth," for example). Although there are still many avenues to be explored where lead seals are concerned, the archaeological recovery of seals at Fort St. Joseph reveals much about textiles at this French colonial site in North America.

Acknowledgments

I would be remiss not to acknowledge the help I have received from my many colleagues and collaborators in the process of carrying out research on this topic. First, I would like to thank Dr. Michael Nassaney for inviting me to share my research in this book, for first setting me on the path that has led to what will surely be a lifelong interest in lead seals and French colonial material culture, and for his continued mentorship and guidance. I would also like to acknowledge the museum specialists who have lent their time and expertise in allowing me access to the lead seals in their collections. These professionals have collaborated on the documentation of lead seals and diffusion of information about them and for that I applaud them. In particular, recognition for help with research leading to this chapter is due to the staff at The History Museum (South Bend, Indiana), the Niles History Center (Niles, Michigan), and Fort Ticonderoga (Ticonderoga, New York). Since no study develops in a vacuum, I am compelled to extend my heartfelt gratitude to faculty and colleagues at the various academic institutions I have been fortunate to attend. I would especially like to thank Dr. Nassaney, Dr. José Brandão, and Dr. David MacDonald for serving as my thesis director and advisors during my undergraduate studies and M. Alain Laberge for his insight and cheerful encouragement during the early stages of my MA research, which contributed to the expansion of ideas present in this chapter. I am also grateful for the support of myriad friends and family members who have patiently listened to my ideas and asked good questions and continue to cheer me on my journey. Not least among them are Mom, Dad, Joseph Gagné, Marie-Hélaine Fallu, Michel Thévenin, my colleagues at the Centre interuniversitaire des études québecoises (Ciéq), and the staff and students, past, present, and future, of the Fort St. Joseph Archaeological Project. *Je vous remercie chaleureusement et de tout mon cœur.*

Notes

1. For the Lakenhal Museum, see Museum de Lakenhal, http://www.lakenhal.nl/en; for the Piece Hall, see "Yorkshire's Most Important Secular Building," The Piece Hall, https://www.thepiecehall.co.uk/heritage.

2. Sometimes this office is referred to as the *bureau de fabrique*, the *bureau de draperie, or* another type of *bureau "communautaire"* (Sabatier 1908, 10).

3. A piece is essentially a piece of textile as it exists when it comes off of the loom. In

France, the size of pieces were not standardized and had varied measures. In addition, each region had its own measurement system (an ell from Paris and one from Languedoc varied by at least several inches, for example). Officials sought to establish a standard measure throughout the seventeenth and eighteenth centuries, but they were not successful until after the Revolution. In *Lead Cloth Seals and Related Items in the British Museum* (London: Department of Medieval and Later Antiquities, British Museum, 1995), Geoffrey Egan defines "piece" as "the complete, uncut length of a textile from the loom" (146).

4. My translation. Original French: "*vûs, visitez & marquez du plomb de Controlle desdits Bureaux, s'ils se trouvent fabriquez, teints & apprestez en conformité des Reglemens: Veut Sa Majesté, que lesdites étoffes soient ensuite emballées dans ces mesmes Bureaux, & les balles cordées & plombées du mesme plomb; au moyen de quoy lesdites balles seront exemptes des visites des Bureaux de Controlle qui se trouveront sur leur route, & pourront aller librement à leur destination, sans estre sujettes à d'autres visites que celles du plomb de Controlle.*"

5. My translation. Original French: "*La Compagnie des Indes donne aux Sauvages des couvertes pour eux, pour leurs femmes, et des machicotés en draps rouges et bleus avec des bandes noires; elle est obligée de les prendre dans les manufactures d'Angleterre; elle a voulu essayer de les prendre dans celles de Carcassonne, mais les Sauvages n'en on pas voulu. Ce n'est pas que les draps n'en fussent meilleures et n'en fussent aussi beaux pour les couleurs, mais on n'a pu encore y faire les bandes d'un beau noir; en général nos marchandises valent mieux pour la qualité que celles des Anglais, mais les Sauvages préfèrent les leurs; ils attrapent mieux leurs goûts.*"

6. My translation. Original French: "*travailler à faire des draps rouges et bleus pour s'attirer cette branche de commerce que l'on fait au Canada, en fournissant des couvertes aux Sauvages.*"

7. Havard (2003, 569–570); Centre d'archives de Québec, Québec City, series C11A, vol. 95, fol. 260–265 and vol. 93, fol. 42–44, Archives de la Ministre de la Marine, Bibliothéque et Archives nationales de Québec. Microfilms of French originals.

8. My translation. Original French: "*Il est important que ces pièces d'Ecarlatine, tant a la couleur qu'a la qualité, soient si bien imitées qu'on ne puisse pas en connoitre la différence parce que les sauvages sont aussy rafinés pour connoitre la qualité de l'Étoffe que les plus habiles negotians, ayant attention de faire bruler le poil d'un echantillon pour en voir la corde.*"

9. Michiana refers to the region of northern Indiana and southwestern Michigan centered on South Bend, Indiana.

10. Letters and numbers in square brackets in transcriptions of the text on lead seals are my insertions.

11. This definition is from *Collins Latin Dictionary Plus Grammar* ([Glasgow]: HarperCollins, 1997).

12. A numismatic term for the dotted borders on coins or seals. When used near the edges of coins, the *grenètis* assured the coin's completeness. The *grenètis* on some seals was used to detect counterfeits; the number of dots or other details allowed the identification of fakes (Sabatier 1912, 23–24).

13. "Histoire de La Grave," Hôpitaux de Toulouse, http://www.chu-toulouse.fr/-histoire -de-la-grave-.

14. *The London Gazette*, January 1–June 28, 1814, 939; *The Commercial Directory for 1818–*

19–20 Containing the Names, Trades, and Situations of the Merchants, Manufacturers, Trades-men, &c. (Manchester: James Pigot & Co., 1918), 144.

15. *The Commercial Directory for 1818–19–20*, 144.

16. "Transcript of the Entry of 'Professions and Trades' for Halifax in Pigot's Directory of 1834," Genuki: UK and Ireland Genealogy, https://www.genuki.org.uk/big/eng/YKS/WRY/Halifax/Halifax34Dry.

17. We can never know with certainty if materials that lack precise provenience data are actually from Fort St. Joseph and not from some other spatial and temporal context.

18. Centre d'archives de Québec, Québec City, series C11A and C11.

6

Crafting Culture at Fort St. Joseph

An Analysis of Tinkling Cone Production

BROCK A. GIORDANO

AND MICHAEL S. NASSANEY

Archaeologists who study craft production often examine changes throughout the life histories of artifacts to determine how they reveal specific choices that people made in daily life and how such goods reproduced social and personal identities (Mullins 2004, 207). An underlying premise in the study of material culture is that artifacts express the practices of the individuals who commissioned, fabricated, purchased or used them, and by extension the cultural values and beliefs of the larger society in which these individuals operated (Neill 2000; Prown 1993, 1). In all societies, the need to adapt to new social, cultural, and economic conditions fosters cultural change, particularly in contexts of cultural interaction (Anderson 1991, 1994; Ehrhardt 2005; White 1991). Studies of artifacts are significant because archaeologists can use them to monitor specific cultural transformations that were taking place and how "new cultural traits were adopted, modified, and created to fit within the underlying ideological structure of both non-European and European peoples" (Lightfoot 1995, 206). While Europeans often maintained Old World technological practices (see Hartley and Nassaney, chapter 4, this volume), empirical evidence suggests that they also embraced more pragmatic choices and opportunistic strategies.

There were many opportunities to adopt new cultural and sartorial practices in the dynamic setting of the North American fur trade, which linked people and regions economically and politically through European mercantile expansion (Becker 2004; Davis, chapter 5, this volume; Loren 2010; Nassaney 2015; Wallerstein 1976; Wolf 1982). In the western Great Lakes region, or *pays d'en haut* of New France, the fur trade provides a lens for examining the impact of cultural interactions and the changing relationships that existed between Native American and European populations. This chapter examines the seventeenth- and eighteenth-century fur trade at the site of Fort St. Joseph and its implications for economic activity associated with the production of tinkling cones.

Located in the interior of the western Great Lakes region in what is now southwest Michigan (Figure 2.1), Fort St. Joseph was the center of religious, military, and commercial activity for local Native American populations and European colonial powers from 1691 to 1781 (Brandão and Nassaney, chapter 2, this volume; Nassaney and Cremin 2004). As a trade outpost, Fort St. Joseph was a site where French and Native Americans intermingled culturally. Archaeological evidence has been recovered that reflects the various functions of the site, including religious paraphernalia (e.g., crosses, medallions), French military buttons and gun parts, and a broad range of domestic and commercial goods that were produced, used, discarded, lost, and abandoned in daily life. Broken, cached, and discarded objects point to the local production of various goods that were likely both used by the fort's inhabitants and intended for exchange. Thus, Fort St. Joseph provides an excellent context for examining the role of craft production and the organization of labor on the colonial frontier because the site contains archaeological evidence of production activities, particularly copper-alloy scrap and other waste products, in addition to finished goods.

Before systematic site investigations began at Fort St. Joseph in 1998, local antiquarians had amassed a significant collection of more than 100,000 artifacts from the site (Beeson 1900; Hulse 1977). Many of these objects were eventually curated locally, including the collection initially used for this study (Giordano 2005). Most of the materials that avocational archaeologists collected from the vicinity of Fort St. Joseph were made from imported raw materials (Nassaney and Cremin 2002b), including tinkling cones.

Documentary evidence of trade reveals there was a strong demand for copper and brass artifacts such as kettles in eastern North America (Anderson 1994); examples of these have been recovered from numerous colonial contexts (Anselmi 2004; Bradley 1987a; Brain 1979, 164–180; Martin 1975; Quimby 1966; Turgeon 1997). Besides being used for their intended utilitarian functions, such as cooking and storage, kettles played a major role in craft production (Morand 1994; Turgeon 1997). As they wore out, they were cut up and readapted for new uses, such as tinkling cones, hair pipes, rivets, and projectile points (Bradley 1987a, Figure 13; Morand 1994; Quimby 1966; Turgeon 1997). Scraps of copper alloy exhibiting cut marks suggest that kettles were recycled and used in ways their original Old World producers did not intend. Evidence for the production of tinkling cones in particular appears in all the stages of the manufacturing process, including finished objects, raw material in various stages of production, and the scrap metal or waste from which the objects were crafted. The production of such material objects illustrates how the French and Native American residents of the fort incorporated and transformed European trade goods into new ornamental, decorative, and symbolic forms (Anselmi 2004; Ehrhardt 2005; Giordano 2005; Miller and Hamell 1986; Nassaney 2009; Nassaney et al. 2007; Turgeon 1997).

Investigating the organization of craft production can provide insight into the demographic composition of the colonial frontier and the activities that were conducted in daily life (Morand 1994). When they examine the organization of labor (also referred to as the organization of production) in complex societies, archaeologists address social, economic, political, and symbolic or religious systems and technological characteristics such as the availability of raw materials and the ability to produce objects under specific requirements to fit demand (Blackman et al. 1993; Brumfiel and Earle 1987; Costin and Hagstrum 1995; Kenoyer et al. 1991; Sinopoli 1988). Interpretations of colonial relations in the western Great Lakes region recognize the complexities and dynamics of the fur trade (Juen and Nassaney 2012; Nassaney 2015; White 1991). Cultural interactions on the frontier spawned dramatic social, political, and economic changes and adoptions of material goods that reinterpreted them in new cultural contexts. In the fur trade of the western Great Lakes region, interactions between Native Americans and Europeans (particularly the French) were mutual endeavors in which accommodations were made in the interests of both parties (Anderson 1994; Nassaney 2009; Sleeper-Smith 2001; White 1991). The fact that interactions among Native Americans and the French often blurred previous cultural boundaries (White 1991) is expressed in novel intercultural artifact forms.

In this chapter, we examine how labor was organized in a multiethnic population in the late seventeenth and eighteenth centuries in the western Great Lakes region. Specifically, we investigate cuprous metalworking practices related to the production of tinkling cones at Fort St. Joseph.

The Spatial, Temporal, and Formal Parameters
of Tinkling Cones in Eastern North America

Tinkling cones, also referred to as tinklers, bangles, dangles, or jingles (Ehr-hardt 2005, 119–120; Good 1972; Jelks 1966; Krause 1972; Odell 2001; Walthall and Brown 2001), are conical decorative objects formed with an open apex by rolling a flat, generally trapezoidal metal blank of cuprous metal cut from sheet metal around a mandrel (Ehrhardt 2005, 120–121). Recycled kettles were often the source of the raw material (Figure 6.1). Kettles were cut into a blank of a desired shape and rolled to form the final cone. A thong or some type of attachment (usually made of leather or animal hair) was threaded through the open tip and knotted on the inside. The tinkling sound comes from individual cones striking one another as they dangle. Tinkling cones were used for adornment as earrings and on clothing, pouches, bags, moccasins, and purses. We have yet to see them appear in trade lists of imported goods, suggesting that they were produced locally.

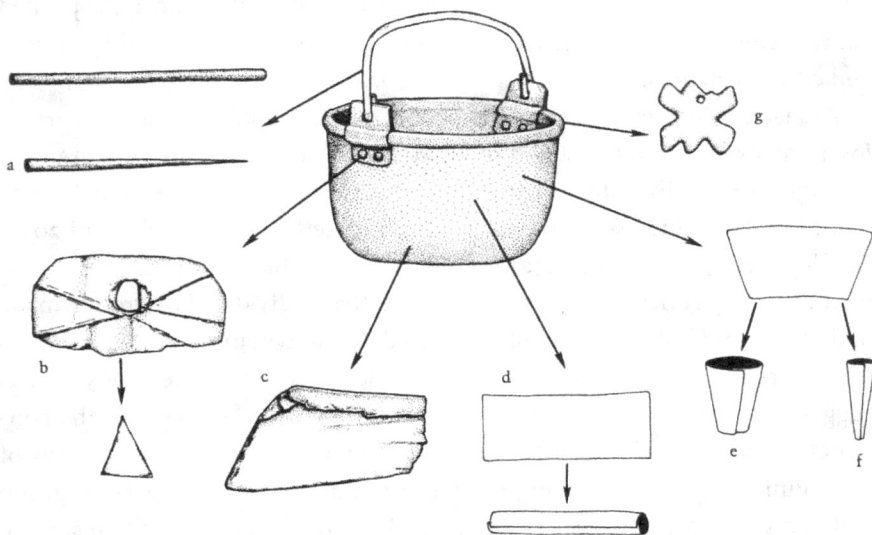

Figure 6.1. In the seventeenth and eighteenth centuries kettles were recycled into a range of useful goods that included (*a*) awls, (*b*) projectile points, (*c*) knives, (*d*) beads, (*e, f*) tinkling cones, and (*g*) pendants. Adapted from Bradley 1987a, Figure 13. Redrawn by Michael S. Nassaney.

The copper-alloy tinkling cone this study examines has organic anteced-ents that stem back to the transitional Early Woodland/Middle Woodland periods. The earliest forms of copper-based metal tinkling cones appear in the lower Great Lakes region as early as AD 1580 and were meant to imitate bangles made from hollowed-out deer phalanxes, which were common at early Ontario Iroquoian sites (Fitzgerald 1990, 503; Willoughby 1922). Wil-loughby (1922, 64) noted that "44 hollow cones made of antler tips" were recovered from Altar 4, Mound 4 at the Hopewellian Turner Mound Group in present-day Ohio. Additional artifacts recovered from Altar 4, Mound 4 at the Turner Group in association with the cone antler tips included numer-ous objects manufactured from Native American copper such as bracelets, beads, and a series of "copper cones" (Willoughby 1922, 66). Although not formally classified as tinkling cones, the morphological attributes of these cones are quite similar: they have a conical shape and an open apex at the proximal end. Similarly, Quimby (1966, 43) noted large tinkling cones made of Native American copper in the Great Lakes region at Late Woodland sites in Michigan and Illinois. He also identified other objects manufactured from Native American copper, including cylindrical hair pipes, finger rings, C-shaped bracelets, and snake effigy pendants (Quimby 1966, 39). Today, tin-kling cones are often made of tin and are used on authentic and appropriated Native American items such as bags, moccasins, pouches, smoking pipes, and dream catchers.

Archaeological evidence for the production of tinkling cones at Fort St. Joseph consists of all the stages of an artifact's life cycle, from procurement through discard. Examples of this at Fort St. Joseph and other French colo-nial outposts include scrap metal, blanks, and kettle patches (Anselmi 2004; Bradley 1987b; Ehrhardt 2005; Morand 1994). As objects of personal adorn-ment, tinkling cones can reveal the choices that individuals or groups made in daily life and how those people perceived themselves in society. Such goods also expressed an assertive and emblemic identity. As White (2005, 7) has suggested, objects of personal adornment can be used "to perceive the con-struction of physical appearance on an individual scale and are a means of communicating and conveying the recognition of status of a person, group affiliation, or other messages extended to all people." The artifacts that survive are the material remains of symbols men and women used that represent the specific choices they made (Nassaney 2009). People choose particular goods for utilitarian reasons, such as providing the goods needed to survive, or for personal or decorative reasons (Nassaney 2009; White 2005). Objects of personal adornment that were created, modified, or purchased reveal the choices individuals made to communicate who they were and who they wished to be seen as (Nassaney 2009). Objects such as beads, earrings, buckles, buttons, and tinkling cones were powerful visual metaphors in the marking of personal identity (Kerr 2012; White 2005). These objects were used to beautify the self in order to convey a particular meaning (Miller and Hamell 1986). Tinkling cones would seem to represent a type of intercultural artifact (see Singleton and Bograd 2000) that emerged from the blending of practices and beliefs that characterize the process of ethnogenesis in fur trade society (Nassaney 2009). A closer look at the materials can suggest how they were produced and used at Fort St. Joseph.

Crafting Tinkling Cones at Fort St. Joseph

To investigate the organization of labor and the role of craft specialization in the context of the colonial fur trade, Giordano (2005) began by examining a collection of 356 complete tinkling cones recovered from the vicinity of Fort St. Joseph that are housed in the Fort St. Joseph Museum. Although these objects lack data on provenience, they are consistent in terms of raw material, size, and other morphological attributes of tinkling cones from archaeological contexts. It is useful to differentiate between centralized production and opportunistic production by identifying any standardization and variation in the manufacturing techniques used and the formal style of the final forms created. Such observations provide insight into the way labor was organized at Fort St. Joseph.

Craft Specialization, Standardization, and Variation

Archaeologists, ethnohistorians, and historians of technology have used multiple lines of evidence to examine the organization of labor. Measurements of standardization, including formal and technological attributes, are often used as reliable indices for identifying specialized production (Blackman et al. 1993; Brumfiel 1980; Costin and Hagstrum 1995; Shafer and Hester 1991). Craft specialization, skill, and the standardization hypothesis provide ways to identify production and labor organization in the archaeological record. Researchers have often created standardized scales of measurements as a way of reliably identifying specialized production (Blackman et al. 1993; Schiffer and Skibo

1997). Standardization of the formal attributes of a final object and the manufacturing sequence used to produce the object are evidence of an artisan's skill, defined as the result of an artisan's repetitive movements that led to consistent outcomes (Costin and Hagstrum 1995, 623). Thus, objects manufactured with a greater degree of skill will exhibit similar formal and technological characteristics. Skill is measured by the degree of repetition in the sequence of production that is often observable in the final form.

To investigate the organization of labor by examining material culture, we applied the standardization hypothesis, which posits that specialized production of a particular form or type of material culture may be "observed in the archaeological record through standardization in raw material and manufacturing techniques, form and dimensions, and surface decoration" (Blackman et al. 1993, 61). In stratified societies where production is strictly controlled, factors such as new technologies, external regulations, and access to raw materials are often seen as indicators of centralized production (Sinopoli 1988).

Competition in the production and widespread distribution of large quantities of goods is also a characteristic of centralized production. Opportunistic production refers to production that takes place in more dispersed workshops in response to the needs of local consumers (Sinopoli 1988, 582). Thus, in an archaeological context it is possible to identify centralized production by observing standardization in the manufacturing techniques used, the formal style of the final forms created, and the spatial distribution of production facilities or waste debris. Conversely, the lack of standardization implies decentralized production.

The distribution of scrap metal and tinkling cones can mark activity areas devoted to production. Limited or isolated areas of production that yield high percentages of scrap metal across the site are indicative of centralized production. Wide distribution across the site is indicative of dispersed workshops and opportunistic production.

To explore these issues, we drew on multiple lines of complementary data, including a detailed technometric analysis (Leader 1988) that included metric analysis, visual inspection techniques, and scratch testing to determine the base metal. The aim was to specifically examine the "technological histories" (Lechtman 1977) of a sizable collection of tinkling cones and conduct a spatial analysis to identify the distribution of production areas and associated activities.

Analytical Methods

This research is based on a combination of archaeometric (laboratory) and visual examination techniques, including metric analysis, macroscopic examination, and low-powered magnification. Leader (1988, 4) refers to the process of recording primary measurements such as length, width, thickness, weight, and observation of surface features as a technometric analysis. This type of material investigation enabled us to construct a typology that reflects morphological variation and distinguishes any technological signatures used in the production of cuprous tinkling cones.

Metric Methodology

In the first stage of material investigation, I (Giordano) measured and recorded the basic morphological attributes of each complete tinkling cone in the collection (Figure 6.2). For each artifact, I recorded both the finished dimensions of the final product and the measurements of the blank that was used to form the tinkling cone. By doing so, I could establish metric comparisons between the blank's size and shape and the finished product. I took measurements of the length, basal diameter, and tip diameter of each finished object.

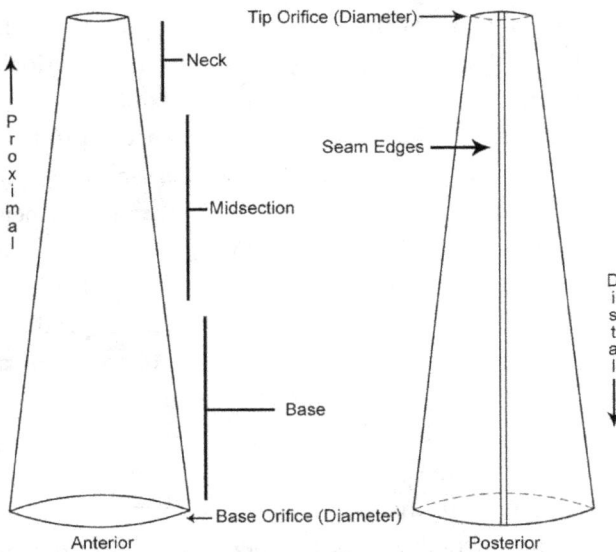

Figure 6.2. The anatomy of a tinkling cone. Drawing by Brock Giordano.

I also measured the finished tinkling cones in an effort to reconstruct the original size and shape of the blank that was used to create the final product. To do this, I recorded measurements of the two horizontal widths (top and bottom) and two vertical lengths (left and right) of each tinkling cone. I measured curved surfaces using adhesive paper that I marked with points and then measured to the nearest millimeter using digital calipers. This revealed the exact size and shape of the original blank. Lastly, I conducted examinations to record the correlation between the blank shape and the finished shape.

Manufacturing Techniques

The second stage of investigation was the visual examination of the collection to record basic metalworking techniques that have been identified in contemporaneous archaeological collections of objects made from modified copper alloy (Anselmi 2004). I examined each finished tinkling cone for eleven manufacturing techniques (see Anselmi 2004, 57), including hammering and flattening, chiseling, scoring, bending, twisting, folding, cutting, sawing, melting, perforating, and grinding, which I then recorded and entered into a database. Upon further investigation, I recorded additional data about posterior bends, anterior crimp marks, seam overlap, and overall symmetry in the final form (see Ehrhardt 2005).

In the manufacturing sequence of an object, any technique could leave a visible scar. These scars may be identifiable markers on the final product, such as a perforated surface or cut edge that is distinguishable from lacerations made by scissors. However, certain manufacturing techniques exhibit a clearer signature or attribute than others. This may be due to the sequence of production processes, the tools used, or the technique of the craftsperson, who may have been Native American or European (male or female). For example, when a blank is cut to the desired shape and size by chiseling, it will often leave a scar along the edge. However, the scar could be removed by grinding. Thus, although a particular manufacturing technique may have been used to produce an object, it may no longer be distinguishable because it was obscured by a subsequent action in the manufacturing sequence. In this particular example, the final morphological attribute would be the comparison between ground seam edges and edges that lack grinding.

In addition to recording manufacturing techniques, I performed a simple scratch test that involves the removal of the patina in order to reveal the original color of the metal (Anselmi 2004; Fitzgerald and Ramsden 1988). Copper yields a reddish color when exposed, whereas brass, sometimes referred to as "yellow copper," yields a yellow tint (Fitzgerald and Ramsden 1988, 154). With the approval of the Fort St. Joseph Museum, I scratched a small line (1–2 millimeters) into the posterior surface of each tinkling cone to visually determine, both with the naked eye and low-powered magnification, the color of the metal.

Fitzgerald and Ramsden (1988) suggest that identifying the raw material is a crucial determinant in identifying the ages of assemblages. During Fort St. Joseph's active period (1691–1781), a wide variety of objects used for various purposes were traded. Copper and brass kettles were among the leading forms of this material culture (Turgeon 1997). The wide distribution of various reworked metal-based artifacts, including tinkling cones, spirals, and projectile points, and the waste or scrap found archaeologically serve as indisputable evidence that European-introduced copper and brass kettles were recycled at the site. In keeping with the goal of this research, I recorded the base metal and the other formal and metric attributes in order to investigate the technological histories of this collection of tinkling cones. Nassaney provided data on the distribution of scrap, preforms, and finished products from controlled excavations to identify spatial patterns that would indicate the degree of specialization.

A Tinkling Cone Typology and Metric Attributes

In this study we identified three distinct types of tinkling cones: conical, extended base (Walthall and Brown 2001, 102), and extended seam (Figure 6.3). The conical form constitutes 94 percent of the collection (n = 334). Conical tinkling cones were constructed by taking a blank of desired shape (332 trapezoidal and two square blanks), and rolling it around a mandrel to form a hollow cone shape, leaving an opening at the tip (proximal) and basal (distal) ends. The symmetry of the cones vary: some are generally symmetrical and some have uneven proportions (Figure 6.4). Extended base types (n = 18) were primarily produced using a square- (n = 17) or diamond-shaped (n = 1) blank (Figure 6.5). Extended base tinkling cones exhibit different basal planes than conical cones because the former involved the use of a diamond-shaped blank that produced a tinkling cone with a wide base and triangular projection facing downward. Finally, the third type (n = 4) is marked by an extended seam that protrudes past the base plane (Figure 6.6).

Statistical analyses of the metric attributes of the 334 conical tinkling cones in this sample were conducted to examine the degree of variation. Their length

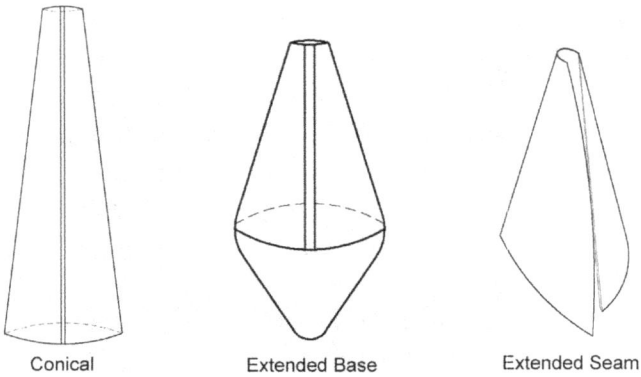

Figure 6.3. Types of tinkling cones identified in this study (*left to right*): conical, extended base, and extended seam. Drawing by Brock Giordano.

Figure 6.4. Conical tinkling cones (catalog numbers 91, 139, 94, 96, 114, 282, and 257). Photo by Brock Giordano.

Figure 6.5. Extended base tinkling cones manufactured with square or kite-shaped blanks. Photo by Brock Giordano.

Figure 6.6. Extended seam tinkling cones. Photo by Brock Giordano.

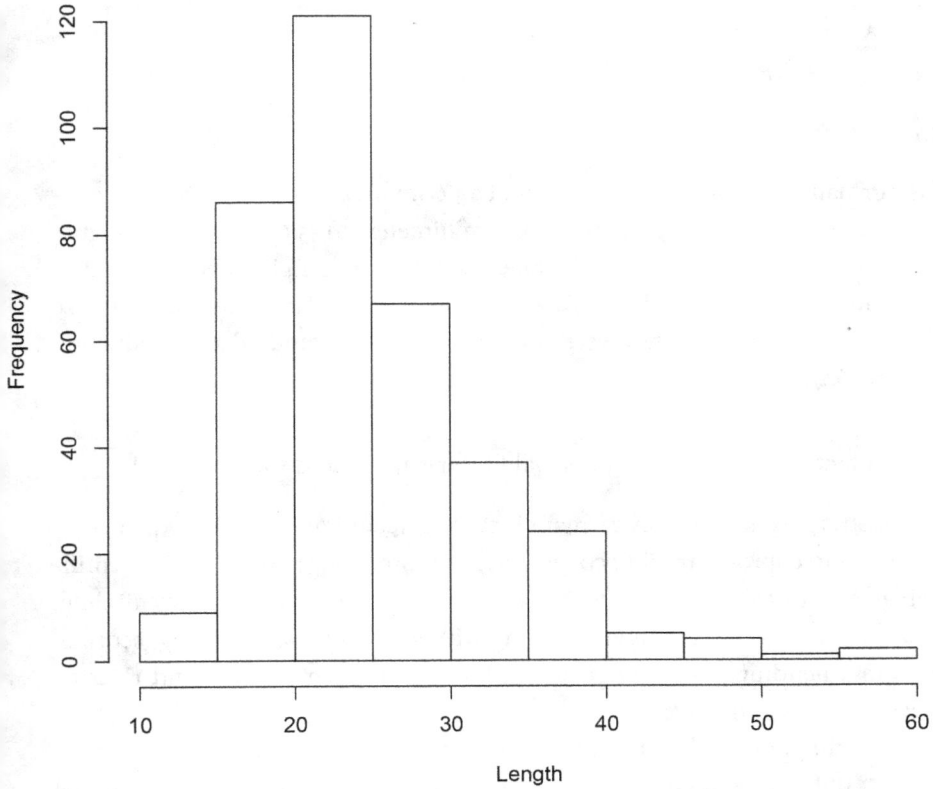

Figure 6.7. Frequency distribution of tinkling cones by length (mm). Histogram by Jason Glatz.

Table 6.1. Metric attributes of conical tinkling cones examined for this study

Conical Tinkling Cones (n = 334)	Minimum	Maximum	Mean	Standard Deviation	Relative Variability (%)
Finished length	10.10	55.60	24.55	7.14	29
Finished tip diameter	0.61	5.93	2.37	0.85	36
Finished base diameter	2.89	24.25	6.37	2.70	42
Blank Length 1—left	10.85	55.51	23.40	6.87	29
Blank Length 2—right	10.65	55.11	23.28	6.67	29
Blank Width 1—proximal	2.52	32.48	10.63	3.78	36
Blank Width 2—distal	10.34	58.03	21.18	7.64	36
Metal thickness	0.20	0.92	0.48	0.15	32

Note: All measurements in mm.

is normally distributed with a mean of 24.6 millimeters, though there is considerable variation, ranging from 10.10 millimeters to 55.6 millimeters (Figure 6.7). The average sheet metal thickness is 0.48 mm, ranging from 0.2 mm to 0.92 mm. The width of the tips and bases exhibit similar variation. Their size variation suggests that they were not the outcomes of standardized production (Table 6.1).

Manufacturing Techniques, Formal Observations, and Raw Material

This study examined eleven manufacturing techniques in the sequence of producing cuprous tinkling cones (after Anselmi 2004) and visually identifiable formal attributes (Table 6.2). Manufacturing techniques include chiseling, cutting using snips or scissors, sawing with a jeweler's saw, melting, scoring, folding, bending, twisting, grinding, hammering, perforating, and riveting (Anselmi 2004, 162–176).

Grinding, defined as the process of repeatedly rubbing two surfaces together until the edges become smooth, was observed on 98.6 percent (n = 351) of the total collection. Grinding was the most frequently observed manufac-

Table 6.2. Observed manufacturing techniques in the production of tinkling cones

Manufacturing Techniques (n = 356)	N	% of Sample Assemblage
Bending	94	26.4
Chiseling	10	3.6
Cutting	86	24.2
Folding	7	2.0
Grinding	351	98.6
Hammering	15	4.2
Melting	0	0.0
Perforating	22	6.2
Sawing	0	0.0
Scoring	80	22.5
Twisting	29	8.1

turing technique in the collection. Possible tools used for grinding are iron files and any type of abrasive stone (see Anselmi 2004, 171, for a discussion of sandstone with clear evidence of grinding). It was expected that there would be a high frequency of grinding because that technique was employed at various stages in the production sequence. For example, after the blank was cut, the edges were ground until smooth. In addition, a finishing touch may have been added to the tinkling cone by grinding the finished seam edge to create a smooth surface plane (Anselmi 2004, 171). This process obscures many of the previous manufacturing techniques such as cutting, chiseling, or scoring.

Bending, as Anselmi (2004) describes it, is the process of repeatedly applying pressure back and forth along a vertical line until the metal becomes weak and breaks. This process leaves a distinctive upturned edge and is not often recognizable. In this collection, bending to alter the morphological appearance was noted in 26.4 percent (n = 94) of the collection. Likewise, twenty-nine specimens (8.1 percent) in the collection exhibit twisting, whereas only seven (2.0 percent) examples of folding were observed among the 356 examined finished tinkling cones.

Eighty (22.5 percent) specimens display scoring lines, primarily along the

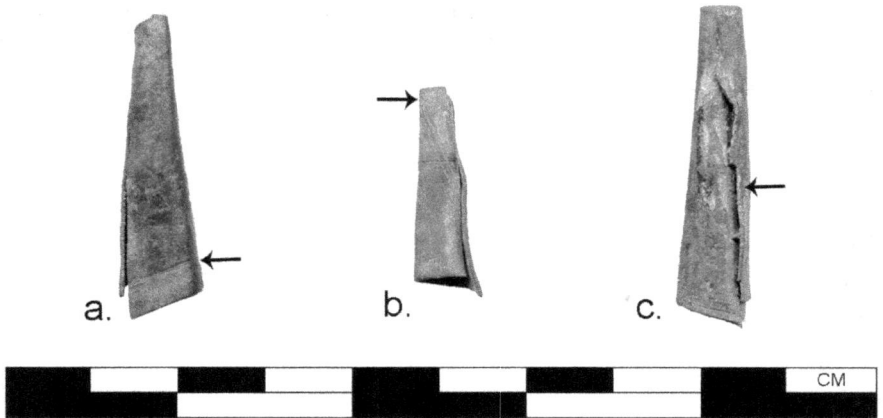

Figure 6.8. Conical tinkling cones showing evidence of scoring and cutting (catalog numbers 294, 335, 295). Photo by Brock Giordano.

surface edges (Figure 6.8). Scoring is the process of inscribing lines into the metal with a sharp instrument in order to create an outline that may be traced by cutting, chiseling, or repeatedly bending metal until it is severed. However, it is likely that in the process of cutting out other cones, score marks were removed and the evidence eliminated in the production sequence.

Only fifteen tinkling cones (4.2 percent) exhibit evidence of hammering (literally flattening), which refers to the initial process for reworking the raw material to form the desired shape of the blank. The visible scars of hammering are identified as multiple indentations along the surface.

Ten specimens (3.6 percent) show evidence of chiseling. Chiseling refers to breaking apart the raw material into the desired shape and size by applying indirect percussion to the surface using a sharp-edged object such as a chisel. This manufacturing technique creates a pattern of breakage marks along the edge of an object (Anselmi 2004, 163). However, it can be difficult to determine when chiseling was used because these markings can be attributed to the use of scissors to cut the raw material. In addition, when the edges are ground smooth before rolling the blank to form the finished cone, the manufacturing techniques are no longer visible. Many of the fragments of scrap metal collected at Fort St. Joseph display evidence of cutting using scissors or snips. In the production sequence of tinkling cones identified in this study, a desired shape blank was cut out from the raw material of a kettle. Cutting, as defined here, was accomplished using scissors or snips that Europeans introduced (Anselmi 2004, 168). As previously discussed, excavations have yielded numerous fragments of scrap metal that exhibit burrs from cutting. In addition, one shear of a scissor has been recovered.

A total of 97 (27.2 percent) tinkling cones exhibited ventral markings and 190 (53.4 percent) had dorsal indentations. Neither can be attributed conclusively to the production sequence because often such markings resulted from attachment to a garment (see Ehrhardt 2005).

Perforating refers to the process of punching or piercing a hole in the surface of an object. Anselmi (2004, 170) suggests that perforating appears to be a secondary manufacturing technique in the sense that it followed other primary methods that were used to shape and form the final object. Within this collection, two morphologically distinctive methods of perforating are present (Figure 6.9). The first method engages the process of riveting in the reuse of kettles. As kettles became worn and in need of repair, rivet holes were punctured into the metal to fasten patches together with locally produced rivets. (The latter have been recovered from excavations at Fort St. Joseph.) This process is represented by scrap metal with rivet holes, locally produced rivets, and fragments of scrap metal that display two sheets of metal that are joined together with rivets.

Figure 6.9. Perforated tinkling cones showing examples of rivet holes (a, d–e) and perforation created by a sharp, pointed object (b–c). Photo by Brock Giordano.

The second example of perforating involves a small hole made using a sharply pointed object such as an awl, a nail, or a drill bit. In cases such as this, it appears that the perforations are made after manufacturing, perhaps to embellish the appearance or sound of the tinkling cones.

As with the size attributes, the manufacturing techniques involved in the production of tinkling cones suggests that they did not result from standardized production conducted by a small segment of the population. This proposition can be tested by examining the spatial distribution of copper-alloy scrap and blanks associated with the production of tinkling cones.

Discussion and Spatial Distribution

The manufacturing techniques, form, and metric attributes of tinkling cones discussed above assist in identifying intra-assemblage variation. Results of the technological and morphological analysis suggest that various techniques were used to produce tinkling cones. Thus, tinkling cones in and around Fort St. Joseph were likely produced by multiple individuals at the fort rather than by specialized artisans. This implies that tinkling cones were manufactured on a relatively small scale by independent producers as opportunistic practices to fit the demands of local consumers in the community, of relatives, and/or even of the producers themselves. It is probable that metal was also used to craft other objects, such as metal projectile points and rivets used to repair kettles.

This pattern also has implications for the spatial distribution of production areas and scrap metal at the site. Controlled excavations can be used to evaluate distribution patterns. Hundreds of objects of personal adornment have been recovered since 2002 (Kerr 2012). Artifacts such as glass beads, scissors, earrings, needles, awls, straight pins, and tinkling cones are material expressions of personal and occupational identity. While a complete analysis of craft production and all craft-related objects found at Fort St. Joseph from controlled excavation has yet to be conducted, distributional and contextual information can contribute to this study of the organization of craft production.

Before 2015, a total of nineteen tinkling cones were recovered through controlled excavations at forty-three excavation units across the site. The distribution of copper-alloy scrap recovered from Fort St. Joseph indicates a similarly dispersed pattern. In nearly all cases, locations that yielded tinkling cones also yielded scrap metal. Thus, production of tinkling cones does not appear to have been confined to discrete production areas, as might be expected if they were the products of craft specialists. Together this evidence suggests that tinkling cones were produced opportunistically in independent workshops, likely at the household scale, to fit the demands of life on the colonial frontier at Fort St. Joseph.

Summary and Conclusions

The analysis of a large assemblage of tinkling cones collected in the late nineteenth and early twentieth centuries from the vicinity of Fort St. Joseph suggests considerable variation in metric attributes, techniques of production, and final form, implying a lack of the standardization one would expect if production was specialized and conducted by a limited number of skilled producers. Data from excavated context, particularly the dispersed spatial distribution of copper-alloy scrap metal that derives from the production of tinkling cones, supports the idea that tinkling cones were produced by most households in the area investigated thus far. Although more rigorous spatial analysis is needed to verify this pattern (see Benston 2010), tinkling cones appear to be associated with houses once occupied by fur traders and their French Canadian and Native American wives, suggesting that these individuals were the makers (and probably the users) of these objects of adornment at Fort St. Joseph.

Regional comparisons are needed to determine whether other sites that vary temporally, spatially, and culturally exhibit similar patterns. Morand (1994) documented patterns of spatial distribution and formal variation at Fort Michilimackinac that are comparable to those inferred at Fort St. Joseph. In addition, Walder (2018) employed a study of technological practices related to copper-base metal artifacts in the Great Lakes region. She also noted similarities between Fort St. Joseph and Fort Michilimackinac, specifically in the proportions of finished to unfinished (i.e., blanks, scrap) artifacts. She interprets the greater quantities of scrap metal at French colonial sites as indicative of a distinctive reworking pattern, perhaps as a result in part of the greater availability of copper-alloy raw material obtained more directly from overseas sources. When she compared the patterns of copper use in the seventeenth and eighteenth centuries between French and Native American sites in the western Great Lakes region, she found significant differences and argued that variability in finished forms is a result of the social, cultural, and ethic affiliations of communities engaged in production.

We cannot predict the spatial extent of the pattern we have observed at Fort St. Joseph because our observations derive from investigations confined to a limited area of the site associated with only a few habitations (see Hartley and Nassaney, chapter 4, this volume). Further work in other areas of the Fort St. Joseph site will be needed to determine whether the pattern observed thus far extends to other precincts and to help refute the idea that production was confined to the households of fur traders who perceived that it was in their interest to craft these intercultural objects.

This study demonstrates that significant technological transformations took place at Fort St. Joseph on the frontier of New France. It also suggests that French Canadians were capable of adopting new economic practices to produce goods desired by their Native American allies, who were likely the major consumers of these objects (Walder 2018). The contingencies of Native American demands, the availability of raw material, new cultural aesthetics, and a host of other factors make it difficult to predict what form technologies took, how labor was organized in colonial contexts, and who used the finished products. Empirical studies such as those conducted here are needed to reveal how people used technologies and resources when they confronted the exigencies of life away from their homeland.

Acknowledgments

Brock Giordano would like to thank many of the people who contributed to the analysis in this research project. This chapter draws on my master's thesis. I would like to thank Dr. Michael Nassaney for his mentorship during numerous presentations, completion of my master's thesis, and now this book chapter. Dr. Lynn Evans served on my thesis committee and provided her expertise and guidance on the material culture of the fur trade. Dr. Fred Smith also served on my thesis committee and provided valuable insight during the study. Special thanks to Dr. Kathy Ehrhardt and Dr. Lisa Marie Anselmi for supplying and discussing their previous work on technological processes for use in this research. This research would not have been feasible without their input and support. Special thanks to my Western Michigan University classmates, especially Rory Becker and Daniel Lynch. Lastly, I would like to thank my family for supporting me throughout the process. Special thanks to my father, Philip, who read countless versions of this research and stuck with me throughout the process. I have been blessed with my wife Christine, my son Luca, and my daughter Liliana, who continue to support me in this research and in life.

7

Hide Processing and Cultural Exchange
in the Fort St. Joseph Community

ERIC TEIXEIRA MENDES AND MICHAEL S. NASSANEY

In a mid-twentieth-century account of Fort St. Joseph, local historian Ralph Ballard (1949, 20) opined that "from 1740 to 1750, there were upwards of fifty families engaged at the fort. These, however, were not all within the fort." His perhaps speculative remark draws attention to the fact that it was not uncommon for fur trade populations to occupy areas beyond the fortification, as demonstrated archaeologically at places like Fort Michilimackinac and Fort Vancouver (Dunnigan n.d.; Mullaley 2011). Fort St. Joseph is no exception, based on the presence of contemporaneous artifacts and features immediately across the river and on the terrace adjacent to the floodplain (Figure 1.2) (Jelinek 1958; Nassaney 2015, 175–177; Nassaney et al. 2000). Some of these materials are arguably associated with Native American components, although little analysis has been conducted to determine their cultural affiliation and chronological placement. Additionally, Native American artifacts and imported goods often co-occur, suggesting their contemporaneity while adding to the complexity of making cultural attributions. The high density of cultural materials east of the river may explain why in 1913 city officials selected a site on the terrace overlooking the floodplain for a 65-ton boulder that commemorates Fort St. Joseph (Figure 1.1; Coolidge 1915). The monument attracted professional archaeologists in the 1930s to this area, where they found (predominantly) Late Woodland pottery and triangular projectile points at what became known as the Lyne site (20BE10) (Michigan State Site files). Limited testing in proximity to the boulder prior to the 1990s failed to locate the fort (Cremin and Nassaney 1999; Cunningham 1961).

The initial survey by Western Michigan University archaeologists in 1998 began by digging shovel test pits on the high ground west of the Fort St. Joseph boulder and state site marker (Figures 1.1, 1.2). But instead of confining the survey to the immediate vicinity of the rock, WMU archaeologists excavated some 350 shovel test pits along transects all the way to the river (Nassaney 1999). Among the materials recovered in 1998 were Late Woodland ceramics and projectile points, considerable amounts of modern debris associated with a nearby twentieth-century landfill, and a small quantity of colonial-era artifacts that included musket balls, white clay pipe stems, hand-blown glass fragments, and other possible eighteenth-century objects (Nassaney et al. 2003). The low density of these latter finds was initially disappointing, although it indicated that Fort St. Joseph was *not* located on the terrace where some believed it had been placed for defensive purposes.

Subsequent intensive survey on the terrace has revealed more eighteenth-century artifacts and several features concentrated in what we have designated Locus II of the Lyne site (Figure 1.2). These archaeological remains have implications for commercial fur-trading activities that took place beyond the fort walls. A considerably longer occupational history and different postdepositional formation processes produced cultural deposits at the Lyne site that vary formally and stratigraphically from the materials recovered from the nearby fort in the floodplain. An array of extant pit features partially truncated by plowing represent a set of activities conducted by a multiethnic segment of the eighteenth-century population. These features and their associations enable us to reconstruct the types of economic activities that were conducted on the margins of a commercial fur-trading post on the edge of empire. In this chapter, we examine and interpret the archaeological remains recovered from this locus and demonstrate their contemporaneity with the fort. We also provide a brief review of the archaeological and ethnographic literature pertaining to these pit features to aid in our interpretation of the features identified at the Lyne site and provide a broader comparative context.

Archaeological Investigations of the Lyne Site (20BE10)

Archaeologists initially dismissed the significance of the eighteenth-century artifacts they encountered at the Lyne site because of their low density and apparent lack of integrity (Nassaney 1999). When subsurface testing in the floodplain to the north in 1998 revealed dense concentrations of French and English colonial artifacts, emphasis shifted away from the terrace to the area that became known as Fort St. Joseph (20BE23). However, similarities between the cultural remains at the Lyne Site and at Fort St. Joseph revealed through subsequent work suggest that the eighteenth-century materials on the terrace resulted from activities conducted by members of the Fort St. Joseph community, albeit for a special purpose. Thus, the Lyne site offers additional opportunities for investigating colonialism and the fur trade in the St. Joseph River valley.

Excavations at the Lyne site conducted under the auspices of the Fort St. Joseph Archaeological Project since 2000 have led to the recovery of a mostly culturally and stratigraphically mixed assemblage of artifacts from four loci (Figure 1.2). Since the initial survey, the plowed terrace and the peninsula to the west (Locus IV) have yielded materials that are likely contemporaneous with the fort occupation, including triangular Madison projectile points, grit- and shell-tempered pottery, several stone smoking pipes, and a range of European imports, including gunflints, flintlock hardware (i.e., a trigger, a side plate), lead shot and musket balls, a pewter brooch, numerous copper alloy scraps, a perforated thimble (Figure 7.1), fragments of hand-blown glass containers, glass beads, and a cut fragment of trade silver perforated for ornamental use (Figure 7.2). The presence of copious amounts of fire-cracked rock, a possible Middle Woodland blade, and a Brewerton Eared projectile point indicates that the Lyne site contains multiple components representing over 3,000 years of human occupation. Most of the cultural materials (except for modern debris associated with dumping and recreational site use) date to the eighteenth century. Much of it also resembles materials found on sites Native Americans inhabited (Quimby 1960, 1966).

The site is currently covered by secondary growth deciduous trees, shrubs, and bushes. Beneath a thin layer of duff there is typically a well-defined plow zone (15–25 cm deep) underlain by a B soil horizon. Because of nineteenth- and twentieth-century plowing, most of the artifacts are confined to the plow zone and the site contains few undisturbed features. However, Locus II contains several clusters of partially overlapping pits filled with carbonized corncobs and charcoal in close proximity (Figure 7.3). While only two of these pits have been excavated in their entirety, their formal attributes (e.g., size, shape) and contents are similar to smudge pits used to tan hides

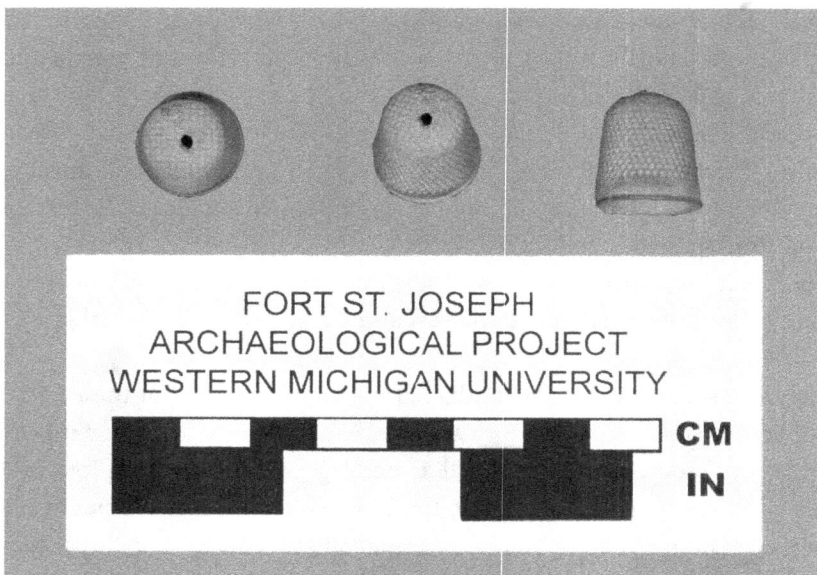

Figure 7.1. Perforated thimble (catalog no. 12-1-14) recovered from Locus III of the Lyne site. Photo by Katelyn Hillmeyer.

Figure 7.2. Trade silver ornament (catalog no. 07-1-86) recovered from Locus II of the Lyne site. Photo by John Lacko.

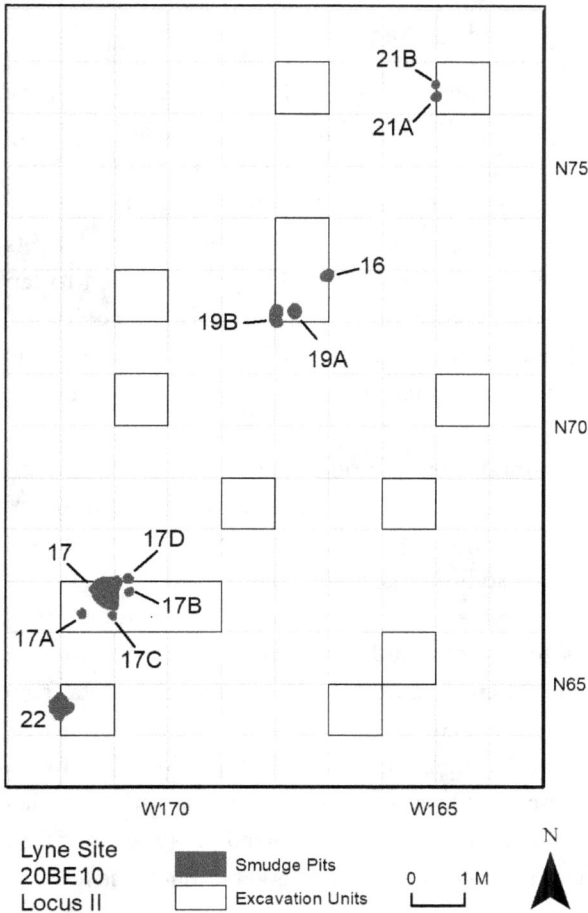

Figure 7.3. The smudge pits in Locus II of the Lyne site. Map by Jason Glatz.

noted at several sites in the region, namely Moccasin Bluff nearby in Berrien County (Ford 1973), Rhoads in central Illinois (Wagner 2011, 98–100), and Gete Odena on Grand Island in Lake Superior (Skibo et al. 2004, 171–174). In the following section, we discuss these features and their contents, their archaeological and ethnographic study, and the role they played in the fur trade at Fort St. Joseph.

Smudge Pits in Ethnographic and Archaeological Perspectives

Smudge pits are common archaeological features in North America. They have been observed ethnographically and documented archaeologically throughout the Eastern Woodlands, especially in the Southeast and the Midwest, including the western Great Lakes region (Bettarel and Smith 1973; Skibo et al. 2004; Skibo et al. 2007; Spector 1975). These small circular pits were used to contain a flameless fire, the smoke of which was used to tan hides, act as insect repellant, and/or smudge ceramic vessels (Munson 1969). The typical fuel source for these pits was maize cobs; however, slow-burning woods, nuts, and pinecones were also used (Binford 1967; Ritzenthaler 1947; Skibo et al. 2007).

Lewis Binford (1967) made smudge pits famous in his discussion of analogical reasoning, where he proposed that analogy should be used to spur inquiry. To illustrate his point, Binford (1967, 3) used smudge pits, which he described as a series of pits that "exhibited so little internal formal variability that there is little doubt that they represent a single type of feature and a single activity." He focused his analysis on fifteen smudge pits from the Toothsome site in southern Illinois but included archaeological and ethnographic data from sites in other regions throughout the continent. Based on his observations, he concluded that smudge pits were roughly a foot in diameter, were filled with charred corncobs as a fuel source, and represented "women's work." He added that hide tanning was an activity that generally occurred at "base camps" in the spring and summer when hunting was less frequent and that these features might vary in fuel source choice and method of placing the hide over the pit. Binford's work brought this type of feature to a broader audience, presented a set of characteristics that could be used to help identify them, and stoked a debate over the function of these "mundane" pits.

Two years after Binford's article, Patrick Munson (1969) published a response. First, Munson criticized Binford for exclusively discussing smudge pits' use for tanning hides, offering data on smudge pits that may have been used for smudging pots, though he admitted that this function would be region specific. Munson also offered additional sites with smudge pits to supplement Binford's survey, adding evidence that suggested the ubiquity of these features. Binford (1972) later acknowledged that ceramic smudging should be considered as a possible function of smudge pits but defended his interpretations given that smudging pots in a pit was an uncommon practice.

At the Moccasin Bluff site on the St. Joseph River about twelve miles downstream from the Lyne site, four classes of pits were uncovered. One of these classes was identified as "smudge pits" (Bettarel and Smith 1973). The two pits that made up this class were roughly 15 and 25 cm in diameter (respectively) and 5 cm deep and contained various types of wood and corncobs as fuel (Table 7.1; Bettarel and Smith 1973). The Moccasin Bluff smudge pits were at the minimum end of the range of smudge pit sizes Binford and Munson had defined. Ford (1973) noted that they were also significantly shallower than most of the pits that had been previously documented. Given their contents, the carbonized fuel sources, and the absence of ash, Bettarel and Smith stated that these were obviously used for smudging, probably for hides. Ford (1973) cautioned that given their shallow depth and the presence of ceramic fragments, these pits may have been used for smudging pots rather than smoking hides, although other sites have revealed equally shallow smudge pits that were interpreted as hide-smoking pits (Cremin and Nassaney 2003; Tordoff 1980).

At the Gete Odena site in Michigan, located on the south shore of Grand Island in Lake Superior, six smudge pits for smoking hides were uncovered (Skibo et al. 2007). These pits, which are thought to have been used during the late eighteenth and early nineteenth centuries, average 36 cm wide and 46 cm deep. These pits are somewhat unique in that their fuel sources were pinecones and pine boughs that were partially burned. Skibo and colleagues (2007) attribute this peculiarity to the site's soft sandy soil, which made for structurally unstable pits. These pits were apparently filled immediately after they served their purpose, before the fuel had been fully combusted. Researchers have discounted the idea that these were used for smudging pots because the Ojibwe were not smudging ceramics then, the mouths of the pits were too large for the "standard Late Woodland vessel" (Skibo et al. 2007, 86), and faunal remains suggest that this site was used for hide processing.

The contemporaneous Crabapple Point site in Jefferson County, Wisconsin, also provides comparative data (Spector 1975). Due to limited excavation, full interpretation of the site's permanence and function remains speculative, but at least two functions have been identified. The Ho-Chunks used this late eighteenth-century site for mining and processing lead and for smoking hides, as evidenced by the presence of four smudge pits. Two of the smudge pits at Crabapple Point were circular and two were ovoid and the fuel sources for all four pits were corncobs (Northern Flint variety) and unidentified charcoal.

Table 7.1. Smudge pit morphology at select colonial-era sites

Site Name	Feature	Length (cm)	Width (cm)	Depth (cm)	Site Location
Moccasin Bluff	Cornhole A	25	25	5	Buchanan, MI
Moccasin Bluff	Cornhole B	15	15	5	Buchanan, MI
Gete Odena	Mean of six features	46	36	46	Grand Island, MI
Crabapple Point	F12W	26	26	26	Jefferson County, WI
Crabapple Point	F12E	60	30	30	Jefferson County, WI
Crabapple Point	F13	32	32	27	Jefferson County, WI
Crabapple Point	F17	27	21	18	Jefferson County, WI
Rhoads	Mean of 79 features	35	23	8	Logan County, IL
Converse	F22	26	23	22	Grand Rapids, MI
Converse	F23 Potential smudge/basin	60	26	13	Grand Rapids, MI
Converse	F30	25	25	12.5	Grand Rapids, MI
Converse	F39	45	41	20	Grand Rapids, MI
Converse	F40	23	20	26	Grand Rapids, MI
Converse	F44	23	23	15	Grand Rapids, MI
Converse	F45	18	16	3, truncated by construction	Grand Rapids, MI
Converse	F47	25	25	20	Grand Rapids, MI
Converse	F48	24	20	3, truncated by construction	Grand Rapids, MI
Lyne	Feature 17	38	38	> 15	Niles, MI
Lyne	Feature 17A	20	20	Excavation stopped at identification	Niles, MI
Lyne	Feature 17B	25	25	> 12	Niles, MI
Lyne	Feature 17C	26	> 10	12	Niles, MI
Lyne	Feature 17D	20	> 10	Excavation stopped at identification	Niles, MI
Lyne	Feature 16	26	> 18	> 21	Niles, MI
Lyne	Feature 19A	>25	20	10	Niles, MI
Lyne	Feature 19B	>35	> 15	> 10	Niles, MI
Lyne	Feature 21A	19	19	> 10	Niles, MI

Site Name	Feature	Length (cm)	Width (cm)	Depth (cm)	Site Location
Lyne	Feature 21B	17	17	Disturbed by bioturbation	Niles, MI
Lyne	Feature 22	> 26	> 15		Niles, MI
Fort St. Joseph	Feature 3	25	20	9	Niles, MI
Fort Ouiatenon	Feature 36	46	46	30	West Lafayette, IN
Fort Ouiatenon	Feature 37	30	30	43	West Lafayette, IN

The two circular pits had a depth of 26 cm and 27 cm and diameters of 26 cm and 32 cm. The ovoid smudge pits were quite unusual in size. One had a depth of 30 cm, a length of 60 cm, and a width of 30 cm and the other a depth of 18 cm, a width of roughly 21 cm, and a length of 27 cm. Each of these smudge pits contained temporally diagnostic artifacts, including fragments of glass containers, glass beads, and lead shot. Additional artifacts included lithic flakes and animal bones. Spector (1975) proposes that this site may be consistent with Binford's notion that smudge pits were present at "base camps" inhabited during the spring and summer, outside hunting season, as the Ho-Chunks mined iron during the summer. However, historical documentation of extensive corn farming in the area suggests that the site may have been a permanent camp rather than a seasonal one.

The greatest number of smudge pits from a single site in the Midwest to date appeared at the Rhoads site, a Kickapoo village in Logan County, Illinois, where seventy-nine pits were identified as the "most ubiquitous feature" (Wagner 2011, 98). These smudge pits ranged in width from 9 to 70 cm (mean 23 cm) and in length from 12 to 84 cm (mean 35 cm). Like the Moccasin Bluff features, the depth of these smudge pits was unusually shallow; their mean depth was only 8 cm (range of 1.5 to 23 cm). Eastern Eight Row maize was used as fuel in at least sixty-four of the pits (81 percent), and a minimum of four pits contained wood charcoal. Another anomaly of the smudge pits at this site was that "at least 16 (21.9 percent) of the smudge pits also had areas of burned red clay either on their sides or base" (Wagner 2011, 100). Given the shallowness of these smudge pits and the fact that the site was excavated using a combination of hand excavation, mechanical stripping, and backhoe trenches, it is possible that more of the smudge pits had corn remains in them than those that were documented. The Rhoads site pits were interpreted as being for "the smoking of animal hides for the fur trade" (Wagner 2011, 103) and for hides the Kickapoo themselves used. This interpretation is supported by the presence of a gun barrel repurposed into a hide flesher and several post molds associated with a cluster of smudge pits near village structures that appeared to be similar to a latticework structure used in the hide-smoking process of the mid-twentieth century Kickapoos living in Mexico (Wagner 2011, 103).

Excavations of a small, early eighteenth-century component of the Converse site in Grand Rapids, Michigan, revealed nine smudge pits, some of which were truncated by historic disturbance (Hambacher et al. 2003). A single radiocarbon date and temporally diagnostic artifacts indicate this occupation most likely took place during the first half of the eighteenth century, possibly in the period 1720 to 1740 (Hambacher et al. 2003, 9–12). Among the associated artifacts were glass seed beads, a British spall-type gunflint, small amounts of trade silver, a thimble, fire-cracked rock, low-fired Native American earthenware, bone fragments, and debitage. Most of the artifacts from these features were found during flotation.

Two of the smudge pits were only 3 cm deep, whereas the other seven ranged from 12.5 to 26 cm. The pits were from 16 to 41 cm wide and from 18 to 45 cm long and were generally circular in shape; most lengths and widths differed by less than 4 cm. Six of the smudge pits featured straight walls with flat bottoms, while the remaining two were basin shaped. One of the smudge pits (Feature 22) was unusual, since it contained cattails, aquatic grasses, and tubers but no charcoal or maize. Hambacher and colleagues (2003) speculate that this smudge pit may have been used for smoking and preserving aquatic tubers and fish, although the exact reasons for its deviation from traditional smudge pits are uncertain. The other smudge pits appear to have been used for tanning hides for both domestic and commercial purposes.

The hide-tanning process is also well documented ethnographically. Ritzenthaler (1947) provides the most detailed and commonly cited work on the process of tanning and smoking hides based on his ethnographic observation of the contemporary practices of the Wisconsin Chippewa Indians. Tanning for these people involved first soaking and washing the hide, then wringing it out and scraping it clean of hair and excess flesh. Next it was washed and soaked it in a solution of water and dried deer brains, then wrung out again and stretched on a frame, where it was further stretched using an axe handle to press and loosen the hide. Then it was left taut on the frame to dry. The hide was then ready to begin the smoking process (Ritzenthaler 1947, 8–11).

For the Chippewas, smoke was created from a smudge produced in a metal bucket placed on the ground. The fuel for the smudge was generally "rotten pine or poplar, although in some cases dried Norway pine cones" were used (Ritzenthaler 1947, 12). The hide to be smoked was sewn into a bag with a single opening about a foot wide. A small band of cloth was sewn onto the hide at the opening as an extension and this cloth was secured around the bucket. This ring of cloth helped ensure that the hide would not be soiled or damaged. The skin was smoked for roughly fifteen minutes on the fur side and twenty on the flesh side, although Ritzenthaler notes that this was the light smoking his informant preferred and that a hide could be smoked for longer. The fuel in the smudge was replenished at unspecified intervals. Once the hide had been smoked on both sides, it was finished and considered fully dressed (Ritzenthaler 1947, 11–13).

Frances Densmore ([1929] 1979) also described the smoking process among early twentieth-century Native Americans. Although less detailed than Ritzenthaler, her discussion of the methods Minnesota Chippewas used offers some variations worth mentioning. Instead of scraping excess flesh, this group laid the hide over a post and used several incisions in combination with a blunt defleshing instrument made of the leg bone of a moose. Additionally, this group rubbed the brains of the deer on the hide instead of soaking it in a mixture of dried deer brains and water. The smoking process also varied for this group in significant ways. First, the smudge was created in a hole in the ground roughly 23 cm deep and 46 cm in diameter. The fuel used for this smudge was dried corncobs, as is commonly observed archaeologically. Over this hole, a frame was placed that "resembled a small tipi" (Densmore [1929] 1979, 164). The hide that was being smoked was sewn into a conical shape. If multiple hides were used, they were sewn together into the same shape and suspended on the frame over the smudge. This group also sewed a small piece of cloth around the opening of the hide so as not to damage or spoil it when it was secured on the ground around the smudge. Densmore ([1929] 1979, 163–165) did not mention smoking time. The variability in processes and methodology in these two accounts reinforces Binford's observation that archaeologists should avoid readily associating specific ethnographic accounts with archaeological interpretations. That being said, these two accounts offer a great deal of insight into potential ways that archaeologically recovered smudge pits may have been made and used.

Smudge pits are also well documented in the Southeast and much has been written about their use among the Creeks. Although Creek environmental and cultural contexts are quite different from those of groups residing in the Great Lakes region, the work done by researchers in the Southeast furthers our understanding of hide processing and the fur trade in general.

Kathryn Braund (1993) details many of the ways that new forms of commerce, specifically the fur trade, affected Creek lives. The attention she gave to modes of hunting, gendered labor, and hide-trading practices is noteworthy. As with other sources, Braund identified fall and winter as the hunting season when bucks were aggressive and careless, frost made travel through thick woods and brush easier, meat was less prone to rotting, and deer skins were thicker and more desirable (Braund 1993, 62). In the fall, Creek hunters left their summer homes and traveled in search of game, sometimes for great distances. This travel was traditionally done on foot, but during the late eighteenth century they began using horses for travel. They would set up a camp and then set out on foot to hunt. When it was considered safe, Native American men would travel with their wives and children. One of the hunting practices of the Creeks was using deerskin to camouflage a hunter pursuing deer. Ehrmann (1940, 64) reported that in Florida Timucua hunters who were adept at this practice could collect "up to four hundred deer in one winter." Women performed multiple roles during the hunting season, including processing deer skins meant for both trade and domestic use (Ehrmann 1940, 68; see Cangany 2012, 268). Although the bulk of trade hides were produced by Native Americans, colonials also hunted commercially. However, colonial hunters evidently did not tan their own hides. In the eighteenth century, selling untanned hides would likely have been an issue for colonial hunters, since the market still valued dressed and half-dressed skins over green (undressed) ones (Ehrmann 1940, 68–69, 88). For many Native American men in the Southeast who did not have wives to process hides, rum was the primary exchange good for the lesser-valued green skins and this exchange caused various problems for Native American groups. European traders could increase the value of these hides by enlisting the help of their Native American wives (Ehrmann 1940, 83–84). It was economically and practically advantageous for English traders to marry Native American women, a practice that was also common throughout New France.

Most observations about smudge pits deal exclusively with their formal characteristics and use their existence as evidence for hide processing. However, smudge pits have broader implications. Claudio Saunt (1998) uses the presence (or absence) of smudge pits to support his analysis of gender conflict within a Creek community. By highlighting the fact that tanning hides was "women's work," Saunt examined the loss of social and economic power Creek women experienced when traders began exchanging liquor for the untanned hides of single men. This was followed by an even greater loss when European companies began requesting untanned hides instead of tanned ones, perhaps coincident with improved tanning practices in Europe. This eliminated the specialized economic work of women, leading to labor reallocation. Saunt demonstrated that both the presence and absence of smudge pits can be used to explore social relations, some of which have implications for Fort St. Joseph.

In 1940, W. W. Ehrmann fused previous ethnographic and archaeological descriptions of the Timucuas of sixteenth-century Florida to produce an overview of their daily lives and practices. He noted that at night the Timucuas "built smudges under their beds to drive away insects" (1940, 177), drawing on previous work by Swanton (1922, 354), who observed that "it is usually necessary for [the Timucuas] to make fires in their houses, absolutely under their beds, . . . to be freed from these vermin ['maringous,' a small biting fly]." No descriptions of these fires were given, but future archaeological reports cited this reference to Timucua behavior when identifying features. For example, Jerald Milanich (1972) identified at least twenty-one features as smudge pits in north-central Florida. The diameters of these pits ranged from about 15.0 to 30.5 cm. They deviated from most smudge pits in that they had a "high" ash content and "large amounts of food bone refuse" (Milanich 1972, 42). Although small quantities of faunal remains are often found in smudge pits, it is rare that a single smudge pit contains any significant quantity of bone. Additionally, smudge pits rarely contain ash since they held oxygen-deprived fires that, ideally, did not flame. Thus, it is strange that the Florida smudge pits contained these elements. Milanich hypothesized that the smudge pits at the Richardson site were repeatedly used and were found "under beds supported by small posts and located inside a house structure" (1972, 42) that the Potanos slept in. Milanich also suggested that these pits offered a convenient place to dispose of food remains. Milanich proposed that as the smudge pits filled over time, either a new pit would be dug or the old one would be emptied and its contents would be dispersed on the ground surrounding the pits, creating what he calls "dark 'bed size' humic areas surrounding the pit" (1972, 42). He does not address the issue of ash in the pits.

Finally, it should be noted that smudge pits are not confined exclusively to Native American contexts, although they represent Native American practice. A widespread distribution of these pits (n = 9) was found in proximity to the eastern wall of Fort Moore, an early eighteenth-century British settlement in South Carolina (Cobb and Sapp 2014). Perhaps most notably, these features suggest an interior presence of Native Americans in the fort, since Europeans generally did not engage in this type of activity.

In sum, archaeological and ethnographic data suggest that smudge pits are ubiquitous in eastern North America and that while they served various functions, they were most often used by Native Americans to tan hides, particularly at the height of the fur trade.

Smudge Pits at the Lyne Site

WMU archaeologists have regularly investigated the Lyne site (20BE10) over the past two decades (Nassaney 2015, 175–177). The sediment at the Lyne site consists of a well-drained, sandy loam that has two strata. The uppermost stratum is a dark-brown sandy-loam plow zone about 20 cm deep that was created by agricultural activity in the nineteenth and early twentieth centuries. It is underlain by a B soil horizon that appears as a light yellow-brown sandy loam. Although the plow zone is disturbed, it contains a low-to-moderate density of artifacts, so the general practice is to excavate both it and the B horizon in five-centimeter arbitrary levels within stratigraphic units. Excavated soil has been dry screened through quarter-inch and eighth-inch mesh. Features typically become visible at the base of the plow zone when dark feature fill can be readily distinguished from the lighter B-horizon matrix. Features are generally pedestaled and cross-sectioned during excavation. Feature fill is collected for flotation to recover botanical remains.

Beginning in 2007, we located a series of definitive pre-nineteenth-century features in Locus II that we have interpreted as smudge pits (Figures 1.2, 7.3). Feature 17 first appeared as a rather large circular feature composed of dark sandy loam mottled with flecks of charcoal and fragments of carbonized corncobs immediately beneath the plow zone. By about 35 cm below the ground surface (BS), this feature could be distinguished as two separate pits, designated Features 17 and 17A. Feature 17A was a circular pit identified as a smudge pit because of the high concentration of carbonized corn and charcoal it contained. Excavations also revealed lithic flakes and a core in proximity. Feature 17A was pedestaled but not excavated further.[1] This unit was expanded into a one- by two-meter unit to further explore Feature 17, which extended into the wall.

At 46 cm BS, Feature 17 appeared as four distinct pits, Features 17, 17B, 17C, and 17D. One of these pits, Feature 17D, appeared as a half-circle that extended into the northern wall of the unit. This feature contained a high density of carbonized corn and charcoal and was identified as a smudge pit. Feature 17D was pedestaled at 46 cm BS and was not excavated further. Feature 17B appeared as a circular pit marked by a high concentration of carbonized corn and charcoal and some oxidized soil. A chert scraper recovered near Feature 17B appears similar to Chickasaw end scrapers found in Mississippi, reinforcing the inference that these pits were used for processing fur.

Feature 17 persisted, gradually diminishing in size. Its shape became more circular until 50 cm BS, when it was clearly a circular pit like the other related features, although this pit contained far more carbonized seeds (n = 171) than the other smudge pits (Martinez 2009, 44). Excavation was terminated at this depth. A final feature, Feature 17C, was identified in the west profile of the unit at 35 cm BS and also appears to be a smudge pit. Several large pieces of unburned bone were uncovered in these smudge pits, including a deer vertebra. Fire-cracked rock was also found in the unit containing this feature cluster, mostly in the southeast corner away from the smudge pits, but some small pieces were found in the smudge pits as well.

Flotation samples were taken from Features 17, 17B, and 17D at multiple levels. Two tubular glass beads (white and black) were recovered while processing two of the flotation samples from this cluster. Analysis also revealed that small amounts of wood charcoal, carbonized walnuts, and raspberry, sumac, and grape seeds were present in the feature fill in addition to the large amounts of carbonized corn (see Hughes-Skallos and Allen 2012; Martinez 2009). A ^{14}C sample taken from this feature cluster yielded a date of AD 1710 ± 50 years. This date and the presence of glass beads from the features and the occurrence of other eighteenth-century artifacts at the site suggest that members of the Fort St. Joseph community used these smudge pits.

Three additional smudge pits were identified approximately 6 meters to the north (Figure 7.3). Before encountering these features, excavations in the plow zone yielded a core, a fragment of low-fired earthenware, clear glass sherds, slag, and a piece of ferrous metal. The first smudge pit in this feature was identified at 35 cm BS and was located in the northeast corner, extending into both the northern and eastern walls. As a result, the unit was expanded to the north. Feature 16 included calcined bone fragments, carbonized seeds, and large amounts of charcoal, carbonized corn, and sherds of clear glass. When excavation was terminated on this unit, Feature 16 appeared to extend into the east wall. At 46 cm BS two additional smudge pits were identified—Features 19A and 19B (Figure 7.4). Both features contained large amounts of charcoal and carbonized corn. Feature 19A also contained a large piece of fire-cracked rock which had an unburned bone underneath it. Feature 19A is only one of two smudge pits fully excavated at the Lyne site (the other being Feature 17C). Both smudge pits featured flat bottoms, and Feature 19A had a thin lens of oxidized soil at its base.

Feature 21 was identified at 30 cm BS. At 35 cm BS, this feature appeared as two smudge pits designated Feature 21A (19 cm in diameter) and Feature 21B

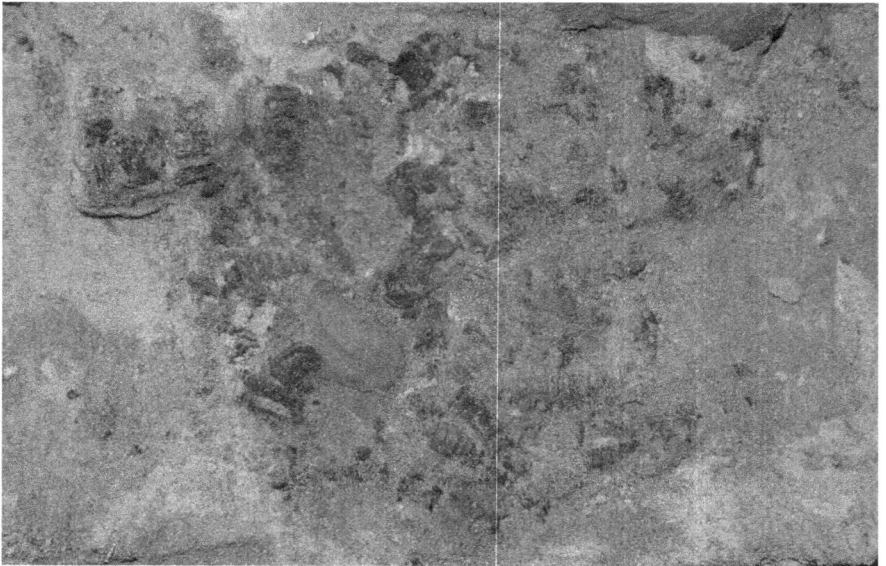

Figure 7.4. Close-up of Feature 19A. Note the high density of carbonized corncobs and charcoal, a common attribute of smudge pits at the Lyne site. Photo by Stephanie Barrante.

(17 cm in diameter). Although these features were pedestaled at 35 cm BS, an animal burrow destroyed the visible remains of Feature 21B to a depth of 40 cm where excavation was terminated. Feature 21A was still present, however, though reduced in size while extending into the west wall. Lithic flakes were also found in the non-feature soil of this unit in the plow zone and B horizon.

In 2010 another smudge pit, Feature 22, was uncovered in Locus II of the Lyne site. As with most smudge pits at the Lyne site, identification of the feature was made at 35 cm BS when a large concentration of carbonized corn and charcoal was observed. Like Features 17, 17B, and 19A, this feature exhibited oxidized soil and contained fire-cracked rock. Unlike most other smudge pits at the Lyne site, however, Feature 22 contained small amounts of calcined bone. Excavation ended at 50 cm BS, before the smudge pit was fully excavated.

To date, smudge pits at the Lyne site share some characteristics. First, of the five smudge pits that were fully exposed in plan, all are circular with diameters ranging from 17 to 38 cm. This is consistent with the other colonial-era smudge pits previously mentioned, with the exceptions of Feature 12E at the Crabapple site and Feature 23 at the Converse site, which was interpreted as a potential smudge pit or basin. The walls of clearly defined smudge pits at the Lyne site are straight, as is typical of similar features elsewhere. Pit depths have been compromised at the Lyne site due to plowing and only two smudge pits have been excavated to their base. That being said, the minimum depths of the smudge pits at the Lyne site are deeper than those at Moccasin Bluff, Fort St. Joseph, and Fort Ouiatenon and exceed the average depth at Rhoads. They are more similar to those at Crabapple Point, Converse, and Gete Odena (see Table 7.1 for a summary of their morphology).

Additionally, the contents and associated artifacts of the Lyne site smudge pits conform to what is traditionally found in colonial-era smudge pits. The fuel in the pits at the Lyne site appears as dense concentrations of carbonized maize and wood charcoal. These are traditional fuel sources for smudge pits, as observed in many smudge pits at contemporaneous sites in Michigan. The flotation samples that have been sorted and analyzed thus far have produced artifacts that are also consistent with other colonial-era smudge pits. These include calcined bone fragments or splinters that are often too small for identification during hand excavation, lithic debitage, fire-cracked rock, and glass seed beads. Furthermore, there is a conspicuous absence of deer bone in smudge pits used for tanning hides. Instead, the bones are generally those of other mammals and fish. Ash and oxidized soil are sometimes found in smudge pits, including those at the Lyne site, although they occur less frequently. Finally, stone or metal hide scrapers have been found in proximity to smudge pits. The Rhoads site yielded a gun-barrel hide flesher and a chert hide scraper was found near Feature 17B at the Lyne site.

In sum, the formal attributes, associations, and location of the pits found at the Lyne site implicate them in the processing of hides in the eighteenth century. People likely affiliated with the Fort St. Joseph community conducted these activities.

Summary and Conclusions

Archaeological evidence of the fur trade is not confined to the European-style structures and associated objects identified in the fortified settlement known as Fort St. Joseph. Artifacts and features in the vicinity of the fort testify to the presence of Potawatomis, Miamis, and perhaps even some French traders who conducted activities that were essential to the fur trade, including processing fur-bearing animals and preparing their hides (see Nassaney et al. 2012; Hoock et al., chapter 8, this volume).

The use of small, shallow pits filled with combustible materials to produce smoky fires is a notably Native American practice throughout eastern North America, as we have discussed. Moreover, these features increase in frequency in the western Great Lakes region in the eighteenth century, when Native Americans were the primary producers in the fur trade. Eleven smudge pits that represent the tanning of hides have been identified at the Lyne site on a terrace in close proximity to Fort St. Joseph. The lack of any other premodern features, their close proximity, the similarities in their contents and formal characteristics, the stratigraphic context, and associated artifacts and a radiocarbon date suggest that the smudge pits at the Lyne site are most likely eighteenth-century features that are contemporaneous with the occupation of Fort St. Joseph.

Ethnographic and ethnohistorical accounts suggest that Native American women were usually responsible for processing hides, including using smudge pits, for both domestic and commercial purposes. Thus, it is reasonable to infer that the smudge pits identified at the Lyne site and in the nearby floodplain (Cremin and Nassaney 2003) represent activities conducted by enslaved Native American women, Native American wives of French traders, and/or the *métis* offspring of these cross-cultural unions. Women were likely directly involved in processing furs to increase their value before the furs were shipped to Detroit, Michilimackinac, and Montreal (see Cangany 2012). This is one of many activities that Native American women contributed to the fur trade, in addition to provisioning Native American hunters and French traders (Nassaney 2015, 56–57, 169–171). The frequency of these features on the terrace may suggest that intensive hide tanning took place in this location, brought about by the increased demands for processed hides and the desire to segregate this activity beyond the fort walls.

In the future, larger sample sizes drawn from sites in the Midwest may provide researchers with data to explore other avenues of labor organization involved in hide processing. For example, future research may examine intrasite variation to ascertain the degree of standardization smudge pits exhibit to determine if they indicate centralized production (see Giordano and Nassaney, chapter 6, this volume). The size of smudge pits may also be correlated with the size of the hide being smoked or the intensity of the activity being conducted. At present, the variability in their size and contents suggest that smudge pits did not require strict guidelines to function effectively.

Furthermore, smudge pits were not excluded from European settlements. In the context of cultural exchanges that characterized fur trade society (Loren 2008; Mann 2003; Nassaney 2015), the French may have also adopted the practice of tanning hides. For example, features identified as smudge pits have been found at European settlements, including Fort Moore (n = 9) (Cobb and Sapp 2014), Fort Ouiatenon (n = 2) (Tordoff 1980, 22, 45), and Fort St. Joseph (n = 1), as mentioned above (Cremin and Nassaney 2003). This may be indicative of European adoption of the practice and/or of Native American activities in previously unsuspected locations. At Fort Ouiatenon and possibly at Fort St. Joseph, the pits are associated with the activities of a blacksmith (Hartley and Nassaney, chapter 4, this volume). Further evidence that blacksmiths may have been involved in hide tanning comes from documentary sources. Fort St. Joseph merchants Louis Hamelin and Louis Gastineau (Gatineau?) supplied blacksmiths Antoine De Lestre and Joseph Lepage with some 500 pounds of deerskins valued at 875 livres in June 1739 (Peyser 1978, document 86). The Crown reimbursed the merchants for these skins, suggesting that De Lestre and Lepage were owed for goods or services that they had provided to local Native American allies (Nassaney 2015, 169). Although the intended use of these skins is unknown, they were likely a medium of exchange. Given their economic significance, the French may have acquired and accepted unprocessed furs with the intention of tanning them to increase their value, thereby competing directly with the labor of Native American women. They did not aim to emulate Native American practices but used them to pursue their own mercantilist agenda deep in the heart of the continent on the frontiers of the French empire (see Nassaney, chapter 10, this volume). The contents and context of rather mundane features such as smudge pits have the potential to reveal significant new information about Native American and French interactions, gendered labor, and the role economic practices played in facilitating cultural exchange in the Fort St. Joseph community.

Acknowledgments

This chapter could not have been completed without the help of my original excavation partner Kelly (Schulze) Rectenwald and the other field school students who excavated and documented these features before and after us. Thanks to Dr. Craig Sheldon for sharing his insights and relevant experiences with us. Special thanks to Dr. LisaMarie Malischke for the assistance, encouragement, and insight she offered through the many iterations and phases of this chapter. Finally, Eric Mendes would like to thank Melissa Musumeci, Nancy and Donald McNinch, Celia and Sergio Mendes, and Scott Wingeier for their encouragement and support in the drafting of this chapter; without them, its completion would not have been possible. Any shortcomings in the chapter belong to the authors and do not reflect on any of the people who helped us bring our research to fruition.

Note

1. Only two smudge pits have been excavated in their entirety at the Lyne site. Typically, we began our field season at the Lyne site and spent less than a week there training novice students in archaeological field techniques. Thus, we have practiced a conservation ethic with regard to the excavation of features and have decided that preservation in place is a viable approach, given that smudge pits are rare in the region, are on municipal property, and are not threatened by imminent destruction.

8

The Changing Cultural Landscape
of the Lower St. Joseph River Valley

MARK HOOCK, ALLISON M. HOOCK,
AND MICHAEL S. NASSANEY

Since the late nineteenth century, when Lewis Henry Morgan (1881) published a comparative study of the indigenous architecture of the New World,
settlement pattern analyses at varying scales have been a vital feature of
anthropological studies (Kowalewski 2008; Nabokov and Easton 1989; Parsons 1972; Trigger 1967). While early twentieth-century spatial studies in the
United States mainly focused on variability in ceramic styles, subsequent
work examined the distribution of sites and features across landscapes to
better understand societal transformations (Feinman 2015; Johnson 1981;
Paynter 1982; Smith 1978). Among the topics of interest are the settlement
strategies that Europeans and Native Americans enacted in the age of exploration and colonization, when Europeans penetrated the continent in search
of profitable goods and Native Americans became involved in global processes of production and resource extraction (Cronon 1983). Many analyses
have emphasized the purported changes in Native American living arrange-
ments, social organization, and political structure in response to European
military, political, and economic activities (see Mintz 1985, 157; Wolf 1982,
145–149; Zinn 1999, 1–22). Less emphasis has been placed on how Native
American peoples sought to maintain access to land, resources, and mobility
patterns in the face of European encroachment (cf. O'Brien 1997). Settlement

systems result from a variety of ecological and social factors (Nassaney et al. 2001). Whatever the causal factors that influenced the movement and emplacement of people, regional settlement analysis can be an effective way of understanding past relationships between Native American and European groups.

Although Native Americans eventually became dispossessed under European and Euro-American policies and practices, they were not passive victims in an inevitable process. Scholars recognize that Native Americans challenged new conditions by adopting technological innovations in order to maintain the traditional cultural values that guided their decisions in daily life (e.g., Hamell 1983), including the locations of their settlements. The persistence of Native American subsistence, settlement, and material practices challenges the idea that interactions with Europeans created a hybrid culture (cf. Nassaney 2008b, 2018b, chapter 10, this volume). Quimby (1966, 140) noted this decades ago when he observed that Native Americans of the region were participating in a pan-Indian culture that involved the wholesale adoption of European goods. Yet as he documented changes in Native American material assemblages, he also noted a number of "old-style native manufactures" that "may reflect a conservatism in some aspects in material culture" (1966, 141–142). Traditional objects included pits filled with charred corn (see Mendes and Nassaney, chapter 7, this volume), birch-bark grave linings, burial furniture, stone pipes, modified brass thimbles reimagined as tinkling cones, hair pipes, wooden spoons, medicine bundles, wampum, and bone handles decorated with a traditional incised zigzag design. In describing the lifeways of the early nineteenth-century Chippewas (based on the ethnohistory of Alexander Henry and the archaeological record), Quimby similarly remarked, "Acculturation applies primarily to material culture. . . . There seems to be a *continuity and conservatism of subsistence and settlement pattern* that is lacking in most aspects of material culture" (Quimby 1966, 179; our emphasis). Indeed, the Ojibwas maintained seasonal mobility so they could secure subsistence resources—a practice that long preceded European contact—well into the mid-nineteenth century in parts of the eastern Great Lakes region (Ferris 2009, 62). These seemingly incongruous patterns eventually led archaeologists to discard the old acculturation paradigm as they began to consider a Native American point of view (see Nassaney 2012a, 2018b).

The complex relations between Native Americans and Europeans undoubtedly influenced the identities, positions of power, legacies, settlement, and histories of all groups. Any community confronting adversities will maintain certain customs and behaviors while changing others. As a consequence, a simple dichotomy of change and continuity is an inadequate way of examining colonialist relations (Silliman 2009, 213, 226). Colonial studies demonstrate that Native American and European cultural practices sometimes blended and sometimes were largely preserved (Hartley and Nassaney, chapter 4, this volume; Nassaney 2015; Nassaney, chapter 10, this volume). The fur trade in the Great Lakes region transformed the ways many Native American groups were organized and how they lived. Some groups such as the Iroquois gained a competitive advantage through the goods they obtained and the alliances they created with European groups (Brandão and Nassaney, chapter 2, this volume). Similarly, Europeans often benefited from relations with Native Americans by adopting their technologies (Mendes and Nassaney, chapter 7, this volume) and learning how to cultivate local subsistence resources, including maize (Cunningham 1961, 72–73; Martin et. al., chapter 3, this volume). Native Americans were also the primary producers in the fur trade and their settlement choices dictated where the French lived. This chapter examines how shifting settlement distributions in the St. Joseph River valley can provide information about the nature of these changing social, political, and economic relationships.

Archaeological evidence from the lower St. Joseph River valley provides a useful case study for examining how Native American groups and European colonists positioned themselves in relation to one another as they pursued overlapping and divergent interests. Fort St. Joseph, which was located in the St. Joseph River valley (Figures 2.1, 8.1), was a node of exchange for local Native Americans and the French for nearly a century. This chapter explores the influence Fort St. Joseph had on settlement patterns in the region, where Native American peoples lived before and after the abandonment of the fort. Systematic and opportunistic survey information collected by the Michigan State Historic Preservation Office and the Indiana Department of Natural Resources, Division of Historic Preservation and Archaeology, has led to data on over 170 archaeological sites that can be used to monitor settlement change and continuity. In this spatial study, we engaged in a longitudinal analysis using a geographic information system (GIS) to examine change and continuity in settlement size and location. This analysis can provide insight into the relationships between groups in the region based on the proximities of settlements to one another, to natural landscape features, and to Fort St. Joseph.

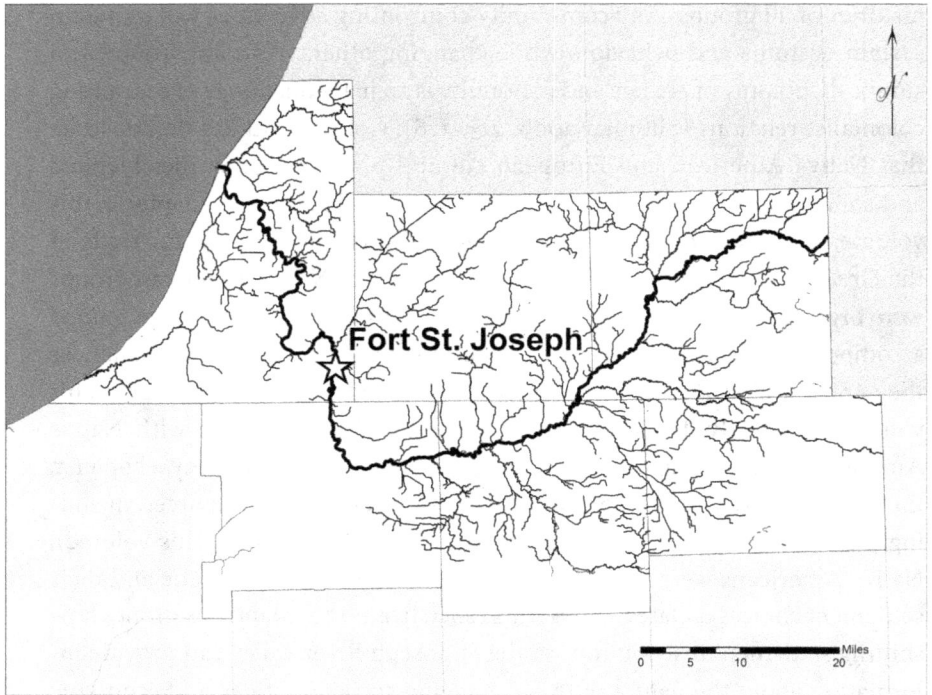

Figure 8.1. Location of Fort St. Joseph in the St. Joseph River valley. Map by Allison Hoock.

Background and Research Approach

Archaeological remains and oral accounts indicate that Native American cultures flourished for thousands of years before Europeans arrived in the western Great Lakes region and the St. Joseph River valley. Archaeologists have documented and investigated some of these sites and their associated activities (see Bettarel and Smith 1973; Cremin 1992, 1996; Garland 1981; Hinsdale 1931; Holman and Brashler 1999; O'Gorman and Lovis 2006; Secunda 2006; Schurr 2006, 2010). By about AD 1000, small, mobile groups of hunter-gatherers with a ceramic tradition of grit-tempered wares occupied the region. Potentially significant additions to their cultural practices before the arrival of the French include the adoption of maize horticulture and shell tempering, both of which diffused into or were carried into the area from regions to the south and west. These adoptions may have increased Native American resource security in a region marked by a natural bounty of plant and animal foods.

The St. Joseph River valley supported seasonally occupied sites; people moved across the landscape in accordance with the shifting availability of resources. Spring was the time for exploiting potamodromous fish such as sturgeon (Martin et al., chapter 3, this volume) and possibly collecting and processing maple sap. In the summer, agricultural villages were established in areas with arable land along rivers. Fall was the time to harvest nuts, store surplus foods in subterranean pits (Dunham 2000), and hunt fur-bearing animals. Populations likely dispersed into small family units in the late fall and winter in order to continue hunting as they subsisted on stored foods. Larger groups aggregated once again in the spring (Holman and Brashler 1999, 215–218). Animal foods were an important part of the diet, as indicated by the wide variety of mammal, bird, fish, and reptile remains recovered from archaeological sites (e.g., Bettarel and Smith 1973; Martin et al., chapter 3, this volume). Typically, Native American peoples moved within a defined homeland to accommodate the seasonal availability of food resources, fluctuations in group size, and different activities. These practices account for much of the settlement variation observed on the landscape.

According to oral tradition and early French documents, the Potawatomis had separated from their Ojibwe and Odawa kin and moved into western Lower Michigan by the early seventeenth century (Clifton 1977, 1986). After they settled, they adopted a mixed economic strategy that included maize agriculture (Nassaney et al. 2012, 58). Historical and archaeological evidence suggests that many Potawatomis relocated to the Green Bay area of Wisconsin in response to pressure from the Iroquois (see Mason 1986; Nassaney et al. 2012). It was here in a multi-ethnic community that the exiled Potawatomis engaged in and perhaps perfected the Algonquin practice of alliance and mediation. This movement to a new area afforded them a social and strategic advantage from their previous homeland by providing temporary security from Iroquois raids, direct access to French trade goods, and a political climate that offered opportunities for expansion and cultural growth (Clifton 1978; Nassaney et al. 2012; White 1991).

In 1679, the French explorer La Salle traveled to the mouth of the St. Joseph River and built Fort Miami, the first European settlement in the region. After constructing the fort, he moved up river in search of a portage near South Bend, Indiana, heading for the Kankakee River, a tributary of the Illinois. Along this route, La Salle came across a mixed community of Miami-Mascouten-Wea Indians located at the southwestern end of the portage near the headwaters of the Kankakee (Anderson 1901). This is one of the few historical references to Native American peoples occupying this region before the 1680s, although there is ample archaeological evidence of Late Woodland occupation (ca. AD 600–1600) on many habitable landforms (see below).

In the 1680s, some Miamis moved to the St. Joseph River from La Salle's Fort St. Louis on the Illinois River (Nassaney et al. 2012, 59). This move may have been facilitated by Father Claude Allouez, who established a Jesuit mission to serve Native Americans close to the portage and the old Sauk trail that connected Lakes Erie and Michigan (Brandão and Nassaney, chapter 2, this volume; Myers and Peyser 1991, 12). According to various historical documents, the earliest Miami village(s) were located on the east side of the river just north of the Michigan-Indiana line (Nassaney et al. 2012, 59–60). However, shortly after Fort St. Joseph was constructed near the Jesuit mission at Niles in 1691, the Miamis moved down river, possibly settling along Brandywine Creek, a tributary stream that enters the St. Joseph from the east only a short distance south of the fort. Later, the Miami groups moved directly across the river from the fort (Cremin 1992; Nassaney et al. 2012). The latter move suggests that the French residents of the fort and the Miamis were forming a mutually advantageous relationship (Nassaney et al. 2012, 60).

In the late seventeenth century, the Potawatomis began to migrate from their refuge in Wisconsin to the St. Joseph River. Some decades later, in 1762, Thomas Hutchins noted a Potawatomi village across the river from the fort on his map of the region and indicated that this settlement included 200 men (Figure 2.2; Nassaney et al. 2012). In the early eighteenth century, the Potawatomis outnumbered but co-existed with small communities of Miamis in the region. However, by mid-century only the Potawatomis remained (Cremin 1992; Kinietz 1972; Nassaney et al. 2012; Temple 1958).

The establishment of the French mission and then Fort St. Joseph in the late seventeenth century marks a major watershed for European influence in the region that was expressed materially by a significant influx of European goods. Fort St. Joseph was established in a strategic position near the portage that linked the St. Joseph River and the Great Lakes basin to the expansive Mississippi drainage basin (Figure 2.1). The fort became pivotal in terms of military, religious, and commercial activity for the local Native American populations. Indeed, the religious role of the fort was soon eclipsed by its military and commercial importance (Nassaney 2015, 168). Given the role of the fort as a center for diplomacy and a distribution point for imported goods such as cloth, kettles, and iron tools, it seems reasonable to hypothesize that it had some influence on the movement and distribution of Native American peoples in the region.

When the British defeated the French in the Seven Years' War and the British came to occupy Fort St. Joseph, relations between the local Native American populations and Europeans soured, precipitating Pontiac's Rebellion (Widder 2013). When the British decided not to regarrison the fort after 1763, predominantly French traders occupied the fort until they were deported in 1780. The fort was apparently abandoned in 1781, soon after it became part of American territory. Trade activity had shifted to other locations in the valley but a significant number of Native American peoples remained in the valley until the 1830s, when the US government acquired much of the land by treaty and forcibly expelled many, although not all, Native Americans to make room for an expanding and land-hungry Euro-American population (Bollwerk 2006; DuLong 2001, 13; Santer 1977, 46; Schurr 2006, 2010; Secunda 2006). Some bands demonstrated that they had taken up farming and adopted Christianity, thereby avoiding the fate of those who were removed to Kansas.

From the precontact period to statehood in 1837, the population of the St. Joseph River valley underwent many transitions in terms of composition, lifestyles, and relationships among various groups. The US doctrine of Manifest Destiny led to questionable treaties in the early nineteenth century that stripped Native American peoples of their land holdings and forced many tribes to move west, leaving only those who were willing to adapt to change or disguise their identity in the wake of tides of immigrants arriving on what had become American soil. Because the federal government appropriated Native American lands and had dispossessed Native Americans by the 1830s, Euro-Americans began to accumulate more power in the newly formed United States. These changes formed the basis of racialized narratives that justified the goal of Manifest Destiny (Nassaney 2012a). However, this does not mean that the government removed all Indians from the St. Joseph River valley during this period. Stuck in a continual process of creating and filling new cultural roles, the Native American inhabitants of the valley experienced rapid change in the nineteenth and early twentieth centuries. By considering multiple lines of evidence, including archaeological remains, we can gain a fuller understanding of Native American actions. These actions often run counter to the information in local histories (see Low 2018).

Data on the distribution of sites in the St. Joseph River valley in the Michigan and Indiana state site files can help us gain a better understanding of site locations and their significance. Some of the 171 recorded sites consist of isolated finds and others are based on documentary sources and have been neither verified in the field nor subjected to thorough archaeological investigations. Despite these limitations, the site files provide a first approximation of the locations of sites in the region. The accessible files contain information on occupants of the St. Joseph River valley from the Late Woodland period until statehood (AD 600–1837). To use these diachronic data to understand change and continuity in settlement patterns, we chose to divide the sample into three temporal periods associated with settlements before the establishment of the fort, while the fort was occupied, and after the fort was abandoned. These periods are thus referred to as the pre-fort period (AD 600–1690); the fort period (1691–1781); and the post-fort period (1782–1850). The latter period is when many Native Americans in the United States were removed from their homelands (1795–1840). The demarcation of these periods helps control for differences in settlement distributions in relation to Fort St. Joseph.

Mapping Colonialism and the Fur Trade in the St. Joseph River Valley

The intent of our research was to construct a more refined picture of how Native Americans and Euro-Americans selected settlement locations in the St. Joseph River valley through a GIS analysis of archaeological data. Toward this end, Kohley (2013) collected spatial data on European and Native American settlements that existed between AD 600 to the mid-nineteenth century from the Michigan State Historic Preservation Office and the Indiana Department of Natural Resources Division of Historic Preservation and Archaeology. These data included 121 sites in Michigan and 50 sites in Indiana. Archival data of all known archaeological sites from these state departments were digitized using Earthpoint.us, Google Earth, and Esri's ArcMap 10.1 on base layer maps downloaded from the state of Michigan Geographic Information System and mapping site and the U.S. Geological Survey national data website.[1] We created an extensive database that included cultural and environmental attributes for each settlement from the site files. The database includes specific characteristics for each site: settlement size, cultural affiliation, professional reports related to specific sites, and samples of artifacts found at smaller sites. We classified each site by temporal period (pre-fort, fort, and post-fort) and cultural affiliation (Native American, European, or Euro-American).

We also placed each site into one of three categories of varying "magnitudes" based on site size and duration of occupation as recorded in the Michigan and Indiana site files. We established settlement size and temporal span through historic records and attributes of the artifact assemblage. These categories aim to be mutually exclusive given the imprecision of the available data and serve as a heuristic device that enabled us to compare the number of sites by size and cultural affiliation over time.

Magnitude 1 consists of sites that have yielded few artifacts and are described in the site files as lithic scatters or isolated finds. Examples include sites that yielded a small quantity of chipping debris, fire-cracked rock, a gun flint, or a finger ring. Magnitude 1 sites were least likely to inform this research due to the paucity of material. Magnitude 2 consists of small, temporary habitations recorded in the site files primarily as "camps" and homesteads, farms, burials, and mill sites. Magnitude 3 sites are recorded in the files as "villages," "forts," trading posts, and missions and as the U.S. General Land Office. The sites in the category of Magnitude 3 were associated with the largest populations.

In addition, we conducted a central feature analysis to track the distribution of sites before Fort St. Joseph was established, while it was occupied, and after it was abandoned. This helped us visualize spatial patterns, since many sites are in close proximity to one another. Central feature analysis illustrates site distribution in a simplified way by identifying a centrally located site for each period for both Europeans and Native Americans. This type of analysis enabled us to track the distribution of sites before Fort St. Joseph was established, while it was occupied, and after it was abandoned and the general movement of population from the pre-fort era to the post-fort era. Although it does not necessarily indicate the most important feature by any classification other than geographic centrality, it does help us visualize patterns of distribution and movement through the three analytical periods. These data also enabled us to chart the proximity of each site to major natural and cultural landscape features (e.g., the St. Joseph River, Lake Michigan, and Fort St. Joseph). This metric helps us understand whether these features were important to settlement decisions and whether the relationships to these features changed over time. These methods gave us a clear way of comparing how Native American and Euro-American groups fluctuated in size and shifted over the landscape at different historical moments.

Results

Pre-Fort Period (AD 600–1690)

Native American settlements were widely distributed during the pre-fort period. We identified 105 Native American sites that included 100 small and widely dispersed isolated sites and temporary encampments (Table 8.1). These sites were occupied in an era marked by the seasonal migration of Native American groups, who relied on the waterways for fishing and transportation (Dunham 2000; Holman and Brashler 1999). Through central feature analysis, we identified a village in the interior of the valley as the geographic center of Native American settlement during this period (Figure 8.2). In addition, the sites were all located on the St. Joseph River or its tributaries or on the portage between the Kankakee and St. Joseph Rivers, a corridor between the St. Joseph River and the Mississippi River drainage (circled in Figure 8.3).

A few Native American sites were located on Lake Michigan. The average distance of these settlements to the lake was 30 miles. The only European

Table 8.1. Number and magnitude of sites by temporal period and cultural affiliation

Time Period	Pre-Fort (AD 600–1690)	Fort (AD 1691–1781)	Post-Fort (AD 1782–1850)
Native American	105	9	25
Magnitude 1[a]	56	2	1
Magnitude 2[b]	44	1	7
Magnitude 3[c]	5	6	17
European	1	12	24
Magnitude 1	0	4	1
Magnitude 2	0	2	9
Magnitude 3	1	6	14

[a] Small settlements (isolates or scatters) that yield a small number of diagnostic artifacts that lack historical context; least likely to inform this research because of the paucity of material.
[b] Temporary habitations such as camps and/ or agricultural fields.
[c] Settlements with longer occupation and larger populations such as villages and forts.

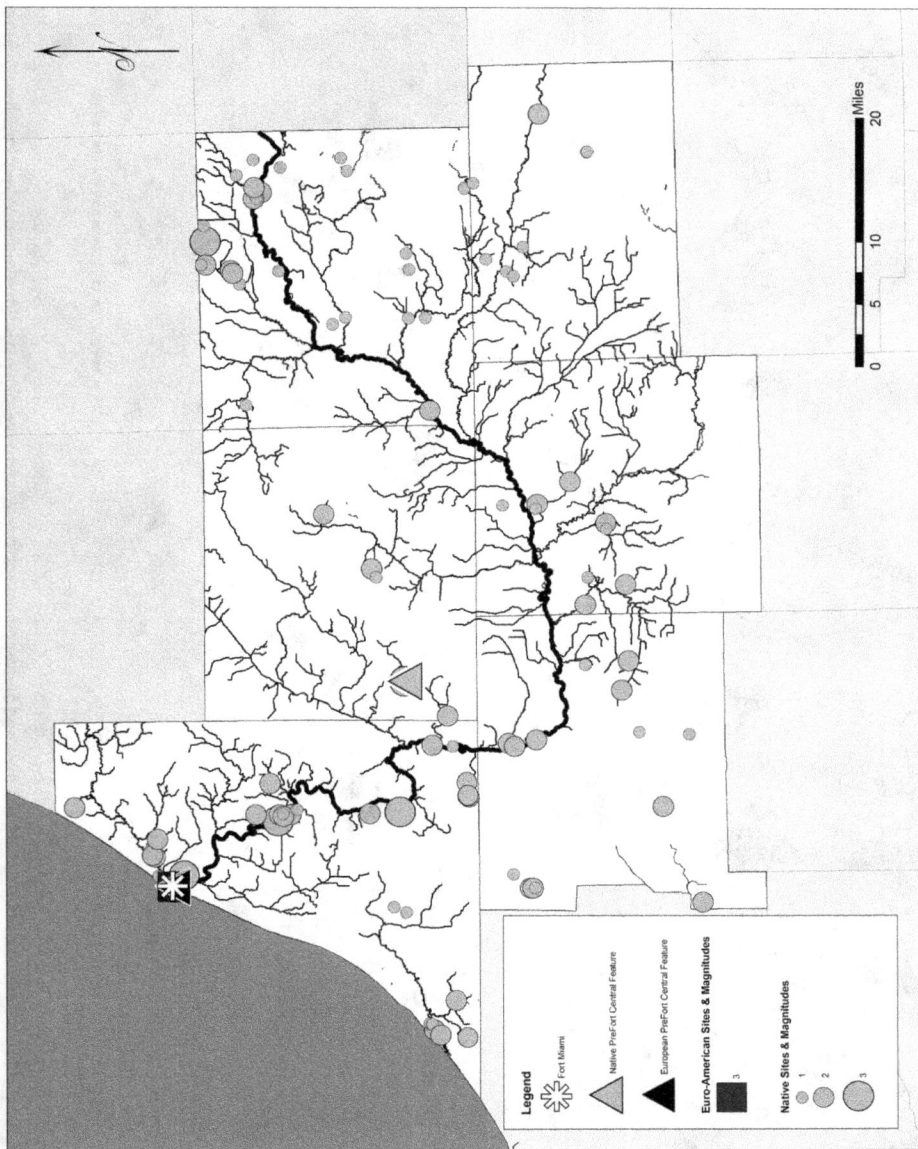

Figure 8.2. Pre-fort period settlements and central features. Map by Allison Hoock.

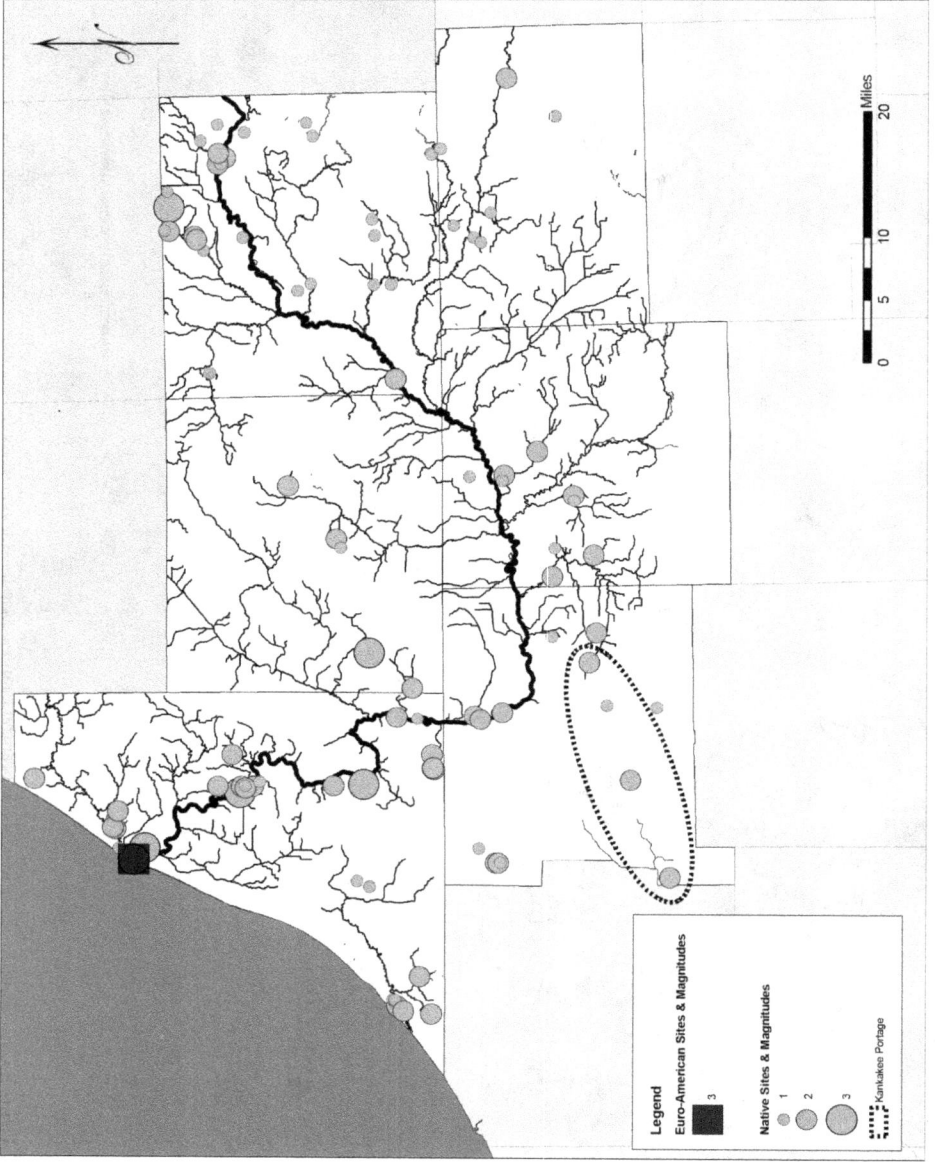

Figure 8.3. The portage connecting the Kankakee and St. Joseph Rivers in relation to pre-fort period settlements. Map by Allison Hoock.

settlement during this period, the French-occupied Fort Miami, was located on the lake at the mouth of the St. Joseph River (Figure 8.2). The locations of all the sites during the pre-fort period suggests that the river was a significant attraction for human habitation.

Fort Period (1691–1781)

After 1690, the number of European settlements increased from one to twelve, all located along the river. This included French Fort St. Joseph, which was established along the St. Joseph River in Niles, about 50 miles away from Lake Michigan (Charlevoix 1761).

While the fort was occupied, the number of Native American sites decreased significantly, from over 100 known sites to only nine sites during this period and the population aggregated into larger settlements clustered around Fort St. Joseph (Figure 8.4). Of these nine sites, six were classified as villages, increasing the proportion of Native American villages from 5 percent to 66 percent (Table 8.1). The Native American sites were located an average of 12 miles away from the fort. However, if two outliers that are located well to the east of Fort St. Joseph are removed from the sample, then the average distance from the Native American sites to the fort was less than a mile.

Central feature analysis further demonstrates that both cultural groups were located quite close to one another. The European central feature was Fort St. Joseph and the Native American central feature, a Miami village that was occupied from 1720 to 1749, were located only 1,400 meters (0.87 miles) apart (Figure 8.4).[2]

The clustering of larger Native American sites so close to the fort suggests that Native American settlement was less dispersed than before the fort was established and the Potawatomis established larger and more permanent settlements to avail themselves of the resources and services associated with the fort (Brandão and Nassaney, chapter 2, this volume). During this period, Native American women sometimes married French or French Canadian men and the Native Americans supplied furs to the French in exchange for a range of manufactured goods and the services of a blacksmith to repair their guns (Nassaney 2015, 168–171). It became more feasible to live in larger groups during the period when the fort was occupied. The close social, political, and economic alliances that developed between the Potawatomis and their French neighbors facilitated this change.

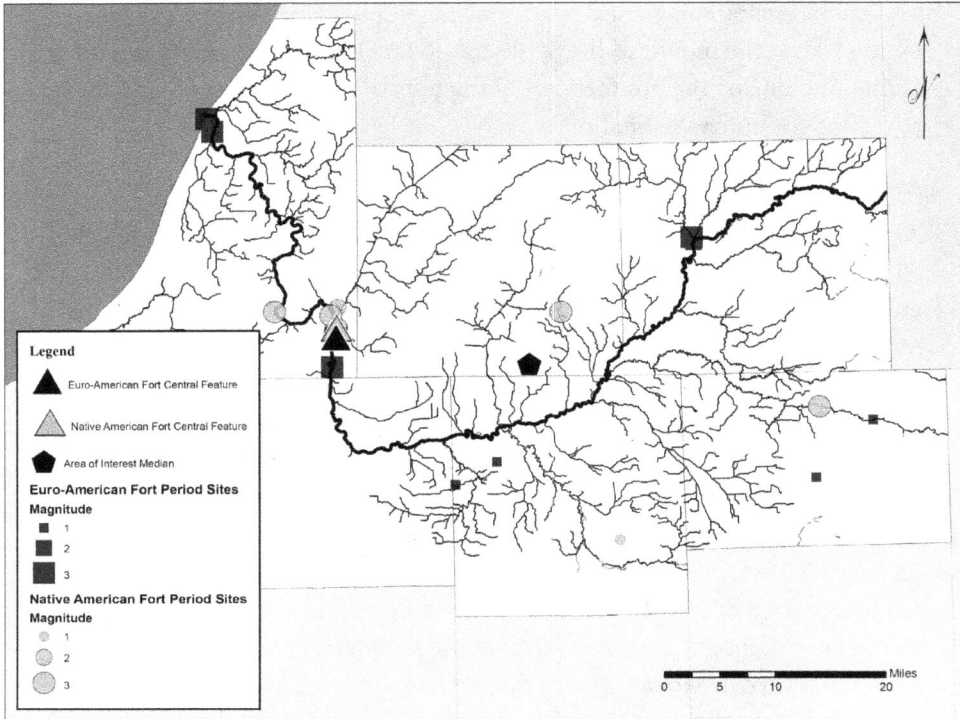

Figure 8.4. Fort period settlements and central features. Map by Allison Hoock.

As was the case during the pre-fort period, both Native American and European settlements were located on the St. Joseph River or its tributaries; waterways were an important consideration for both Europeans and Native Americans when they chose settlement sites. Two European sites were located on Lake Michigan, but no Native American sites were located near the lake after Fort St. Joseph was established (Figures 8.2, 8.4).

Post-Fort Period (1782–1850)

After Fort St. Joseph was abandoned in 1781, Euro-American and Native American settlements again became more widely dispersed throughout the St. Joseph River valley. According to the data from the Michigan State Historic Preservation Office and the Indiana Department of Natural Resources, Division of Historic Preservation and Archaeology, in the period 1782 to 1850, Euro-Americans occupied twenty-four clearly identifiable sites and Native

Americans occupied twenty-five (Figure 8.5). Most Euro-American and Native American sites were magnitude 3 settlements (one fort, six trading posts, five towns, one Baptist mission, the U.S. General Land Office, and the Native American sites were all villages) (Table 8.1). Euro-Americans settled throughout the St. Joseph River valley, establishing sites mainly along the river and its tributaries (Figure 8.5). Many Native American settlements remained close to the area where Fort St. Joseph had been while others spread throughout the St. Joseph River valley, as widely distributed as they had been before the establishment of Fort St. Joseph.

In addition, many of the Native American groups that moved away from the immediate vicinity of the fort remained in close proximity to other Euro-American groups. The continuing relationship between Native Americans and Euro-Americans in the nineteenth century is spatially illustrated through the proximity of Native American sites to newly established Euro-American trading posts. Some Native American groups settled near Euro-American sites where there is no evidence of Native American groups settling there before. This suggests the importance of Native American/Euro-American relationships. These settlement locations include historic Charleston, Michigan (circled in Figure 8.6), Rennsaw's trading post (indicated by the southernmost arrow in Figure 8.6), which was established in 1830 (Indiana Department of Historical Preservation and Archaeology);[3] Hatch Trading Post (indicated by the arrow farthest east in Figure 8.6), an American trading post that was established in 1831 (Cutler 1906; Cremin and Quatrin 1987); and a trading post operated by a descendant of a French settler (indicated by middle arrow in Figure 8.6; surveyed by Thomas J. Todd, General Land Office 1830).[4]

In the late eighteenth and early nineteenth centuries, the cultural landscape of the St. Joseph River valley underwent a drastic transformation. Sustained interactions with Euro-Americans at Fort St. Joseph contributed significantly to Native American settlement patterns throughout the valley. However, the abandonment of the fort led, in part, to a return to the settlement patterns that existed before the fort was established. After 1781, Native American communities once again dispersed throughout the St. Joseph River valley.

Summary and Conclusions

Prior to the establishment of Fort St. Joseph, Native American settlements were widely distributed across the landscape of the lower St. Joseph River valley,

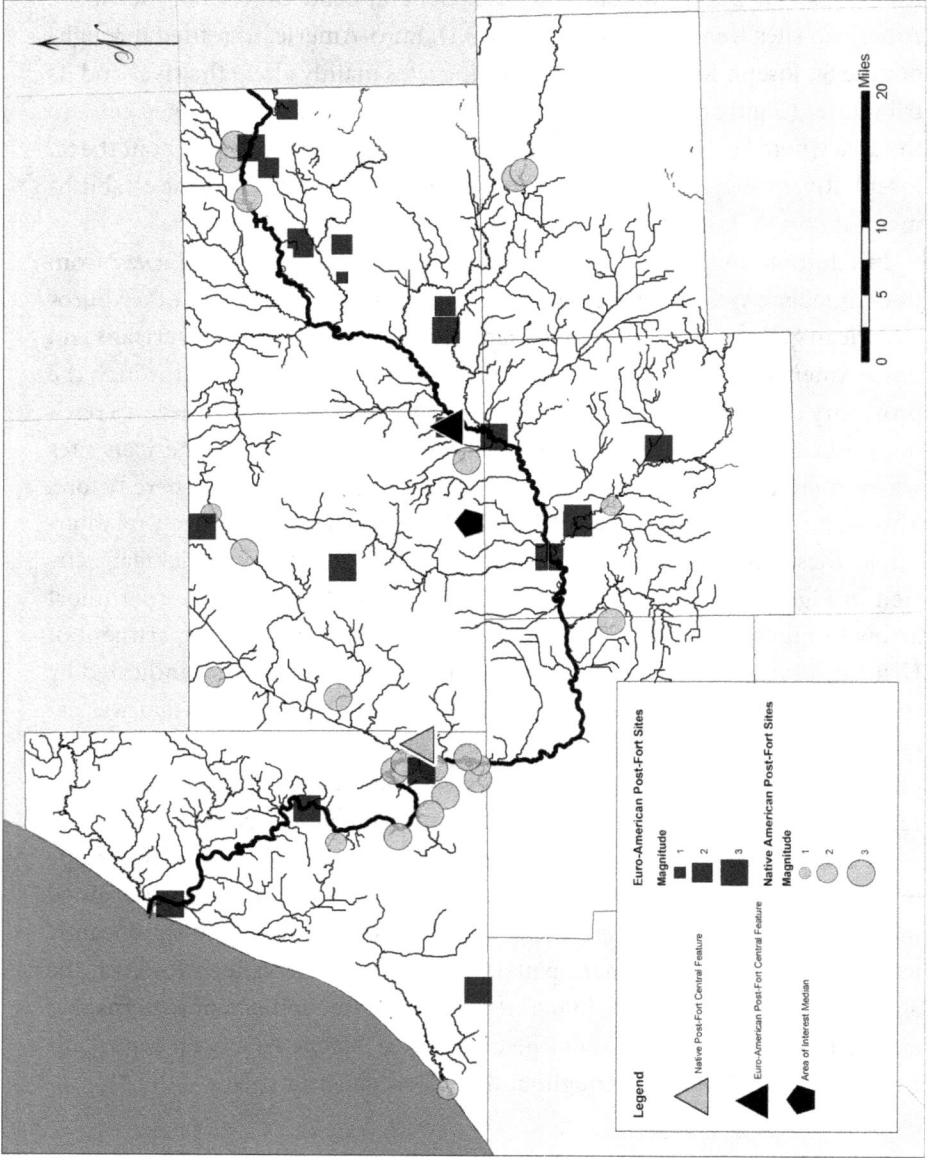

Figure 8.5. Post–fort period settlements and central features. Map by Allison Hoock.

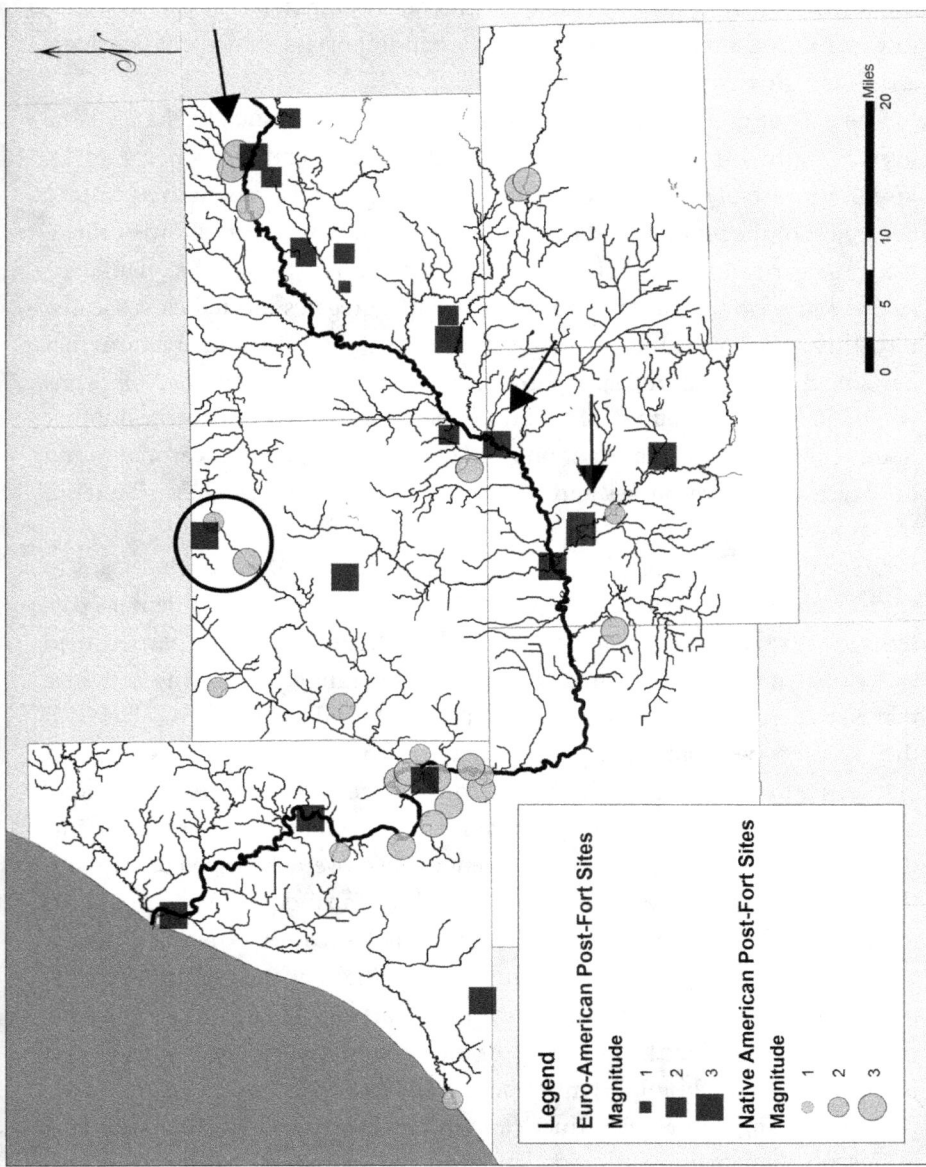

Figure 8.6. Post–fort period Native American/Euro-American settlement proximities. Map by Allison Hoock.

although most were located in close proximity to the St. Joseph River and its tributaries. Native American populations were transitory, relying on a seasonal round and largely occupying small, ephemeral encampments. Access to waterways for transportation and resources was an important settlement consideration for Native American groups.

The arrival of Europeans in southwest Michigan drastically changed the lives of Native Americans, ultimately to their detriment. Yet when Fort St. Joseph was established in 1691, Native American groups reorganized to take advantage of the political and economic opportunities the fort afforded them. Native American sites changed from the small and dispersed that characterized the pre-fort period to larger population aggregates located closer to the fort. This spatial proximity facilitated the economic and social interactions that developed between Europeans, particularly the French, and Native Americans while the fort was occupied. Fort St. Joseph appears to have become another node—a particularly important one—in the Native American seasonal round to obtain various resources and services (Brandão and Nassaney, chapter 2, this volume).

Once the fort was abandoned, there was no need for Native Americans to aggregate at a central place on a periodic basis. Instead, their settlement patterns in the valley again became widely dispersed, suggesting that they resumed traditional activities associated with their annual movements. The activities that Native American peoples conducted, how they identified themselves, and the ways they were alternately integrated into and shunned by the dominant culture are topics in need of further exploration (see Clifton 1978, 1986; Schurr 2006, 2010; Secunda 2006; Sleeper-Smith 2001; Tanner 1987). This study demonstrates that Native American settlement patterns were dispersed throughout the St. Joseph River valley after Fort St. Joseph was abandoned. However, some groups still chose to settle, at least temporarily, near Euro-American sites in the first half of the nineteenth century suggesting that the relationships between these cultural groups was for the most part amicable. Furthermore, our research suggests that the proximity of the two groups implies that trade and interaction remained important to both Native Americans and Euro-Americans. The changes in Native American settlement size and location after Fort St. Joseph was abandoned marks an effort on the part of Native American groups to resume their traditional lifeways. However, those lifeways became increasingly difficult to maintain as their land base shrank through treaties that led up to the forced displacement of much of their population.

The changing distribution of human populations in the St. Joseph River valley illustrates more than just the displacement of indigenous peoples by groups seeking to obtain land at any cost. First, scholars have noted elsewhere that Native American peoples were essential to the fur trade (Gilman 1982). Although the environmental degradation and dwindling number of animal species by the middle of the nineteenth century played a central role in the demise of the fur trade, Native American displacement was also a fundamental cause—no Indians, no trade (Nassaney 2015, 68). Unlike the land-hungry pioneers of the early nineteenth century who sought to transform the landscape to suit their agricultural needs, the fur traders of previous decades had been comfortable co-existing with Native American populations who were the primary producers in their trade.

Second, spatial analysis of both Native American and European sites in the St. Joseph River valley reveals that the relationship between the two groups was more complex than one built simply on invasion and removal. Native American sites during the Late Woodland period (AD 600–1690) were generally small and widely dispersed, reflecting the seasonal round that nuclear and extended family units practiced. When the fort was occupied (1691–1781), sites tended to cluster close to it and were larger, perhaps indicating aggregations of multifamily units. Once the fort was abandoned (post-1781), Native American sites are again widely dispersed but seem to have been located in proximity to new Euro-American sites in the region, perhaps indicating the continued importance of the fur trade and the desire of Native Americans to obtain imported and manufactured goods. The dispersed pattern suggests that Native Americans maintained their seasonal round and incorporated European sites as just another node in their scheduling of activities, so long as they had access to land and could remain mobile (Nassaney 2015, 177).

Finally, these data indicate that Native American peoples exercised agency when they made decisions about settlement that took into account new opportunities that the French and Fort St. Joseph offered and were able to revert to older practices under new economic and political conditions. Shifting settlement patterns remind us that the cultural landscape of the St. Joseph River valley today is the product of a long series of decisions, choices, and negotiations that were never inevitable and led to outcomes that were often unintended and unpredictable. In hindsight, using empirical evidence and analytical tools like GIS, we can begin to decipher the material traces our ancestors left to reveal the meaning of these patterns in the contemporary world and the importance of Fort St. Joseph for both the French and their Native American allies.

Acknowledgments

Mark Hoock acknowledges the research, analysis, academic labor, and consideration that Allison Hoock (née Kohley) contributes, for which she rarely receives her deserved credit. This publication demonstrates the effort and talent Allison offers. Mark also thanks Dr. Michael Nassaney for his invaluable input while developing this chapter and Drs. LouAnn Wurst and Dan Sayers for guiding him through the academic process and nurturing his perceptions of historical and contemporary social organization and his understanding of what archaeology can contribute to help us better understand it. Allison Hoock acknowledges Dr. Michael Nassaney for the assistance and encouragement he provided during her MA thesis research and Drs. Kathleen Baker and Gregory Veeck for guidance in professional development and knowledge of spatial analysis. She would also like to thank the Michigan State Historic Preservation Office and the Indiana Department of Natural Resource Division of Historic Preservation and Archaeology for providing access to data for this project. Mark and Allison Hoock appreciate the invitation to contribute to this volume. All the authors also thank Doug Wilson and Elizabeth Scott for their comments on an earlier draft of this chapter. We dedicate this paper to our predecessors in the St. Joseph River valley, who left us a piece of their history in the detritus scattered throughout the region that marks where they were and what they did.

Notes

1. State of Michigan Geographic Information Systems (https://www.michigan.gov/som/0,4669,7-192-78943_78944---,00.html); "GIS Data," USGS: Science for a Changing World, https://www.usgs.gov/products/maps/gis-data.

2. 20BE218 Michigan State Archaeological Site Files, Office of the State Archaeologist, Lansing, Michigan.

3. Site 12EO328, Indiana State Archaeological Site Files (SHAARD Database), 2012, Indiana Department of Natural Resources Division of Historic Preservation and Archaeology, Indianapolis, Indiana.

4. Site 12EO327, Indiana State Archaeological Site Files (SHAARD Database), 2012, Indiana Department of Natural Resources Division of Historic Preservation and Archaeology.

9

Public Archaeology at Fort St. Joseph

Past, Present, and Future

ERICA A. D'ELIA, KELLEY BERLINER,
SUE REICHERT, AND MICHAEL S. NASSANEY

The focus of public archaeology has shifted over the past three decades from the stewardship of archaeological resources to educating the public about archaeological findings to creating long-term community partnerships that serve to empower disenfranchised groups and decolonize the discipline (Atalay 2006; Belford 2014; Colwell-Chanthaphonh and Ferguson 2008b; Kerber 2003, 2006; Little 2007; Nassaney 2012b, 2018a; Shackel and Chambers 2004; Skeates et al. 2012). In addition to reading about archaeology and viewing it on TV, people are visiting archaeological sites and experiencing cultural heritage tourism in growing numbers (Gazin-Schwartz 2004; Holtorf 2007). A study conducted at the beginning of this millennium (Mandala 2009) found that 78 percent of all US leisure travelers (118.3 million adults each year) are participating in cultural and/or heritage activities; they are not just passively absorbing the information (Atalay 2012). Archaeologists have advocated many different approaches to meeting the public's interest. These are referred to variously as community archaeology, collaborative archaeology, community-based participatory research, and covenantal archaeology, among others (see Atalay 2012; LaRoche and Blakey 1997; Little 2007; Little and Shackel 2007; McDavid 2002; McManamon 1991; Saitta 2007). What these approaches have in common is sensitivity to the needs and interests of nonprofessionals and an acknowledgment that archaeologists are not the only stewards of the past. Here, we use the broad term public archaeology to encompass these various approaches. Instead of parsing the differences among the various terms for public outreach, we recognize that public archaeology takes many forms along a collaborative continuum from site visits and public lectures to community involvement in the design of archaeological research, site investigation, analysis, interpretation, and the dissemination of results (Atalay 2012; Colwell-Chanthaphonh and Ferguson 2008a).

As local and descendant communities become involved and invested in the study of the past, they bring valuable and diverse perspectives to the archaeological endeavor and compel professionals to consider viewpoints other than their own regarding heritage management and site interpretation. This creates a richer and more authentic history—one that is more relevant to public audiences. Public archaeology necessitates a balance between community needs and archaeological goals—a balance that depends on establishing working relationships between archaeologists and communities (Marshall 2002). Over the past three decades, community groups have increasingly become the impetus for archaeological investigations and some have even insisted on full control of the archaeological enterprise (Atalay 2012; LaRoche and Blakey 1997). Many archaeologists welcome public interest, recognizing that community groups can be more than just consumers of archaeological knowledge (Berliner and Nassaney 2015). Contemporary trends in public archaeology and community service learning have inspired the goals and practices of the Fort St. Joseph Archaeological Project (see Atalay 2012; Nassaney 2012b, 2018a; Nassaney and Levine 2009). It is useful to assess how the project engages with community groups to fulfill the goals of public archaeology. An assessment can ensure that the project is responsive to community needs and can contribute to the growing literature on the contributions of public archaeology.

Public Outreach and the Fort St. Joseph Archaeological Project

The project began in 1998 when a 501(c)(3) nonprofit organization, Support the Fort, Inc. (STF), invited Michael Nassaney, then an associate professor of anthropology at Western Michigan University (WMU), to help them find the lost eighteenth-century French Fort St. Joseph (see Nassaney, chapter 1, this volume). What STF did *not* tell him was that amateur and professional archaeologists had been looking for the site for nearly a century! When Nassaney agreed to help, it was clear that the project would be a collaborative venture between community members and researchers. Locals had conducted the background research, secured access to the survey area, and had a vested interest in the outcome (Peyser 1992). Community volunteers assisted with the archaeological survey that led to the recovery of eighteenth-century French and English artifacts along the St. Joseph River in present-day Niles, Michigan, by contributing physical labor and providing meals for the field crew. A major community goal after the remains of the fort were located was to collect spatial and architectural data to aid in a reconstruction that would attract heritage tourists (Hartley and Nassaney, chapter 4, this volume).

Excavations and analysis conducted since 1998 have led to the recovery of information about the fort's inhabitants, their daily activities, and the material conditions of their lives, considerably expanding our understanding of colonialism and the fur trade in New France in the eighteenth century (Nassaney 2015, 164–196). The chapters in this volume and numerous theses and publications on topics such as subsistence, trade goods, social relations, religiosity, and the role of women on the frontier (Becker 2004; Brandão and Nassaney 2006; Davis 2014; D'Elia 2013; Giordano 2005; Hearns 2015; Kohley 2013; Loveland and Nassaney 2017; Malischke 2009; Nassaney 2008b; Nassaney and Brandão 2009; Nassaney and Martin 2017; Nassaney et al. 2007, 2012) attest to the range of subjects that this work has addressed. While many of these publications are oriented toward professionals, the project has also emphasized other media to reach nonprofessional audiences including public lectures, booklets written for a general audience (see Godbout 2018), a fifth grade school curriculum (Reichert 2016), an interactive Minecraft map (Schwaderer 2017), DVDs, a website, and social media platforms. All of these seek to increase public awareness of local history and instill an appreciation for the archaeological past. While the recovery and analysis of the remains of Fort St. Joseph are important components of the project, interpretation, heritage tourism, and public education are equally important and are made possible through the continued support of, and collaboration with, the local community.

Collaboration and public participation in the project take many forms and continue to grow. Volunteer labor in the initial survey enabled the community to become invested in the search and assume a role in unearthing and interpreting local history. Locating the fort marked the beginning of a fruitful, if sometimes challenging, relationship between WMU archaeologists and the citizens of Niles (see Berliner and Nassaney 2015). For the volunteers, their participation was profound; not only had they located Fort St. Joseph, but they could claim ownership over its discovery. Local pride in the find is evident in their continued engagement in the project and their attendance at numerous public outreach activities that we co-sponsor with community partners such as the Niles District Library and the Niles History Center. Volunteers regularly participate in clearing the site each season, installing the dewatering system, providing housing and food for field school students, planning the annual open house, and helping archaeologists collect more data. The annual dig is a highly visible component of our work that continues to attract visitors and partners who discover their self-interest in the site and the stories it contains.

The project has developed several public outreach strategies to reach people of all ages and backgrounds. Not all potential stakeholders will choose to become involved in the project in similar ways. We discuss some of the more significant opportunities for public engagement along a ladder of citizen participation that ranges from "nonparticipation" to "citizen power" (Nevell 2013). Citizens have more authentic input into the archaeological process as they move "up" the ladder and become more involved in offering recommendations that might influence decision making.

While we profess to welcome public participation, in truth most of our outreach efforts are predominantly aimed at rectifying a deficit in our audience's knowledge by providing them with information about the history and archaeology of Fort St. Joseph (see Merriman 2004; Wilson 2015). These programs include a lecture series, social media outlets, and the annual open house. For example, the summer archaeology lecture series (which began in 2009) was developed to bring nationally and internationally known scholars to Niles to present their research to field school students and the public. These lectures, which have had different themes, have been co-sponsored with community partners such as the Niles District Library and the Niles Senior Center. This forum gives members of the public an opportunity to learn from specialists in a congenial and somewhat informal setting that encourages discussion and interactions among presenters, students, and community members. Prior to the lecture, the principal investigator (Nassaney) invites students to share information about their ongoing field and lab activities to give them the opportunity to practice public speaking and to entice the public to visit the dig and learn more about our work.

Because many people are unable to attend the lectures or visit the dig, we have used our web site and social media pages to disseminate information about the project. Regular postings to our blog and to our Facebook and Instagram accounts are most frequent when we are in the field, although updates occur throughout the year. During the field season, students take turns preparing blog posts and posting images that showcase our most recent finds, our fieldwork, and related events. This enhances interest among our followers and raises awareness about our lecture series, public tours, and the open house through their comments and "likes" on our posts. While it can be difficult to draw a connection between the number of "likes" or views and real engagement, it seems like these platforms have been popular for those with an interest in the project. As of the summer of 2018, the blog had more than 154,000 page views and the Facebook page had 1,400 followers. Many comments consist of inquiries about daily artifact finds or guesses about what mystery artifacts are. Even if most of these viewers and followers engage passively, this demonstrates that they are seeing what we have to share and are interested in our message.

The annual archaeology open house is the culmination of our fieldwork each season. The open house, which we first held in 2001 and expanded in 2006, has become an opportunity for the archaeologists and their supporters to showcase the results of their work, discuss recent discoveries with the public, and demonstrate firsthand the techniques of archaeological excavation and interpretation. The event is authorized by the Fort St. Joseph Archaeology Advisory Committee, a city-appointed group that makes recommendations for site investigation and interpretation in the public interest (see below). In addition to open excavations and recent artifact finds, the open house focuses on a different theme each year that also informs public lectures, children's activities, artifact displays, informational panels and banners, demonstrations, and activities conducted by eighteenth-century living history reenactors. The open house is an informal forum for public input as the students, staff, and demonstrators engage in conversations with and listen intently to the public. For the past several years, we have used a written survey to collect demographic and other data to ascertain how visitors learn about the event, where they come from, what they like most, and what needs improvement. While preparation for the open house reduces the amount of time the archaeologists can devote to excavation each season, the net effect is overwhelmingly positive for students and the public, as everyone's spirits are buoyed by the collective interest and enthusiasm that permeates the event.

198 Erica A. D'Elia, Kelley Berliner, Sue Reichert, and Michael S. Nassaney

During the open house, field school students enjoy the chance to explain the significance of their work and how it has contributed to the overall understanding of the site. We intend the open house to be more than just a place where archaeologists showcase their work for public consumption. The open house enables members of the archaeological community to interact with each other and with the public as they share ideas about the past and the future while relating what they learn to their lives in the present. For example, when we focused on shelters in New France in 2016, we asked visitors how they would have selected a place to live in the eighteenth century, how they would have constructed their homes in the absence of hardware and home improvement stores, and what life would be like without electricity and thermostats.

Open house attendees also gain some appreciation of eighteenth-century life by interacting with our living history reenactors. While archaeology enables us to understand the past by unearthing and studying the physical remains of human activities, historical reenactors understand the past by adopting the persona, technology, and mannerisms of our ancestors. Historical interpreters may be nonspecialists (see Berliner and Nassaney 2015) in the field of archaeology, but they are often knowledgeable about the past and ensure the authenticity of their reenactment, from the clothes they wear to the food they eat and the temporary shelters they occupy.

Although STF sponsored a rendezvous for the public featuring local historical reenactors in the 1990s before the archaeology began, the project's current relationship with the living history community developed by chance when LisaMarie Malischke, a WMU graduate student involved in the project, invited several of her reenacting associates to visit the site in colonial garb and accoutrements in 2004. Two years later we hosted over 100 reenactors at the open house and reenactors have since become a regular component of this event. Historical interpreters ably demonstrate to visitors the sounds, smells, and appearance of eighteenth-century life and contribute to the milieu and overall success of the affair.

In some cases, the living history interpreters and the archaeologists have different expectations of the event. For the archaeologists, good public outreach enables the community to witness the literal recovery of the past. Visitors want to be able to see the archaeological process, and the tours of the dig site are consistently rated in surveys and informal conversations as one of the public's most enjoyable activities. However, for historical interpreters, "modern" booths and activities (e.g., T-shirt sales) detract from the immersive experience of eighteenth-century food, music, dance, and activities that the open house offers the public. For example, in 2012 we invited the Northwest Territorial Alliance, a group of historical reenactors, to portray events on the eve of the American Revolution by creating an authentic military encampment near the fort. The ambiance they aimed to create was incompatible with several dozen project archaeologists and historical scholars in modern dress giving lectures and tours about the fort in the past tense. Due to both the large size of the reenacting contingent and the desire to keep the eighteenth-century encampment free of modern intrusions, a larger space for the reenactors was secured in a park not far from the excavation site. This is just one example of the many ways project stakeholders must continually negotiate and compromise to meet the needs of everyone involved. Ultimately, this decision preserved the authenticity of the military encampment while still allowing the archaeologists to provide a link to how the past is understood and interpreted in the present.

The open house is a culmination of our field season and is eagerly anticipated each summer in the city of Niles. There was considerable disappointment in the community in 2014 when supporters learned that there would be a year-long hiatus from fieldwork and the open house since Nassaney was on sabbatical leave for the academic year while writing a book on the fur trade (Nassaney 2015). Instead, Nassaney invited the Midwest Historical Archaeology Conference to convene at the Niles District Library to examine the future of the past at Fort St. Joseph. Archaeologists, historians, preservationists, educators, environmentalists, geographers, and other members of the community attended and generated useful ideas that formed the basis of a strategic plan that students in Nassaney's Historical Archaeology class compiled (Loveland et al. 2015). Work resumed the following summer, reinvigorating interest in the project and reassuring the community that there is still much to be learned at the site. For most visitors, the open house is not just the chance to see archaeology in action, it is also a complete learning experience. The community has a strong desire to learn about the past and the open house instructs the public about how the artifacts unearthed from the ground are instrumental in telling the story of Fort St. Joseph. Of course, as the partnership grew so did a need for central coordination of the project so it could effectively meet the needs of various stakeholders.

The Fort St. Joseph Archaeology Advisory Committee

The project began somewhat informally as a partnership involving STF, a representative of the city of Niles (Carol Bainbridge, director of the Fort St. Joseph Museum), and a representative from WMU (Michael Nassaney, professor of anthropology). As interest in and visibility of the project increased, the city and WMU signed a formal ten-year agreement (2008; renewed in 2017 for five years) stipulating that WMU was committed to investigating and interpreting the site for the public good and that the city would permit and support those efforts. A year earlier, the city had recognized the importance of Fort St. Joseph as a potential heritage tourist destination and had appointed the official committee to oversee and coordinate the excavation and operation of the project. The committee's changing membership has included local citizens, educators, city officials, the director of the Fort St. Joseph Museum (now the Niles History Center), WMU faculty and staff, representatives of the Pokagon Band of the Potawatomi, the Niles District Library, Niles Public Schools, and the Center for History (now the History Museum) in nearby South Bend, Indiana (Low 2018; Nassaney 2012b). Although individuals may have their own specific interest in and priorities for the project, the committee is united by a shared commitment to presenting the history and interpretation of Fort St. Joseph for the public good.

The committee is instrumental in defining annual project goals and determining how to achieve those goals. It is also an official body that can make recommendations to the City Council, which can authorize funding and provide administrative support. Since 2007 the committee has

- worked to secure funding from the city for the open house, archaeology camps for middle schoolers, and an annual Fort St. Joseph Museum intern;
- offered logistical support at the annual open house and at the Midwest Historical Archaeology Conference (in 2014);
- made educational and experiential programs and exhibits available to the community;
- obtained necessary permits from local and state offices as required; provided staffing, marketing, and administrative support for the project through the Niles History Center;
- ensured that artifacts are properly curated and that associated documentation from the excavations is completed;

- persuaded the city to install electricity at the site to replace the diesel pumping system;
- mobilized city support for site maintenance (Department of Public Works), the dewatering process (wastewater treatment plant); site security during the open house (Police Department), access to potable water and electricity (Utilities Department); and a suitable venue for the lecture series (Niles District Library);
- encouraged the community to participate in providing meals and hosting events for WMU staff, students, and fort followers;
- contributed to the annual report; and
- assisted in solving problems that inevitably arise.

Discussions, negotiations, and recommendations regarding project priorities are the purview of the committee. To ensure that a wide range of perspectives are represented, the committee attempts to be inclusive in its membership. For example, we have welcomed a representative from the local Native American tribe since the inception of the committee. The committee invites members of the public to participate at its bimonthly meeting and welcomes their input (Berliner and Nassaney 2015). However, despite efforts to involve a cross-section of the population in archaeology at the fort, including in excavations, some segments of the local population remain underrepresented, including the business community and people of color, a challenge many heritage organizations face (Black 2005, 17).

Opportunities to Practice Archaeology

There is a long tradition within archaeology of training students of all ages to conduct archaeological fieldwork (Baerreis 1963 cited in Krass 2000; Nassaney 2004). Universities and professional organizations have long hosted field schools to teach novices how to practice archaeology responsibly by using proper techniques for recovering and recording information (Sullivan and Childs 2003, 10), but the opportunity to participate in an archaeological dig is appealing to a much wider audience, most of whom are not students and have no intention of pursuing archaeology as a profession. Indeed, there are benefits to participating in archaeology even for nonprofessionals.

To make fieldwork accessible to a wider audience, we developed a summer camp program (in 2002) and created an archaeology curriculum (in 2004) to encourage more active and engaged learning. The aim is to reach beyond the local community of history enthusiasts through formalized educational partnerships. Recognizing that students and teachers are an essential audience for targeted outreach programs, we first piloted a week-long program for middle and high school students in 2002 and formalized the program two years later with a curriculum a WMU graduate student developed as part of her internship (Hagenmaier 2005). A week-long archaeology day camp for middle and high school students and lifelong learners has been held regularly since then. In 2006, we expanded our educational focus to include educators and began offering continuing education credits. Since the inception of the archaeology summer camp program, over 300 participants have learned about local history and archaeology through classroom lectures and hands-on excavations.

While the camps have been very successful in attracting interest, efforts have also been developed to expand our influence by working directly with educators and schools to establish programs that meet the needs of students. The goal is to move beyond merely learning about the fort to using archaeological methodology as a tool for engaging students in critical thought and experiential learning (Bartoy 2012). In this way, the project will be relevant to a much larger audience and have the potential to make a long-lasting impact that goes well beyond the borders of Niles and southwest Michigan. The work of two graduate students who participated in the project, Erica D'Elia and Sue Reichert, has been instrumental in transforming the educational goals of the project and serve as illustrative examples.

Archaeologists have a history of seeing K-12 schools as fertile markets for outreach. Yet often those who try to develop school programs overlook collaborating with educators because teachers are typically seen as the audience when they should be thought of as partners (Jeppson and Brauer 2007). Teachers decide what is to be taught when the door to the classroom closes. When a program or curriculum is developed to incorporate archaeology into classroom lessons, it is essential that archaeologists and educators work together in a fully collaborative manner. It is also important for archaeologists to understand the current political drive for assessment and accountability in the classroom (Davis 2000). Archaeologists must realize that although they may believe archaeology is hugely important, its benefits are not self-evident. As archaeologists, we must assume the responsibility of providing classroom teachers, who are already overburdened, with clear and effective reasons for making room in their curriculum for new material (Smardz and Smith 2000). Teachers will use only the programs that fall within the Common Core guidelines (Davis 2000).

For archaeologists, the challenge is to find ways to package archaeology to meet state and national educational standards while also providing a foundation that will drive critical thought and lead to interdisciplinary problem-solving skills. These concerns informed recent efforts to better integrate Fort St. Joseph archaeology into local classrooms (D'Elia 2013; Reichert 2016).

D'Elia (2013) evaluated the archaeology summer camp program to assess the needs of educators and the prospects for and impediments to implementing archaeology in K-12 classrooms. One of the continued goals of the education programs is to provide teachers with the knowledge and resources to use archaeology in their classrooms. This comes with the recognition that teachers most likely will not (and perhaps should not) teach archaeology to their students. Rather, they can use the information they have learned and archaeological methodologies to enhance lesson plans for their students. This approach also recognizes that teachers are themselves specialists (Jeppson 2010) and are best suited to assess their classroom needs and formulate lessons that adhere to pedagogical standards and their own teaching philosophies. Educators who participated in the 2012 summer camp were interviewed to provide insight into classroom realities in the communities the project serves and to explore the potential for new partnerships. Additionally, surveys were sent to all educators who had previously participated in summer camps that asked them to evaluate the program and provide feedback about how they use what they learned in the camp to create viable and effective lesson plans (D'Elia 2013).

In general, the interviews and surveys revealed that teachers thought the camp program successfully communicates the benefits of using archaeology in their classrooms and that it gave them knowledge to help with its implementation. Nearly all respondents found ways to bring archaeological topics and methods into their classrooms. The teachers' uses typically fell into three categories: teaching topics derived from archaeology; using artifacts as examples to help students relate to history; and using archaeology to teach other subjects. Perhaps predictably, social studies teachers were able to directly incorporate material about Fort St. Joseph when they taught about the early colonial history of Michigan. But teachers of other subjects found uses for archaeology as well. Some language arts teachers have students write essays about how artifacts may symbolize their own lives and math teachers used archaeology examples in their word problems and geometry (D'Elia 2013).

What was most apparent about some of the lessons is that the teachers used artifacts in much the same way as archaeologists do: not as ends in and of themselves but to help students understand and relate to people. For example, when students are asked to write about which contemporary artifacts best represent themselves, they begin to consider how their material goods tell a story about who they are. They also make connections with the past through artifacts, especially in lessons such as the one used in a Catholic school classroom where students related the eighteenth-century crosses and medallions of the French Jesuits to symbols of their own faith. In another lesson, students were asked to examine an artifact and think about who might have used it and how. When the focus is placed on people as the object of study, the artifact is transformed into a source of historical information. History in schools is often taught using a textbook and sometimes with the addition of archival or documentary sources. This limits both what topics students learn and what they understand to be valid sources about the past. Although the teachers did not explicitly teach archaeology, they introduced students to the concept of material objects as sources of information. The teachers' uses of artifacts begins to break down the idea that written sources are the only way to learn about the past (D'Elia 2013).

An equally important focus of D'Elia's work centered on reasons why teachers may not use archaeology in their classrooms. Many of the teachers attend the archaeology camp because it provides continuing education credits and they were personally interested in the subject. They were less certain about how it fit into their classrooms (although follow-up surveys suggest that most teachers soon discover uses for the information). Most teachers expressed concerns that they simply did not have time to incorporate more topics into their already content-heavy curricula, in some cases explicitly because of the time they must devote to standardized content and mandated testing (D'Elia 2013). Archaeology, therefore, must be tailored for classroom use.

One way to ensure a good fit with the curriculum is to get teachers involved in archaeology curricular development. Reichert (2016) built on these earlier insights and worked with several Michigan schools to design lessons and field trips. The goals were to expand the successful educational programs the project hosts, reach a broader audience beyond Niles, and teach young people about the importance of heritage. In the spring of 2015, the project offered field trips to the Fort St. Joseph Museum and ongoing excavations at the fort (Reichert 2016). Over 900 third through sixth grade students attended this program, which consisted of a tour of the Fort St. Joseph Museum where the museum staff presented their fur trade program to introduce students to Fort St. Joseph through interactive pedagogy (Figure 9.1). Students were able to

Figure 9.1. A school group visiting the Fort St. Joseph Museum to learn about the fur trade before visiting the excavations at the fort site. Photo by Sue Reichert.

handle real furs, learn about their value in the eighteenth century, and conduct other activities that involved artifacts housed in the museum.

After this orientation, students visited the archaeological site, where WMU student archaeologists explained how archaeologists practice their craft (Figure 9.2). This snapshot of Fort St. Joseph, the fur trade, and archaeology was intended to spark interest in history and archaeology. This program expanded the number of students who were exposed to Fort St. Joseph beyond the few who attend the summer camp. This prompted us to consider how we might collaborate with educators to incorporate archaeology in their classrooms.

Reichert worked with teachers from Climax-Scotts, a small school district in Kalamazoo County, Michigan, who understood that archaeology could provide their students with an interdisciplinary opportunity to make inferences and develop critical thinking and analytical reasoning skills. These are all key elements of the standards they are required to teach. Archaeology can be used

Figure 9.2. University field school students demonstrate the process of wet-screening sediments to grade school children at Fort St. Joseph. Photo by Sue Reichert.

to support state curricula requirements in science, social studies, language arts, and mathematics (e.g., scientific inquiry, problem solving, and higher thinking skills) at the upper elementary to junior high grades because those students have the cognitive skills to engage with such topics (Farr and Teach for America 2010; Smith et al. 1996). Reichert (2016) worked with fourth grade, fifth grade, and junior high teachers to learn about the state standards that need to be at the forefront of creating lessons and where archaeology might fit in best with those standards. Looking across disciplines, they agreed that archaeology would fit well in the fifth grade curriculum.

Each lesson explicitly stated what the learning objectives were and what materials the teacher and the students would need, provided a list of vocabulary words, listed the subjects covered in each lesson, listed the state standards, provided recommendations about the duration of each class, and information about the optimal class size for the lesson. For the teacher, the curriculum provides background information, discussion information, and all worksheets needed to teach each lesson. Final assessments were also created to evaluate student progress. For example, the lesson titled "Observation, Inference and Evidence" covers the subjects of social studies, language arts, and science. Each lesson covers at least five of the Common Core and Next Generation Science Standards. Students work on skills in the areas of remembering, understanding, applying, analyzing, and evaluating. The students also gain experience in explanation, interpretation, application, and self-knowledge. In the fall of 2015, Reichert collaborated with teachers to introduce the lessons to two fifth grade classes as a pilot study. The lessons were presented mainly by the classroom teacher with the archaeologist as an observer. This gave us an opportunity to work with the students and teachers and identify key learning goals that will enhance the program for the following years.

Lessons build on previous ones, giving students the skills needed to develop the critical thinking, problem-solving, and analytical reasoning skills that are mandatory in the Michigan public school curriculum. Students learn what archaeology is and what an archaeologist does. They learn how to make observations and inferences using the evidence they obtain, the importance of context when learning about past people, and how archaeologists use stratigraphy to establish relative age. They also learn how to survey and grid a site. The highlight for the students was the opportunity to use these skills to conduct a simulated dig in which they were expected to use proper techniques, including documentation, to make inferences about the activities the materials they recovered represented (Figure 9.3).

These examples demonstrate that we have the potential to bring archaeology into our schools to benefit both the students and the future of archaeology. However, without collaboration between educators and archaeologists, the potential for success is slim. It is essential that the lessons developed fit within the core curriculum and the standards to which teachers are required to teach. Although both archaeologists and educators see the importance of bringing archaeology to students across disciplines, unless archaeologists and educators work together to develop a program that fits within all the standards that the teachers need, efforts to develop an archaeology curriculum will not succeed.

Our experience has shown us that teachers want to embrace archaeology. Despite some of the impediments teachers face, including time constraints, narrow curricular goals, and the need to cover tested topics, archaeological lesson plans can be designed to meet curricular needs that spark an interest in the past

Figure 9.3. Students making inferences using objects and notes from a simulated dig. Photo by Sue Reichert.

and enhance students' critical thinking. One of the major accomplishments of these educational initiatives is the creation of a network of teachers who are interested in archaeology, know a little about it, and are willing to experiment with it in their classrooms. The next step the project can take is to create a forum for continued contact within this network to encourage the sharing of ideas and facilitate discussion and collaboration between archaeologists and educators. In this way, knowledge about Fort St. Joseph can be shared with a wider audience and the lessons and network will persist even after the excavations end.

The Mutual Benefits of Public Archaeology

Public archaeology at Fort St. Joseph provides benefits for both professionals and community members. The people of Niles are gaining a deeper understanding and appreciation of their history. The founders of the city named local streets for the fort, a commemorative boulder was dedicated in 1913 to honor the fort (Figure 1.1), and Niles earned its moniker as the "City of Four Flags" in recognition of the various nations that struggled for control of the fort. With the rediscovery of the fort, Niles has a deeper connection to its past. The city is an active partner in the project and aspires to become a heritage tourism destination and research center. Thousands of local residents and others have visited the site for an authentic experience and to learn how archaeology contributes to our nation's heritage at the open house and related activities. The excavations have added thousands of artifacts to the Niles History Center's collection, many of which are on display and are available for scholarly research. The collections and exhibits are a magnet for hundreds of schoolchildren each year who come to the center to learn about Fort St. Joseph and tour the site. Finally, the camp program gives young people, educators, and lifelong learners the opportunity to work alongside archaeologists.

Archaeology students, faculty, and the discipline also benefit from the working relationships professionals maintain with the community. The service-learning pedagogy of the field school gives students the opportunity to provide service in a real-world setting and reflect on the contingencies associated with an evolving research project (Nassaney 2004). For example, students are charged with teaching proper field techniques to novice campers, which reinforces their newly acquired skills in troweling, mapping, and record keeping. Students also begin to see the different ways people identify with Fort St. Joseph and their visions for the site's future.

Faculty and professional archaeologists are no longer the sole stewards of the past at Fort St. Joseph. They can turn to community partners for assistance with logistics (e.g., student housing, dewatering installation), collections curation, and promotion of the project to wider audiences, as just some examples. Some partners become co-teachers; they mobilize their knowledge, collections, and resources to assist faculty in creating learning opportunities for students. For example, a local historian and collector of antique firearms and his wife, herself a historian, repeatedly hosted the archaeological field school for dinner and allowed students to wander through their home, identifying the attributes of distinctive seventeenth- and eighteenth-century muskets, swords, and daggers, many of which were similar to components students could encounter in their excavations at the fort. Community members have contributed their skills and worked with students in the production of an annual series of informational panels and banners that highlight various themes related to the history and archaeology of the fort. They have also been willing to edit the text of these panels and the contents of three issues in the Archaeological Booklet Series to ensure that these works are written in jargon-free prose for a general audience (e.g., Juen and Nassaney 2012; Loveland and Nassaney 2017).

Finally, community partnerships also benefit the discipline of archaeology. In addition to creating an audience for the work we do, heightened awareness of archaeology as an exacting science that requires patience, intuition, and inference demystifies the process of recovering and writing history, humanizes the archaeological endeavor, and challenges the myths that are rampant about archaeology. The realization that Niles is home to an archaeological site listed on the National Register of Historical Places enables people to envision archaeology as a part of their lives and not just an irrelevant practice in some foreign land. When people see the care that students and professionals take in the recovery and curation of long-lost artifacts, they adopt a sense of ownership toward the materials and become protective, particularly individuals and groups who have a connection to the site. This fosters the desire to see the site treated properly and the collections conserved for future generations.

The Conundrum of Collaboration

Various community organizations have been involved in the project over the years. Beyond STF, groups such as the Fort St. Joseph Museum, the city of Niles, the Kiwanis Club, the local chapter of the Daughters of the American Revolution, the Society of Colonial Wars in Michigan, the French-Canadian Heritage Society of Michigan, the Michigan Humanities Council, the Pokagon Band of Potawatomi Indians, and the now-defunct Fort St. Joseph Historical Association have partnered with WMU to support the investigation and interpretation of the fort. Volunteer efforts, university field schools, and partnerships with community groups have been a successful formula for the project. Two decades of collaborative archaeology at Fort St. Joseph provides us with the perspective to evaluate the successes and challenges of a long-term community archaeology program. The lessons learned provide a source of reflection for everyone involved in this project. WMU archaeologists continue to fulfill their commitments to investigate the site and interpret their findings to the public, and the city of Niles appears to be pleased with the relationship (Christina Arseneau, personal communication 2018). Regular and transparent communication and willingness to work together and compromise when necessary to meet goals is crucial to a successful outcome.

Lest we paint an overly positive picture, public archaeology and collaboration with community groups in Niles is not without its challenges and contradictions (Low 2018, 112–113). This stems from the diversity of the groups who represent different interests and goals. For example, archaeologists are generally committed to conducting excavations to answer research-oriented questions in order to gain a better understanding of the past, in this case the role of the fort in the fur trade and colonialism. In contrast, many in the city of Niles are interested in how the fort can draw heritage tourists to the area and stimulate the local economy (see Nassaney 2018a). For many years, some STF members envisioned a reconstruction of the fort similar to that at Fort Michilimackinac in northern Michigan (Evans 2013). Although these goals are not necessarily contradictory, accomplishing them requires different timelines. Both WMU and community partners want continued site investigations in order to encourage visitors to come to Niles. Some citizens would prefer to see quicker results leading to reconstruction and interpretation, while the archaeological team wants to conduct more in-depth research to better situate any reconstruction and interpretive efforts in an appropriate historical context.

The specific goals of each field season are largely driven by the archaeologists, although members of the committee have input in the process and sometimes compromises must be made. For example, in 2012 the archaeologists proposed an attempt to define the southern boundary of the site, which has not yet been established. A mid-twentieth century landfill is located immediately to the south of the current excavation area. The archaeologists proposed excavations through the landfill to search for colonial deposits in this area. Even before the bureaucratic challenges of such excavations were brought to our attention by the Michigan Department of Environmental Quality, some committee members did not see the need to explore new areas of the site. They hoped that archaeologists would return to areas where architectural features had been found so they could unearth evidence of a complete building. While a large-scale reconstruction is still a long way off, this would make it possible to reconstruct at least a single building—a tangible outcome of years of work. In the end, the committee recommended excavations to identify further architectural evidence *and* to survey to the southwest to establish the site's boundaries.

That same year, the five-year permit to excavate on the floodplain was about to expire. The new permitting process raised concerns about the safety of conducting excavations in an old landfill and fears about contamination. It was necessary to hire an environmental firm to test the groundwater beneath the site before it could be pumped back into the river. Because the environmental firm determined that the groundwater contained unacceptable levels of heavy metals, it was necessary to pump it to the city's wastewater treatment facility. The city has since incurred the ongoing cost of water treatment to help ensure that excavations could take place—a testimony to their commitment to the project.

In an effort to be inclusive, the city invited a representative of the Pokagon Band of the Potawatomi to serve on the advisory committee at the time the committee was established (Low 2018, 112–113). Historically, the Potawatomis and Miamis were the tribal nations who lived in the southwest Michigan area and would have lived near, traded with, and married the French fur traders at Fort St. Joseph. Given the central role that Native Americans played in the fur trade and the relatively recent efforts to involve Native American peoples generally in the archaeological process (Colwell-Chanthaphonh and Ferguson 2008b; Nassaney 2015; Robinson et al. 1985; Silliman 2008), we understood that Native American partners could make valuable contributions and were essential voices if we were to be truly inclusive.

Soon after the committee was established, the Pokagon Band provided a representative. This proved to be a series of new members over the next decade, making it difficult to maintain continuity. This could be interpreted as ambivalence on the part of the Pokagons, although they cannot be solely blamed. A lack of cultural sensitivity and awareness on the part of some members of the committee may thwart the relationship. References by committee members to "rain dances" and "talking sticks" come off as insensitive attempts to appropriate Native American culture and ascribe them to local tribes when these practices are not actually part of Pokagon history. This can damage already-fragile relationships and provide disincentive for further collaborative work.

At times, Native American representatives have participated in the open house. They prefer to discuss contemporary Native culture and language to remind their audiences that Native American culture is not dead and relegated to the past. In 2015, the Pokagon Band agreed to construct a Native American-style structure of bent poles covered with elm bark in keeping with the season's

Figure 9.4. Replica of a Native American–style structure built by Pokagon Band citizens for the 2015 archaeology open house. Photo by John Cardinal.

architectural theme (Loveland and Nassaney 2017). Among the band members who constructed this building was Amelia Harp, a Georgia State University graduate student enrolled in the field school. She was able to both assist the band with the construction and interpret it to the public from the perspective of an indigenous archaeologist. This generated considerable interest among visitors (Figure 9.4). Her subsequent research explored the relationship between archaeologists and tribal citizens in an effort to gauge the interest of Native American peoples in the project and what archaeology can reveal about Native American history and culture. She concluded that although the project has made important inroads in collaborating with various community groups, considerable work needs to be conducted to involve the Pokagon Band as an authentic partner in creating a decolonized history of the Fort St. Joseph community (Harp 2017; see also Low 2018).

There are important lessons here. Working with the Pokagon Band may mean recognizing that their interests in the project will deal more with contemporary issues they face rather than exploring their past archaeologically. It is entirely possible that some tribal citizens feel the project does not apply to them significantly as its focus is on the past, which could be seen as helping to reinforce the stereotype that Native Americans are stuck in history. Moving forward, closer collaboration with indigenous partners that allows them to express their real needs could help researchers explore ways the work at Fort St. Joseph could directly benefit and engage these groups. A stronger emphasis on finding ways to make archaeology meaningful for band citizens may encourage more Native American involvement in the discipline while also strengthening community outreach efforts. What we view as disinterest by indigenous partners may really represent a failure on the part of the project to work collaboratively with these communities. A true partnership should have mutual benefits, yet the project primarily asks indigenous people to participate in archaeology events without reciprocal offers.

The members of the committee are not necessarily a cross-section of the community and some segments are clearly underrepresented. Committee members often have divergent interests and values, although they generally come to a consensus in their deliberations. Collaboration cannot be forced and it is well within the rights of autonomous partners to choose when to participate and when not to participate. Additionally, frequent staff changes (both of Pokagon Band representatives and the continual revolving door of WMU graduate and undergraduate student archaeologists) make these relationships even harder to maintain. Specific activities and programs are often designed and implemented based on interests that appear to be timely and then are abandoned as students graduate and move on with their careers and others leave the committee. Greater continuity can be achieved by adopting a strategic plan that all members agree to follow (see Loveland et al. 2015).

Lessons from Public Archaeology at Fort St. Joseph

The lessons of the project discussed in this chapter illustrate its successes and challenges (see also Berliner and Nassaney 2015; Nassaney 2011, 2012b). As we look to the future, we need to think about ways to sustain the project and the extent to which it meets the expectations of various and shifting publics. This issue is particularly pertinent when considering institutional support for the project, since WMU is not immune to the challenges many educational institutions face, such as reductions in funding, turnover and loss of faculty, and declining student interest in the humanities and social sciences. While these have not been serious issues for the project over the past twenty years, it is ethically responsible to ask how the project might continue under changing conditions. One way the project can remain resilient is to ensure that the community continues to support its mission. For archaeologists to retain this support, we must ensure that the community continues to view the project and, more generally, archaeology as valuable and relevant to their interests (see Belford 2014). As discussed previously, education is one avenue that enables the project to grow beyond its small audience of archaeologists and immediate partners in the local community. While various community groups appreciate and support the project's efforts, it is less clear if all of their expectations have been met.

For example, most partners recognize the need for long-term curation of the archaeological collections, including artifacts, notes, and samples. From its inception, one of the central goals of the project was to create an interpretive center where collections could be stored and exhibited, a central place where scholars and the public could come to learn about the importance of Fort St. Joseph in the fur trade, colonialism, and our nation's patrimony. One of the primary responsibilities of the committee is to attempt to resolve the logistical challenges associated with ongoing excavations and research. Proper curation and exhibition facilities are arguably as important, as these will persist long after excavations have terminated (Sullivan and Childs 2003). A small municipality and a stressed state university must develop creative solutions to preserve and protect this legacy well into the future (see Berliner and Nassaney 2015). The city of Niles faces economic challenges as a postindustrial town and understandably expects an economic return from the project. The most often imagined way of fulfilling this need is some type of reconstruction of the fort and/or an interpretive center where materials from the site could be curated and the results of the archaeology at the site could be presented to the public. However, reconstructions of wood and *bousillage* may be outmoded interpretive platforms in a digital era and they may not align with the goals of archaeologists who are dedicated to researching a site in its entirety and not just focusing on building foundations (Berliner and Nassaney 2015). Any local constructions in Niles will have to be supported predominantly by the local community; WMU is unlikely to undertake the expense associated with the construction, maintenance, and staffing of a facility at this location unless it makes a serious effort to expand its influence into Michiana (the region of northern Indiana and southwest Michigan centered on the city of South

Bend). While Niles is aware of the need for proper storage facilities, limited resources make it difficult to meet these standards. We remain hopeful that a central repository will become a reality, but at this point it is helpful to consider other ways that the project can have a sustained impact on the Niles community.

While the focus of the project has been on investigations of Fort St. Joseph, there is potential for research on related topics and other archaeological sites. In addition, the nearly half a million objects recovered thus far provide a mountain of data to be mined for decades to come and a source of materials for a large number of exhibits. It is incumbent upon the various community partners to determine how to build relationships to promote new initiatives and concerns as they arise in Niles and beyond.

The theme of the 2017 field season was "Community Partnerships: Building Meaningful Connections through Archaeology." That spring, upper-level undergraduate and graduate students in Nassaney's Anthropology in the Community course contacted some of the communities that have a vested interest in the history and archaeology of Niles to explore how the project could establish and strengthen our collaborations. The results appeared in a series of banners that were displayed at the annual open house (Figure 9.5; see http://www.wmich.edu/fortstjoseph/about/panels). Among our partners were living history reenactors, religious leaders and parishioners of St. Mary's Catholic Church, the staff of the Fernwood Botanical Garden and Nature Preserve, Niles High School teachers, and citizens of the Pokagon Band. Students interviewed members of these groups to identify community goals and assets and to determine what interests anthropologists and communities share and how specific communities can benefit, if at all, from anthropological studies. What emerged was an understanding of the overlapping interests among these groups and the desire to collaborate and learn from each other.

For example, our discussions with religious community members revealed a series of possible collaborative projects that have the potential to strengthen our working relationship. We learned that the project's findings about religious practices are important contributions to the understanding of the history of the Catholic faith in the region. This may explain the large number of St. Mary's parishioners who volunteer at the open house and their broader interest in supporting further study, interpretation, and preservation of the site. Some members proposed a historical places tour to showcase locations related to the shared history of the church and the fort and suggested that an

Figure 9.5. The introductory Community Partnerships banner prepared for the 2017 archaeology open house. Design by Michael Worline.

outdoor mass be held at the archaeology open house to serve Catholics (and others). They would welcome guest speakers to reach youth groups and potentially wider audiences about the religious history and significance of the fort. They also suggested that we create a traveling teacher's trunk with artifacts and materials related to Fort St. Joseph to supplement the St. Mary's School curriculum.

The Fort St. Joseph Archaeological Project and the religious community of Niles are working toward defining and achieving mutual goals using the tenets of collaborative, community-based research. The potential collaborative efforts we have mentioned await operation, but a shared interest in the history of Fort St. Joseph and in community-based learning initiatives are likely to drive the partnership forward for years to come in whatever forms they may take. Similar bonds should be explored and strengthened among new and existing partners to ensure that the project remains sustainable.

Project participants who aim to bring the past alive in Niles are limited only by their imaginations. The committee is discussing the design and placement of a permanent ghost structure (a partial reconstruction of a building's framework) near the excavation site to serve as a focus of interpretive activities and provide a space that replicates a French colonial habitation. (Students and volunteers constructed a temporary ghost structure for the 2018 open house that was very well received by the public; see Figure 9.6.) Interpretive signage could also extend from the site along the river to the downtown area to provide information on local heritage, including the history and archaeology of the fort. An interpretive trail would make the history of the fort visible on the landscape and encourage residents and visitors to seek out more information on the region's rich history.

Municipal archaeology can also be explored to expand the research potential and audience for the archaeological work conducted in Niles (see Appler 2012). While the project has focused on the eighteenth-century fort, archaeological remains are clearly not restricted to this chapter of the city's history. The region has evidence of precontact Native American settlements, early business and industrial ventures, and connections to the Underground Railroad, to name just a few examples of important heritage topics. Although admittedly pursuing these will require significant restructuring of the project, it accords with promoting the history and character of this small midwestern town. Beyond Niles, the regional significance of Fort St. Joseph is increasingly apparent. Research is showing how populations in this region interacted with

Figure 9.6. A temporary ghost structure constructed for the 2018 open house. Photo taken by Shelby Johnson.

one another over a significant span of time (see Hoock at el., Chapter 8, this volume). Geospatial analysis of indigenous settlement patterns near the fort show how Native American communities adapted to and incorporated newcomers in the region into their seasonal movements. Further research could be conducted to examine how these communities interact with other populations in the present and expand this analysis to more recent waves of immigrants such as African Americans. Broadening the project's reach can engage a wider audience as it situates Fort St. Joseph in a larger landscape history.

One of the widest-reaching contributions the project could make is an education program for teachers and students. This would include ways to align archaeological research with Common Core curriculum requirements. Using archaeological methods in teaching has much to offer as it allows children to learn in a haptic multidisciplinary environment. Importantly, there are opportunities to use archaeology on a smaller scale than the full field school conducted at the fort site through mock excavations. These could be conducted at any time of the year to teach math and science skills and do not require professionals to be present. Additionally, the use of artifacts and the idea of discovering history in one's own backyard could also be used to cultivate an interest in timely themes like immigration, cultural diversity, and sustainability, to name just a few. In the long term, incorporating archaeology into the curriculum will have at least two benefits. First, it will satisfy educational requirements in an interesting and engaging way. Second, it will help instill in students an understanding of the importance of archaeology and the past as we chart our way into an unknown future. Research shows that one of the best predictors of adult interest in heritage is exposure during childhood (Black 2005, 26). The future of the past and the sustainability of public archaeology lies with our youth.

The Future of the Past at Fort St. Joseph

Twenty years of public archaeology at Fort St. Joseph has been a rewarding and challenging learning experience for all involved. The support of the city of Niles, WMU, and various stakeholders has been vital to the success of the project. The collaborative partnerships that have been formed draw on a mutual commitment to the ultimate mission of the project: discovering and interpreting the remains of colonial Fort St. Joseph in the public interest. Every year, new goals and smaller projects are developed in pursuit of that mission. And every year we negotiate and make compromises in order to reach our goals. The project continues to be successful because of the commitments both stakeholder organizations and individuals have made to it. The continuity of key staff members, such as the principal investigator (Nassaney) and the director of the Niles History Center (formerly Carol Bainbridge, now Christina Arseneau), makes it possible to develop long-term relationships. It can be difficult to form such relationships when frequent changes of students and other staff members mean some small projects are short-lived. As it becomes necessary to consider if and when the project will ultimately end, educational outreach has emerged as one particularly promising area to continue its legacy. Educational programs enable archaeologists to give the public the tools for interpreting the past for themselves, which, in turn satisfies a major goal of public outreach: archaeologists sharing control and creating a past that reflects multiple voices.

Archaeologists recognize that partnerships can be fragile relationships that are difficult to nurture and sustain over time. In this chapter, we have tried to identify some of the strategies that we have used in our practice of public archaeology. Although we cannot predict whether these approaches will serve us into the future, we can summarize what currently works in Niles:

Professional research: Faculty and student archaeologists use professional research protocols to investigate and interpret the site;

Open communication: Members of the committee work in a spirit of cooperation and transparency;

Mutual benefits: Collaborators come to the project with the understanding that their interests will be heard and they will benefit from the resource in some tangible or intangible way;

Shared vision: Those who work to investigate, interpret, and benefit from the resource share a vision pertaining to heritage and its role in the community;

Trust: Various stakeholders understand that while they may have divergent interests, they trust that they will be heard and that those in positions of power have everyone's best interests in mind;

Inclusivity: Efforts are made to offer inclusive interpretations and empower people to have some control over the production of knowledge about the past; and

Balance: The concerns of locals and experts are weighed against each other to ensure that the site and the data are accessible to all.

These values are the glue that binds together researchers, community partners, and the public. If they erode, the project will likely collapse and its legacy will diminish in importance. We cannot say for certain if we will continue to achieve our goals in the future. Heritage decisions are based on a consideration of the value of heritage to diverse and changing constituents. They require regular review to determine if they meet the needs of contemporary society (Harrison 2013). In the Fort St. Joseph Archaeological Project, we have tried to be ever vigilant and self-reflective in our efforts to develop authentic and sustainable practices for responsible heritage management in the public interest.

Acknowledgments

Christina Arseneau and Erika Hartley reviewed and commented on an earlier draft of this chapter. We are grateful for their willingness to share their time and talents, a practice we have also encountered from so many people who have participated in the Fort St. Joseph Archaeological Project since its inception in 1998. Carol Bainbridge, Barb Cook, the late Grif Cook, the late Bill Cremin, Mary Ellen Drolet, Juan Ganum, Ric Huff, Michael McCauslin, the late Jan Personette, the late Joseph Peyser, Larry Sehy, and Sanya Vitale have been among our staunchest supporters in the community. A heartfelt thank-you to the entire Niles community who welcomes us each summer, especially Barb Cook and the Layman family for opening their homes to us. Finally, our gratitude goes out to our anonymous supporters for your interest, dedication, and commitment to preserving and interpreting the history of a small French fort on the edge of empire.

10

Fort St. Joseph Revealed Then and Now

MICHAEL S. NASSANEY

Revelation in historical and archaeological inquiry is not an instantaneous act, as it is in theology, where an essential truth is disclosed through communication with a supernatural being. Rather, it is a social process by which those in the present attempt to comprehend the past and create a narrative to serve their shifting needs at particular historical moments. In this concluding chapter, I reflect on our current understandings of Fort St. Joseph as revealed through two decades of sustained archaeological investigations and over a century of historical research and antiquarian collecting. The fort and material evidence of it have long been familiar to scholars and to members of the public, some of whom have used it as a trope for varying political purposes. It is instructive to review how the fort has figured and been configured in local, regional, and national narratives since it was abandoned, repeatedly rediscovered, and reimagined from the early nineteenth century through the present.

Fort St. Joseph in southwest Michigan serves as a useful case study to illuminate how a community has forgotten, remembered, and embraced its past (Nassaney 2008a). For over a century, this French colonial outpost has been a defining element in the creation of community identity and a community's sense of place. This process has arguably accelerated with ongoing excavation and interpretation. Suffice it to say that Fort St. Joseph has sustained multiple narratives simultaneously and sequentially for varying audiences; every generation and varying segments of the population reimagine Fort St. Joseph and put it to a different use. To a great extent, the meaning, significance, and potential of Fort St. Joseph are always in the eyes of the beholder.

Early Discovery and Manifest Destiny

Sites associated with the early European exploration of the Midwest piqued the interest of nineteenth-century pioneers who first identified these places through documentary sources (e.g., historical maps) and archaeological remains that were often accidentally unearthed by plowing (e.g., Beeson 1900; McCoy 1907; Nassaney 2009). Squire Thompson found numerous relics associated with Fort St. Joseph in the ash and mold of the old fort as early as the 1820s while he was clearing land and conducting agricultural activities along the St. Joseph River (Beeson 1900). Similarly, imported glass beads from Venetian workshops were impaled on newly sprouted blades of grass each spring in West Lafayette, Indiana, betraying the location of a related French fort known as Ouiatenon (Figure 2.1). These materials were mere curiosities at the time and were not yet considered evidence that could shed light on the history of the colonial period. Early white visitors to Niles also took note of a burial place, allegedly of Father Allouez, who was one of the fort's first priests and an important figure in local history.[1] Antiquarians were soon attracted to these archaeological sites because of their antiquity and legacy; they were the oldest *European* settlements in the region, established by intrepid explorers who paved the way for subsequent land-hungry pioneers (Nassaney 2008a). Leading up to and in the wake of the centennial celebrations of 1876, historians and preservationists throughout the nation mounted a concerted effort to identify and commemorate sites associated with early European settlements and America's forefathers. These were "places where national values and ideals were formed and shaped on an everyday basis" (King 2006, 295; see also Gillam 1915; Kammen 1991; Woodruff 1999, 10).

Among the early antiquarians who sought to identity and preserve relics from Fort St. Joseph was Lewis H. Beeson, who was raised on Bond Street just south of the site and later became president of the Michigan Historical Society. In the late nineteenth and early twentieth centuries, Beeson and three associates (E. H. Crane, a Mr. Lombard, and W. Hillis Smith) banded together under the name of the Miami Cross Society to explore their shared interest in the history of the fort (Gillam 1915, 281). They amassed significant collections of fur trade-era relics (Beeson 1900, 186) that were later donated or sold to local museums in southwest Michigan and northern Indiana, with the majority going to the Fort St. Joseph Museum in Niles. Beeson (1900, 186) provided a precise legal description of the greatest concentration of his finds and he may have drawn the anonymous turn-of-the-century map that shows the location of the fort.[2]

The work of Beeson and his associates was instrumental in keeping the memory of the fort alive and culminated in 1913 when the Fort St. Joseph Historical Society commemorated the site by placing a 65-ton "boulder, considered by many to be the finest and largest" in the state, at the corner of Fort and Bond Streets (Figure 1.1; Gillam 1915, 280). The dedication took place with considerable fanfare on July 4, 1913, and included a celebration with floats and a parade over two miles long followed by songs, a prayer, speeches, and the ceremonial unveiling of the big rock from beneath an American flag draped over it. Among the more emotionally moving addresses was that delivered by Judge Coolidge (1915, 290–291), who expressed patriotic notions that were current in early twentieth-century discourse. Most important, he heralded the Jesuits for introducing Christianity to the heathens and the French for bringing civilization to the savages. He opined that the commemorative boulder would memorialize the process of civilizing the American wilderness to all those in attendance and for generations to come. Either local Native American peoples were not invited or they chose (understandably) to avoid the ceremony.

The concept of the wilderness has loomed large in histories that justify the exploration, settlement, and appropriation of New World lands (Nash 1982). Fort St. Joseph played a role in this process by symbolizing a place where civilization had tamed the wilderness (Nassaney 2008a). Coolidge (1915, 284) noted somewhat paradoxically that "a natural alliance" developed and was strengthened between the French *coureurs de bois* and the western Indians by intermarriage. While the willingness of French men to intermarry with Native American women distinguished them from other white colonists, its importance was soon surpassed by the civilizing effect of missions and forts (Coolidge 1915, 284).

Coolidge (1915, 290) offered the conversions the missionaries made as a measure of the positive impact of the French. He noted that "a large portion of the Pottawatomies were converted to Christianity and became to a considerable degree civilized and accustomed to industrial pursuits." The baptisms and marriages the priests at the fort performed are well documented throughout the mid-eighteenth century (Paré and Quaife 1926). Most of the Native American baptisms involved dying babies, women marrying French men, or young female servants. Although the extent of Native American Christian piety remains unknown, much of the conversion that Coolidge emphasized may have been actually performed by Protestant missionaries in the early nineteenth century (see Brandão and Nassaney 2008; Secunda 2006). Coolidge (1915, 290) saw the French, who "treated the Indians with kindness and forbearance," as different from other New World colonizers such as the Spaniards, English, and even the Americans, arguing that "that innate courtesy, tact and power of adaptation to attract other races which have characterized the French race beyond

Figure 10.1. La Salle monument at the mouth of the St. Joseph River in St. Joseph, Michigan, near the location where Fort Miami once stood in the seventeenth century. Photo by Michael S. Nassaney.

all other races, were inherent in the missionary, the explorer and soldier alike." In the early twentieth century, the disposition of the French toward Native American peoples was attributed to their inherent (read: inborn) characteristics rather than to their demographic, economic, and/or social circumstances.

The achievements of the French and other early European explorers were widely commemorated in the early twentieth century and contributed to national pride (Kammen 1991; Nassaney 2009, 45–47). In 1902, the Daughters of the American Revolution dedicated a monument on the bluff at the mouth of the St. Joseph River (in St. Joseph, Michigan) to recognize La Salle's accomplishments in paving the way for European penetration of the continent (Figure 10.1; Woodruff 1999, 10). Such celebratory events were always politically charged, however benign they may have appeared. Commemoration served to legitimize the appropriation of territory by symbolically reenacting and reinforcing the claims European forebears had staked at the "dawn of history." These memorializing events occurred during a perceived peak period of foreign immigration as a way of reasserting the American ideals of ownership and private property and a particular vision of heritage in the nationalist project that defined contemporary citizenship through racial exclusion (see Camp 2013; McGuire 1992; Orser 2007). The events that occurred in Niles on July 4, 1913, sanctified the rock, thereby transforming it into a representation of the fort and a hallowed American symbol. Meanwhile, the precise location of the fort was fading into memory.

The Dawn of Professional Archaeology at Fort St. Joseph

In the first decades of the twentieth century, archaeology was emerging as a professional pursuit. Its focus was generally on pre-Columbian sites that had only recently become recognized as associated with the ancestors of contemporary Native Americans. Historical archaeology was in its infancy and was confined to documenting material traces of significant people and places, predominantly in Anglo America. In New England and Virginia, archaeologists joined preservationists in excavating to aid in the reconstruction of buildings associated with the nation's forefathers (Hicks and Horning 2006, 274–275).

Native American peoples who had been the target of systemic genocide for centuries were at a population nadir in the United States. This demographic trend reinforced the myth of the vanishing Indian. Anthropologists were engaged in salvage ethnography in an effort to document cultural practices that were believed to be rapidly disappearing. Little attention was paid to the archaeological remains of postcontact Native American peoples because archaeologists working under the acculturation paradigm "equated Native American utilization of European-made goods with technological decay, social disintegration, and dependence" (Wagner 2011, 12). George Quimby was one of a few archaeologists with an interest in the imported materials Native American peoples acquired from Europeans, although his work was admittedly conducted for chronological purposes. He reasoned that European goods from independently dated sites such as missions and forts could serve as index specimens to establish the age of lesser-known historic-era Native American sites. In the summer of 1937, Quimby and Glenn A. Black of the Indiana Historical Society examined sites and collections in the St. Joseph River valley with "particular attention to the locus of Fort St. Joseph" (Quimby 1993, 10). Quimby used the collections of Beeson and others from the Fort St. Joseph Museum (in Niles) to help him develop a chronology of postcontact artifacts in the western Great Lakes region with the goal of linking prehistoric and historic groups through the direct historical approach (Quimby 1966). Most of the artifacts from Fort St. Joseph were temporally diagnostic of his Middle Historic Period (1670–1760), since the site was occupied from about 1691 to 1781. Although the artifacts in the museum lacked precise provenience information, Quimby recognized their broader comparative research potential. His chronological framework is reliable to this day, although he was unable to recognize anomalous patterns that challenged his notions of acculturation (see Nassaney 2018b).

In the late 1940s, interest developed in locating and excavating the fort site to recover materials for display purposes and to document architectural features to supplement the limited information that was available on the appearance of the fort. Alexis A. Praus, director of the Kalamazoo Public Museum (Michigan), who had field experience with the Yale Peabody Museum and the University of Nebraska supervising the excavation of Indian village sites and mounds, began a 20-year campaign to get permission to excavate the fort, although he was never successful.[3] He corresponded with Lewis Beeson, Ralph Ballard, and Gertrude Johnston (then director of the Fort St. Joseph Museum), among others; expressed an interest in excavating and preserving the fort for posterity; and sought local approval for his proposed actions. Through his experience, Praus understood how important careful recovery and documentation was for future efforts to reconstruct the fort. He tried to reassure the Fort St. Joseph Historical Association of his credentials and intentions by stating that "once dug, the record will be gone forever. There is a lot of information: post-moulds, building outlines, pits, etc., to be secured from the ground that is just as important as trade and Indian materials that may be found."[4] It was not uncommon for museums to acquire collections through fieldwork and he was willing to share his findings with the local historical association. Praus finally convinced an unnamed Kalamazoo benefactor to provide up to $50,000 to purchase the site to allow preliminary testing.[5] His efforts to excavate were thwarted, however, because the site owners at the time were unwilling to sell and refused to give him permission to excavate.

A flurry of fort-related activity occurred in the 1970s, instigated by a former director of the Fort St. Joseph Museum (D. Wayne Stiles), the Four Flags Historical Study Committee of the city of Niles, and the Greater Niles Recreation Board. Presumably these efforts were the culmination of years of anticipating a systematic search for the fort and the upcoming bicentennial, which heightened interest in history throughout the country. In 1973, Fort St. Joseph was listed on the National Register of Historic Places at a time when a three-page nomination form was adequate to establish eligibility. The Michigan Department of Natural Resources recommended that the area be developed as a future state park, even though it was still in private hands (Ballard 1973). The Greater Niles Recreation Board hired Victor Hogg (1975), a consultant for Mackinac State Historic Parks, to prepare a physical feasibility study for the development of historic Fort St. Joseph and they hired an engineering firm to bore through the twentieth-century landfill to ascertain its depth and the potential of the substrate to support a reconstruction in an area where the fort was believed to be located (Cremin and Nassaney 1999, 27). Lyle Stone (1974a), a well-known historical archaeologist who had worked at Fort Michilimackinac, conducted a preliminary inventory of the artifacts from the vicinity of the fort that were curated in Niles and South Bend. In 1977, the Four Flags Historical Study Committee invited Dr. Joseph L. Peyser, professor of French at Indiana University-South Bend, to identify and translate French-language documents pertaining to Fort St. Joseph (Peyser 1978, 1992). In the course of his research, Peyser examined some 2,000 pages of documents and hundreds of maps and concluded that Fort St. Joseph was indeed located in Niles along the east bank of the river, despite claims to the contrary (e.g., Webster and Krause 1990). Michigan State University archaeologists expressed an interest in locating the site on the ground in the early 1970s (Cremin and Nassaney 1999, 29). Although they did not undertake any fieldwork, a graduate student (Hulse 1977, 1981) cataloged the artifacts from the fort that were curated in the Fort St. Joseph Museum for his MA thesis using the typology that Stone (1974b) had developed for Fort Michilimackinac. University of Notre Dame archaeologists conducted some test excavations near the boulder and on the east side of Bond Street but found no related materials (Ballard 1973). Thus, despite the scholarly interest in and historical significance of the site, material evidence of the site remained elusive and inaccessible. The area's French heritage was all but forgotten until a local community group, Support the Fort., Inc., was formed in 1991. Dedicated to keeping the memory of Fort St. Joseph alive, the group sponsored several annual living history events in the mid-1990s and invited WMU archaeologists to conduct a survey to locate the fort in 1998 (Nassaney 1999, chapter 1, this volume; Nassaney et al. 2003).

The Intellectual Climate of Colonial Archaeology in the Late Twentieth Century

Once WMU archaeologists identified undisturbed archaeological remains associated with Fort St. Joseph (Nassaney 1999, chapter 1, this volume; Nassaney and Cremin 2002b), Support the Fort and local citizens authorized them to recover architectural data that would be useful in creating a reconstruction of the fort (see Hartley and Nassaney, chapter 4, this volume). Archaeologists came to the project with an academic interest in examining the relationships that resulted from interactions between the French and their Native American allies in the context of the fur trade (Nassaney 2015). This research question had emerged from long-standing anthropological interests that had formed the basis for the development of historical archaeology, which was focused at the time on cultural change and continuity in response to European colonialism (Deetz 1977). Colonial archaeology was experiencing a fundamental shift in perspective in the late twentieth century as researchers began to incorporate postcolonial thinking into their work (Gosden 2002). In brief, researchers began to challenge the notion that culture change merely flowed from colonizers to the colonized. This conceptual shift created space for the agency of the subaltern. In other words, scholars were receptive to seeing a blending of cultural traditions in colonialist settings in a process referred to variously as hybridity, ethnogenesis, creolization, and *métissage* (Dawdy 2000; Hu 2013; Turgeon et al. 1996).

The ethnohistorian Richard White's seminal work (1991) had a significant influence on the how scholars understood interactions between the French and Native American peoples in the western Great Lakes region and early interpretations of the archaeology of Fort St. Joseph. White posited a middle ground—a metaphorical space of accommodation that was created through the cultural exchanges between the French and their Native American allies— and viewed the fur trade in the region as less an economic relationship than an ever-evolving arena of cultural negotiation. The Indians and French who initially shared neither cultural values nor assumptions about the appropriate ways of acting toward each other developed novel ways of communicating their cultural needs and desires as they forged a middle ground and created new social identities in the process of ethnogenesis (see also Sleeper-Smith 2001, 21). The practices that emerged in fur trade society were neither French nor Native American but a distinctive blending of cultural traditions. This perspective challenged earlier notions of the French who, even as they were courteous, kind, and forbearing to the Indians and became accustomed to Native American practices, attempted to reproduce their so-called civilizing ways. Native Americans similarly grafted French practices onto their own traditions as they accommodated to the new material, economic, and religious realities in which they were entangled. Moreover, the archaeological evidence could be interpreted to support this scenario (Nassaney 2008b).

French official diplomacy rested on the loyalties of their Native American allies. Although the French claimed an enormous territory that greatly exceeded that of the English, they had a much smaller population that remained dispersed with few exceptions in the St. Lawrence River Valley. In an effort to confine the English to the eastern seaboard, the French allied themselves with the western Indians by creating mutually beneficial exchange relationships that were often reinforced through intermarriage (Havard and Vidal 2006; Sleeper-Smith 2001). Unlike Britain, France lacked a sufficient population to appropriate Native American surpluses, dispossess Native Americans of their lands, or establish relations of dominance and did not aim to do so. Eligible spouses for the predominantly male population of New France were also in short supply, leading to the common practice of unions with Native American women—marriage à la façon du pays. Men sometimes found refuge in their wives' households, where they accommodated to a world structured by Native American customs and traditions. Marriage transformed French traders into Indian husbands, fathers, and brothers (Ekberg 2007,

24; Sleeper-Smith 2001, 42). The offspring of Indian women and French men were often raised biculturally, and they "might identify themselves as either Indian or French," depending on the social context (Sleeper-Smith 2001, 46, 49). They may have also developed an entirely new identity (see Murphy 2014; Peterson 1981).

The vast majority of the artifacts that we have recovered are imported goods that indicate that commodity production and European building styles were transplanted to the New World along with a desire for technologies like iron knives and brass kettles. But in addition to these objects, we have also recovered evidence that suggests a Native American presence and/or the French adoption of Native American practices at the fort. For example, excavations have yielded several metal and triangular stone (Madison) and bone projectile points—components of an effective technology for damp weather in which flintlocks might fail (Figure 3.2). Fragments of hematite recovered from the site, some ground, could have been used to produce a red pigment. Numerous fragments of stone smoking pipes have been found in proximity to white clay European forms (Nassaney 2008b, figure 8). Two bone or antler gaming pieces (Figure 3.4) that are remarkably similar to those still used by Potawatomi women in the 1960s, attest to new forms of recreation, as does a modified deer phalanx that was an element of the well-known cup-and-pin game (Figure 3.5). The vast majority of the animal bones recovered are well preserved but highly fragmented, as if they were intentionally broken to facilitate the extraction of marrow or bone grease for tallow. Moreover, preliminary analysis indicates that most of the bones represent predominantly deer and other native species; there are few elements from domesticated animals (Martin et al., chapter 3, this volume; Nassaney and Martin 2017). Finally, there is the smudge pit that was used to tan hides (Cremin and Nassaney 2003; Mendes and Nassaney, chapter 7, this volume).

These artifacts, features, and ecofacts were associated with French-style buildings and do not derive from earlier pre-European components. They also point to technologies, practices, and resources that were foreign to the French. While any of these individual artifacts, features, or ecofacts could represent isolated incidents of deposition, taken as a whole they raised some intriguing possibilities regarding the identities of the site occupants. For example, we surmised that the hematite could have been ground by a French *voyageur* to produce face paint in imitation of his Native American kin. In a description of the commandant of the French post of Natchitoches in the Lower Mississippi

Valley, a French priest noted that "many Frenchmen . . . can scarcely be distinguished from the Indians . . . they imitate them not only in their nakedness, but even in painting their faces" (Hackett 1934 quoted in Loren 2005, 310). The smudge pit appeared to represent the work of a fur trader's Native American spouse or perhaps his *métis* daughter. Alternately, the French (perhaps the blacksmith Antoine D'Haitre) might have been using Native American practices to tan their own hides. The prevalence of wild animal species represented by the faunal remains suggested that the French adopted a new cuisine on the frontier. Furthermore, the highly fragmented animal bones suggest intentional breakage to render grease and tallow to process hides and produce commodities (Nassaney and Martin 2017).

Collectively, these data suggested that the blending of French and Indian cultures was well under way at Fort St. Joseph. We observed no discrete patterns in the distribution of these materials that would suggest the maintenance of cultural boundaries. Instead, it appeared that "Native American activities" were being integrated into "French" households, resulting in syncretic cultural and material practices (see Deagan 1996 for parallels in New Spain). The archaeological and documentary records suggested that the interaction of these two cultural groups at Fort St. Joseph led to a distinctive blending of practices and beliefs that characterize the process of ethnogenesis (Nassaney 2008b). This interpretation contrasts markedly with the image that the commemorative boulder was meant to convey and celebrate, namely the civilized French as the donor culture and the Indians as the passive recipients. Rather, Fort St. Joseph appeared to be a multiethnic community in which French and Native American peoples were mutually dependent on each other and were able to transcend cultural boundaries in the context of the fur trade.

Interpreting identity is not without its caveats. It always runs the risk of reification and essentialism (see Brandão and Nassaney, chapter 2, this volume). We must avoid projecting our own categories onto the past. We also need to beware of facile linkages between material objects and ethnic groups. For example, archaeologists recognize that artifact makers, users, and viewers often reuse and impose new meanings on objects. Beads, buttons, and bangles are often transformed once they are appropriated by new cultural groups and are used in new social settings. More refined information about their contexts of use is often needed to interpret their meanings. Nevertheless, it seemed reasonable to infer that many of the locally produced objects—including those made of imported raw materials (e.g., tinkling cones; see Giordano and Nassaney, chapter 6, this volume)—represent socially transformative intercultural practices that contributed to the process of ethnogenesis.

Undoubtedly, the challenge for a social archaeology is to develop a methodology to decode the complex meanings related to identity formation from material culture. In the end, one may have to conclude that identity—being symbolically constituted, fluid, situational, malleable, and contested—is subject to fewer constraints than, say, technology, thus reaffirming Hawkes's ladder of inference (1954). Nevertheless, our interpretations are still constrained by the material evidence such that we can only begin to approach identity in all its myriad forms through the archaeological record. Moreover, how we see the evidence is equally dependent on the social relations in which we are embedded (Nassaney 2012a; Saitta 2007).

Much of our practice is guided by the tenets of a collaborative archaeology in which we aim to be receptive to the voices of various stakeholders (D'Elia et al., chapter 9, this volume). In an effort to align ourselves with an indigenous perspective we may have overemphasized the similarities between the French and their Native American allies in the eighteenth century. Thus, in my assessment of identity formation at Fort St. Joseph I concluded that

> the material assemblage from excavations forces us to challenge essentialist categories of French and Indian. The archaeological and documentary records suggest that the interaction of these two cultural groups at Fort St. Joseph led to a distinctive blending of practices and beliefs that characterize the process of ethnogenesis. . . . I am not saying that the occupants of Fort St. Joseph were not signaling any form of ethnicity. Rather, they were constructing a new ethnic identity *in relationship to others.* The Fort St. Joseph community had a shared political purpose—to defend itself from the onslaught of their Native foes and the English and their allies; in the process of this alliance they used material culture and daily practices to distinguish themselves from outsiders and reinforce social solidarity (see Johnson 2000). This is not to say that the French were trying to become Indian nor the Indians French, but in the process of social interactions they made conscious choices with unintentional consequences that fundamentally altered their conceptions of themselves. (Nassaney 2008b, 314)

A postcolonial perspective underscores the extensive borrowing of cultural traits that took place in the process of creolization, leading to the emergence of new cultural forms. The blurring, mixing, and blending that occurred in fur trade society (*métissage*) challenges essentialized categories such as dominant/subordinate, colonized/colonizer, and even Native American /newcomer that were familiar dichotomies in colonial discourse. Postcolonial theory compels us to view identities as increasingly fluid and situational and no more fixed in matters of policy than in material practices. Material remains from archaeological contexts can be reimagined from this perspective, as expressed in the borrowing and blending of sartorial styles, the adoption of body piercing and face painting, and other cross-cultural material exchanges (Loren 2009; see also White 2012). Subsistence patterns, cloth adoption, tinkling cone production and use, and hide tanning are among the practices that archaeologically reinforce this scenario (Davis, chapter 5, this volume; Giordano and Nassaney, chapter 6, this volume; Martin et al., chapter 3, this volume; Mendes and Nassaney, chapter 7, this volume).

Thus, the archaeological record raised some intriguing possibilities regarding the activities and identities of the people who resided at Fort St. Joseph. The data suggested that Fort St. Joseph was a multiethnic community of French *and* Indians in which kin relations and political alliances transcended racial and ethnic categories (Nassaney 2012a). Moreover, I have argued (Nassaney 2012a) that essentialist categories like "French" and "Indian" do not capture the subtle ethnic expressions in the pluralistic society of Fort St. Joseph because ethnogenesis on the frontier had eliminated ethnic distinctions within the St. Joseph community (see Mann 2003, 2008; Silliman 2005). I have also emphasized that the French were more accommodative and less civilizing than earlier historians were willing or able to admit (Nassaney 2008b). They had, after all, established close personal, social, and political ties and relations of mutual dependency with their Native American allies. This interpretation is consistent with "archaeological practice that aims to decolonize the discipline, pay homage to hybridity, emphasize cultural fluidity, acknowledge human agency, and empower contemporary cultural groups who have a stake in the history of the fur trade and the colonial enterprise" (Nassaney 2012a, 16–17).

Beyond Ethnogenesis at Fort St. Joseph

A critical outcome of this postcolonial narrative of fur trade society at Fort St. Joseph and elsewhere is that it elides a number of anomalies that point to significant ethnic differences that cannot be ignored (see Nassaney 2018b; Nassaney and Brandão 2009). It also suggests that cultural mimicry was a form of naïve emulation, that each group was consciously or unconsciously imitating the other (see Havard 2008). Furthermore, the *métissage* trope carries considerable ideological baggage. It contributes to the idea that New France offered a kinder and gentler form of colonialism (see Volo and Volo 2002, xxi; Nassaney et al. 2012, 56). After all, the French and Indians created a middle ground to facilitate political alliance, economic exchange, and intermarriage. Yet when we examine the evidence from a different (post-postcolonial?) perspective, we are compelled to scrutinize and reconsider these apparent similarities and the motivations that led to a superficial uniformity in the material world of the fur trade. Conversely, various data classes can be interpreted to reveal an ethnic separation between Native American and white society. Despite the evidence for "cross-cultural exchange, distinctive colonist and Indian identities were not entirely muffled" (White 2012, 213).

When we examine the former model of close affinity, emulation, and mutual admiration in the light of glocalization, which focuses on the articulation of global processes at the local scale, anomalies emerge that challenge this postcolonial narrative (Nassaney 2015, 2018b). Cross-cultural adoptions were undoubtedly common, yet the materiality of Fort St. Joseph suggests equally important continuities and retentions of traditional practices that cannot be dismissed. Artifacts, features, and ecofacts and their contextual relationships can also be interpreted to indicate that the French and the Native Americans operated within distinct cultural realms, attempted to maintain daily practices, and were reluctant to relinquish them. They attempted to preserve and use their own materiality to ensure survival and well-being in the colonial encounter. Borrowing was often an expedient strategy that furthered the interests of each group. In other words, French *voyageurs* adopted birch-bark canoes, for example, because they were the most effective means of transporting goods to ensure a profit, not because they wanted to imitate the Indians. This perspective shifts attention away from the amicable relations researchers like me have previously posited and toward an understanding grounded in more pragmatic solutions that agents employ when new cultural alternatives are presented that can be used to further old ways of being. Even as the French relied on Native Americans for cartographic knowledge and military support, often learned native languages to facilitate trade and religious conversion, and borrowed selected forms of material culture (e.g., birch-bark canoes, moccasins, snowshoes) and practices (e.g., hide tanning) in the course of their interactions (Delâge and Warren 2008, 310; Heidenreich 1978), they doggedly

maintained various architectural, technological, sartorial, and religious practices that served to reproduce their traditional cultural identities.

For example, the most conspicuous archaeological features at Fort St. Joseph are the fireplaces and architectural remains associated with a series of
habitation structures. As Hartley and Nassaney (chapter 4, this volume) argue,
these materials are evidence of permanent European-style structures that derive from building traditions developed in northwest France. Their rectilinear
form and permanence connote the proper French (or, more precisely, Canadian) way to construct a house (Moogk 2002). French Canadian construction techniques persisted into the nineteenth century in parts of the Midwest,
reflecting the importance of an architectural style in expressing ethnicity, one
that contrasted with Native American, English, and later American building
forms (see Mann 2008).

Domestic and commercial activities were conducted in these buildings, as
evidenced by associated artifacts. Many domestic items such as cloth, kettles,
and iron tools were among the durable goods that the French traded to Native Americans and also used themselves on a daily basis, typically in ways
their makers intended (Figure 10.2). Various products of Old World technol-

Figure 10.2. Iron tools, like this ax from Fort St. Joseph, were among the European imports fort
occupants used and exchanged for furs with Native Americans. Photo by Cathrine Davis.

ogy such as iron and brass kettles for cooking and iron-edged tools for cutting (knives), tilling (hoes), and chopping (axes) were essential. Similarly, a blacksmith produced goods (e.g., nails) and provided services (e.g., gun repair) as needed (Brandão and Nassaney, chapter 2, this volume). A large cache of gun parts from Fort St. Joseph suggests the importance of the blacksmith's role in daily life (Nassaney 2015, 181–182).

In addition to these prosaic objects, some artifacts recovered from the fort have distinctive ideological meanings grounded in Old World beliefs. For example, a French flintlock butt plate recovered from the site exhibited a series of scratches that were later determined to be intentional file(?) marks (n = 119) along its margins, carefully organized into groups of ten—a pattern indicative of a computation system imported from the Old World (Figure 10.3). The French also carried other time-honored notions to New France, including sumptuary laws to reinforce positions of social status as expressed in the raw materials, styles, and colors of clothing and personal adornment (cf. Davis, chapter 5, this volume; Loren 2010). Many personal adornment objects recov-

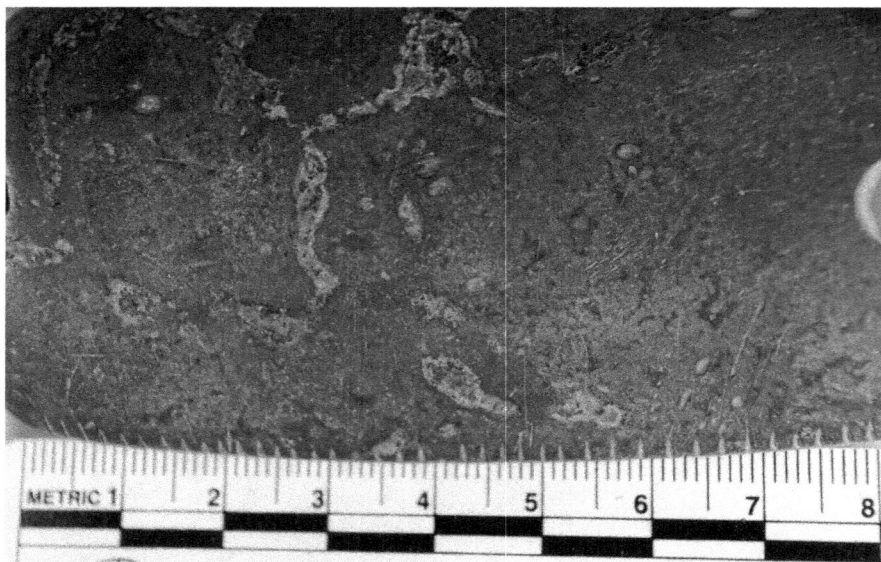

Figure 10.3. Eighteenth-century French flintlock butt plate with computational marks along its margins. Photo by Kevin Jones.

ered from the fort (e.g., buckles, buttons, finger rings) were likely the possessions of fort occupants that they used to signal identity and construct an image
of the self. More important, some of these objects were selected by individuals
to adopt, maintain, or reintroduce symbolic meanings from distant markets,
perhaps to broadcast notions of gentility and refinement in a frontier context.
Sleeve buttons on tailored shirts and buckles attached to leather shoes were
clothing styles connected to Montréal, Québec, and perhaps French towns and
cities. Even if they were confined to the commandant and other representatives
of the Crown, these styles indicate that at least some of the denizens of the
fort retained European sensibilities regarding proper attire even at a frontier
fortification. Catholic crucifixes and medallions were also common at the fort,
testimony that core beliefs and values such as those relating to monogamy and
religious conversion had survived (Hulse 1981; Brandão and Nassaney 2008).
Although it is difficult to assess the sincerity of religious beliefs in a society
(past or present), French material culture and its symbolism are clear evidence
that piety persisted at Fort St. Joseph.

Archaeologists have often highlighted the imported goods found at Native
American sites in the postcontact period as evidence that traditional society
gradually changed under the onslaught of economic, political, and social influences. For example, in his study of changes in material culture and Native
American lifestyles brought about by the fur trade in the western Great Lakes
from the seventeenth through nineteenth centuries, George Quimby (1939,
1966) observed that by 1760, Native American peoples of the western Great
Lakes had been changed by their involvement in the fur trade because they had
adopted imported goods that had produced a cultural uniformity throughout
the region. One anomalous observation was rather telling in hindsight, yet
Quimby was unable to grasp its implications for challenging his assumptions.
He noted that despite significant material culture change, Chippewa (Ojibwe)
economic activities of the 1760s "were still linked to [the] physical environment and the seasons, probably much as they had been in pre-European times.
*Thus there seems to be a continuity and conservatism of subsistence and settle-
ment pattern that is lacking in most aspects of material culture*" (Quimby 1966,
179; my emphasis).

Prior to the appropriation of Native American lands by treaty and other
nefarious means, Native American peoples could maintain a dispersed settlement pattern within a homeland and schedule their activities in accordance
with the seasonal availability of resources (Hoock et al, chapter 8, this volume).

As a result, they constructed temporary houses as a practical response to seasonal mobility (Loveland and Nassaney 2017). Native Americans constructed houses made of bent saplings covered with bark and other organic materials until they were forced to adopt plow agriculture in the early nineteenth century, which led to more permanent European habitation styles. One early exception is worth noting. In the 1740s, a Native American leader asked the French to build him a home in the European style. It required 400 linear feet of squared timber and had two doors (Peyser 1978, document 123, page 2). It is not known what compelled this desire.

Settlement patterns are sensitive indicators of cultural conceptions of ownership, mobility, and resource use. In a systematic analysis of settlement patterns at the regional scale to determine if Fort St. Joseph influenced the distribution of Native American population in the valley from northern Indiana to the mouth of the St. Joseph River, Hoock and colleagues (chapter 8, this volume) demonstrated that Late Woodland sites (AD 600–1690) were generally small and widely dispersed, reflecting the seasonal round nuclear and extended family units practiced, just as Quimby observed. However, sites tended to cluster close to the fort during its occupancy (1691–1781), and were larger, perhaps reflecting aggregations of multifamily units. Once the fort was abandoned (post-1781), Native American sites were again widely dispersed but seem to have been located in proximity to new Euro-American sites in the region, perhaps indicating the continued importance of the fur trade and the desire to obtain imported and manufactured goods. Dispersal suggests that Native Americans maintained their seasonal round and incorporated European sites as just another node in their scheduling of activities so long as they had access to land and could remain mobile (Nassaney 2015, 176–177).

Less is known about Native American subsistence strategies in the eighteenth century, although judging from the animal bone assemblage at Fort St. Joseph it seems likely that wild food resources continued to play a dominant role in the diet. The English surveyor Thomas Hutchins remarked on the resident community of the fort during his 1762 visit, noting that the French fur traders engaged in limited agriculture and had few domesticated animals; they generally subsisted much as their Native American allies did, who had not adopted domesticated animals or imported cultigens to any significant degree (Cunningham 1961, 72–73).

Native Americans were more apt to adopt imported durable goods, many of which were substitutes for objects they were already familiar with. Native Americans often acquired manufactured goods such as cloth, kettles, iron tools, and sundry objects in exchange for furs, as indicated by the recovery of such items from mortuary and habitation contexts throughout the region (Mainfort 1979; Mason 1986; Nassaney et al. 2000; Walder and Yann 2018). Some of these goods replaced traditional technologies such as leather clothing, stone tools, and low-fired earthenware ceramics, suggesting that Native Americans generally chose to adopt materials that fit their worldview (see Nassaney and Volmar 2003). Studies repeatedly demonstrate that Native American peoples were active and discerning consumers who pitted French against English traders, walked miles to strike a fair bargain, and selectively adopted goods into their material repertoire (see Bradley 1987a; Kehoe 2000; Ray 1974, 1980).

Goods were sometimes put to use in ways their makers or traders had not intended. Native Americans often reinterpreted objects such as glass beads, copper kettles, and thimbles on their own terms (e.g., Bradley 1987a; Hamell 1983; Langford 2011, 38). Fort St. Joseph has yielded thousands of glass beads (Malischke 2009). Many of these were destined for Native American hands, where they would have been used in much the same ways that Native Americans had previously used seeds, bone, shell, and other natural materials to embellish themselves in traditional ways. In some cases, Native American peoples viewed trade goods as raw materials. For example, James Bradley (1987a, 146) examined how the Onondagas dismembered and modified axes from their original form to fabricate more "useful" implements. They bent knives into curved shapes to form crooked knives that were used for woodcarving (Bradley 1987a, 149). Far from being seduced by these "toil-alleviating tools" (Ritchie 1954, 1), Native American people seem to have been more interested in adapting these implements into useful forms (Bradley 1987a, 152).

A striking example comes from the Lyne site (20BE10) on the terrace above the floodplain at Fort St. Joseph. The site has yielded a wide range of Native American stone and ceramic artifacts, including lithic debitage, triangular Madison projectile points, low-fired grit-tempered earthenware, several stone smoking pipes, copious amounts of fire-cracked rock, and a series of smudge pits used for smoking hides (Mendes and Nassaney, chapter 7, this volume). We have also recovered various European imports such as gunflints, flintlock hardware (i.e., a trigger, a sideplate), lead shot and musket balls, a pewter brooch, numerous copper-alloy scraps, fragments of hand-blown glass containers, and a cut fragment of trade silver perforated for ornamental use (Figure 7.2), among other probable eighteenth-century artifacts, including a thimble (Figure 7.1). This assemblage, the presence of fire-cracked rock, the smudge pits, and the absence of evidence of European-style buildings suggests that this area was occupied by small, seasonal households that included Native American peoples. Several thimbles have been recovered from our excavations. The thimbles from the floodplain are intact and were probably used with needles for baling furs and making and repairing clothing, whereas the thimble found in Locus III on the terrace is perforated, suggesting reuse for a decorative function (Figure 7.1; see also Langford 2011, 38; Quimby 1966, 76). This telling example illustrates how Native American peoples reimagined and repurposed artifacts for culturally appropriate uses.

Clothing and objects of personal adornment such as a perforated thimble are particularly revealing about ethnic identity because these materials were literally personal embodiments (see Loren 2001). Unfortunately, cloth seldom preserves in the archaeological record, leaving us to ponder the meaning of buttons, buckles, bracelets, finger rings, and similar objects (see Davis, chapter 5, this volume). Archaeologists with access to paintings and other lines of evidence have argued that Native Americans made pragmatic choices in daily attire (e.g., Kehoe 2000). Their willingness to wear foreign clothing does not represent a rejection of their culture but an adoption of desired innovations or rare and novel styles to increase social status. Native American women often selected objects that were suitable substitutes for goods that already existed in their own societies or modified unfamiliar goods to satisfy their own needs. They were not drawn to frivolous ornaments and other trifles (Nassaney 2015, 111). Loren (2009, 120) discussed the role a French frock coat served for a Tunica chief in the 1720s in Louisiana. She suggested that rather than a civilizing object, as Father Charlevoix believed, it "was an endlessly useful object," manipulated "for a particular audience to allow for certain kinds of interactions to take place" (Loren 2009, 120). This points to the multivalence of the material world and the ways that materiality can be manipulated to maintain identity and attract social approval and admiration in the face of changing circumstances. The cultural persistence of Native American descendants in the region to the present day suggests that eighteenth-century Native Americans did not adopt the accoutrements and assume the conditions of modernity (Delâge and Warren 2008, 314).

Concluding Thoughts

Fort St. Joseph has been good for archaeologists and the public to think with and about for over a century. The ways we envision this place are assuredly a function of the discoveries revealed in the documents and in the ground. Yet the meanings we ascribe to historical accounts, soil stains, trinkets, trifles, and other small things forgotten are dependent on the social relationships in which we are embroiled. Whereas once we viewed the French at Fort St. Joseph as the literal saviors of the area's original inhabitants, we no longer find such an interpretation tenable for epistemological, social, ethical, and moral reasons. An appreciation of cultural diversity and a recognition that both the French and the local Native Americans were active agents who were conservative in their outlook and resistant to cultural change sheds new light on the detritus of over a century of occupation along the St. Joseph River and its environs. It demonstrates how they could be similar and yet so different.

Archaeologists aim to understand what happened in the past and who conducted the activities represented by the materials we recover. There is no simple relationship between the objects that were made, used, and discarded at this old French fort and their meanings in the present because the archaeological record is underdetermined. In other words, because bias can creep into this ambiguity, archaeologists often struggle with the conceptual and methodological challenges of interpreting identity from the archaeological record in the context of shifting social and political conditions (Ferris et al. 2014, 3). When archaeologists consider the material remains from multiple perspectives, they can begin to weave a braided narrative of the outcomes of cultural interactions (Atalay 2012) that does justice to the activities of the French *and* Indians in the past and their descendants in the present.

The history and archaeology of Fort St. Joseph teaches us that the French and Native Americans built conceptual bridges to facilitate the exploitation of North America's natural resources (Delâge and Warren 2008, 309). These bridges were essential for each group's survival. Yet despite the sharing of material goods and cultural practices, Indian and white worlds often remained distinct (Havard 2008). Neither the French nor the Native Americans were altruistic, even in selecting marriage partners. For example, French men sought to marry Native American women because of the imbalanced ratio of white men to white women on the frontier and to gain access to Indian property and political processes (Maher 2016, 115). Successful fur traders in the St. Joseph

River valley relied on their wives to mediate the sometimes tentative and potentially explosive alliances between neighboring villages (Sleeper-Smith 2001, 90). Success in the increasingly competitive market economy of the region in the late eighteenth century depended on the kin network of a trader's wife and her own skills as a trader (Sleeper-Smith 2001, 91). Traders might also rely on the agricultural prowess of their wives' household to produce sufficient corn, wheat, and maple sugar to feed their own household and to produce a surplus for regional markets (Sleeper-Smith 2001, 91). Advantages also accrued to Native American wives who married French men. For example, they gained ready access to objects from distant markets that they could distribute within their own kinship networks.

Religious differences also persisted in the middle ground of cultural exchange. Jesuit missionaries, for instance, recognized that religious *métissage*—the weaving of contrary truths into a new fabric—was impossible (Warkentin and Podruchny 2008, 12–13). Their mission also helped them see their own culture from a different perspective. Although they lived among "primitive tribes," it was actually in their own culture that they "discovered ridiculous mores, shameful social ideas, and amoral policies" (Delâge and Warren 2008, 310).

Simple daily practices, such as those related to personal hygiene, can be particularly insightful in distinguishing French and Indian worldviews. Sophie White (2012) has argued that in French colonial Louisiana, material culture—especially dress—was central to the elaboration of discourses about race and physical difference. Because "notions of cleanliness in Europe since the seventeenth century privileged laundering linens over cleaning bodies," bodily contact with water was generally avoided because of unfounded ideas about the transmission of disease (White 2012, 191). This belief contrasts markedly with archaeological and ethnohistoric evidence that demonstrates that Algonquian peoples emphasized washing their bodies (White 2012, 198) and using sweat lodges for hygienic, medicinal, and ritual purification for millennia in the western Great Lakes region (Quattrin and Cremin 1988). Seemingly taken-for-granted ideas about personal cleanliness are in fact historically and culturally constituted and reveal the cultural chasm that existed between the French and Native Americans when they encountered each other at places like Fort St. Joseph. In the absence of motivation or force, cultural change can be an extremely slow process and is often resisted when agents are politically autonomous.

In the end, researchers must reflect on their own subject positions and the relationships they have with the communities they study and those who have a stake in their work to actively determine how the stories they tell about the archaeology of places like Fort St. Joseph illuminate contemporary conditions and position us to make better-informed decisions as we move forward. Revealing Fort St. Joseph is a serious enterprise that has implications for the ways we see the past, live in the present, and envision the future. Our investigations and reflections reveal that our understandings of Fort St. Joseph are constantly in flux and that the next generation will be attracted to this place for reasons that we cannot imagine.

Acknowledgments

Portions of this chapter appeared in a special issue of *Historical Archaeology* devoted to forts and identities (Nassaney 2019). Permission to reprint this material has been granted by the Society for Historical Archaeology thanks to *Historical Archaeology*'s editor, Chris Matthews. Doug Wilson provided a careful reading and useful comments on a previous draft of this chapter, for which I am appreciative. The ideas expressed here have slowly evolved over the nearly two decades since we first identified material evidence of this long-lost fort. The colleagues, associates, and friends who lent support and inspired my thinking are too numerous to name. Thank you all for your continued interest and support for the investigation and interpretation of Fort St. Joseph.

Notes

1. Cunningham (1961, 80). See also "Map of Location of Old Fort St. Josephs and the Miamis Village in the City of Niles, Michigan," 1900, on file at the Fort St. Joseph Museum, Niles, Michigan; Coolidge (1915, 289).

2. "Map of Location of Old Fort St. Josephs and the Miamis Village"; Nassaney et al. (2002–2004, Figure 2).

3. Nowicki (2001); Alexis A. Praus to Lewis Beeson, May 22, 1947; Alexis A. Praus to Herbert Barber, August 20, 1947, both on file in the Kalamazoo Valley Museum, Kalamazoo, Michigan.

4. Praus to Barber, August 20, 1947.

5. Alexis A. Praus to Gertrude Johnston, May 20, 1965, on file in the Kalamazoo Valley Museum, Kalamazoo, Michigan.

References Cited

Académie Française. 1694. *Le dictionnaire de l'Académie Française*. Vol. 1. Paris: Chez la Veuve de J. B. Coignard et J. B. Coignard.

Adams, Diane L. 1987. Lead Seals from Fort Michilimackinac, Mackinaw City, Michigan. MA thesis, Western Michigan University, Kalamazoo.

———. 1989. *Lead Seals from Fort Michilimackinac, 1715–1781*. Archaeological Completion Report Series no. 14. Mackinac Island, MI: Mackinac State Historic Parks.

Allaire, Bernard. 1999. *Pelleteries, manchons et chapeaux de castor: Les fourrures nord-américaines à Paris, 1500–1632*. Sillery, QC: Septentrion, and Paris: Presses de l'Université de Paris-Sorbonne.

Allaire, Gratien. 1980. Les engagements pour la traite des fourrures. *Revue d'histoire de l'Amérique française* 34(1): 3–26.

———. 1987. Officiers et marchands: Les sociétés de commerce des fourrures, 1715–1760. *Revue d'histoire de l'Amérique française* 40(3): 409–28.

Anderson, Dean L. 1991. Variability in Trade at Eighteenth-Century French Outposts. In *French Colonial Archaeology: The Illinois Country and the Western Great Lakes*, edited by John A. Walthall, 218–236. Urbana: University of Illinois Press.

———. 1994. The Flow of European Trade Goods into the Western Great Lakes Region, 1715–1760. In *The Fur Trade Revisited: Selected Papers of the Sixth North American Fur Trade Conference*, edited by Jennifer S. H. Brown, William J. Eccles, and Donald P. Heldman, 93–115. East Lansing: Michigan State University Press, and Mackinac Island, MI: Mackinac State Historic Parks.

Anderson, Fred. 2001. *Crucible of War: The Seven Years' War and the Fate of Empire in British North America, 1754–1766*. New York: Random House.

Anderson, Melville B. 1901. *Relation of the Discoveries and Voyages of Cavelier de La Salle from 1679 to 1681*. Chicago: The Caxton Club.

Anderson, Virginia DeJohn. 2004. *Creatures of Empire: How Domestic Animals Transformed Early America*. New York: Oxford University Press.

Anselmi, Lisa Marie. 2004. New Materials, Old Ideas: Native Use of European-Introduced Metals in the Northeast. PhD diss., University of Toronto.

Appler, Douglas R. 2012. Municipal Archaeology Programs and the Creation of Community Amenities. *Public Historian* 34(3): 40–67.

Armour, David. 2000. *Colonial Michilimackinac*. Mackinac Island, MI: Mackinac State Historic Parks.

Atalay, Sonya. 2006. Indigenous Archaeology as Decolonizing Practice. *American Indian Quarterly* 30(3–4): 280–310.

———. 2012. *Community-Based Archaeology: Research with, by, and for Indigenous and Local Communities*. Berkeley: University of California Press.

Atkinson, Frank. 1956. *Some Aspects of the Eighteenth Century Woolen and Worsted Trade in Halifax*. Halifax, UK: Halifax Museums.

Auer, Nancy. 2013. Form and Function in Lake Sturgeon. In *The Great Lake Sturgeon*, edited by Nancy Auer and Dave Dempsey, 9–19. East Lansing: Michigan State University Press.

Baart, Jan M. 2005. Cloth Seals at Iroquois Sites. *Northeast Historical Archaeology* 34: 77–88.

Babits, Lawrence E., and Stephanie Gandulla, eds. 2013. *Archaeology of French and Indian War Forts*. Gainesville: University Press of Florida.

Baerreis, D. A. 1963. Teaching Techniques. In *The Teaching of Anthropology*, edited by D. G. Mandelbaum, G. W. Lasker, and E. M. Albert, 247–252. Memoir 94. Washington, DC: American Anthropological Association, and Berkeley: University of California Press.

Baker, George A. 1899. *The St. Joseph-Kankakee Portage: Its Location and Use by Marquette, LaSalle and the French Voyageurs*. Northern Indiana Historical Society Publication no. 1. South Bend, IN: Northern Indiana Historical Society.

Baker, Rollin H. 1983. *Michigan Mammals*. East Lansing: Michigan State University Press.

Balkwill, Darlene McCuaig, and Stephen L. Cumbaa. 1992. *A Guide to the Identification of Postcranial Bones of Bos taurus and Bison bison*. Syllogeus no. 71. Ottawa: Canadian Museum of Nature.

Ballard, Ralph. 1949. *Old Fort St. Joseph*. Niles, MI: Niles Printing Company.

———. 1973. *Old Fort St. Joseph*. Berrien Springs, MI: Hard Scrabble Books.

Bamforth, Douglas B., Mark Becker, and Jean Hudson. 2005. Intrasite Spatial Analysis, Ethnoarchaeology, and Paleoindian Land-Use on the Great Plains: The Allen Site. *American Antiquity* 70: 561–580.

Barrows, Walter Bradford. 1912. *Michigan Bird Life*. Special Bulletin of the Department of Zoology and Physiology, Michigan Agricultural College, East Lansing.

Bartoy, Kevin. 2012. Teaching through Rather than About: Education in the Context of Public Archaeology. In *The Oxford Handbook of Public Archaeology*, edited by Robin Skeates, Carol McDavid, and John Carman, 552–565. New York: Oxford University Press.

Beaudoin, Matthew A. 2013. A Hybrid Identity in a Pluralistic Nineteenth-Century Colonial Context. *Historical Archaeology* 47(2): 45–63.

Beauchamp, Pierre, Hubert Charbonneau, and Bertrand Desjardins. 1978. Le comportement démographique des voyageurs sous le régime français. *Histoire sociale/Social History* 11(21): 120–133.

Becker, Rory J. 2004. Eating Ethnicity: Examining Eighteenth-Century French Colonial Identity through Selective Consumption of Animal Resources in the North American Interior. MA thesis, Western Michigan University, Kalamazoo.

Beeson, Lewis H. 1900. Fort St. Joseph—The Mission, Trading Post and Fort, Located about One Mile South of Niles, Michigan. *Collections of the Michigan Pioneer and Historical Society* 28: 179–186.

Beik, William. 2000. *Louis XIV and Absolutism: A Brief Study with Documents*. New York: Bedford/St. Martins.

Belford, Paul. 2014. Sustainability in Community Archaeology. *AP: Online Journal of Public Archaeology* 4(2): 21–44.

Bense, Judith A. 2003. *Presidio Santa María de Galve (1698–1719): A Struggle in Survival in 18th Century Pensacola, Florida*. Gainesville: University Press of Florida.

Benston, Susan. 2010. Using GIS to Describe and Understand Archaeological Site Distribution: Mapping Fort Saint Joseph. MA thesis, Western Michigan University, Kalamazoo.

Bentley, Jerry H., and Herbert F. Ziegler. 2003. *Traditions and Encounters: A Global Perspective on the Past*. 2nd ed. Boston: McGraw Hill.

Berliner, Kelley, and Michael S. Nassaney. 2015. The Role of the Public in Public Archaeology: Ten Years of Outreach and Collaboration at Fort St. Joseph. *Journal of Community Archaeology and Heritage* 2(1): 3–21.

Berthong, Donald J. 1974. *Indians of Northern Indiana and Southwestern Michigan*. New York: Garland Publishing.

Bettarel, Robert L., and Hale G. Smith. 1973. *The Moccasin Bluff Site and the Woodland Cultures of Southwestern Michigan*. Anthropological Papers 49. Ann Arbor: Museum of Anthropology, University of Michigan.

Billeck, William T. 2016. Ethnographic and Historical Evidence for Glass Pendant Function in the Plains. *Plains Anthropologist* 61(240): 410–424.

Binford, Lewis R. 1967. Smudge Pits and Hide Smoking: The Use of Analogy in Archaeological Reasoning. *American Antiquity* 32(1): 1–12.

———. 1972. *An Archaeological Perspective*. New York: Seminar Press.

———. 1978. *Nunamiut Ethnoarchaeology*. New York: Academic Press.

Black, Graham. 2005. *The Engaging Museum: Developing Museums for Visitor Involvement*. London: Routledge.

Blackman, James M., Gil Stein, and Pamela Vandiver. 1993. The Standardization Hypothesis and Ceramic Mass Production: Technological, Compositional, and Metric Indexes of Craft Specialization at Tell Leilan, Syria. *American Antiquity* 58(1): 60–80.

Bollwerk, Elizabeth. 2006. Controlling Acculturation: A Potawatomi Strategy for Avoiding Removal. *Midcontinental Journal of Archaeology* 31(1): 117–141.

Bosher, J. F. 1987. *The Canada Merchants, 1713–1763*. New York: Clarendon Press.

Bougainville, Louis-Antoine de. 1757. Memoire de Bougainville sur l'état de la Nouvelle-France a l'époque de la guerre de sept ans (1757). In *Relations et mémoires inédits pour servir à l'histoire de la France dans les pays d'outremer*, edited by Pierre Margry. Paris: Challamel Aimé.

———. 2003. *Écrits sur le Canada*. Sillery, QC: Septentrion.

Bourdieu, Pierre. 1970. The Berber House or the World Reversed. *Social Science Information* 9(2): 151–170.

Bradley, James W. 1987a. *Evolution of the Onondaga Iroquois: Accommodating Change, 1500–1655*. Syracuse, NY: Syracuse University Press.

———. 1987b. Native Exchange and European Trade: Cross-Cultural Dynamics in the Sixteenth Century. *Man in the Northeast* 33: 31–46.

Brain, Jeffrey P. 1979. *The Tunica Treasure*. Cambridge, MA: Peabody Museum of Archaeology and Ethnology, Harvard University, and Andover, MA: Peabody Museum of Salem.

———. 1988. *Tunica Archaeology*. Papers of the Peabody Museum of Archaeology and Ethnology no. 78. Cambridge, MA: Harvard University Press.

Brandão, J. A. 1997. *"Your fyre shall burn no more": Iroquois Policy towards New France and Its Native Allies to 1701*. Lincoln: University of Nebraska Press.

———. 2008. Introduction: New France, the Fur Trade, and Michilimackinac. In *Edge of Empire: Documents of Michilimackinac, 1671–1716*, edited and translated by Joseph L. Peyser and J. A. Brandão, xxiii–xliii. East Lansing: Michigan State University Press, and Mackinac Island: Mackinac State Historic Parks.

Brandão, José António, and Michael S. Nassaney. 2006. A Capsule Social and Material History of Fort St. Joseph and Its Inhabitants (1691–1763). *French Colonial History* 7: 61–75.

———. 2008. Suffering for Jesus: Penitential Practices at Fort St. Joseph (Niles, Michigan) during the French Regime. *Catholic Historical Review* 94(3): 476–499.

Branstner, Susan. 1992. Tionontate Huron Occupation at the Marquette Mission. In *Calumet and Fleur-De-Lys: Archaeology of Indian and French Contact in the Midcontinent*, edited by John Walthall and Thomas Emerson, 177–202. Washington, DC: Smithsonian Institution Press.

Braund, Kathryn. 1993. *Deerskins & Duffles: The Creek Indian Trade with Anglo-America, 1685–1815*. Lincoln: University of Nebraska Press.

Brazier, Jennifer. 2013. The Development of the Architectural Styles of New France. *Le Journal* 29(3): 2–9.

Brewer, Richard. 1991. Original Avifauna and Postsettlement Changes. In *The Atlas of Breeding Birds of Michigan*, edited by Richard Brewer, Gail A. McPeek, and Raymond J. Adams, Jr., 33–58. East Lansing: Michigan State University Press.

Brewer, Richard, Gail A. McPeek, and Raymond J. Adams Jr., eds. 1991. *The Atlas of Breeding Birds of Michigan*. East Lansing: Michigan State University Press.

Brown, Margaret Kimball. 1971a. Glass from Fort Michilimackinac: A Classification for Eighteenth Century Glass. *Michigan Archaeologist* 17(3–4): 97–215.

———. 1971b. An Eighteenth-Century Trade Coat. *Plains Anthropologist* 16: 128–133.

———. 2002. *The Voyageur in the Illinois Country: The Fur Trade's Professional Boatman in Mid America*. Center for French Colonial Studies Extended Publication Series no. 3. Naperville, IL: Center for French Colonial Studies.

Brumfiel, Elizabeth. 1980. Specialization, Market Exchange, and the Aztec State: A View from Huexotla. *Current Anthropology* 21(4): 459–478.

Brumfiel, Elizabeth, and Timothy Earle. 1987. Specialization, Exchange, and Complex Societies: An Introduction. In *Specialization, Exchange, and Complex Societies*, edited by Elizabeth Brumfiel and Timothy Earle, 1–10. New York: Cambridge University Press.

Calver, William L., and Reginald Bolton. 1950. *History Written with Pick and Shovel: Military Buttons, Belt-Plates, Badges and Other Relics Excavated from Colonial, Revolutionary, and War of 1812 Camp Sites by the Field Exploration Committee of the New York Historical Society*. New York: New York Historical Society.

Camp, Stacey. 2013. *The Archaeology of Citizenship*. Gainesville: University Press of Florida.

Cangany, Catherine. 2012. Fashioning Moccasins: Detroit, the Manufacturing Frontier, and the Empire of Consumption, 1701–1835. *William and Mary Quarterly* 69: 265–304.

———. 2014. *Frontier Seaport: Detroit's Transformation into an Atlantic Entrepôt*. Chicago: University of Chicago Press.

Carlson, Jenna K. 2012. *Culinary Creolization: Subsistence and Cultural Interaction at Fort Michilimackinac, 1730–1761.* Archaeological Completion Report Series no. 18. Mackinac Island, MI: Mackinac State Historic Parks.

Cassel, Jay. 1987. Troupes de la marine in Canada, 1683–1760: Men and Material. PhD diss., University of Toronto.

Cazals, Rémy. 1992. *Histoire de Castres, Mazamet, La Montagne.* Toulouse: Privat.

Charlevoix, Pierre-François-Xavier. 1761. *Journal of a Voyage to North America.* 2 vols. London: R. and J. Dodsley.

Claussen, Erin, Erica D'Elia, and Michael S. Nassaney. 2013. How Can Archaeology Help Itself and Others? 21st Century Relevancy at Fort St. Joseph. *Society for Applied Anthropology Newsletter* 24(4): 27–29.

Cleland, Charles E. 1966. *The Prehistoric Animal Ecology and Ethnozoology of the Upper Great Lakes Region.* Anthropological Papers no. 29. Ann Arbor: Museum of Anthropology, University of Michigan.

———. 1970. Comparison of the Faunal Remains from French and British Refuse Pits at Fort Michilimackinac: A Study in Changing Subsistence Patterns. *Canadian Historic Sites Occasional Papers in Archaeology and History* 3: 8–23.

Clifton, James A. 1977. *The Prairie People: Continuity and Change in Potawatomi Indian Culture, 1665–1965.* Lawrence: Regents Press of Kansas.

———. 1978. Potawatomi. In *Northeast,* edited by Bruce G. Trigger, 725–742. Vol. 15 of *Handbook of North American Indians.* Washington, DC: Smithsonian Institution Press.

———. 1986. Potawatomi. In *People of the Three Fires: The Ottawa, Potawatomi, and Ojibway of Michigan.* [Grand Rapids, MI]: Grand Rapids Inter-Tribal Council.

Clute, Janet R., and Gregory A. Waselkov. 2002. Faunal Remains from Old Mobile. In "French Colonial Archaeology at Old Mobile: Selected Studies," edited by Gregory A. Waselkov. Special issue, *Historical Archaeology* 36(1): 129–134.

Cobb, Charles R., and Stephanie Sapp. 2014. Imperial Anxiety and the Dissolution of Colonial Space and Practice at Fort Moore, South Carolina. In *Rethinking Colonial Pasts through Archaeology,* edited by Neal Ferris, Rodney Harrison, and Michael V. Wilcox, 212–231. New York: Oxford University Press.

Cole, Charles Woolsey. (1939) 1964a. *Colbert and a Century of French Mercantilism.* Vol. 1. Hamden, CT: Archon Books.

———. (1939) 1964b. *Colbert and a Century of French Mercantilism.* Vol. 2. Hamden, CT: Archon Books.

Colwell-Chanthaphonh, Chip, and T. J. Ferguson. 2008a. Introduction: The Collaborative Continuum. In *Collaboration in Archaeological Practice: Engaging Descendant Communities,* edited by Chip Colwell-Chanthaphonh and T. J. Ferguson, 1–32. Lanham, MD: AltaMira Press.

Colwell-Chanthaphonh, Chip, and T. J. Ferguson, eds. 2008b. *Collaboration in Archaeological Practice: Engaging Descendant Communities.* Lanham, MD: AltaMira Press.

Conseil d'État de la France. 1730. *Arrêt du conseil d'etat qui ordonne que les draps, serges et autres étoffes de laine ou fil et laine marqués du plomb de fabrique et qui, après avoir reçu leur dernier apprêt, seront destinés soit pour les villes du royaume y mentionnés ou pour l'étranger, seront préalablement apportés dans les bureaux des marchands drapiers et merciers desdites villes, pour, avant leur départ, y être visités et marqués du plomb de contrôle desdits bureaux, s'ils se trouvent fabriqués, teints et apprêtés en conformité des règlements.* Paris: Imprimerie royale. http://catalogue.bnf.fr/ark:/12148/cb336907029.

———. 1743. *Arrêt du conseil d'état qui ordonne la confiscation de 3 pièces de serge de la manufacture d'Hanvoile, envoyées de Beauvais à l'adresse du Sieur Le Roy marchand drapier de Paris et saisies à la halle aux draps de cette ville, tant pour s'être trouvées trop étroites et grasses que pour autres défauts.* Paris: Imprimerie royale. http://catalogue.bnf.fr/ark:/12148/cb33694304v.

———. 1754. *Arrêt du conseil d'état du Roy qui réforme une ordonnance de M. de Saint-Fiest, intendant de la province du Languedoc du 18 avril 1754 qui avait réduit à la troisième classe des articles 2, et 89 des tarifs de 1722, les droits de controlle et d'insinuation du testament de la femme du sieur Forret, marchand fabriquant de Draps de la ville de Carcassonne, et ordonne que les dits droits seront payés sur le pied de la première chasse des dits articles, et décharge le fermier des dépens ausquels il avait été condamné par ladite ordonnance.* Paris: Imprimerie de P. Prault. http://catalogue.bnf.fr/ark:/12148/cb336972180.

Cook, Darious B. (1889) 1974. *Six Months among Indians in the Forests of Allegan County, Michigan in the Winter of 1839 and 1840.* Berrien Springs, MI: Hardscrabble Books.

Coolidge, Orville W. 1915. Address at the Dedication of the Boulder Marking the Site of Fort St. Joseph. *Collections of the Michigan Pioneer and Historical Society* 39: 283–291.

Costin, Cathy L., and Melissa Hagstrum. 1995. Standardization, Labor Investment, Skill, and the Organization of Ceramic Production in Late Prehispanic Highland Peru. *American Antiquity* 60(4): 619–639.

Cremin, William M. 1992. Researching the Void between History and Prehistory in Southwest Michigan. *Michigan Archaeologist* 38(1–2): 19–37.

———. 1996. The Berrien Phase of Southwest Michigan: Proto-Potawatomi. In *Investigating the Archaeological Record of the Great Lakes State: Essays in Honor of Elizabeth Baldwin Garland*, edited by Margaret Holman, Janet Brashler, and Kathryn Parker, 383–413. Kalamazoo, MI: New Issues Press.

Cremin, William M., and Michael S. Nassaney. 1999. Background Research. In *An Archaeological Reconnaissance Survey to Locate Remains of Fort St. Joseph (20BE23) in Niles, Michigan*, edited by Michael S. Nassaney, 7–30. Archaeological Report no. 22. Kalamazoo: Department of Anthropology, Western Michigan University.

———. 2003. Sampling Archaeological Sediments for Small-Scale Remains: Recovery, Identification and Interpretation of Plant Residues from Fort St. Joseph (20BE23). *Michigan Archaeologist* 49(3–4): 73–85.

Cremin, William M., and Dale W. Quattrin. 1987. *An Archaeological Survey of the Middle St. Joseph River Valley in St. Joseph County, Michigan.* Archaeological Report 17. Kalamazoo: Department of Anthropology, Western Michigan University.

Cronon, William. 1983. *Changes in the Land: Indians, Colonists, and the Ecology of New England.* New York: Hill and Wang.

Crompton, Amanda J. 2012. The Historical Archaeology of a French Fortification in the Colony of Plaisance: The Vieux Fort Site (ChA1–04), Placentia, Newfoundland. PhD diss., Memorial University of Newfoundland.

Cummings, Kevin S., and Christine A. Mayer. 1992. *Field Guide to Freshwater Mussels of the Midwest.* Manual 5. Champaign: Illinois Natural History Survey.

Cunningham, Wilbur M. 1961. *Land of Four Flags: An Early History of the St. Joseph Valley.* Grand Rapids, MI: William B. Eerdmans.

Cunningham, Wilbur M., ed. 1967. *Letter Book of William Burnett: Early Fur Trader in the Land of Four Flags.* St. Joseph, MI: Fort Miami Heritage Society of Michigan.

Cutler, H. G. 1906. *History of St. Joseph County.* Chicago: S. J. Clarke Publishing Company.

D'Elia, Erica A. 2013. An Assessment of Public Outreach with Children and Educators Conducted by the Fort St. Joseph Archaeological Project. MA thesis, Western Michigan University, Kalamazoo.

Davis, Cathrine M. 2014. Lead Seals from Colonial Fort St. Joseph (20BE23). Honors thesis, Western Michigan University, Kalamazoo.

Davis, M. Elaine. 2000. Governmental Educational Standards and K-12 Archaeology Programs. In *The Archaeology Education Handbook: Sharing the Past with Kids*, edited by Karolyn Smardz and Shelly J. Smith, 54–71. New York: AltaMira Press.

Dawdy, Shannon Lee. 2008. *Building the Devil's Empire: French Colonial New Orleans.* Chicago: University of Chicago Press.

———. 2010. "A Wild Taste": Food and Colonialism in Eighteenth-Century Louisiana. *Ethnohistory* 57: 389–414.

Dawdy, Shannon Lee, ed. 2000. "Creolization." Special issue, *Historical Archaeology* 34(3).

Deagan, Kathleen. 1996. Colonial Transformations: Euro-American Cultural Genesis in the Early Spanish Colonies. *Journal of Archaeological Research* 52(2): 135–160.

Dechêne, Louise. 1974. *Habitants et marchands de Montréal au XVIIe siècle.* Montréal: Librarie Plon.

———. 1988. *Habitants et marchands de Montréal au XVIIe siècle.* Montreal, QC: Les Éditions du Boréal.

Deetz, James. 1977. *In Small Things Forgotten: The Archaeology of Early American Life.* Garden City, NY: Doubleday.

Delâge, Denys. 1992. L'influence des Amérindiens sur les Canadiens et les Français au temps de la Nouvelle-France. *LEKTON* 2(2): 103–191. http://classiques.uqac.ca/contemporains/delage_denys/influence_amerindiens/influence_amerindiens.pdf.

Delâge, Denys, and Jean-Philippe Warren. 2008. Amerindians and the Horizon of Modernity. In *Decentering the Renaissance: Canada and Europe in Multidisciplinary Perspective, 1500–1700*, edited by Germaine Warkentin and Carolyn Podruchny, 305–317. Toronto: University of Toronto Press.

Densmore, Frances. (1929) 1979. *Chippewa Customs.* St. Paul: Minnesota Historical Society Press.

De Vries, Jan. 1976. *The Economy of Europe in An Age of Crisis, 1600–1750.* Cambridge: Cambridge University Press.

Dodge, Wendell E. 1982. Porcupine (*Erethizon dorsatum*). In *Wild Mammals of North America: Biology, Management, and Economics*, edited by Joseph A. Chapman and George A. Feldhamer, 355–366. Baltimore: Johns Hopkins University Press.

DuLong, John P. 2001. *French Canadians in Michigan.* East Lansing: Michigan State University Press.

Dunham, Sean B. 2000. Cache Pits: Ethnohistory, Archaeology, and the Continuity of Tradition. In *Interpretations of Native North American Life: Material Contributions to Ethnohis-*

tory, edited by Michael S. Nassaney and Eric S. Johnson, 225–260. Gainesville: University Press of Florida.

Dunnigan, James. N.d. Those Beyond the Walls: An Archaeological Examination of Michilimackinac's Extramural Domestic Settlement, 1750–1781. MA thesis, Western Michigan University, Kalamazoo, MI (in preparation).

DuPlessis, Robert S. 2009. Cottons Consumption in the Seventeenth- and Eighteenth-Century North Atlantic. In *The Spinning World: A Global History of Cotton Textiles, 1200–1850*, edited by Giorgio Riello and Prasannan Parthasarathi, 227–246. Oxford: Oxford University Press.

———. 2015. *The Material Atlantic: Clothing, Commerce, and Colonization in the Atlantic World, 1650–1800*. Cambridge: Cambridge University Press.

Eccles, William J. 1964. *Canada under Louis XIV, 1663–1701*. New York: Oxford University Press.

———. 1978. *The Canadian Frontier, 1534–1760*. Albuquerque: University of New Mexico Press.

———. 1987. *Essays on New France*. Toronto: Oxford University Press.

———. 1997. French Exploration in North America, 1700–1800. In *North American Exploration*. Vol. 2, *A Continent Defined*, edited by John Logan Allen, 149–202. Lincoln: University of Nebraska Press.

———. 2003. *Frontenac: The Courtier Governor*. Introduction by Peter Moogk. Lincoln: University of Nebraska Press.

Edmunds, R. David, and Joseph L. Peyser. 1993. *The Fox Wars: The Mesquakie Challenge to New France*. Norman: University of Oklahoma Press.

Edwards, Jay. 1986. French. In *America's Architectural Roots: Ethnic Groups that Built America*, edited by Dell Upton, 62–67. Washington, DC: Preservation Press.

Egan, Geoffrey, Michael Cowell, and Hero Granger-Taylor. 1995. *Lead Cloth Seals and Related Items in the British Museum*. London: Department of Medieval and Later Antiquities, British Museum.

Ehrhardt, Kathleen. 2005. *European Metal in Native Hands: Rethinking Technological Change*. Tuscaloosa: University of Alabama Press.

Ehrmann, W. W. 1940. The Timucua Indians of Sixteenth Century Florida. *Florida Historical Quarterly* 18(3): 168–191.

Ekberg, Carl J. 1985. *Colonial Ste. Genevieve: An Adventure on the Mississippi Frontier*. Carbondale: Southern Illinois University Press.

———. 1998. *French Roots in the Illinois Country: The Mississippi Frontier in Colonial Times*. Urbana: University of Illinois Press.

———. 2007. *Stealing Indian Women: Native Slavery in the Illinois Country*. Urbana: University of Illinois Press.

Enloe, James G., Francine David, and Timothy S. Hare. 1994. Patterns of Faunal Processing at Section 27 of Pincevent: The Use of Spatial Analysis and Ethnoarchaeological Data in the Interpretation of Archaeological Site Structure. *Journal of Anthropological Archaeology* 13(2): 105–124.

Evans, Lynn. 2013. Michilimackinac, a Civilian Fort. In *The Archaeology of French and Indian War Frontier Forts*, edited by Lawrence Babits and Stephanie Gandulla, 216–228. Gainesville: University Press of Florida.

Farah, Lelia Marie. 2011. *Food Paths, Architecture and Urban Form: A Case Study*. PhD diss., McGill University, Montreal.

Faribault-Beauregard, Marthe. 1982. *La population des forts français d'Amérique (xviiie siècle)*. 2 vols. Montreal: Éditions Bergeron.

Farr, Stephen, and Teach for America. 2010. *Teaching As Leadership: The Highly Effective Teacher's Guide to Closing the Achievement Gap*. San Francisco: Jossey-Bass.

Faulkner, Alaric. 1986. Maintenance and Fabrication at Fort Pentagoet 1635–1654: Products of an Acadian Armorer's Workshop. *Historical Archaeology* 20(1): 63–94.

Feinman, Gary M. 2015. Settlement and Landscape Archaeology. In *International Encyclopedia of the Social and Behavioral Sciences*, 2nd ed., edited by James Wright, 654–658. Amsterdam: Elsevier.

Ferris, Neal. 2009. *The Archaeology of Native-Lived Colonialism: Challenging History in the Great Lakes*. Tucson: University of Arizona Press.

Ferris, Neal, Rodney Harrison, and Michael V. Wilcox, eds. 2014. *Rethinking Colonial Pasts through Archaeology*. Oxford: Oxford University Press.

Fitzgerald, William. 1990. Chronology to Cultural Process: Lower Great Lakes Archaeology. PhD diss, McGill University, Montreal.

Fitzgerald, William, and Peter Ramsden. 1988. Copper Based Metal Testing as an Aid to Understanding Early European Amerindian Interaction: Scratching the Surface. *Canadian Journal of Archaeology* 12: 153–161.

Ford, Richard I. 1973. The Moccasin Bluff Corn Holes. In Robert L. Bettarel and Hale G. Smith, *The Moccasin Bluff Site and the Woodland Cultures of Southwestern Michigan*, 188–197. Anthropological Papers 49. Ann Arbor: Museum of Anthropology, University of Michigan.

Gallup, Andrew, and Donald F. Shaffer. 1992. *La Marine: The French Colonial Soldier in Canada, 1745–1761*. Westminster, MD: Heritage Books.

Garland, Elizabeth B. 1981. A Cultural Resource Survey of the Proposed Alternative Routes of M-60, Niles to Cassopolis, Cass County, Michigan. Technical Report 5. Department of Anthropology, Western Michigan University, Kalamazoo, MI.

Garland, Elizabeth B., Kathryn E. Parker, Terrance J. Martin, and Arthur L. DesJardins. 2001. The Wymer West Knoll Site (20BE132): An Upper Mississippian Habitation in a Multicomponent Site on the Lower St. Joseph River in Berrien County, Michigan. Completion report prepared for the Michigan Department of Transportation. Department of Anthropology, Western Michigan University, Kalamazoo.

Gauthier-Larouche, Georges. 1974. *Évolution de la maison rurale traditionnelle dans la région de Québec*. Québec: Les presses de L'Université Laval.

Gazin-Schwartz, Amy. 2004. Mementos of the Past: Material Culture of Tourism at Stonehenge and Avebury. In *Marketing Heritage: Archaeology and the Consumption of the Past*, edited by Yorke Rowan and Uzi Baram, 93–102. Lanham, MD: AltaMira Press.

Gillam, Rena B. 1915. Marking Fort St. Joseph. *Collections of the Michigan Pioneer and Historical Society* 39: 280–282.

Gilman, Carolyn. 1982. *Where Two Worlds Meet: The Great Lakes Fur Trade*. Museum Exhibit Series no. 2. St. Paul: Minnesota Historical Society.

Giordano, Brock. 2005. Crafting Cultural at Fort St. Joseph: An Archaeological Investigation of Labor Organization on the Colonial Frontier. MA thesis, Western Michigan University, Kalamazoo, MI.

Gladysz, Kevin. 2011. *The French Trade Gun in North America, 1662–1759*. Woonsocket, RI: Andrew Mowbray Publishers.

Godbout, Geneviève. 2018. Review of the Fort St. Joseph Archaeological Project Booklet Series. *Historical Archaeology* 52(3): 632–634.

Good, Mary E. 1972. *Guebert Site: An 18th Century Historic Kaskaskia Indian Village in Randolph County, Illinois*. Central States Archaeological Society Memoir 2. N.p.: Central States Archaeology Society Memoir.

Gosden, Christopher. 2002. Postcolonial Archaeology: Issues of Culture, Identity, and Knowledge. In *Archaeological Theory Today*, edited by I. Hodder, 241–261. Malden, MA: Blackwell.

Gousse, Suzanne. 2013. *Les Couturières de Montréal au XVIIIe siècle*. Sillery, QC: Septentrion.

Grayson, Donald K. 1973. On the Methodology of Faunal Analysis. *American Antiquity* 38: 432–439.

———. 1984. *Quantitative Zooarchaeology: Topics in the Analysis of Archaeological Faunas*. Orlando, FL: Academic Press.

Greer, Allan. 1997. *The People of New France*. Toronto: University of Toronto Press.

Grinnell, George B. 1972. *The Cheyenne*. Vol. 2. Lincoln: University of Nebraska Press.

Gums, Bonnie L. 2002. Earthfast (*Pieux en Terre*) Structures at Old Mobile. *Historical Archaeology* 36(1): 13–25.

Gums, Bonnie L., William R. Iseminger, Molly E. McKenzie, and Dennis D. Nichols. 1991. The French Colonial Villages of Cahokia and Prairie du Pont, Illinois. In *French Colonial Archaeology: The Illinois Country and the Western Great Lakes*, edited by John A. Walthall, 85–122. Urbana: University of Illinois Press.

Hackett, Charles Wilson. 1934. *Pichardo's Treatise on the Limits of Louisiana and Texas*. 5 vols. Austin: University of Texas Press.

Hagenmaier, Kelly. 2005. Designing and Implementing a Public Archaeology Program for Fort St. Joseph in Niles, Michigan. MA internship report, Department of Anthropology, Western Michigan University, Kalamazoo.

Hambacher, Michael J., Janet G. Brashler, Kathryn C. Egan-Bruhy, Daniel R. Hayes, Bruce Hardy, Daniel G. Landis, Terrance E. Martin, G. William Monaghan, Kimmarie Murphy, James A. Robertson, and Diane L. Seltz. 2003. *Phase III Archaeological Data Recovery for the U.S. 131 S-Curve Realignment Project Grand Rapids, Michigan: Volume 1*. Site report for State of Michigan Department of Transportation. Prepared by Commonwealth Cultural Resources Group, Jackson, MI.

Hamell, George. 1983. Trading in Metaphors: The Magic of Beads. In *Proceedings of the 1982 Glass Trade Bead Conference*, edited by Charles F. Hayes III, 5–28. Research Records no. 16. Rochester, NY: Rochester Museum and Science Center.

Harding, James H. (1997) 2006. *Amphibians and Reptiles of the Great Lakes Region*. Ann Arbor: University of Michigan Press.

Harp, Amelia. 2017. Matters of Perspective: An Assessment of Cross-Cultural Collaboration on the Fort St. Joseph Archaeological Project. MA practicum, Georgia State University, Atlanta.

Harris, R. Cole, ed. 1987. *Historical Atlas of Canada*. Vol. 1, *From the Beginning to 1800*. Toronto: University of Toronto Press.

Harrison, Rodney. 2013. *Heritage: Critical Approaches*. New York: Routledge.

Havard, Gilles. 2000. Postes français et village indiens: Un aspect de l'organisation de l'espace colonial français dans le Pays d'en Haut (1600–1715). *Recherches Amerindiennes au Quebec* 30(2): 11–22.

———. 2003. *Empire et métissages: Indiens et Français dans le Pays d'en Haut, 1660–1715*. Québec City: Septentrion, and Paris: Presses de l'Université de Paris-Sorbonne.

———. 2008. "So Amusingly Frenchified": Mimetism in the French-Amerindian Encounter (XVIIth–XVIIIth c.). *Le Journal* 24(1): 1–7.

Havard, Gilles, and Cécile Vidal. 2006. *Histoire de l'Amérique Française*. Paris: Éditions Flammarion.

Hawkes, Christopher. 1954. Archaeological Theory and Method: Some Suggestions from the Old World. *American Anthropologist* 56: 155–168.

Hearns, Joseph. 2015. Patterns in Faunal Remains at Fort St. Joseph (20BE23), a French Fur Trade Post in the Western Great Lakes. MA thesis, Western Michigan University, Kalamazoo.

Heidenreich, Conrad E. 1978. Seventeenth-Century Maps of the Great Lakes: An Overview and Procedures for Analysis. *Archivaria* 6(Summer): 83–112.

———. 1987. Settlements to 1760. In *The Historical Atlas of Canada: From the Beginning to 1800*, vol. 1, edited by Richard C. Harris, plate 37. Toronto: University of Toronto Press.

———. 1997. Early French Exploration in the North American Interior. In *North American Exploration*, vol. 2, *A Continent Defined*, edited by John Logan Allen, 65–148. Lincoln: University of Nebraska Press.

Heidenreich, Conrad E., and Françoise Noël. 1987. The Fur Trade, ca. 1755. In *The Historical Atlas of Canada: From the Beginning to 1800*, vol. 1, edited by Richard C. Harris, Plate 40. Toronto: University of Toronto Press.

Heldman, Donald P. 1991. The French in Michigan and Beyond. In *French Colonial Archaeology: The Illinois Country and the Western Great Lakes*, edited by John A. Walthall, 201–217. Urbana: University of Illinois Press.

Henry, Alexander. 1985. Massacre at Michilimackinac. In *Captured by the Indians: 15 Firsthand Accounts, 1750–1870*, edited by Frederick Drimmer, 73–104. Mineola, NY: Dover Publications.

Hesselton, William T., and RuthAnn Monson Hesselton. 1982. White-Tailed Deer, *Odocoileus virginianus*. In *Wild Mammals of North America: Biology, Management, and Economics*, edited by Joseph A. Chapman and George A. Feldhamer, 878–901. Baltimore, MD: Johns Hopkins University Press.

Hicks, Dan, and Audrey Horning. 2006. Historical Archaeology and Buildings. In *The Cambridge Companion to Historical Archaeology*, edited by Dan Hicks and Mary C. Beaudry, 273–292. Cambridge: Cambridge University Press.

Hinsdale, Wilbert B. 1931. *Archaeological Atlas of Michigan*. Ann Arbor: University of Michigan Press.

Hockett, Bryan Scott. 1998. Sociopolitical Meaning of Faunal Remains from Baker Village. *American Antiquity* 63: 289–302.

Hodson, Christopher, and Brett Rushforth. 2010. Absolutely Atlantic: Colonialism and the Early Modern French State in Recent Historiography. *History Compass* 8(1): 101–117.

Hogg, Victor. 1975. The Development of Historic Fort St. Joseph. Report prepared for the Greater Niles Recreation Board. On file at the Niles District Library, Niles, MI.

Holman, Margret B., and Janet G. Brashler. 1999. Economics, Material Culture, and Trade in the Late Woodland Lower Peninsula of Michigan. In *Retrieving Michigan's Buried Past: The Archaeology of the Great Lakes State*, edited by John R. Halsey and Michael D. Stafford, 213–227. Bloomfield Hills, MI: Cranbrook Institute of Science.

Holtorf, Cornelius. 2007. *Archaeology Is a Brand! The Meaning of Archaeology in Contemporary Popular Culture*. Walnut Creek, CA: Left Coast Press.

Hu, Di. 2013. Approaches to the Archaeology of Ethnogenesis: Past and Emergent Perspectives. *Journal of Archaeological Research* 21(4): 371–402.

Hughes-Skallos, Jessica, and Susan E. Allen. 2012. Analysis of Feature 21, A Smudge Pit from the Lyne Site, Michigan (20-BE-10). Manuscript on file, Department of Anthropology, Western Michigan University, Kalamazoo.

Hulse, Charles A. 1977. An Archaeological Evaluation of Fort St. Joseph: An Eighteenth Century Military Post and Settlement in Berrien County, Michigan. MA thesis, Michigan State University, East Lansing.

———. 1981. An Archaeological Evaluation of Fort St. Joseph (20BE23), Berrien County, Michigan. *Michigan Archaeologist* 27(3–4): 55–76.

Hume, Ivor Noël. 1969. *A Guide to Artifacts of Colonial America*. Philadelphia: University of Pennsylvania Press.

Hutchins, Thomas. (1778) 1904. *A Topographic Description of Virginia, Pennsylvania, Maryland, and North Carolina*. Edited by Frederick Charles Hicks. Cleveland, OH: Burrows Brothers Company.

Idle, Dunning. 2003. *The Post of the St. Joseph River during the French Regime*. Niles, MI: Fort St. Joseph Museum.

Innis, Harold A. 1962. *The Fur Trade in Canada: An Introduction to Canadian Economic History*. New Haven, CT: Yale University Press.

———. 2001. *The Fur Trade in Canada*. Toronto: University of Toronto Press.

Jean, Régis, and André Proulx. 1995. *Le commerce à Place-Royale sous le Régime français*. Québec: Gouvernement du Québec, Ministère de la culture et des communications.

Jelinek, Arthur. 1958. A Late Historic Burial from Berrien County. *Michigan Archaeologist* 4(3): 48–51.

Jelks, Edward B. 1966. The Gilbert Site. *Bulletin of the Texas Archaeological Society* 37.

Jelks, Edward B., Carl J. Ekberg, and Terrance J. Martin. 1989. *Excavations at the Laurens Site: Probable Location of Fort de Chartres I*. Studies in Illinois Archaeology no. 5. Springfield: Illinois Historic Preservation Agency.

Jenks, William A. 1926. The "Hutchins" Map of Michigan. *Michigan History Magazine* 10(34): 358–373.

———. 1931. Supplementary Note: The "Hutchins" Map of Michigan. In *Bibliography of the Printed Maps of Michigan, 1804–1880*, edited by Louis Karpinsky, 71–79. Lansing: Michigan Historical Commission.

Jeppson, Patrice L. 2010. Doing Our Homework: Reconsidering What Archaeology Has to

Offer Schools. In *Archaeologists as Activists: Can Archaeologists Change the World?* edited by Jay M. Stottman, 63–79. Tuscaloosa: University of Alabama Press.

Jeppson, Patrice L., and G. Brauer. 2007. Archaeology for Education Needs: An Archaeologist and an Educator Discuss Archaeology in the Baltimore County Public Schools. In *Past Meets Present: Archaeologists Partnering with Museum Curators, Teachers, and Community Groups,* edited by John H. Jameson Jr. and Sherene Baugher, 231–248. New York: Springer.

Johnson, Eric. 2000. The Politics of Pottery: Material Culture and Political Process among Algonquians of Seventeenth-Century Southern New England. In *Interpretations of Native North American Life: Material Contributions to Ethnohistory,* edited by Michael S. Nassaney and Eric S. Johnson, 118–145. Gainesville: University Press of Florida.

Johnson, Gregory A. 1981. Monitoring Complex System Integration and Boundary Phenomena with Settlement Size Data. In *Archaeological Approaches to the Study of Complexity,* edited by Sander E. van der Leeuw, 144–188. Amsterdam: Van Giffen Institut, University of Amsterdam.

Johnson, Ida Amanda. 1919. *The Michigan Fur Trade.* Lansing: Michigan Historical Commission.

Jones, Kevin. N.d. An Examination of Flintlock Musket Components at Fort St. Joseph (20BE23), Niles, Michigan. MA thesis, Western Michigan University, Kalamazoo (in preparation).

Jones, Olive, and Catherine Sullivan. 1989. *The Parks Canada Glass Glossary for the Description of Containers, Tableware, Flat Glass, and Closures.* Quebec: Canadian Parks Service.

Jordan, Kurt A. 2008. *The Seneca Restoration, 1715–1745: An Iroquois Local Political Economy.* Gainesville: University Press of Florida.

———. 2009. Colonies, Colonialism, and Cultural Entanglements: The Archaeology of Postcolumbian Intercultural Relations. In *International Handbook of Historical Archaeology,* edited by Teresita Majewski and David R. M. Gaimster, 31–49. New York: Springer.

Juen, Rachel B., and Michael S. Nassaney. 2012. *The Fur Trade.* Fort St. Joseph Archaeological Project Booklet Series no. 2. Kalamazoo: Western Michigan University.

Kalm, Peter. 1937. *Peter Kalm's Travels in North America.* 2 vols. Edited by A. B. Benson. New York: Wilson-Erickson.

Kammen, Michael. 1991. *Mystic Chords of Memory: The Transformation of Tradition in American Culture.* New York: Knopf.

Kehoe, Alice B. 2000. François' House, A Significant Pedlars' Post on the Saskatchewan. In *Interpretations of Native North American Life: Materials Contributions to Ethnohistory,* edited by Michael S. Nassaney and Eric S. Johnson, 173–187. Gainesville: University Press of Florida.

Kenoyer, Jonathon, M. Massimo Vidale, and Kuldeep Kumar Bhan. 1991. Contemporary Stone Beadmaking in Khambhat, India: Patterns of Craft Specialization and Organization of Production as Reflected in the Archaeological Record. *World Archaeology* 23(1): 44–63.

Kent, Timothy J. 2001. *Ft. Ponchartrain at Detroit: A Guide to the Daily Lives of Fur Trade and Military Personnel, Settlers, and Missionaries at French Posts.* Ossineke, MI: Silver Fox Enterprises.

Kerber, Jordan E. 2003. Community Based Archaeology in Central New York: Workshops Involving Native American Youth. *Public Historian* 25(1): 83–90.

Kerber, Jordan E., ed. 2006. *Cross-Cultural Collaboration: Native Peoples and Archaeology in the Northeastern United States.* Lincoln: University of Nebraska Press.

Kerr, Ian B. 2012. An Analysis of Personal Adornment at Fort St. Joseph (20BE23), an Eighteenth-Century French Trading Post in Southwest Michigan. MA thesis, Western Michigan University, Kalamazoo.

King, Julia A. 2006. Household Archaeology, Identities and Biographies. In *The Cambridge Companion to Historical Archaeology*, edited by Dan Hicks and Mary C. Beaudry, 293–313. Cambridge: Cambridge University Press.

Kinietz, W. Vernon. 1972. *The Indians of the Western Great Lakes, 1615–1760.* Ann Arbor: University of Michigan Press.

Kohley, Allison M. 2013. Change and Continuity: Euro-American and Native American Settlement Patterns in the St. Joseph River Valley. MA thesis, Western Michigan University, Kalamazoo.

Kornwolf, James D. 2002. France in North America, 1562–1763. In *Architecture and Town Planning in Colonial North America*, vol. 1, by James D. Kornwolf, 185–376. Baltimore, MD: Johns Hopkins University Press.

Kowalewski, Stephen A. 2008. Regional Settlement Pattern Studies. *Journal of Archaeological Research* 16: 225–285.

Krause, Richard A. 1972. *The Leavenworth Site: Archaeology of an Historic Arikara Community.* University of Kansas Publications in Anthropology no. 3. Lawrence: University of Kansas.

Langford, Theresa E. 2011. Identity: Using Objects to "Fit In" and "Stand Out." In *Exploring Fort Vancouver*, edited by Douglas C. Wilson and Theresa E. Langford, 29–50. Vancouver, WA: Fort Vancouver National Trust, and Seattle: University of Washington Press.

Lapham, Heather A. 2005. *Hunting for Hides: Deerskins, Status, and Cultural Change in the Protohistoric Appalachians.* Tuscaloosa: University of Alabama Press.

LaRoche, Cheryl J., and Michael L. Blakey. 1997. Seizing Intellectual Power: The Dialogue at the New York African Burial Ground. *Historical Archaeology* 31(3): 84–106.

Lavender, David S. 1964. *The Fist in the Wilderness.* Garden City, NY: Doubleday.

Leader, Jonathan Max. 1988. Technological Continuities and Specialization in Prehistoric Metalworking in the Eastern United States. PhD diss., University of Florida.

Lechtman, Heather. 1977. Style in Technology—Some Early Thoughts. In *Material Culture: Styles, Organization and Dynamics of Technology*, edited by H. Lechtman and R. Merrill, 3–20. St. Paul, MN: West Publishing Co.

LeFever, Gregory. 2008. Side by Side: Forged and Cut Iron Nails. *Early American Life* 39(3): 60–69.

Lemire, Beverly. 2009. Revising the Historical Narrative: India, Europe and the Cotton Trade. In *The Spinning World: A Global History of Cotton Textiles, 1200–1850*, edited by Giorgio Riello and Prasannan Parthasarathi, 205–226. Oxford: Oxford University Press.

Lessard, Michel, and Huguette Marquis. 1972. *Encyclopédie de la maison Quebecoise: 3 siècles d'habitations.* Montreal: Les Éditions de L'Homme.

Lewis, Kenneth E. 2002. *West to Far Michigan: Settling the Lower Peninsula, 1815–1860.* East Lansing: Michigan State University Press.

Lightfoot, Kent G. 1995. Culture Contact Studies: Redefining the Relationship between Pre-historic and Historical Archaeology. *American Antiquity* 60(1): 199–217.

———. 2005. *Indians, Missionaries, and Merchants: The Legacy of Colonial Encounters on the California Frontiers.* Berkeley: University of California Press.

Little, Barbara J. 2007. Archaeology and Civic Engagement. In *Archaeology as a Tool of Civic Engagement,* edited by Barbara J. Little and Paul A. Shackel, 1–22. Lanham, MD: AltaMira Press.

Little, Barbara J., and Paul A. Shackel, eds. 2007. *Archaeology as a Tool of Civic Engagement.* Lanham, MD: AltaMira Press.

Logan, Brad. 1998. Fat of the Land: White Rock Phase Bison Hunting and Grease Production. *Plains Anthropologist* 43: 349–366.

Lohse, E. S. 1988. Trade Goods. In *History of Indian-White Relations,* edited by Wilcomb E. Washburn, 396–403. Vol. 4 of *Handbook of North American Indians.* Washington, DC: Smithsonian Institution Press.

Loren, Diana DiPaolo. 2001. Manipulating Bodies and Emerging Traditions at the Los Adaes Presidio. In *The Archaeology of Traditions: Agency and History Before and After Columbus,* edited by Timothy R. Pauketat, 58–76. Gainesville: University Press of Florida.

———. 2005. Creolization in the French and Spanish Colonies. In *North American Archaeology,* edited by Timothy R. Pauketat and Diana D. Loren, 297–318. Oxford: Blackwell.

———. 2009. Material Manipulations: Beads and Cloth in the French Colonies. In *The Materiality of Individuality: Archaeological Studies of Individual Lives,* edited by Carolyn L. White, 109–124. New York: Springer.

———. 2010. *The Archaeology of Clothing and Bodily Adornment in Colonial America.* Gainesville: University Press of Florida.

Loren, Diana DiPaolo, and Mary C. Beaudry. 2006. Becoming American: Small Things Remembered. In *Historical Archaeology,* edited by Stephen W. Silliman and Martin Hall, 251–271. Oxford: Blackwell.

Lotbinière, Michel Chartier de. 1976. *Fort Michilimackinac in 1749: Lotbinière's Plan and Description.* Edited and translated by Marie Gérin-Lajoie. Mackinac Island, MI: Mackinac Island State Park Commission.

Loveland, Erika K. 2017. Archaeological Evidence of Architectural Remains at Fort St. Joseph (20BE23), Niles, MI. MA thesis, Western Michigan University, Kalamazoo.

Loveland, Erika K., and Michael S. Nassaney. 2017. *Sheltering New France.* Fort St. Joseph Archaeological Project Booklet Series no. 3. Kalamazoo: Western Michigan University.

Loveland, Erika, James Schwaderer, Shanna Baldwin, John Cardinal, Aaron Howard, Nick Reimers, Alicia Russell, Katie Schinske, and Mike Stampfler. 2015. Fort St. Joseph Strategic Plan. Manuscript on file, Department of Anthropology, Western Michigan University, Kalamazoo.

Low, John N. 2018. A Native's Perspective on Trends in Contemporary Archaeology. In "Encounters, Exchange, Entanglements: Current Perspectives on Intercultural Interactions throughout the Western Great Lakes," edited by Heather Walder and Jessica Yann. Special issue, *Midwest Archaeological Conference Occasional Papers* 2: 105–115.

Lucas, Stephen. 1986. Proper Syntax When Using aff. and cf. in Taxonomic Statements. *Journal of Vertebrate Paleontology* 6(2): 202.

MacDonald, David. 2012. A French Cloth Seal Recovered at Fort St. Joseph, Michigan. *Le Journal* 28(1): 8.

Maher, Daniel R. 2016. *Mythic Frontiers: Remembering, Forgetting, and Profiting with Cultural Heritage Tourism*. Gainesville: University Press of Florida.

Mainfort, Robert C., Jr. 1979. *Indian Social Dynamics in the Period of European Contact*. Anthropological Series 1, no. 4. East Lansing: Michigan State University Museum.

———. 1985. Wealth, Space, and Status in a Historic Indian Cemetery. *American Antiquity* 50(3): 555–579.

Malchelosse, Gérard. 1957. La Salle et le fort Saint-Joseph des Miamis. *Les Cahiers des Dix* 22: 83–103.

———. 1958. Le Poste de la Rivière Saint-Joseph (Mich.) (1691–1781). *Les Cahiers des Dix* 23: 139–186.

———. 1979. Genealogy and Colonial History: The St. Joseph River Post (Michigan). *French Canadian and Acadian Genealogical Review* 3–4: 173–209.

Malischke, LisaMarie. 2009. The Excavated Bead Collection at Fort St. Joseph (20BE23), and Its Implications for Understanding Adornment, Ideology, Cultural Exchange, and Identity. MA thesis, Western Michigan University, Kalamazoo.

Mandala, L. 2009. The Cultural and Heritage Traveler, 2009 Edition. Tourism report by Mandala Research LLC.

Mann, Rob. 2003. Colonizing the Colonizers: Canadien Fur Traders and Fur Trade Society in the Great Lakes Region, 1763–1850. PhD diss., Binghamton University, Binghamton, New York.

———. 2008. From Ethnogenesis to Ethnic Segmentation in the Wabash Valley: Constructing Identity and Houses in Great Lakes Fur Trade Society. *International Journal of Historical Archaeology* 12(4): 319–337.

Margry, Pierre, ed. 1867. *Relations et mémoires inédits pour servir à l'histoire de la France dans les pays d'outremer*. Paris: Challamel Aimé.

———. 1876–1886. *Découvertes et établissements des Français dans l'ouest et dans le sud de l'Amérique septentrionale, 1614–1754*. 6 vols. Paris: D. Jouaust.

Marshall, Yvonne. 2002. What Is Community Archaeology? *World Archaeology* 34(2): 211–219.

Marshall, Yvonne, Chris Gosden, Barry Cunliffe, and Rosemary A. Joyce, eds. 2009. *The Oxford Handbook of Archaeology*. New York: Oxford University Press.

Martin, Calvin. 1975. The Four Lives of a Micmac Copper Pot. *Ethnohistory* 22: 111–133.

Martin, Terrance J. 1986. A Faunal Analysis of Fort Ouiatenon, an Eighteenth Century Trading Post in the Wabash Valley of Indiana. PhD diss., Michigan State University.

———. 1988. Animal Remains from the Cahokia Wedge Site. In *Archaeology at French Colonial Cahokia*. Studies in Illinois Archaeology no. 3. Springfield: Illinois Historic Preservation Agency.

———. 1991a. An Archaeological Perspective on Animal Exploitation Patterns at French Colonial Sites in the Illinois Country. In *French Colonial Archaeology*, edited by John A. Walthall, 189–200. Urbana: University of Illinois Press.

———. 1991b. Modified Animal Remains, Subsistence, and Cultural Interaction at French Colonial Sites in the Midwestern United States. In *Beamers, Bobwhites, and Blue-Points: Tributes to the Career of Paul W. Parmalee*, edited by James R. Purdue, Walter E. Klippel, and Bonnie W. Styles, 409–419. Scientific Papers vol. 23. Springfield: Illinois State Museum.

———. 2003. Animal Remains from the 2002 Investigation of the Moccasin Bluff Site, Berrien County, Michigan. *Michigan Archaeologist* 49(1–2): 57–68.

———. 2008a. The Archaeozoology of French Colonial Sites in the Illinois Country. In *Dreams of the Americas: Overview of New France Archaeology*, edited by Christian Roy and Hélène Coté, 185–204. Archéologiques, Collection Hors Série 2. Québec: Association des archéologues du Québec.

———. 2008b. Subsistence Strategies in Southwestern Michigan and the Spiritual Importance of Lake Sturgeon. In "The Tie That Binds: Essays in Honor of Margaret B. Holman," edited by Janet G. Brashler and William A. Lovis. Special issue, *Michigan Archaeologist* 54: 61–72.

———. 2010. Animal Remains from the Duckhouse Site and Their Implications for Eighteenth-Century Foodways in French Cahokia. In *Constructing the Past: Essays in Honor of John A. Walthall*, edited by Thomas E. Emerson. Special issue, *Illinois Archaeology* 22: 186–226.

———. 2015. Foodways and the Illinois: Archaeozoological Samples from Grid A. In *Protohistory at the Grand Village of the Kaskaskia: The Illinois Country on the Eve of Colony*, edited by Robert F. Mazrim, 65–88. Studies in Archaeology no. 10. Urbana: Illinois State Archaeological Survey, University of Illinois.

Martin, Terrance J., and Dennis F. Lawler. 2014. Animal Pathologies at French Colonial Sites in the Midwest: Case Studies of White-Tailed Deer at Forts St. Joseph and Ouiatenon. Paper presented at the 79th annual meeting of the Society for American Archaeology, Austin, Texas.

Martin, Terrance J., and Mary Carol Masulis. 1988. Preliminary Report on Animal Remains from Fort de Chartres (11R127). In *Archaeological Excavations at Fort de Chartres: 1985–87*, by David Keene. Technical Report submitted to the Illinois Historic Preservation Agency, Springfield.

Martin, Terrance J., J. Chris Richmond, and Erin Brand. 2003. An Archaeozoological Analysis of 23CK116, the Illini Village of the Marquette and Jolliet Voyage of 1673. Landscape History Technical Report 2003-1478-8. Submitted to the Missouri Department of Natural Resources, Jefferson City.

Martinez, David Jordan. 2009. Dirt to Desk: Macrobotanical Analyses from Fort St. Joseph (20BE23) and the Lyne Site (20BE10). MA thesis, The Ohio State University.

Mason, Ronald J. 1986. *Rock Island: Historical Indian Archaeology in the Northern Lake Michigan Basin*. Midcontinental Journal of Archaeology, Special Paper 6. Kent, OH: Kent State University Press.

Maucomble, Jean François Dieudonné. 1767. *Histoire abrégée de la ville de Nîmes avec la description de ses antiquités*. Amsterdam.

Mazrim, Robert F. 2011. *At Home in the Illinois Country: French Colonial Domestic Site Archaeology in the Midwest 1730–1800*. Urbana: Illinois State Archaeological Survey.

McCoy, Daniel. 1907. Old Fort St. Joseph. *Collections of the Michigan Pioneer and Historical Society* 35: 545–553.

McDavid, Carol. 2002. Archaeologies that Hurt; Descendants that Matter: A Pragmatic Approach to Collaboration in the Public Interpretation of African-American Archaeology. *World Archaeology* 34(2): 303–314.

McGuire, Randall H. 1992. Archaeology and the First Americans. *American Anthropologist* 94(4): 816–836.

McManamon, Francis P. 1991. The Many Publics for Archaeology. *American Antiquity* 56(1): 121–130.

Ménard, Léon. 1856. *Histoire des antiquités de la ville de Nîmes.* Nîmes: Chez l'Auteur.

Merriman, Nicholas, ed. 2004. *Public Archaeology.* London: Routledge.

Milanich, Jerald. 1972. Excavations at the Richardson Site, Alachua County, Florida: An Early 17th Century Potano Indian Village (with Notes on Potano Culture Change). *Florida Bureau of Historic Sites and Properties Bulletin* 2: 35–61.

Miller, Christopher L., and George R. Hamell. 1986. A New Perspective on Indian-White Contact: Cultural Symbols and Colonial Trade. *Journal of American History* 73(2): 311–328.

Minard, Philippe. 1998. *La Fortune du Colbertisme: État et industrie dans la France des Lumières.* Paris: Fayard.

Mintz, Sidney W. 1985. *Sweetness and Power: The Place of Sugar in Modern History.* New York: Penguin Books.

Mitchell, Jimmie. 2013. N'me. In *The Great Lake Sturgeon*, edited by Nancy Auer and Dave Dempsey, 21–25. East Lansing: Michigan State University Press.

Moogk, Peter. 2000. *La Nouvelle-France: The Making of French Canada—A Cultural History.* East Lansing: Michigan State University Press.

———. 2002. *Building a House in New France: An Account of the Perplexities of Client and Craftsmen in Early Canada.* Markham, Ontario: Fitzhenry and Whiteside.

Morand, Lynn L. 1994. *Craft Industries at Fort Michilimackinac, 1715–1781.* Archaeological Completion Report Series no. 15. Mackinac Island, MI: Mackinac State Historic Parks.

Morgan, M. J. 2010. *Land of Big Rivers: French and Indian Illinois, 1699–1778.* Carbondale: Southern Illinois University Press.

Mullaley, Meredith J. 2011. Rebuilding the Architectural History of the Fort Vancouver Village. MA thesis, Portland State University, Oregon.

Mullins, Paul R. 2004. Ideology, Power, and Capitalism: The Historical Archaeology of Consumption. In *A Companion to Social Archaeology*, edited by Lynn Meskell and Robert W. Preucel, 195–211. Oxford: Blackwell.

Munson, Patrick. 1969. Comments on Binford's "Smudge Pits and Hide Smoking: The Use of Analogy in Archaeological Reasoning." *American Antiquity* 34(1): 83–85.

Murphy, Lucy Eldersveld. 2014. *Great Lakes Creoles: A French-Indian Community on the Northern Borderlands, Prairie du Chien, 1750–1860.* New York: Cambridge University Press.

Myers, Robert C., and Joseph L. Peyser. 1991. Four Flags over Fort St. Joseph. *Michigan History Magazine* 75(5): 11–21.

Nabokov, Peter, and Robert Easton. 1989. *Native American Architecture.* New York: Oxford University Press.

Nash, Roderick. 1982. *Wilderness and the American Mind.* New Haven, CT: Yale University Press.

Nassaney, Michael S. 2004. Implementing Community Service Learning through Archaeological Practice. *Michigan Journal of Community Service Learning* 10(3): 89–99.

————. 2008a. Commemorating French Heritage at Fort St. Joseph, an Eighteenth-Century Mission, Garrison, and Trading Post Complex in Niles, Michigan. In *Dreams of the Americas: Overview of New France Archaeology*, edited by Christian Roy and Hélène Côté, 96–111. Archéologiques, Collection Hors Série 2. Québec: Association of Archaeologists of Quebec.

————. 2008b. Identity Formation at a French Colonial Outpost in the North American Interior. *International Journal of Historical Archaeology* 12(4): 297–318.

————. 2009. Fort St. Joseph Site, Niles, Michigan: An Early European Trade Site. In *Midwest and Great Plains/Rocky Mountains*, 184–187. Vol. 2 of *Archaeology in America: An Encyclopedia*, edited by Francis P. McManamon, Linda S. Cordell, Kent G. Lightfoot, George R. Milner. Westport, CT: Greenwood.

————. 2011. Public Involvement in the Fort St. Joseph Archaeological Project. *Present Pasts* 3: 42–51.

————. 2012a. Decolonizing Archaeological Theory at Fort St. Joseph, an Eighteenth-Century Multi-Ethnic Community in the Western Great Lakes Region. *Midcontinental Journal of Archaeology* 37(1): 5–23.

————. 2012b. Enhancing Public Archaeology through Community Service Learning. In *The Oxford Handbook of Public Archaeology*, edited by Robin Skeates, Carol McDavid, and John Carman, 414–442. New York: Oxford University Press.

————. 2015. *The Archaeology of the North American Fur Trade*. Gainesville: University Press of Florida.

————. 2018a. Problematizing Heritage Authenticity and Sustainable Practices in Public Archaeology: A North American Case Study. Manuscript on file, Department of Anthropology, Western Michigan University, Kalamazoo.

————. 2018b. Embracing Anomalies to Decolonize Archaeology. In "Encounters, Exchange, Entanglements: Current Perspectives on Intercultural Interactions throughout the Western Great Lakes," edited by Heather Walder and Jessica Yann. Special issue, *Midwest Archaeological Conference Occasional Papers* 2: 55–66.

————. 2019. Social Identity and Materiality at French Fort St. Joseph (20BE23), Niles, Michigan. In "Disrupted Identities: Colonialism, Personhood, and Frontier Forts," edited by Mark Tveskov and Chelsea Rose. Special issue, *Historical Archaeology* 53(1): 56–72.

Nassaney, Michael S., ed. 1999. *An Archaeological Reconnaissance Survey to Locate the Remains of Fort St. Joseph (20BE23) in Niles, Michigan*. Archaeological Report no. 22. Department of Anthropology, Western Michigan University, Kalamazoo.

Nassaney, Michael Shakir, and José António Brandão. 2009. The Materiality of Individuality at Fort St. Joseph: An Eighteenth-Century Mission-Garrison-Trading Post Complex on the Edge of Empire. In *The Materiality of Individuality: Archaeological Studies of Individual Lives*, edited by Carolyn L. White, 19–36. New York: Springer.

Nassaney, Michael S., José António Brandão, William M. Cremin, and Brock Giordano. 2007. Archaeological Evidence of Economic Activities at an Eighteenth-Century Frontier Outpost in the Western Great Lakes. *Historical Archaeology* 41(4): 3–19.

Nassaney, Michael S., and William M. Cremin. 2002a. Realizing the Potential of the Contact Period in Southwest Michigan through the Fort St. Joseph Archaeological Project. *Wisconsin Archaeologist* 83(2): 123–134.

————. 2002b. Fort St. Joseph is Found! *Michigan History* 86(5): 18–27.

Nassaney, Michael S., William M. Cremin, and Renee Kurtzweil, and José António Brandão. 2003. The Search for Fort St. Joseph (1691–1781) in Niles, Michigan. *Midcontinental Journal of Archaeology* 28(2): 107–144.

Nassaney, Michael S., William M. Cremin, and Daniel Lynch. 2002–2004. The Archaeological Identification of Colonial Fort St. Joseph, Michigan. *Journal of Field Archaeology* 29(3–4): 309–321.

Nassaney, Michael S., William M. Cremin, and LisaMarie Malischke. 2012. Native American-French Interactions in Eighteenth-Century Southwest Michigan: The View from Fort St. Joseph. In *Contested Territories: Native Americans and Non-Natives in the Lower Great Lakes, 1700–1850*, edited by Charles Beatty-Medina and Melissa Rinehart, 55–79. East Lansing: Michigan State University Press.

Nassaney, Michael S., and Mary Ann Levine, eds. 2009. *Archaeology and Community Service Learning*. Gainesville, University Press of Florida.

Nassaney, Michael S., and Terrance J. Martin. 2017. Food and Furs at French Fort St. Joseph. In *Archaeological Perspectives on the French in the New World*, edited by Elizabeth M. Scott, 83–111. Gainesville: University Press of Florida.

Nassaney, Michael S., Daniel Osborne, and Stacy Bell. 2000. *Salvage Excavations near the Junction of French and St. Joseph Streets, Niles, Michigan*. Report of Investigations no. 108. Department of Anthropology, Western Michigan University, Kalamazoo.

Nassaney, Michael S., Deborah Rotman, Daniel Sayers, and Carol Nickolai. 2001. The Southwest Michigan Historical Landscape Project: Exploring Class, Gender, and Ethnicity from the Ground Up. *International Journal of Historical Archaeology* 5(3): 219–261.

Nassaney, Michael S., and Michael Volmar. 2003. Lithic Artifacts in Seventeenth-Century Native New England. In *Stone Tool Traditions in the Contact Era*, edited by Charles R. Cobb, 78–93. Tuscaloosa: University of Alabama Press.

Neill, Susan M. 2000. Emblems of Ethnicity: Ribbonwork Garments from the Great Lakes Region. In *Interpretations of Native North America Life: Material Contributions to Ethnohistory*, edited by Michael S. Nassaney and Eric S. Johnson, 146–170. Gainesville: University Press of Florida.

Nevell, Michael. 2013. Archaeology for All: Managing Expectations and Learning from the Past for the Future—the Dig Manchester Community Archaeology Experience. In *Archaeology, the Public and the Recent Past*, edited by Chris Dalglish, 65–75. Suffolk, UK: The Boydell Press.

Noble, Vergil E. 1983. Functional Analysis and Intra-Site Analysis in Historical Archaeology: A Case Study from Fort Ouiatenon. PhD diss., Michigan State University, East Lansing.

Nowicki, Joshua Stanley. 2001. The Kalamazoo Valley Public Museum's Collection from Fort St. Joseph: An Inventory and Preliminary Assessment. Manuscript on file, Department of Anthropology, Western Michigan University, Kalamazoo.

O'Brien, Jean M. 1997. *Dispossession by Degrees: Indian Land and Identity in Natick, Massachusetts*. New York: Cambridge University Press.

O'Gorman, Jodie A., and William A. Lovis. 2006. Before Removal: An Archaeological Perspective on the Southern Lake Michigan Valley. *Midcontinental Journal of Archaeology* 31(1): 21–56.

Odell, George H. 2001. The Use of Metal at a Wichita Contact Settlement. *Southeastern Archaeology* 20(2): 173–186.

Olsen, Stanley J. 1959. Similarity in the Skull of the Bison and Brahman. *American Antiquity* 14: 321–322.

———. (1960) 1974. *Post-Cranial Skeletal Characters of* Bison *and* Bos. Millwood, NY: Kraus Reprint Co.

Orser, Charles E., Jr. 2007. *The Archaeology of Race and Racialization in Historic America*. Gainesville: University Press of Florida.

Panich, Lee M. 2013. Archaeologies of Persistence: Reconsidering the Legacies of Colonialism in Native North America. *American Antiquity* 78(1): 105–122.

Paradiso, John L., and Ronald M. Nowak. 1982. Wolves, *Canis lupus* and Allies. In *Wild Mammals of North America: Biology, Management, and Economics*, edited by Joseph A. Chapman and George A. Feldhamer, 460–474. Baltimore, MD: Johns Hopkins University Press.

Paré, George, and Milo M. Quaife. 1926. The St. Joseph Baptismal Register. *Mississippi Valley Historical Review* 13(September): 201–239.

———. 1930–31. The St. Joseph Mission. *Mississippi Valley Historical Review* 17(1): 24–54.

Parmalee, Paul W., and Walter E. Klippel. 1983. The Role of Native Animals in the Food Economy of the Historic Kickapoo in Central Illinois. In *Lulu Linear Punctated: Essays in Honor of George Irving Quimby*, edited by Robert C. Dunnell and Donald K. Grayson, 253–324. Anthropological Papers no. 72. Ann Arbor: University of Michigan, Museum of Anthropology.

Parsons, Christopher M. 2017. Wildness without Wilderness: Biogeography and Empire in Seventeenth-Century French North America. *Environmental History* 22: 643–667.

Parsons, Jeffery R. 1972. Archaeological Settlement Patterns. *Annual Review of Anthropology* 1: 127–150.

Paynter, Robert. 1982. *Models of Spatial Inequality: Settlement Patterns in Historical Archaeology*. New York: Academic Press.

Peterson, Charles. 1965. *Colonial St. Louis: Building a Creole Capital*. Tucson, AZ: The Patrice Press.

Peterson, Jacqueline C. 1981. The People in Between: Indian-White Marriage and the Genesis of a Métis Society and Culture in the Great Lakes Region, 1680–1830. PhD diss., University of Illinois, Chicago Circle.

Peuchet, Jacques. 1799. *Dictionnaire universel de la géographie commerçante*. Tome 5. Paris: Blanchon. http://gallica.bnf.fr/ark:/12148/bpt6k9735315c.

Peyser, Joseph L., ed. 1978. Fort St. Joseph Manuscripts: Chronological Inventory of French-Language Manuscripts and Their Translations and Abstracts. Compiled for the Four Flags Historical Study Committee. Translated by Joseph L. Peyser. Manuscript on file, Niles District Library, Niles, Michigan.

———. 1992. *Letters from New France: The Upper Country, 1686–1783*. Urbana: University of Illinois Press.

Peyser, Joseph L., and José António Brandão, eds. and trans. 2008. *Edge of Empire: Documents of Michilimackinac, 1671–1716*. East Lansing: Michigan State University Press, and Mackinac Island: Mackinac State Historic Parks.

Peyser, Joseph L., and Robert C. Myers. (1991) 1997. *Fort St. Joseph, 1691–1781: The Story of Berrien County's Colonial Past*. Niles, MI: Support the Fort Inc.

Pouchot, Pierre. 2003. *Mémoires sur la dernière guerre de l'Amérique septentrionale*. Sillery, Québec City: Septentrion.

Pritchard, James. 2004. *In Search of Empire: The French in the Americas, 1670–1730*. Cambridge: Cambridge University Press.

Prown, Jules. 1993. The Truth of Material Culture: History or Fiction? In *History From Things: Essays on Material Culture*, edited by Steven Lubar and W. David Kingery, 1–19. Washington, DC: Smithsonian Institution Press.

Purdue, James R. 1983. Epiphyseal Closure in White-Tailed Deer. *Journal of Wildlife Management* 47: 1207–1213.

Quattrin, Dale, and William M. Cremin. 1988. A Possible Sweatlodge at the Schilling Site (20KZ56), Kalamazoo County, Michigan. *Midcontinental Journal of Archaeology* 13(1): 29–39.

Quimby, George I. 1939. European Trade Articles as Chronological Indicators for Archaeology of the Historic Period in Michigan. *Papers of the Michigan Academy of Science, Arts, and Letters* 24: 25–31.

———. 1960. *Indian Life in the Upper Great Lakes: 11,000 B.C to A.D 1800*. Chicago: University of Chicago Press.

———. 1966. *Indian Culture and European Trade Goods: The Archaeology of the Historic Period in the Western Great Lakes Region*. Madison: University of Wisconsin Press.

———. 1993. A Thing of Sherds and Patches. *American Antiquity* 58(1): 7–21.

RAPQ. 1928. *Rapport de l'Archiviste de la Province de Quebec pour 1927–1928*. Québec: L.-Amable Proulx, Imprimeur de Sa Majesté le Roi.

Raudot, Antoine. 1904. *Relation par lettres de l'amerique septentrionale*, éditée et annotée par Le P. Camille de Rochemonteix. Paris: Letouzey et Ané.

Ray, Arthur J. 1974. *Indians in the Fur Trade*. Toronto: University of Toronto Press.

———. 1980. Indians as Consumers in the Eighteenth Century. In *Old Trails and New Directions: Papers of the Third North American Fur Trade Conference*, edited by Carol M. Judd and Arthur J. Ray, 255–271. Toronto: University of Toronto Press.

Ray, Arthur J., and Donald Freeman. 1979. *Give Us Good Measure: An Economic Analysis of Relations between the Indians and the Hudson's Bay Company before 1763*. Toronto: University of Toronto Press.

Reichert, Sue K. 2016. Collaborating with Educators to Create a Program to Include Archaeology for 5th Grade in the Southwest Michigan Public Schools' Curriculum (aka Archaeology CSI, Cultural Scene Investigation). MA internship report, Department of Anthropology, Western Michigan University, Kalamazoo.

Reitz, Elizabeth J., Irvy R. Quitmyer, H. Stephen Hale, Sylvia J. Scudder, and Elizabeth S. Wing. 1987. Application of Allometry to Zooarchaeology. *American Antiquity* 52: 304–317.

Reitz, Elizabeth J., and C. Margaret Scarry. 1985. *Reconstructing Historic Subsistence with an Example from Sixteenth-Century Spanish Florida*. Special Publication Series no. 3. Glassboro, NJ: Society for Historical Archaeology.

Reitz, Elizabeth J., and Elizabeth S. Wing. 1999. *Zooarchaeology*. Cambridge: Cambridge University Press.

Rice, Prudence M. 1981. Evolution of Specialized Pottery Production: A Trial Model. *Current Anthropologist* 22(3): 219–240.

Ritchie, William A. 1954. Dutch Hollow, an Early Historic Period Seneca Site in Livingston County, New York. *Researches and Transactions of the New York State Archaeological Association* 13(1).

Ritzenthaler, Robert. 1947. The Chippewa Indian Method of Securing and Tanning Deerskin. *Wisconsin Archaeologist* 28(1): 6–13.

Roache-Fedchenko, Amy S. 2013. Technological Adaptation on the Frontier: An Examination of Blacksmithing at Fort Michilimackinac, 1715–1781. PhD diss., Syracuse University.

Robinson, Paul A., Marc A. Kelley, and Patricia E. Rubertone. 1985. Preliminary Biocultural Interpretations from a Seventeenth-Century Narragansett Indian Cemetery in Rhode Island. In *Cultures in Contact: The European Impact on Native Cultural Institutions in Eastern North America, A. D. 1000–1800*, edited by William W. Fitzhugh, 107–130. Washington, DC: Smithsonian Institution Press.

Rogers, E. S. 1978. Southeastern Ojibwa. In *Northeast*, edited by Bruce G. Trigger, 760–771. Vol. 15 of *Handbook of North American Indians*. Washington, DC: Smithsonian Institution Press.

Ruggles, Richard I., and Conrad E. Heidenreich. 1987. French Exploration. In *The Historical Atlas of Canada: From the Beginning to 1800*, vol. 1, edited by Richard C. Harris, Plate 36. Toronto: University of Toronto Press.

Sabatier, Antoine. 1908. Étude Révisionnelle des Sceaux de Plomb Fiscaux et Commerciaux. *Bulletin de la Société des Sciences & Arts de Beaujolais* 33(January–March): 5–30.

———. 1912. *Sigillographie historique des administrations fiscales, communautés ouvrières et institutions diverses ayant employé des sceaux de plomb (XIV–XVIII siècles): plombs historiés de la Saône et de la Seine*. Paris: H. Champion.

Saitta, Dean J. 2007. *The Archaeology of Collective Action*. Gainesville: University Press of Florida.

Sakaguchi, Takashi. 2007. Site Formation Processes and Long-Term Changes in Land Use among Maritime Hunter-Gatherers: A Case Study at the Hamanaka-2 Site, Reuben Island, Hokkaido. *Arctic Anthropology* 44: 31–50.

Santer, Richard A. 1977. *Michigan, Heart of the Great Lakes*. Dubuque, IA: Kendall/Hunt.

Saunt, Claudio. 1998. "Domestick . . . Quiet Being Broke": Gender Conflict among Creek Indians in the Eighteenth Century. In *Contact Points: American Frontiers from the Mohawk Valley to the Mississippi, 1750–1830*, edited by Andrew Cayton and Fredrika Teute, 151–174. Chapel Hill: University of North Carolina Press.

Savary des Bruslons, Jacques. 1732a. *Dictionnaire Universel de commerce, contenant tout ce qui concerne le commerce qui se fait dans les quatre parties du monde*. Tome 1. Amsterdam: Chez les Jansons. http://gallica.bnf.fr/ark:/12148/bpt6k5833070b.

———. 1732b. *Dictionnaire Universel de commerce, contenant tout ce qui concerne le commerce qui se fait dans les quatre parties du monde*. Tome 2. Amsterdam: Chez les Jansons. http://gallica.bnf.fr/ark:/12148/bpt6k5835437q.

Schiffer, Michael B. 1987. *Formation Processes of the Archaeological Record*. Albuquerque: University of New Mexico Press.

Schiffer, Michael Brian, and James Skibo. 1997. The Explanation of Artifact Variability. *American Antiquity* 62(1): 27–50.

Schurr, Mark R. 2006. Untangling Removal Period Archaeology: The Complexity of Potawatomi Sites. *Midcontinental Journal of Archaeology* 31(1): 5–19.

———. 2010. Archaeological Indices of Resistance: Diversity in the Removal Period Potawatomi of the Western Great Lakes. *American Antiquity* 75(1): 44–60.

Schwaderer, James B. 2017. Minecrafting Archaeology: An Experimental Pedagogy for an Eighteenth-Century French Trading Post in Niles, Michigan. MA thesis, Western Michigan University, Kalamazoo.

Scott, Elizabeth M. 1985. *French Subsistence at Fort Michilimackinac, 1715–1781: The Clergy and the Traders.* Archaeological Completion Report Series no. 9. Mackinac Island, MI: Mackinac Island State Park Commission.

———. 1991. "Such Diet as Befitted His Station as Clerk": The Archaeology of Subsistence and Cultural Diversity at Fort Michilimackinac, 1761–1781. PhD diss., University of Minnesota.

———. 2001. Faunal Remains from House D of the Southeast Rowhouse, British Period (1760–1781), Fort Michilimackinac. In *House D of the Southeast Row House: Excavations at Fort Michilimackinac, 1989–1997,* by Lynn L. M. Evans, 60–66. Archaeological Completion Report Series no. 17. Mackinac Island, MI: Mackinac Island State Historic Parks.

Scott, Elizabeth M., and Shannon Lee Dawdy. 2011. Colonial and Creole Diets in Eighteenth-Century New Orleans. In *French Colonial Archaeology in the Southeast and Caribbean,* edited by Kenneth G. Kelly and Meredith D. Hardy, 96–116. Gainesville: University Press of Florida.

Secunda, W. Ben. 2006. To Cede or Seed? Risk and Identity among the Woodland Potawatomi during the Removal Period. *Midcontinental Journal of Archaeology* 31(1): 57–88.

Séguin, Robert-Lionel. 1967. *La civilisation traditionelle de l'"habitant" aux XVIIe et XVIIIe siècles.* Montreal: Éditions Fides.

Shackel, Paul A., and Erve Chambers, eds. 2004. *Places in Mind: Public Archaeology as Applied Anthropology.* New York: Routledge.

Shafer, Harry J., and Thomas Hester. 1991. Lithic Craft Specialization and Product Distribution at the Maya Site of Colha, Belize. *World Archaeology* 23(1): 79–97.

Sheldon Craig T., Jr., Ned J. Jenkins, and Gregory Waselkov. 2008. French Habitations at the Alabama Post, ca. 1720–1763. In *Rêves d'Amériques: Regard sur l'archéologie de la Nouvelle-France/Dreams of the Americas: Overview of New France Archaeology,* edited by Christian Roy and Hélène Côté, 112–126. Québec: Association des archéologues du Québec.

Silliman, Stephen W. 2005. Culture Contact or Colonialism? Challenges in the Archaeology of Native North America. *American Antiquity* 70(1): 55–74.

———. 2009. Change and Continuity, Practice and Memory: Native American Persistence in Colonial New England. *American Antiquity* 74(2): 211–230.

Silliman, Stephen W., ed. 2008. *Collaborating at the Trowel's Edge: Teaching and Learning in Indigenous Archaeology.* Tucson: University of Arizona Press.

Singleton, Theresa A., and Mark Bograd. 2000. Breaking Typological Barriers: Looking for the Colono in Colonoware. In *Lines That Divide: Historical Archaeology of Race, Class, and Gender,* edited by James A. Delle, Stephen A. Mrozowski, and Robert Paynter, 3–21. Knoxville: University of Tennessee Press.

Sinopoli, Carla M. 1988. The Organization of Craft Production at Vijayanagara, South India. *American Anthropologist* 90(3): 580–597.

Skeates, Robin, Carol McDavid, and John Carman, eds. 2012. *The Oxford Handbook of Public Archaeology*. New York: Oxford University Press.

Skibo, James, John Franzen, and Eric Drake. 2007. Smudge Pits and Hide Smoking Revisited. In *Archaeological Anthropology: Perspectives on Methods and Theory*, edited by James Skibo, Michael Graves, and Miriam Stark, 72–92. Tucson: University of Arizona Press.

Skibo, James M., Terrance J. Martin, Eric C. Drake, and John G. Franzen. 2004. Gete Odena: Grand Island's Post-Contact Occupation at Williams Landing. In Grand Island Archaeology, edited by Sean B. Dunham, 167–190. *Midcontinental Journal of Archaeology* 29(2).

Sleeper-Smith, Susan. 2001. *Indian Women and French Men: Rethinking Cultural Encounter in the Western Great Lakes*. Amherst, MA: University of Massachusetts Press.

Smardz, Karolyn, and Shelley J. Smith, eds. 2000. *The Archaeology Education Handbook: Sharing the Past with Kids*. Walnut Creek, CA: AltaMira Press.

Smith, Bruce D., ed. 1978. *Mississippian Settlement Patterns*. New York: Academic Press.

Smith, Cameron M. 2006. Formation Processes at a Lower Columbia River Plankhouse Site. In *Household Archaeology on the Northwest Coast*, edited by Kenneth M. Ames, E. A. Sobel, and A. Trieu, 233–269. International Monographs in Prehistory, Archaeological Series 16. Ann Arbor: University of Michigan Press.

Smith, Gerald R. 2010. *Guide to Great Lakes Fishes*. Ann Arbor: University of Michigan Press.

Smith, S. J., Jeanne M. Moe, K. A. Letts, and D. M. Paterson. 1996. *Intrigue of the Past: A Teacher's Activity Guide for Fourth through Seventh Grades*. Delores, CO: Bureau of Land Management, Anasazi Heritage Center.

Sobolik, Kristin D., and D. Gentry Steele. 1996. *A Turtle Atlas to Facilitate Archaeological Identifications*. Mammoth Site of Hot Springs, SD, Inc. Rapid City, SD: Fenske Companies.

Sommerville, Suzanne Boivin. 2014. My Relatives at Fort St. Joseph: French? Indian? Some Important Interconnections. *Michigan's Habitant Heritage: Journal of the French-Canadian Heritage Society of Michigan* 35(1): 22–31.

Spector, Janet. 1975. Crabapple Point (Je 93): An Historic Winnebago Indian Site in Jefferson County, Wisconsin. *Wisconsin Archaeologist* 56: 270–345.

Starbuck, David R. 2011. *The Archaeology of Forts and Battlefields*. Gainesville: University Press of Florida.

Still, Michael Charles William. 1995. Roman Lead Sealings. 2 vols. PhD diss., University College, London.

Stone, Lyle M. 1974a. A Review of the Fort St. Joseph Artifact Collections: Niles, Michigan and South Bend, Indiana. Manuscript on file, Niles District Library, Niles, Michigan.

———. 1974b. *Fort Michilimackinac, 1715–1781: An Archaeological Perspective on the Revolutionary Frontier*. Anthropological Series vol. 1. East Lansing: Publications of the Museum, Michigan State University.

Styles, Bonnie Whatley. 1981. *Faunal Exploitation and Resource Selection: Early Late Woodland Subsistence in the Lower Illinois Valley*. Scientific Papers no. 3. Evanston, IL: Northwestern Archeological Program.

Sullivan, Lynne P., and S. Terry Childs. 2003. *Curating Archaeological Collections: From the Field to the Repository*. Walnut Creek, CA: AltaMira Press.

Surrey, N. M. Miller. (1916) 2006. *The Commerce of Louisiana during the French Régime, 1699–1763*. Tuscaloosa: University of Alabama Press.

Swanton, John R. 1922. Early History of the Creek Indians and Their Neighbors. *Smithsonian Institution Bureau of American Ethnology Bulletin* 73: 1–491.

Tanner, Helen H. 1987. *Atlas of Great Lakes Indian History*. Norman: University of Oklahoma Press.

Teit, James. 1900. *The Thompson Indians of British Columbia*. Memoirs of the American Museum of Natural History, Vol. 2, Part IV, 163–392. New York: N.p.

Temple, Wayne C. 1958. *Indian Villages of the Illinois Country: Historic Tribes*. Illinois State Museum Scientific Papers, Vol. 2, Part 2. Springfield: Illinois State Museum.

Thurman, Melburn D. 1984. *Building a House in 18th Century Ste. Genevieve*. Ste. Genevieve, MO: Pendragon's Press.

Thwaites, Reuben G., ed. 1896–1901. *The Jesuit Relations and Allied Documents, 1610–1791*. 73 vols. Cleveland: Burrows Bros.

Tichenor, Harold. 2002. *The Blanket: An Illustrated History of the Hudson's Bay Point Blanket*. Toronto: Hudson's Bay Company/Quantum Press.

Tordoff, Judith Dunn. 1980. *Excavations at Fort Ouiatenon, 1974–76 Seasons: Preliminary Report*. The Museum, East Lansing: Michigan State University.

———. 1983. An Archaeological Perspective on the Organization of the Fur Trade in Eighteenth Century New France. PhD diss., Michigan State University, East Lansing.

Trigger, Bruce G. 1967. Settlement Archaeology—Its Goals and Promise. *American Antiquity* 32: 149–160.

———. 1986. *Natives and Newcomers: Canada's "Heroic Age" Reconsidered*. Montreal: McGill-Queen's University Press.

Trouillot, Michel-Rolph. 1995. *Silencing the Past: Power and the Production of History*. Boston: Beacon Press.

Turgeon, Laurier. 1997. The Tale of the Kettle: Odyssey of an Intercultural Object. *Ethnohistory* 44(1): 1–29.

Turgeon, Laurier, Denys Delâge, and Réal Ouellet, eds. 1996. *Cultural Transfer, America and Europe: 500 Years of Interculturation*. Québec City, Québec: Les Presses de l'Université Laval.

Tveskov, Mark, and Chelsea Rose. 2019 "Thematic Collection: Disrupted Identities: Colonialism, Personhood, and Frontier Forts." Special issue, *Historical Archaeology* 53(1): 41–180.

Vehik, Susan C. 1977. Bone Fragments and Bone Grease Manufacturing: A Review of Their Archaeological Uses and Potential. *Plains Anthropologist* 22: 169–182.

Volo, James M., and Dorothy D. Volo. 2002. *Daily Life on the Old Colonial Frontier*. Westport, CT: Greenwood Press.

Wagner, Mark J. 2011. *The Rhoads Site: A Historic Kickapoo Village on the Illinois Prairie*. Studies in Archaeology no. 5. Urbana: Illinois State Archaeological Survey, University of Illinois.

Walder, Heather. 2018. Picking up the Pieces: Intercultural Interaction in the Great Lakes Region Examined through Copper-Base Metal Artifacts. *International Journal of Historical Archaeology*. Published online July 7.

Walder, Heather, and Jessica Yann, eds. 2018. "Encounters, Exchange, Entanglements: Current Perspectives on Intercultural Interactions throughout the Western Great Lakes." Special issue, *Midwest Archaeological Conference Occasional Papers* 2(Spring).

Wallerstein, Immanuel. 1976. A World-Systems Perspective on the Social Sciences. *British Journal of Sociology* 27(3): 343–352.

Walthall, John A., ed. 1991. *French Colonial Archaeology: The Illinois Country and the Western Great Lakes*. Urbana: University of Illinois Press.

Walthall, John A., and Elizabeth B. Benchley. 1987. *The River L'Abbe Mission: A French Colonial Church for the Catholic Cahokia Illini on Monks Mound*. Studies in Illinois Archaeology 2. Springfield, IL: Illinois Historic Preservation Agency.

Walthall, John A., and Thomas E. Emerson, eds. 1992. *Calumet and Fleur-de-Lys: Archaeology of Indian and French Contact in the Midcontinent*. Washington, DC: Smithsonian Institution Press.

Walthall, John A., and Margaret Kimball Brown. 2001. French Colonial Material Culture from an Early Eighteenth-Century Outpost in the Illinois Country. *Illinois Archaeology* 13(1–2): 88–126.

Warkentin, Germaine, and Carolyn Podruchny. 2008. Introduction: "Other Land Existing." In *Decentering the Renaissance: Canada and Europe in Multidisciplinary Perspective, 1500–1700*, edited by Germaine Warkentin and Carolyn Podruchny, 3–16. Toronto: University of Toronto Press.

Waselkov, Gregory A. 1991. Review of *Tunica Archaeology*. *Ethnohistory* 38 (3): 345–347.

Webster, Mildred E., and Fred Krause. 1990. *French Saint Joseph: Le Poste De La Rivière St. Joseph, 1690–1780*. N.p.: Mildred E. Webster.

Wesley, Jay K., and Joan E. Duffy. 1999. *St. Joseph River Assessment*. Fisheries Division Special Report no. 24. Ann Arbor: Michigan Department of Natural Resources.

White, Bruce. 1998. The Trade Assortment: The Meaning of Merchandise in the Ojibwa Fur Trade. In *Vingt ans après Habitants et marchands. Lectures d'histoire des XVIIe et XVIIIe siècles canadiens*, edited by Sylvie Depatie et al., 115–137. Montreal: McGill-Queen's University Press.

White, Carolyn L. 2005. *American Artifacts of Personal Adornment 1680–1820: A Guide to Identification and Interpretation*. Lanham, MD: Rowman & Littlefield.

White, Richard. 1991. *The Middle Ground: Indians, Empires, and Republics in the Great Lakes Region, 1650–1815*. Cambridge: Cambridge University Press.

———. 2011. *The Middle Ground: Indians, Empires, and Republics in the Great Lakes Region, 1650–1815*. New York: Cambridge University Press.

White, Sophie. 2012. *Wild Frenchmen and Frenchified Indians: Material Culture and Race in Colonial Louisiana*. Philadelphia: University of Pennsylvania Press.

Widder, Keith R. 2013. *Beyond Pontiac's Shadow: Michilimackinac and the Anglo-Indian War of 1763*. East Lansing: Michigan State University Press.

Willoughby, Charles. 1922. The Turner Group of Earthworks, Hamilton County, Ohio. *Papers of the Peabody Museum of American Archaeology and Ethnography* 8(3).

Wilson, Douglas C. 2015. A Mongrel Crowd of Canadians, Kanakas, and Indians: The United States National Park Service Public Archaeology Programme and Fort Vancouver's Village. *Journal of Community Archaeology and Heritage* 2(3): 221–237.

Witgen, Michael J. 2012. *An Infinity of Nations: How the Native New World Shaped Early North America*. Philadelphia: University of Pennsylvania Press.

Wolf, Eric R. 1982. *Europe and the People without History*. Berkeley: University of California Press.

Woodruff, James C. 1999. La Salle's Walk on the Wild Side. *Michigan History Magazine* 83(2): 6–15.

Zinn, Howard. 1999. *A People's History of the United State: 1492–Present*. New York: Harper Collins Publishers.

Zitomersky, Joseph. 1994. *French Americans-Native Americans in Eighteenth-Century French Colonial Louisiana: The Population Geography of the Illinois Indians, 1670s-1760s*. Lund, Sweden: Lund University Press.

Zoltvany, Yves F. 1974. *Philippe de Rigaud de Vaudreuil, Governor of New France, 1703–1725*. Toronto: McClelland and Steward.

Contributors

RORY J. BECKER is associate professor of anthropology at Eastern Oregon University, where his research interests include historical archaeology of the contact period with a focus on the Rocky Mountain fur trade and remote sensing techniques.

KELLEY BERLINER is the eastern field representative for the Archaeological Conservancy. Her interests include public archaeology, community engagement with academia, preservation, cultural resource management, and archaeology of the northeastern United States and Canada.

JOSÉ ANTÓNIO BRANDÃO is professor in the Department of History at Western Michigan University. His research focuses upon interactions between the French and Native Americans in the Great Lakes region, and he serves as the Fort St. Joseph Archaeological Project ethnohistorian.

CATHRINE DAVIS is a doctoral student in anthropology at the College of William and Mary. Her research focuses on the material culture of the seventeenth- and eighteenth-century French and Native American presence in North America, historic sigillography, commerce and merchant ties in the French Atlantic, and textile production and inspection in pre-revolutionary France.

ERICA A. D'ELIA worked in various roles for the Fort St. Joseph Archaeological Project from 2010 to 2012. She received her MA in anthropology from Western Michigan University in 2013, where she specialized in public archaeology.

BROCK A. GIORDANO, RPA, presently works as an archaeologist for FEMA in Region II, New York, NY. He is the supervisor for Hurricane Sandy, New York (DR-4085), in the Environmental and Historic Preservation department. His research interests include historical archaeology of the Northeast, culture contact, and historic preservation of colonial burying grounds.

ERIKA K. HARTLEY earned her MA in anthropology from Western Michigan University. Her interests include historical archaeology, public archaeology, colonialism, trade, identity, and regional analysis.

JOSEPH HEARNS earned his MA in anthropology from Western Michigan University, where he focused on historical archaeology, zooarchaeology, and the fur trade at Fort St. Joseph. He currently is completing his initial teacher certification in social studies for the state of Michigan.

ALLISON M. HOOCK earned her MA degree in geography from Western Michigan University. Her interests include the material evidence of the construction of social and physical boundaries.

MARK HOOCK is a doctoral candidate in anthropology at American University. His interests include the variety of ways archaeology can explore transformations in social organization, class relations, and the hidden mechanisms of ideological common sense.

TERRANCE J. MARTIN is emeritus curator of anthropology at the Illinois State Museum and is interested in osteological evidence for animal exploitation in the greater Midwest, especially at Native American and Euro-American archaeological sites of the seventeenth through nineteenth centuries.

ERIC TEIXEIRA MENDES holds an MA in comparative religion and a BA in anthropology. His research focuses on Buddhist and Shinto amulets in Japan and the relationships between popular culture and religion.

MICHAEL S. NASSANEY is professor emeritus of anthropology at Western Michigan University and the principal investigator of the Fort St. Joseph Archaeological Project. He is the author of *The Archaeology of the North*

American Fur Trade. His research interests include the archaeology of colonialism, material analysis, ethnohistory, and social relations in eastern North America.

SUE REICHERT received her MA in anthropology in 2016 from Western Michigan University. She was a member of the 2012 Fort St. Joseph Archaeological Project team and has continued volunteering since then.

Index

The letter *f* following a page number denotes a figure; the letter *t* following a page number denotes a table.